Socialist Constitutionalism and the Communist Polity

This collection of specially commissioned essays provides the first incisive collaborative intervention to ongoing debates about law and politics under capitalism from an explicitly socialist constitutionalist perspective.

Heterodox literature on constitutional studies, to a large extent and with a few notable exceptions, shares a rejection of Marxist analytical principles. Moving beyond the formalism and instrumentalism, this volume will engage with the question: what differentiates a Marxist conception of socialist constitutionalism and the role of institutional forms in building socialism, from republican and post-Marxist conceptions? Drawing inspiration from socialist thinkers and historical attempts to build socialism, the contributors explain the relevance of socialist conceptions of democracy and rights for contemporary struggles for social emancipation. They combine historical and theoretical analyses to review socialist constitutional theory and practice, while thinking about the future of democracy and rights in a communist polity. The contributions deal with a variety of topical issues, including the relationship between state, law, and society; the relationship between constitutional law and revolutionary social change; right as legal superstructure and right as a form of social consciousness; the ethical grounds of communism; socialist conceptions of right; and principles for a socialist constitutionalism.

Consolidating Marxist approaches to public law and constitutional theory, *Socialist Constitutionalism and the Communist Polity* offers both a rigorous contribution to the elaboration of Marxist theory and a re-examination of foundational constitutional concepts, questions, and debates that will help to orient non-specialist readers.

Alexandros Chrysis is Professor of History of Ideas and Philosophy of History at Panteion University of Social and Political Sciences. His main research interests refer to Enlightenment and Marxism. While dealing with theories of state and revolution, Chrysis published *True Democracy as a Prelude to Communism: The Marx of Democracy* (2018) and *The Marx of Communism: Setting Limits in the Realm of Communism* (2022).

Dimitrios Kivotidis is Senior Lecturer in Constitutional Law at City St George's, University of London. His research explores themes related to public law, constitutional theory, democracy, rights, and social change from a critical perspective. He is the author of *The Dialectics of Democracy: Towards a Socialist Constitutionalism* (Routledge, 2024), *Dictatorship* (Routledge, 2021), and several articles in peer-reviewed journals and book chapters.

Marx and Marxisms: New Horizons

Edited by Marcello Musto

The peer-reviewed series *Marx and Marxisms: New Horizons* (edited by Marcello Musto, with Francesca Antonini as Assistant Editor) comprises rigorous scholarly books, accessible to general readers, that offer innovative and critical works in the field of Marx studies and Marxisms. The series publishes monographs, edited collections, and anthologies, by both prestigious and emerging international experts, in the fields of political theory, history of political thought, sociology, political philosophy, and heterodox economics. The books in this series provide original investigations within the Marxist tradition, push the boundaries of accepted interpretations and existing literatures, bring different concepts and thinkers into new relationships, and inspire significant conversations for today. They come from a wide range of academic disciplines, subject matters, political perspectives, cultural backgrounds, and geographical areas, producing an eclectic and informative collection that appeals to a diverse and international audience.

The Biopolitical Body of Capital
From Labour Value to Labour Legislation
Jacques Bidet

Gramsci and the Colonial Question
Sardinia, Subalternity, and the Global South
Gianni Fresu

Subversive Negri
From the Refusal of Work to the Multitude
Roberto Nigro

Socialist Constitutionalism and the Communist Polity
Edited by Alexandros Chrysis and Dimitrios Kivotidis

For more information about this series, please visit: https://www.routledge.com/Marx-and-Marxisms/book-series/MM

Socialist Constitutionalism and the Communist Polity

Edited by Alexandros Chrysis and Dimitrios Kivotidis

Routledge
Taylor & Francis Group
NEW YORK AND LONDON

First published 2027
by Routledge
605 Third Avenue, New York, NY 10158

and by Routledge
4 Park Square, Milton Park, Abingdon, Oxon, OX14 4RN

Routledge is an imprint of the Taylor & Francis Group, an informa business

ISBN: 978-1-032-62160-9 (hbk)
ISBN: 978-1-032-62163-0 (pbk)
ISBN: 978-1-032-62162-3 (ebk)

DOI: 10.4324/9781032621623

Typeset in Times New Roman
by codeMantra

Contents

Contributors

Cosmin Cercel is Professor of Law at the University of Ghent. His main research explores the nexus between law and authoritarian ideologies with a specific focus on continental legal theory and constitutional history. He is the author of *Towards a Jurisprudence of State Communism: Law and the Failure of Revolution* (2018). Recently, he has co-edited (with Gian-Giacomo Fusco and Simon Lavis) *States of Exception: Law, History, Theory* (2020).

Alexandros Chrysis is Professor of History of Ideas and Philosophy of History at Panteion University of Social and Political Sciences. He has written a number of books and articles on Enlightenment and Marxism, including *True Democracy as a Prelude to Communism: The Marx of Democracy* (2018) and *The Marx of Communism: Setting Limits in the Realm of Communism* (2022).

Radha D'Souza is Professor of Law at the University of Westminster, London. She is a social justice activist, writer, critic, and commentator. She is the author of *What's Wrong with Rights?* (2018) and *Interstate Disputes Over Krishna Waters* (2006) and works with the Campaign Against Criminalising Communities (CAMPACC) in the United Kingdom.

Dimitrios Kilakos is Adjunct Lecturer and Postdoctoral Researcher in the Department of Primary Education, University of Athens, Greece. He is also a member of the Centre for Philosophical Studies of History, University of Oulu, and a collaborating member of the Institute for Philosophical Studies, Faculty of Arts and Humanities, University of Coimbra. His research focuses on social aspects of scientific cognition and cognitive aspects of the techno-scientific transformation, science and religion, science and culture, science and politics, as well as the relationship between social consciousness and the superstructure of the society, from a Marxist perspective.

Dimitrios Kivotidis is Senior Lecturer in Constitutional Law at City St George's, University of London. His research explores themes related to public law, constitutional theory, democracy, rights, and social change from a critical perspective. He is the author of *The Dialectics of Democracy: Towards a*

Socialist Constitutionalism (Routledge, 2024), *Dictatorship* (Routledge, 2021), and several articles in peer-reviewed journals and book chapters.

Paul O'Connell is Reader in Law at SOAS, University of London. He is a socialist activist, trade unionist, and legal academic who has published extensively on issues of public law, human rights, and the relationship between law and social change. His publications include *Masking Barbarism: Human Rights in the Contemporary Global Order* (2017) and *Vindicating Socio-Economic Rights: International Standards and Comparative Experiences* (2012), while he is the co-editor of the *Research Handbook for Law and Marxism* (2021).

Igor Shoikhedbrod is Assistant Professor of Political Theory in the Department of Political Science, St. Francis Xavier University. He is also the author of *Revisiting Marx's Critique of Liberalism: Rethinking Justice, Legality and Rights* (2019) and several academic articles focused on legal and political theory in *History of Political Thought, Contemporary Political Theory, Critical Horizons, Canadian Journal of Law & Jurisprudence, Critical Analysis of Law,* and *Canadian Journal of Political Science.*

Tony Smith is Emeritus Professor of Philosophy and Political Science at Iowa State University. He is the author of *Beyond Liberal Egalitarianism: Marx and Normative Social Theory in the Twenty-First Century*, *Globalisation: A Systematic Marxian Account*, *Technology and Capital in the Age of Lean Production: A Marxian Critique of the "New Economy"*, *Dialectical Social Theory and Its Critics: From Hegel to Analytical Marxism and Postmodernism*, *The Role of Ethics in Social Theory*, and *The Logic of Marx's Capital: Replies to Hegelian Criticisms*, along with numerous articles on Marxism, the philosophy of technology, and normative social theory. He has also co-edited four collections (*The Oxford Handbook of Karl Marx*, *Hegel's Logic and Marx's Capital: A Reexamination*, *Dialectics for a New Century*, and *Philosophy Against Empire*).

Mehmet Tabak is Clinical Assistant Professor at the Program in International Relations, New York University. He is the author of several books on the philosophies of Plato, Hegel, and Marx, including *Marx's Philosophy of Revolution and Freedom: A Critical Reconstruction*, *Dialectic in Hegel's History of Philosophy, Vol. 1*, *The Doctrine of Being in Hegel's Science of Logic: A Critical Commentary*, and *Dialectics of Human Nature in Marx's Philosophy*.

Maria Tzanakopoulou is Senior Lecturer at the School of Law, Birkbeck. She studied law in Athens (National and Kapodistrian University) and London (UCL), during which time she also became a member of the Athens Bar Association. She previously taught European Law and Human Rights Law at King's College London and University College London. She specialises in Public Law and European Public Law and has published mainly in the area of constitutional law and constitutionalism in the state and beyond. She is the author of *Reclaiming Constitutionalism: Democracy, Power and the State* (2018).

Editors' Introduction

The contemporary historical conjuncture is marked by a profound structural crisis of capitalism that encompasses overlapping catastrophes: spiralling inequality, climate breakdown, economic stagnation, the resurgence of imperialist wars, and a generalised shift towards authoritarianism. While the discourse of democracy and rights was a driving force of the bourgeois revolutions of the seventeenth and eighteenth centuries, the institutionalised form of these ideals – the liberal democratic state – has signally failed to deliver its promises of popular self-government and social justice. In the wake of the Great Recession, political decision-making has increasingly shifted from representative to allegedly technocratic institutions, while the political spectrum has shifted to the right, with far-right parties forming or threatening to form government in multiple countries.

This process is accommodated, at least for the time being, within the liberal constitutional framework. The rise of authoritarianism is not yet occurring via an explicit suspension of the constitutional order; however, multiple developments threaten and qualify the major coordinates of the liberal democratic order. From limiting fundamental rights (like the generalised restrictions to the right to protest, the freedom of assembly, and the right to take industrial action), to governments ignoring judicial decisions on the effects of legislative measures on fundamental rights (e.g. the Rwanda Bill in Britain), to extremely politicised judiciaries overturning long-established precedents of human rights protection (e.g. overturning of *Roe v. Wade* in the US), to explicit defiance of international law (e.g. President Trump's 'Louis Quatorze' statement that his own morality is the only restraint he knows regarding annexing foreign territory), the main pillars of modern liberalism seem to be hanging by a thread, facing collapse to a state not encountered since the interwar period.

Meanwhile, mainstream liberal constitutionalism cannot account for these developments, as it tends to resort to apologetics of the current institutional arrangements, which it accepts together with the socio-economic reality they seek to reproduce. The awkward and inert response of liberal constitutionalism to these has led to the exploration of alternative constitutional arrangements by

DOI: 10.4324/9781032621623-1

alternative 'heterodox' constitutionalisms which seek to rethink the main principles of state organisation and interaction between state and citizen. Yet, even these heterodox approaches to constitutionalism and the dominant institutional arrangements of public power ultimately remain trapped in the framework of modern political institutions, which they take for granted and hesitate to radically challenge.

The present edited volume is part of this growing exploration of alternative constitutionalisms but it tries to do things a bit differently. It adopts a historical and theoretical perspective; we dare say a historical materialist perspective, which is based on a historical analysis of class struggle and a dialectical exploration of the socialist tendencies and communist potential for overcoming contemporary politico-economic and juridico-political contradictions. In that sense, it provides a critique of liberal constitutionalism that seeks to reignite the vision and enhance the normative appeal of an alternative which started materialising about a century ago, and which liberal constitutionalism has exorcised ever since, namely the communist alternative.

This book is essentially about the Left's approach to the constitutional phenomenon. Yet, what exactly is meant by 'the Left' is far from a settled issue. We use the term 'Left' here with a clear class reference. The Left is the political movement that, historically and within the context of capitalist society where it originates, sides with the people and their interests, with the popular classes, with the 'sans-culottes', the proletariat, the workers, in other words, against capitalism. This Left has since the publication of the 'Manifesto of the Communist Party' believed in and struggled for social emancipation and a future without exploitation and domination of human by human. This goal necessitates the assessment of legal and political institutions based on their class function and capacity to promote that goal.

But there is another Left, which we would call 'social-democratic' Left, which sees modern liberal democracy and the rule of law as universal ideas and necessary (and most of the time adequate) conditions of achieving social emancipation. This Left functions as an organic part of the bourgeois political system and an active manager of the contradictions of capitalist society, strategically aiming to ameliorate them rather than radically overcome them. This social-democratic Left uses the language of socialism, the language of critique inherited from Marx, in order to promote what we could call 'egalitarian capitalism', a kind of Weimar-style social democracy, a capitalism with a human face.[1]

In the field of constitutional studies, this social-democratic Left is manifested in 'radical' or 'socialist' constitutional currents, which are mainly inspired by the social-democratic, socialist republican, and post-Marxist traditions. These currents reject the revolutionary aspects of Marxist thought. Most influential among these is the current associated with the Law and Political Economy (LPE) group.[2] In the symposium that relaunched the concept of 'socialist constitutionalism' in the summer of 2020, organised by the LPE group, there were two points of general agreement: (i) there is no such thing as capitalism but only conjunctural products of legal ordering and contingent legal arrangements (Moyn 2014, 49), and (ii) whoever controls the apparatus of 'legal ordering' can steer society to more equitable outcomes (Pistor 2019, 8).

Social democracy and the LPE understand socialism as an improved version of capitalism or a mixed economy. This view is intrinsically linked with LPE's methodological axiom that 'law constitutes society'. Since there is no such thing as 'economic laws of capitalism', there is nothing that 'determines' the function of legal and political institutions; these are just 'contingent effects of legal rules and legal choice' (Pistor 2019, 8). Consequently, socialism can simply be the result of taking control of the apparatus of legal ordering and altering the legal coordinates. Socialism is not, from this standpoint, a long historical process of radical restructuring of every aspect of socio-economic relations that rests on the struggle conducted by socially subordinate classes; it is rather reduced to market regulation which blunts the edges of capitalist inequality.

LPE's 'socialist' constitutionalism is part and parcel of the social-democratic instrumentalist view that the state is a neutral 'tool' that can be captured via bourgeois elections to initiate socialist change. This instrumentalist view of the state, law, and the constitution suffers from a lack of form analysis and fails to see how the structural characteristics of the bourgeois state form are resistant to socialist reform. In her contribution to this volume, Maria Tzanakopoulou examines the instrumentalist logic of social democracy as it has appeared in the British labour movement, from the Chartists to Corbyn.

From a constitutionalist standpoint, relevant to this edited volume, social democracy fails to see that market constitutionalism is the true essence of modern liberal constitutionalism. Market constitutionalism is here understood as the instrumentalisation of law (legislation and judicial interpretation) to promote market imperatives and maximise capital's profitability. It does not refer to a distorted version of liberal constitutionalism, but to those aspects of it that are necessary for the reproduction of the capitalist economy. Market constitutionalism, in this light, involves the consolidation and prioritisation of legal principles that enable profitable investment of capital, such as property rights, economic initiative, free trade, security of contract, labour market flexibility, fiscal discipline, and the creation of appropriate institutional forms (consensual and authoritarian) to facilitate this process.

This explains why, to the extent that they are even recognised in it, social rights are only given a subordinate role in bourgeois constitutions. This also explains why, from a market constitutionalist standpoint, political institutions should not be able to decide on the allocation of economic resources. Generally speaking, the role and place of democracy and rights in a country's constitution is, in the last instance, determined by this country's economic constitution, i.e. the rules and principles that determine how a constitution relates to the economy (Prosser 2014). A key question that arises in this context is whether a constitution should, in principle, provide the people with the necessary institutions that ensure the allocation of resources to meet social needs. The answer to this question depends largely on the perspective adopted. From a market perspective, the answer would be negative, while from a socialist perspective, it would be positive. Consequently, defending the place of democracy and rights in modern constitutions necessitates questioning the fundamental principles of liberal market constitutionalism. Genuine socialist constitutionalism is radical in the sense that it takes the analysis to the root of the problem, i.e. the relations of production and distribution.

From a Marxist standpoint, socialist constitutionalism refers to a new social system altogether, a system that supersedes the contradictions of capitalist society, where the politico-economic elements of production for the purpose of satisfying needs (rather than for the purpose of exchange), common ownership of the means of production (rather than private or group ownership), and focus upon development of human potential (rather than upon the production for profit) are combined with the juridico-political elements of democratic decision-making within the workplace (instead of capitalist direction and supervision) and democratic direction by the community of the goals of activity (in place of direction by capitalists) (Lebowitz 2006, 66–67). As socialism is a transitional society, a society in its transition to communism, these principles are to act as benchmarks, not as given abstract ideals.

Socialist constitutionalism is here defined as the theoretical current that explores the institutional forms and principles that challenge and aim at the transformation of the extant social order, from a jurisprudential and constitutionalist perspective. In that sense, socialist constitutionalism must engage with hitherto historical processes of building socialism and socialist constitutions. 'Social-democratic' constitutionalism, of the LPE kind, often dismisses historical attempts at building socialism as a series of betrayals and failures that gave rise to bureaucratic, totalitarian regimes. On the contrary, as Radha D'Souza puts it in the opening chapter, this volume rests on the assumption that the Bolshevik revolution and subsequent historical attempts at building socialism introduced an *epistemic leap* in theories of democracy, the state, and law.

This *epistemic leap* allows us to assess socialist transitions in their own terms, rather than projecting liberal concepts onto Marxist theories. Prior to the socialist revolutions, Marxist analysis focused primarily on the role of legal and political institutions in the reproduction of capitalism. The Bolshevik victory created a qualitatively new situation where the question shifted to what kind of law and institutions are necessary for socialist construction and the exercise of state power by the working class. This break is manifested in three primary areas: (i) a reconceptualisation of democracy, (ii) the nature of the state, and (iii) the function of constitutions.

Bourgeois revolutions articulated democracy through universalistic language, while in practice excluding propertyless men, women, and colonised subjects.

The Bolshevik revolution introduced a break by anchoring democracy in class characteristics, introducing the Soviet form of council democracy. Forms of socialist democracy sought to promote actual participation of the people in decisions that affect all aspects of social life. In this volume, Paul O'Connell discusses the need to develop an understanding of socialist democracy focused on institutional forms of working-class power, while Dimitrios Kivotidis critiques the liberal view that approaches the Soviet system as a bureaucratic antithesis of democracy. Last but not least, Tony Smith explores the role of decentralised democratic institutions engaged in the process of socialist planning in a future socialist society.

The socialist constitutionalist approach to constitutions is linked to the Marxist view of the state. The epistemic leap revealed that states are not neutral arbiters but possess distinct class characteristics defined by the social class wielding power. Additionally, from a socialist constitutionalist standpoint, the socialist state is viewed as a transitory institution that, unlike the 'immortal' bourgeois state, must eventually work towards its own historical demise. If the capitalist state is a top-down apparatus functioning to ensure the reproduction of capital's reproduction and profitability, the socialist state is its inversion, a bottom-up (as well as top-down) transitional institution committed to leading society towards a people-centric future.

If the state is that fundamentally different, then the rulebook, the Constitution, has to change too. Socialist revolutions fundamentally changed the meaning and social function of constitutions. In the liberal tradition, bourgeois constitutions are tied to the idea of constitutionalism as a fundamental law that restricts the state and whose main job is to use the public-private divide to keep private property safe from democracy. As mentioned above, the liberal constitution is, first and foremost, a fence around capital, just spoken in very high-minded language. Socialist constitutions, on the other hand, are seen as practical administrative tools, as blueprints which codify the gains of the revolution and give effect to the political and economic goals of the working people.

The notion of the epistemic leap introduced by socialist revolutions to the study of constitutions is crucial for grasping the raison d'être for this edited volume and other similar studies that have started appearing (Smith 2025; Platenkamp 2025; Shoikhedbrod 2019; Chrysis 2022; Kivotidis 2024). If traditional political theory is a map that assumes the world is flat (the 'flatness' representing formal, universal liberal rights), the Bolshevik epistemic break is the discovery that the world is spherical and governed by the 'gravity' of class struggle. You cannot use the old flat map to navigate a three-dimensional terrain without getting lost or miscalculating your destination entirely.

***

Equally important as the new map that socialist constitutionalism provides is the vision that guides the project of social emancipation. The vision of a communist polity that actualises emancipation is important for enhancing the normative appeal of socialism, which has suffered greatly in the context of the counterrevolution undertaken for the last several decades. This is another front that this edited volume wishes to contribute towards. Exploring the role of institutional forms in communist society is important not least because of the growing literature engaging with this issue. Nevertheless, approaching this question needs to be done with extreme care. The fact that the classics of Marxism were very reluctant to predict or describe the possible relations of communist society testifies to this.

A historical materialist approach is the only way to properly discuss the issue of institutional forms in communist society. In mature communism, decision-making forms may continue to exist, as well as coercion, but their form and operation may be qualitatively different, and the latter's role in reproducing social relations will not be determinant. Contributions by Igor Shoikhedbrod, Mehmet Tabak, and Tony Smith in the final part of the volume explore alternative approaches to the future of rights, the normative grounding of revolutionary communism in human flourishing, and a wide variety of constitutional principles that would safeguard and promote this human flourishing in the context of full-blown socialism.

Investigating the future of the constitutional form in a society engaged in the process of overcoming the contradictions of capitalism necessitates an examination of Marxist analyses of the legal form. Chapters by Dimitrios Kilakos and Igor Shoikhedbrod contribute to this analysis, while Cosmin Cercel's contribution also focuses on the future of a specific aspect of the constitutional form and its implications for socialist constitutionalism. Two issues are essential to note in this respect. First, that law and politics – as primary spheres that converge in the constitutional form – are here approached not only in their institutional capacity but also as forms of social consciousness (Ilyenkov 1982). Law and politics are commonly perceived as objective and ineradicable forms of the external world, based on which we understand and analyse the totality of socio-political processes. Yet, they are only the objectified forms of collectively organised experience, which have crystallised in social consciousness and are reinforced by the force of habit and tradition (Ilyenkov 1982). However, forms of social consciousness are historical.

This brings us to the second issue: an investigation of the constitutional form in socialism must necessarily engage with the Marxist discussion of the legal form and the work of Evgeny Pashukanis on this topic, a task performed by Shoikhedbrod and Kilakos in the present volume. Pashukanis defined the legal form as a 'specific set of relations which [human beings] enter into not by conscious choice, but because the relations of production compel them to do so' (Pashukanis 2003, 68). For him, 'the conflict of private interests' is the basic prerequisite for legal regulation, and consequently, it is the origin of the legal form (Pashukanis 2003, 80–81). The legal form is the inevitable reflex of the commodity relation (Pashukanis, 82).

At a high level of abstraction, we could argue that the legal form, as a form of social consciousness, is characterised by *formalism* (which obscures social and economic divisions and contradictions), *systematicity* (which precludes inconsistency due to internal contradictions), *individualism* (which presents social processes from the standpoint of self-interested individuals), and a *conflictual intersubjective relationship* (which involves an adversarial setting for dispute resolution in the social sphere) (Althusser 2014, 57–69). These characteristics are common in bourgeois law and the law of precapitalist social formations. The element that gives bourgeois law its distinct identity is the *universality* of the principles of *freedom*, *equality*, and *property*. This universality is an essential element for the reproduction of the capitalist mode of production, where expropriation of surplus value is carried out primarily through economic means. These principles are essential to the process of capital's valorisation because they sustain a false consciousness of social production and mask the reality of exploitation. The final element, essential to the legal form, is *coercion*, since the law has historically existed as a means of regulating social relations in class-divided societies, where social groups with conflicting interests often resist rules that adversely affect their living conditions. Cosmin Cercel explores the coercive aspect of the legal form as it manifests in the public law institution of emergency powers.

This analysis brings to the fore important issues regarding the nature of the legal form and the role of the constitutional form in socialism. For it seems to be accepted by all contributors to this volume (especially those contributing to the second and third parts) that the legal form does not wither away, at least in the first initial phase of immature communism. In the 'Critique of the Gotha Programme', Marx comments on the continuous operation of law's abstract formalism during the process of socialist construction. Systematicity and coercion are also continuing characteristics of law in socialism, as they constitute essential elements of any historical legal system.

Nevertheless, there is also discontinuity between bourgeois and socialist law. For one, socialist law promotes the overcoming of the fundamental limitation of bourgeois law, namely abstract formalism, by prioritising the 'human flourishing' and approaching individuals as many-sided personalities with multiple needs. Socialist constitutionalism is essentially a set of navigational principles to guide the long and arduous process of building a communist polity, where human flourishing has replaced profit as the main criterion of social activity. This radically different social goal determines the different roles for democracy, state, and constitution. Socialist constitutionalism is necessary because communist social relations don't just spring up out of nowhere. They have to be built, practised, and learned. The socialist state and law are necessary, but their role isn't just coercive; it is, more importantly, educative.

The true democratic content found in the active, ongoing, mass participation of the working class in the act of governing is crucial in that respect. Socialist constitutionalism is built on the assumption that the process of socialist construction ultimately leads to a point where the formal institutions of law and government can begin to fade away or are overcome and sublated into other forms of consciousness and social interaction. Therefore, the benchmark for this socialist transition isn't just about economic growth. It is, fundamentally, about the capacity of the working class and the popular strata to organise, to struggle, and to develop their own power. In that sense, socialism is the path to a different way of being human.

***

The volume is organised into three parts that track the movement from the critique of capitalism through the process of socialist construction to the ultimate vision of the communist polity. The opening chapters of Part A situate the debate by clarifying the line between socialist and bourgeois constitutions. Professor Radha D'Souza opens the volume by identifying the 'Scholastic turn' in Marxism and arguing that socialist revolutions constitute an epistemic leap that renders the liberal perspective inadequate for evaluating democracy and the state in the 'epoch of imperialism'. She asserts that while bourgeois democracy excludes large swathes of people in practice while speaking in universalist language, socialist democracy anchors rights in the liberation of working people and freedom from colonial oppression.

In the same spirit, Dr. Paul O'Connell provides a critical analysis of rights as 'weapons in the class struggle'. Using the draconian sentencing of climate protesters in Britain as a starting point, he argues that the classics of Marxism had no illusions about bourgeois rights; they saw them as the 'air to breathe' necessary for working-class self-emancipation. In an era of rising authoritarianism, he argues for a 'shield' of democratic forms to allow movements to develop and a 'sword' of radical, transgressive rights to offensive against neoliberal hegemony. Dr. Maria Tzanakopoulou examines the specific history of British socialism, identifying a recurring trap of 'constitutional maximalism' – the overinvestment in the ability of the constitution to yield socialist results if correctly 'tweaked'. She critiques the instrumentalist logic from the Chartists to Corbynism, arguing that treating superstructural institutions as neutral tools obscures the structural realities of class as a social relation constitutive of capitalism.

Part B pivots to the 'cogwheel mechanism' of the socialist state. Professor Alexandros Chrysis explores socialist constitutionalism from a Gramscian perspective. Investigating the role and place of the state and the constitution in socialism, Chrysis enriches Marx and Lenin's analysis of the dictatorship of the proletariat by introducing the Gramscian distinction between 'statolatry' (the citizens' active love for and devotion to their newly founded republic) and 'statism' (the pathological condition that suffocates mass activity). In so doing, he revisits classical oppositions of modern political theory (civil and political society, institutional and ethical) and inquires upon the role of the party in socialism and the withering away thesis. The role of the party and other institutions that have been described as authoritarian is further discussed by Dr. Dimitrios Kivotidis who addresses the 'authoritarian/bureaucratic' critique of socialism furthering D'Souza's point on liberalism's inadequacy to examine socialist institutions. Bringing the debate up to date, Kivotidis explores how socialist constitutionalism can resolve the tension between workplace democracy and central planning by leveraging the digital 'feedback infrastructure'. Additionally, foreshadowing the discussion of Part C, he argues that unlike the market, which is determined by the 'need' for valorisation, socialist constitutionalism is governed by the principle of human flourishing.

The next two chapters deal more explicitly with the constitutional form in socialism. Dr. Dimitrios Kilakos delves into the philosophical foundations of socialist legality, focusing on the development of social consciousness. He argues for a radical discontinuity between the bourgeois and socialist contexts, asserting that socialist legality is the preparation for a non-legal social order in communism where the need for external coercion is abolished. Professor Cosmin Cercel investigates further the relationship between bourgeois and socialist legal form by focusing on the role of emergency powers in socialist constitutionalism. Drawing from bourgeois reactionary (Carl Schmitt) and critical (Giorgio Agamben) as well as Marxist (Pashukanis) analyses on emergency powers, he inquires upon the possibility of reclaiming a progressive element in the suspension of the constitutional order for the purposes of emancipatory revolutionary politics. Cercel sees this as a step that potentially contradicts the core of Pashukanis' theory of the legal form albeit one in the right direction that overcomes Pashukanis's shortcomings and awkwardness regarding public law.

The final part looks towards the 'true realm of freedom'. Dr. Mehmet Tabak reconstructs Marx's revolutionary communism as a constitutional theory focused on overcoming 'political alienation'. He defines communist constitutionalism as a transformative theory that replaces the bureaucratic state with a network of self-governing political and economic communes. Dr. Igor Shoikhedbrod surveys the 'alternative futures' of right in the works of Pashukanis, Kojève, and Bloch. He moves beyond Pashukanis' 'technical regulation' to find in Ernst Bloch a 'natural law from below' that retrieves the 'upright carriage' of human dignity and the right to resistance as ineliminable elements of socialist construction. Finally, Professor Tony Smith provides a set of concrete proposals for a socialist constitution. He outlines an internationalist framework based on a variety of constitutional principles (like socialised investment, 'media for the people', and the 'subsidiarity principle') where communities have weight in decisions affecting them. Most crucially, he envisions a politics of time where the 'realm of necessity' contracts and the 'realm of freedom' expands, allowing for the 'absolute unfolding of man's creative abilities'.

Notes

1 On the split between revolutionary/communist and reformist/social-democratic Left, which dates back to the social-democratic parties' stance on WWI, see Lenin (1976, 126–127).
2 For the inaugural essay that launched the Symposium see Forbath (2020). The collection of essays presented at the Symposium is available at https://lpeproject.org/symposia/socialist-constitutionalism/.

References

Althusser, L. (2014) *On the Reproduction of Capitalism* (Verso).

Chrysis, A. (2022) *The Marx of Communism: Setting Limits in the Realm of Communism* (Palgrave Macmillan).

Forbath, W. (2020) 'Socialism Past and Future, Part I', available at https://lpeproject.org/blog/socialism-past-and-future-part-i-of-ii/.

Ilyenkov, E. (1982) *Leninist Dialectics and the Metaphysics of Positivism* (New Park Publications).

Kivotidis, D. (2024) *The Dialectics of Democracy: Towards a Socialist Constitutionalism* (Routledge).

Lebowitz, M. (2006) *Build It Now: Socialism for the Twenty-First Century* (Monthly Review Press).

Lenin, V. I. (1976) 'Extraordinary Seventh Congress of the R.C.P. (B.)', in V. I. Lenin, *Collected Works: Volume 27*, 49–55 (Progress Publishers).

Moyn, S. (2014) 'Thomas Piketty and the Future of Legal Scholarship', 128 *Harvard Law Review*.

Pashukanis, E. (2003) *The General Theory of Law and Marxism* (Transaction Publishers).

Pistor, K. (2019) *The Code of Capital: How the Law Creates Wealth and Inequality* (Princeton University Press).

Platenkamp, T. (2025) *The Constitution of Socialism: A World without Capital* (Brill).

Prosser, T. (2014) *The Economic Constitution* (Oxford University Press).

Shoikhedbrod, I. (2019) *Revisiting Marx's Critique of Liberalism: Rethinking Justice, Legality and Rights* (Palgrave Macmillan).

Smith, T. (2025) *A Socialism for the Twenty-First Century: Towards the 'Full and Free Development of Every Individual'* (Brill).

1 Democracy, State, and Constitutions in Socialist Transition

Socialist Revolutions as the Benchmark?

Radha D'Souza

> In the first half-century of its existence (from the 1840s on) Marxism was engaged in combating theories fundamentally hostile to it. [...] By the nineties this victory was in the main completed. [...] But after Marxism had ousted all the more or less integral doctrines hostile to it, the tendencies expressed in those doctrines began to seek other channels. [...] And the second half-century of the existence of *Marxism began (in the nineties) with the struggle of a trend hostile to Marxism within Marxism itself.* [...]
>
> (Lenin 1908 [1973]) (italics added)

1.1 Situating the Debate on Socialist Constitutions

This volume on socialism and constitutional change sets up the problematic on a confounding historical, theoretical, conceptual and methodological canvas by inviting contributors to reflect on the role of institutions *as well as* the place of rights and democracy in the transition. Rights and democracy are concepts steeped in liberalism, the ideology of capitalism. If the socialist project is work-in-progress and destined to remain so for a long historical period, the canvas presents a conceptual and methodological quagmire. In theory, a study of socialist transitions and constitutional changes ought to begin with the Bolshevik revolution, or at the earliest from the Paris Commune, moving on to the experiences of the former USSR, Cuba, Vietnam, Laos, Cambodia, East Germany, Eastern European states, North Korea and China, to the more complex contemporary debates on the constitutional reforms spearheaded by Communist Party of China (CPC) under Xi Jinping at the time of writing. This is a period spanning over a century when successful revolutions prompted socialists leading them to attend to socialist construction in the wider context of the 'epoch of imperialism' (Lenin's phrase) (D'Souza 2018b, Ch.3). Instead, we find that the approaches to socialism and constitutional changes encompass a wide array of ideological and theoretical orientations ranging from demands for socialist constitutions in

DOI: 10.4324/9781032621623-2

countries where no socialist revolution has yet taken place such as the United States (LPE Project 2020) to Latin American countries where any progressive or radical liberal constitutional change passes for socialist constitutions – e.g. Venezuela (1999), Ecuador (2008) and Bolivia (2009) (Fernández 2012, Cobos 2018, Bilchitz 2014). These approaches confuse egalitarian capitalism and Weimar style social democracy that promote capitalism with a human face with socialism. What is absent in this literature is the application of key conceptual categories of Marxism: class, capitalism, colonialism, imperialism, the state and the political economy being the most important ones to the problem of socialist constitutional changes rendering such analysis Marxism without Marx.

In Asia, in contrast, constitutions with explicit commitments to socialism (of whatever type) adopted after independence are being rolled back by ethnocentric fundamentalist movements and states in the name of 'decolonisation'. For example, very few socialists today remember that in Afghanistan, the 1923 constitution abolished the veil and the 1963 constitution saw the state as socialist (Ahmed 2016, Kamali 1985). In India, a country where communist parties ruled two states and the post-independence constitution describes itself as socialist, ethno-nationalist forces have introduced piecemeal repeal of the constitution in the name of 'decolonisation' (Fuchs 2024, Khaitan 2020, Menon 2022). Constitutional changes in countries like Afghanistan, Iran and India transform the meaning of decolonisation in fundamental ways. In the South Asian context, demands for constitutional change call for the restoration of liberal constitutions. Between these two ends of constitutional changes, there is what is called 'transitional constitutionalism' that refers to former socialist countries, mainly Eastern European ones that 'transitioned' to liberal constitutionalism. In these countries, legacies of socialist constitutionalism persist and present new problems for liberal democracy after the restoration of capitalism (e.g. Bui 2021, Leskinen 2015, Teitel 1994, Tkatova 2010). This short sketch presents a blurred picture of the relationship of socialism to constitutional changes in the present times. The blurred relationship invites us to clarify the line between socialist constitutions and bourgeois (neo)liberal constitutions.

The chapter will argue that the Bolshevik revolution introduced an epistemic break in theories of liberalism such that socialist ideas of democracy, state and constitutions cannot be understood using liberal theoretical lenses; in other words, liberal concepts and methods cannot be projected onto Marxist theories of socialism and constitutions. The chapter begins by locating the question of socialist transitions and constitutional change within the emerging field of Marxism and Law, a subfield of Legal Studies in academia (Section 1.2). Using the Bolshevik and Chinese revolutions, the two most important socialist revolutions, as bookends, this chapter outlines the differences between bourgeois and socialist ideas of democracy (Section 1.3), state, the single most important institution (Section 1.4) and constitutions (Section 1.5). The chapter argues that the epistemic breaks introduced by the Bolshevik revolution provide benchmarks to assess what is socialist and liberal in democracies, states and constitutions. These benchmarks provide the tools for evaluating socialist transitions in the present conjuncture and form the basis for a future research agenda on socialism and law. The chapter concludes with reflections on the meaning of socialist transition in the long term and approaches to the question in the epoch of imperialism.

1.2 Scholastic Marxism and Socialist Construction

There is a resurgence in the field of Law and Marxism in recent years (e.g. O'Connell and Özsu 2021). The theoretical porousness in the scholarship permits liberal ideas to seep through and masquerade as Marxism. Broadly generalising, whatever the themes, approaches and politics, the field of Law and Marxism in academia is marked by what I shall call 'the scholastic turn' in Marxism.[1] Scholastic Marxism is disengaged from socialist and national liberation practices and politics and dislocated from the concrete historical contexts of the struggles against capitalism and imperialism. Marxist philosophy explicitly postulates practice as the source and inspiration for theory (Marx and Engels 1981 [1846], expanded in Mao 1965). In so doing, Marxism distinguishes itself from feudal and bourgeois theories grounded in metaphysical and/or nominalist sources for theories. These metaphysical/nominalist theories in turn became sources for feudal and bourgeois law such as canon law in the past and doctrinal or positivist 'black letter' modern law.

Any engagement with the problems of law in socialist transition invites, as the first step, a critical assessment of socialist revolutions, their failures *and* successes in the post-revolutionary period, an assessment that must necessarily be grounded in political practices of socialist construction from a standpoint that is sympathetic to the historical socialist project. Delinking Marxist theory from practical problems of socialist construction redirects Scholastic Marxism to 'purist' approaches to Marxist theory. Consequently, as Dominico Losurdo (2000) argues, Western Marxist intellectuals see the attempts to build socialism as a series of 'betrayals' or 'failures' of socialism. This unsympathetic evaluation of socialist practices arises because when disengaged from practice and history, the only reference point that remains to assess socialist practices is to rely on classical Marxist texts, in Losurdo's (2000, 4) words by a 'return to the "authentic" Marx', and interpret classical Marxist texts in scholastic ways. It will not be a caricature to say that this tendency to look back without the impulse to move forward is a characteristic feature of Scholastic Marxism. Scholastic Marxism aborts a scientific and systematic assessment of the problems of socialist construction. Learning from past struggles is a necessary condition for the historical socialist project, not least because going forward entails periodic review of the road travelled and rectification of errors along the way. Undermining the gravity of the problems, failing to acknowledge the contributions, exaggerating the role of individuals by deifying or demonising them sans the context, prevents learning from past experiences of struggles. In turn, this inability to learn makes 'betrayals' and 'failures' into a self-fulfilling prophecy (Losurdo 2000, 2003). Worse still, scholastic approaches disengaged from practice and history lead socialists to frequently, as Losurdo points out, fall behind imperialist agendas of their own states in their political practices (Losurdo 2000, 2003). Consequently, socialism becomes an eschatological incantation that is at best aspirational or utopian and at worst unfaithful deviance from the teachings of Marx and/or Engels.

Historically, questions about Marxist approaches to law *as a specific field* of knowledge arose only *after* the Bolshevik revolution. Marx and other socialist thinkers in pre-Bolshevik era addressed the role of law in capitalism as presuppositions or preconditions that are essential for capitalist processes to operate the way they do, or what I have called the legal and institutional infrastructures for capitalism (D'Souza 2018b, Ch.3). Their focus was on bourgeois law. Neither Marx nor Lenin omits or leave out the operation of bourgeois law in their accounts of capitalism. Prominent amongst these are property rights, wage regulations, stock exchanges, labour markets, land laws, rents and much else that explain the operational aspects of capitalist economy. Volumes 1, 2 and 3 of Marx's *Capital* are replete with observations and interjections on the legal order in the individual and social circuits of capital, far too many to list here. The issues at stake were bourgeois law in capitalist processes of production, exchange, consumption and circulation or the theoretical foundations of bourgeois constitutions; they were not concerned with the existence of law as a distinct scholarly discipline, law for law's sake, as in the canonical and nominalist traditions of bourgeois law (D'Souza 2021). If anything, their theoretical writings on bourgeois law criticised the metaphysical foundations of bourgeois law (Marx 1833–1844).

Necessarily generalising, Scholastic Marxism's engagement with Law and Marxism begins with the Bolshevik revolution and ends with the New Economic Policy (NEP) era (e.g. Head 2020, Marković 2017, Tomba 2017). The NEP divided Marxists in Russia and Europe between those who defended purist/idealist ideas of Marxist conceptualisation of socialism and those who prioritised defending the revolution in practice. After the Bolshevik revolution, the question for Bolsheviks was no longer about how law operated within capitalism but rather what kind of law was needed for socialist construction, how state power *ought* to be exercised and what kind of institutions were necessary for socialist construction. This was a *qualitatively* different question and a *new* question without historical precedents at that.

By not drawing a clear line marking the epistemic break that the revolution had introduced as discussed in the sections below, Law and Marxism literature projects Marx, Engles and Lenin's observations about bourgeois law and institutions under capitalism unproblematically onto problems of post-revolutionary state and socialist construction (e.g. Piers Beirne and Hunt 1988). In so doing, the Law and Marxism scholarship tends to obscure necessity and freedom in specific historical circumstances, the historical inheritances of the Bolsheviks and the constraints they imposed on them, even when quoting the well-rehearsed lines by Marx that: 'Men make their own history, but they do not make it as they please; they do not make it under self-selected circumstances, but under circumstances existing already, given and transmitted from the past' (Marx 1950 [1851]). Scholastic Marxism obscures the next logical question for socialists : what were the historical inheritances of the Bolsheviks, what constraints did they impose on them and what scope for actions did it permit?

The task of addressing the problem of Law and Marxism in aid of socialist construction after the revolution fell on Stalin, a Marxist leader who remains a red rag as it were to most Scholastic/Western Marxists (Losurdo 2023 [2008]). Omitting the Stalin era from the study of constitutions aborts the study of Law and Marxism in socialist construction at its birth. Worse still, considering the setbacks during the Stalin era without considering its successes, especially in the anti-colonial struggles and the defeat of Nazism (see Losurdo 2023 [2008]), obscures Marxist understandings of the role of law in the epoch of imperialism. Scholastic Marxism trivialises problems of socialist construction on the one hand and imperialist aggression on the other. Besides, by omitting to consider developments during and after Stalin's state building era, by omitting socialist experiences in other countries, and most of all omitting the robust debates on Law and Marxism especially since the Reform and Opening Up era under Deng Xiaoping's leadership in China, and more recently under Xi Jinping's leadership, Marxists write-out the most serious debates on questions of the role of law in socialist construction, transition, democracy and constitutions. Socialist transition is by its very nature about the nitty-gritty of resolving practical problems of socialist construction after a successful revolution. Like everything else, Scholastic Marxism too is grounded in the materiality of class and neocolonial relations in the 'epoch of imperialism' but that is a different question for another time.

1.3 Epistemic Break 1: Bourgeois and Socialist Democracy

Bourgeois revolutions in the seventeenth and eighteenth centuries were made possible by the coming together of merchants, a section of the aristocracy and a new breed of anti-feudal intellectuals in Europe. This coming together prepared the economic and political, legal, institutional, ideological and cultural grounds for the revolutions. These social groups characterised the revolutions led by them as 'democratic', which they articulated in universalistic language of all 'mankind' and iconic phrases like 'liberty, equality and fraternity' (Paine), or 'man is born free' (Rosseau) or the idea that all human beings were motivated by a natural propensity to 'truck, trade and barter' (Adam Smith) even while excluding large swathes of people, e.g. propertyless men, women, colonised subjects, slaves and indigenous people from the definitions of 'mankind'. These new social groups projected the merchant's world view as the *human* world view (D'Souza 2010, 2013).

Socialism broke with the merchant's world view and presented the world view of working people as the *human* world view and, in so doing, changed the meaning of democracy. 'Democracy is human existence while in the other political forms man has only legal existence. That is the fundamental difference of democracy,' Marx wrote (Marx 1833–1844, 30). The Paris Commune, for the first time in history, actualised the idea that working people can govern themselves in practice. In his postscript to Marx's *Civil War in France* on the Paris Commune, Engels (1891) described the Paris Commune as the first 'dictatorship of the proletariat' and a true democracy of working people.

> Of late, the Social-Democratic philistine has once more been filled with wholesome terror at the words: Dictatorship of the Proletariat. Well and good, gentlemen, do you want to know what this dictatorship looks like? Look at the Paris Commune. That was the Dictatorship of the Proletariat.
>
> (Engels 1891)

The Bolsheviks, learning from the Paris Commune, extended Marx and Engels' insights to resolve practical problems of the Bolshevik revolution. A European style bourgeois democratic revolution like the French revolution was not possible in Russia, Lenin argued, where the bourgeoisie were weak and 'naturally and inevitably tends to come under the wing of liberal monarchist party' (Lenin 1970 [1905], 529) and therefore 'the proletariat must carry the *democratic revolution* to completion, allying to itself the mass of the peasantry in order to carry the autocracy's resistance by force and paralyse the bourgeoisie's instability' (p.530 italics added). The Bolsheviks defended the idea that democracies were imbued with distinct class characteristics that need to be recognised theoretically and asserted in political practices; and that socialists could and must complete the democratic revolution where their bourgeoisie failed to do so. The issue at stake here was building the economic base and the material foundations for socialist democracy. In the absence of material economic, legal and technological foundations, formal democracy could not bridge the gap between legal and real freedoms.

The Chinese revolution, learning from Marxism and the Bolshevik revolution, further extended theories and practices of democracy to colonial contexts. The Bolshevik Revolution had created a new historic condition for anti-colonial movements. As Mao wrote, '[T]he first imperialist world war and the first victorious socialist revolution, the October Revolution, have changed the whole course of world history and ushered in a new era (Mao 1975 [1940]).' Unlike the Bolshevik revolution which was against a feudal-imperialist regime, the Chinese revolution against a semi-feudal, semi-colonial regime brought the national liberation struggle typical of the era after World War I under the ideological and political umbrella of the struggle for historic socialism. Establishing a modern democratic society, meaning a society free from feudalism *and* imperialism, was the first step towards socialist democracy. To achieve this first step, the Chinese revolution made temporary united fronts and class alliances a historic necessity to resolve the national question, thus making class *and* national liberation in the colonies a precondition for democracy of the working people.

> Being a bourgeoisie in a colonial and semi-colonial country and oppressed by imperialism, the Chinese national bourgeoisie retains a certain revolutionary quality at certain periods and to a certain degree–even in the era of imperialism–in its opposition to the foreign imperialists and the domestic governments of bureaucrats and warlords (instances of opposition to the latter can be found in the periods of the Revolution of 1911 and the Northern Expedition), and it may ally itself with the proletariat and the petty bourgeoisie against such enemies as it is ready to oppose. In this respect the Chinese bourgeoisie differs from the bourgeoisie of old tsarist Russia. Since tsarist Russia was a military-feudal imperialism which carried on aggression against other countries, the Russian bourgeoisie was entirely lacking in revolutionary quality. There, the task of the proletariat was to oppose the bourgeoisie, not to unite with it. But China's national bourgeoisie has a revolutionary quality *at certain periods and to a certain degree*, because China is a colonial and semi-colonial country which is a victim of aggression. Here, the task of the proletariat is to form a united front with the national bourgeoisie against imperialism and the bureaucrat and warlord governments without overlooking its revolutionary quality.
>
> (Mao 1975 [1940]) (Italics added)

Therefore,

> [T]he historical characteristic of the Chinese revolution lies in its division into the two stages, democracy and socialism, the first being no longer democracy in general, [i.e. like bourgeois revolutions note added] but democracy of the Chinese type, a new and special type, namely, New Democracy.
>
> (Mao 1975 [1940])[2]

If the Bolshevik revolution established the principle that democracies have class characteristics, the Chinese revolution established that democracy was contingent on freedom from colonial oppression.

> 'In this era, any revolution in a colony or semi-colony that is directed against imperialism, *i.e.,* against the international bourgeoisie or international capitalism, no longer comes within the old category of the bourgeois-democratic world revolution, but within the new category. It is no longer part of the old

> bourgeois, or capitalist, world revolution, but is part of the new world revolution, the proletarian-socialist world revolution.
>
> (Mao 1975 [1940])

The concept of New Democracy broke decisively with bourgeois democracy conceptually, theoretically and in political practice. The reconceptualisation of bourgeois democracy as freedom from class *and* imperialist oppression had a profound influence on the anti-colonial struggles around the world giving new meaning to democracy, where democracy included not only working-class authority but *also* freedom from national oppression. These developments draw a clear line between the bourgeois democracy of the past and the democracy of working people and demonstrate the impossibility of repeating classical liberal democracies in the epoch of imperialism.

By bringing the concept of democracy down to earth from abstract philosophical ideas in bourgeois revolutions in Europe and anchoring it to the social classes and class struggles, and later to national liberation struggles against imperialism, Marxism introduced an epistemic break in theories of democracy. If bourgeois democracy articulated democracy theoretically as a universalist idea while excluding large swathes of people in political practices, socialist democracy did the opposite by including all working people and freedom from national oppression in political practices, but articulating those practices as 'dictatorship of the proletariat'. Socialist democracy can be understood only if its epistemic break with bourgeois democracy is recognised and the qualitatively different type of democracy the break introduced. My point is not that the democracy in the former USSR or China or Cuba or Venezuela or anywhere else cannot be criticised or evaluated critically. Rather, my point is that this task cannot be done without recognising the epistemic break in the very meaning of democracy that the Bolshevik revolution introduced. The class content of democracy is just what is missed in contemporary analysis. Instead, Scholastic Marxism delinks democracy from class struggles, imperialism and national oppression (D'Souza 2017); harks back to bourgeois democracy of the eighteenth century (D'Souza 2018b); and fetishises the state as an institution (D'Souza 2021). After successful revolutions, the former USSR and China were confronted with the task of consolidating the gains of their revolutions and build institutions that actualised the enlarged meaning of democracy, or what the CPC under Mao called 'People's Democracy' to differentiate it from bourgeois democracy. The most important of these institutions was the state, to which I turn next.

1.4 Epistemic Break 2 – Capitalist and Socialist States

Authority in pre-modern Europe was pyramid shaped derived from transcendental sources like God at the pinnacle followed by the Roman Church with Europe-wide authority, the monarch, and at the base, a territorially dispersed collection of manors, fiefs and estates. Pre-modern feudal societies everywhere were land-centric orders that were decentralised and territorially dispersed where each estate or manor was what Marx called 'a state within a state' (1833–1844, 69). The transition from land-centric feudal orders to a commodity-centric capitalist order called forth a new type of state: the modern nation-state. The modern nation-state is a centralised, abstract entity wherein the bureaucracy and military/police are the centralising pillars and the constitution, the abstracting device. Marx noted '[T]he abstraction of the state as such belongs only to modem times because the abstraction of private life belongs only to modem times. The abstraction of the political state is a modern product' (Marx 1833–1844, 32).

The new bourgeois intellectuals did not extricate the state from its transcendental roots, however. Instead, they substituted old mysticism with new ones. For example, Hobbes called the new state 'Powers Invisible', by which humans 'stand in awe of their own imaginations' (quoted in Loughlin 2022, 51); for Hegel, it was the transcendental Spirit of history; and for Rosseau, it was an imagined 'social contract'. Feudal states *invested* authority in the states of their times. Modern states, in contrast, *divested* the states of its traditional authority, ceding parts of it to the 'invisible hand of the market' (Adam Smith) and turning its role to that of a 'nightwatchman' (Adam Smith). The state in liberal theories appeared to stand above society as a result. The device of legal personality gave the institution of the state the appearance of being above society and veiled the real interests that established it and the reasons for establishing it.

Marx and Engels broke with the transcendental and mystical theories of the state and put it on materialist philosophical and sociological foundations (Marx 1833–1844, Engels 1972 [1891]). Marx and Engles, for the first time, introduced the idea that states possess class characters (Marx 1950 [1851]). The classes that wield state power characterise the nature of the state by defining its purpose, its modes of governance and its institutions. This was a historic epistemic break from previous theories of state and the justifications for its existence. 'The executive of the modern state is but a committee for managing the common affairs of the whole bourgeoisie.' Marx and Engels wrote (Marx and Engels 1969 [1848]). The epistemic break in theories of the state developed by Marx and Engels in their critique of capitalism was one thing, but establishing a new type of socialist state that openly confessed its class character was another matter.

Internally, inside the USSR, the success of the October Revolution was followed by military invasion, civil war and economic blockades (The Central Committee of the C.P.S.U (B) 1945, Ch.8). The Bolsheviks mobilised working people to defeat the imperialist Whiteguard offensives, thus giving the October Revolution a decisive victory. Having accomplished socialist victory in war, the Bolsheviks were confronted with the challenge of socialist construction in a context where imperialist encirclement, economic collapse, sanctions, embargos, incitement of nationalities in the Union and starvation stared the party and country in the face (The Central Committee of the C.P.S.U (B) 1945, Ch.9, Losurdo

2023 [2008], Ch.4). The challenge of socialist construction presented new questions about the nature and role of the state *after* a socialist revolution. The question of the state became one of the most contentious issues for Bolsheviks. Marxist theories of state *before* the Revolution focused on bourgeois states. The idea that working people could govern themselves was a historic epistemic break in theories of the state. Soon after the Bolshevik revolution, Lenin observed,

> […] the question of the state is a most complex and difficult one, perhaps one that more than any other has been confused by bourgeois scholars, writers and philosophers.
>
> (Lenin 1971 [1920])

Capitalism also underwent historic transformations in the early twentieth century, and the Bolsheviks had to understand those changes together with the writings of Marx and Engles on the Paris Commune. The Bolshevik revolution occurred within the interstices of a world-wide crisis of capitalism culminating in World War I. Lenin's theoretical extensions of Marxism, including his theorisation of the state, were shaped by the conditions of imperialism.

The rise of transnational monopoly finance capitalism called forth the state as the *universal form* in the epoch of imperialism beginning in the early twentieth century. The state as the universal form was a condition for new legal and institutional regimes for transnational monopoly finance capitalism and the transformation of old colonialism to neocolonialism (D'Souza 2018b). The neocolonial state that emerged after the end of World War II was formally equal and sovereign but remained politically, economically and militarily subordinated to the economic and military power of a handful of imperial states (Nkrumah 1968). Capitalism too reconfigured the old liberal bourgeois state, calling into existence the Hayekian neoliberal state. Extending Marxism to the new historical transformations underway, Lenin wrote, 'Imperialism is oppression of nations on a new historical basis' (Lenin 1974, 736), and furthermore, whereas unequal relations between small and big states have always existed,

> […] during the period of capitalist imperialism they become a general system, they form part of the process of 'dividing the world,' they become a link in the chain of operations of world finance capital.
>
> (Lenin 1970 [1917], 707)

Whereas imperialist leaders like Woodrow Wilson argued for formal legal equality of states, Lenin insisted that sovereignty was a political question, not a legal one, and that it must be asserted economically, politically and culturally in political practices. The emergence of the state as the universal form in the epoch of imperialism, objectively, and national liberation struggles asserting statehood as the institutional form for self-determination, subjectively, put the national question front and centre of the socialist project alongside the class question. The Bolshevik successes were not without setbacks. These setbacks too provided important lessons in the conceptualisation of the role of the state in socialist transitions.

Believing, as many Marxists did at that time, that socialism was the natural political trajectory for the so-called 'advanced' proletariat of the industrialised capitalist countries, the Bolsheviks under Lenin's leadership believed that the communist parties in the rest of 'advanced' Europe would follow the Bolsheviks, and revolutions would break out across Europe notably in Germany, France, Italy, Austria, Greece, the Eastern European states and others. During the first and second Congresses of the COMINTERN (the Communist International), it became clear to the Bolsheviks that European communists would not follow the Bolshevik Road (Riddell 2015). The reasons need not be digressed into here, except to note that the retreat of the socialist revolutions in Europe presented an existential crisis for the Bolsheviks portending the same fate for the revolution that met the Communards of Paris on a much larger scale.

World War I had unleashed waves upon waves of anti-colonial movements for national liberation. Many of these national liberation struggles were inspired by the Bolshevik revolution. These national liberation struggles turned to Soviet Russia for support and solidarity. Their overtures offered the Bolsheviks the opportunity to turn to national liberation struggles for the survival of *their own* revolution (D'Souza 2018a). The national question became a question for the Bolshevik Revolution from the Third International of the COMINTERN onwards introducing new questions about class in socialist inspired anti-colonial revolutions (D'Souza 2018a). Unlike 'advanced' Europe, the peasantry was the bulwark of anti-colonial struggles across the colonial world. This reality posed new theoretical problems for Marxists about the class character of socialist states after revolution, their relations to colonial states seeking freedom at a particular historical conjuncture and the place of the peasantry in those revolutions. The epistemic break in theories of the state introduced by Marxism had to move forward, but do so by learning from theories and practices of the past. In the epoch of imperialism, class struggles and national liberation struggles had to walk hand in hand. The class composition of a decolonised state had to be reworked in the light of the peasantry's role but without throwing out class analysis all together. This was necessary because only the end of imperialism could create the conditions for socialist construction. These formulations had a profound influence on national liberation struggles across the colonial world, most of which were influenced by socialism to a greater or lesser extent, ranging from Nehruvian Fabian socialism in India to Marxism-Leninism and Mao-Tse-tung Thought in China. The Chinese revolution, more than any other, made agrarian reform and combating feudalism the cornerstone of their national liberation struggle led by socialists. Thus, the Bolshevik and Chinese revolutions, and those in between, introduced a fundamentally *new* question for Marxism: the relationship between class and nation. The design of the state was pivotal for this relationship.

The task of establishing the first socialist state in human history fell on Stalin, a name that remains a taboo in Scholastic/Western Marxism as stated above. It must be noted, however, that this is not the case in many parts of the Third World. The character of the state became a contentious issue after the Bolshevik revolution. There were several assassination attempts on Lenin, the hero of the revolution, by the Socialist Revolutionaries, of which the one in August 1918 proved so serious that Lenin never recovered completely from it and eventually died in 1924 (Marx-Engels-Lenin Institute 1943, 147). One reason for these assassination attempts was the disillusionment of sections of revolutionaries with his tentative shifts in the role of the state after the revolutionary takeover of power, which was dictated by the needs of socialist construction and the NEP to meet the basic needs of working people after the end of wars and economic collapse. After the revolution, Lenin turned to the rudimentary experiences of the Paris Commune from which he developed two tentative approaches to the state in socialist construction. The first was that the institution of the state as a centralised entity was still necessary to lead socialist construction at home and resist imperialist encirclement externally because the state system cannot be abandoned at will. Many socialist/anarchist revolutionaries took a literal and utopian view of Marx and Engels' writings and believed that the state would 'wither away' after the socialist revolution. The revolution brought home the realisation that socialism could not be willed into existence. A socialist state must necessarily attend to the immediate needs of people facing starvation, a collapse of economy due to revolutionary upheavals and the encirclement by forces determined to subvert and defeat the revolution. It required an extended period of struggle going through many phases involving the defeat of imperialism externally and developing the economic conditions (productive forces) necessary for socialism internally, both being intrinsically entwined.

The second lesson from the Paris Commune was that the Soviet system was the best form of state for democratic socialism (Stalin 1974 [1927], 16–17).

> The essence of Soviet power consists in the fact that these most all-embracing and most revolutionary mass organizations of precisely those classes that were oppressed by capitalists and landlords are now "*permanent and sole basis* of the whole power of the state, of the whole state apparatus";[…]. That is why Soviet power is a *new form* of state organization, different in principle from the old bourgeois democratic and parliamentary form, a *new type* of state, adapted not to the task of exploiting and oppressing labouring masses, but to the task of completely emancipating them from all oppression and exploitation, to the tasks of the dictatorship of the proletariat.
>
> [49]

The Bolshevik revolution and the defeat of White Power of imperialist states and the Russian bourgeoisie occurred within a compressed temporal conjuncture from 1917 to 1921. In contrast, the revolutionary takeover of power in China occurred over an extended period, amidst tumultuous global events spanning two world wars, three civil wars and unified resistance to Japanese invasion. These differences had ramifications for state building. By the time of independence in 1949, the CPC had gained 32 years of experience in governance, had trialled and tested land reform schemes, established institutions of the state and the CPC at the grass-root levels and gained experience in managing class alliances, the cornerstone of the New Democratic Revolution. Retreating into rural hinterlands, the CPC established rural Soviets in pockets of 'red bases' with support from the former USSR (Mao 1977 [1928]).

Whereas the Bolsheviks under Stalin did not have a body of pre-existing theory or experience of building a socialist state and socialist economic construction, China had the benefit of the theoretical and political experiences of the Bolsheviks. The new socialist state had a different role.

> The people's state protects the people. Only when the people have such a state can they educate and remould themselves by democratic methods on a country-wide scale, with everyone taking part, and shake off the influence of domestic and foreign reactionaries [...] rid themselves of the bad habits and ideas acquired in the old society, not allow themselves to be led astray by the reactionaries, and continue to advance – to advance towards a socialist and communist society.
>
> (Mao 1969 [1949], 418)

Distinctions between bourgeois and socialist states emerge from these historical experiences of two major socialist revolutions which are summarised briefly below.

a The socialist state was not inherited from previous/ancient regimes. It was built bottom-up during and in the process of the revolutionary takeover of power in their name *as* class power. The bourgeois state, on the other hand, inherited the feudal state which was modified and adapted from the top by a small group of privileged social classes by extricating the feudal state from theology and church and retaining its main institutional features.

b Bourgeois states put the defence of private property at the heart of the institution's purpose, whereas socialist states put the defence of people, not property, at the centre of the institution's rationale for existence.

c Socialist states see themselves as a transitory institution committed to leading the societies they govern to a socialist future – by which is meant a social order that is not land-centric as feudal orders were, not commodity-centric as capitalist societies are, but rather working people-centric, a social system where working people form the pivot for organising society. Bourgeois states, on the other hand, see their role as regulating and managing the contradictions of capitalism, which is ever present in capitalist societies. The unstated assumption, in this role for the state, is that capitalism as a social order is eternal and immutable.

d Bourgeois states invest their institutions with legal personality as a legal artefact to give bourgeois institutions immortality, a device it took from the Catholic Church (Penington 1931). Socialist states see the institution of the state as an ever-changing, transient institution that, far from being immortal, must work towards its own historical demise eventually.

e Socialist states are developmental states, whereas bourgeois states are regulatory states where private property is a holy cow placed on par with human rights. Socialist states do not privilege private property, using it instead as a necessity during the period of historical socialist transition.

f A developmental socialist state directs the economy leading key sectors of the economy in national and class interests. Economic planning was a Bolshevik innovation, developed from close readings of Marx's *Capital*. Bourgeois states idealise 'free market', i.e. giving capitalists a free rein except in times of systemic crises when it steps in temporarily to prevent systemic collapse.

g Socialisation of capital in socialist states occurs through state mobilisation of capital for national development, whereas socialisation of capital in capitalist economies occurs through capitalist competition and formation of oligarchies and monopolies.

h Socialist states base their interstate relations with other states on solidarity against imperialism and capitalism at best and at the least respect for national sovereignty of other states, emphasising real, not formal equality. Interstate relations of bourgeois states are based on national self-interest which is not necessarily the same as respect for national sovereignty. The so-called Realist and Globalist Schools in international relations, both defend the interest of capital and promote national oppression and wars while also promoting formal equality simultaneously.

i Socialist states put socialist ideology front and centre of governance seeing ideological education as a key component of state function. Bourgeois democracies, on the other hand, proclaim that ideology is somehow bad and that liberalism, the ideology of capitalism, is not ideological.

j Socialist states are established through a process of struggle in which the armed forces are democratised and politicised (Mao 1969 [1949], 191). This is a taboo in bourgeois states where the armed forces ideally remain out of politics and neutral in any infightings between fractions of the bourgeoisie and instead focus on disciplining working people and subjugating other nations.

k Socialist states promote a new type of federalism, e.g. the Union of Soviet Socialist Republics, which combines confederal ideas with modern-day federal institutions. Broadly generalising the new type of federalism gives nationalities greater freedom, economically, politically and culturally. Federalism in

> capitalist states is not based on recognition of nationalities. In the US, federalism consolidated the splintered and unequal settler colonial occupation of North America by diverse mercantile groups. In the UK's unitary system, economic power is concentrated in the Union government and local powers devolved to the states can be taken back by the Union. In all cases, the Westphalian model of statehood reduces nationalities within the state to 'minorities', who retain cultural freedom on the condition that they are loyal to the nation-state of the majority nationality (Mahmood Mamdani 2020). In the US, federal state formation is based on recognition of colonised territories, whereas the Soviet Republics of the USSR were founded after repealing old Tsarist treaties – i.e. derecognition of Russian colonies.

These normative differences in the character of the state as an institution based on the idea that people, not property, must be the rationale and purpose of the state had profound influence on the institutional architectures of the socialist states that were formalised in socialist constitutions, a theme considered in the next section.

1.5 Epistemic Break 3: Bourgeois and Socialist Constitutions

What distinguishes a modern state from pre-modern ones, according to Marx (1833–1844, 33) is,

> [...] not that the various moments of the constitution are formed into particular actuality, as Hegel would have it, but rather that the constitution itself has been formed into a particular actuality alongside the real life of the people, the political state has become the constitution of the rest of the state.

Constitutions mirror the political life of the state; indeed, they are the legal foundations on which the political institution of the state is erected. Bourgeois constitutional theorists see the constitution as the instrument that settles the state, and many socialists and democracy activists see the constitution as the vehicle for social change. The reality is the opposite. In what follows, I sketch the characteristic features of bourgeois and socialist constitutions with the aim of providing benchmarks against which to evaluate liberal and socialist constitutions.

1.5.1 Constitutions and Constitutionalism

A distinction must be made between constitutions as rules about governance, and constitutionalism as an ideological artefact. Constitutionalism is traceable to the European Enlightenment thinkers and synthesised in the United States in the Madison papers of 1787 as a universal political philosophy about governance and institutions (Loughlin 2022). In contrast, socialist constitutions are practical administrative tools of governance that give effect to political goals formulated by working people through their organisations, notably the communist parties, which operate in society outside the apparatuses of the state; goals that must be adapted, modified and amended periodically in the course of social practices enroute the historical socialist transition. Marxism is the philosophical and ideological guide including in the legal sphere, not the constitution.

Constitutionalism as a modernist project reconstituted relations between the state, its people, different nationalities and its rationale for and modes of governance (Loughlin 2022, 9). Bourgeois democratic revolutions captured key constitutional ideas in slogans like 'liberty, equality, fraternity' in the French Revolution and 'no taxation without representation' in the American Revolution, which transformed ideas of democracy and private property into an ideological slogan supportive of the bourgeoisie. In the epoch of imperialism, following the Hayekian idea that 'society can be constructed anew through an exercise of human reason' (Loughlin 2022, 68), constitutionalism as ideology, and constitutions as neoliberal artefacts reconstituted the relations between state, society and nationalities by embedding markets as the Basic Law of society and subjecting the state including legislature to the authority of a Constitutional Court tasked with policing the Basic Law (Loughlin 2022).

Socialist countries steered constitutional developments in the opposite direction from constitutionalism. Socialist revolutions fought and won class and national liberation wars *first*, before writing constitutions. During those struggles, they established alternate institutions and systems of governance bottom-up. Socialist constitutions consolidated and codified the successes of socialist revolutions. Constitutional developments in China occurred over a century in four phases, each phase accompanying particular stages in socialist construction: (i) the New Democratic Revolution phase when institutions and systems of governance were established during the course of three civil wars; (ii) the Socialist Revolution phase after national liberation which laid the institutional foundations for socialist economic and social development; (iii) the Reform and Opening Up phase which modernised the economy including legal frameworks for economic development; and lastly (iv) the current Rule of Law phase when constitutional developments based on the history of class and national liberation struggles in China (Chinese characteristics) over a century (Gong 2023). Key aims of the Rule of Law era are to:

> [...] uphold, implement and develop the systems and principles set forth in the Constitution, namely, the basic system and basic tasks of the state, the core leadership and theoretical guidance of the state, the state system which is a socialist state under the people's democratic dictatorship led by the working class and based on the alliance of workers and farmers, the system of people's congresses as the system of government, the system of multiparty cooperation and political consultation under the leadership of the CPC, the system of

> regional ethnic autonomy, the system of community level self-governance, the patriotic united front, the socialist legal system, the principle of democratic centralism, and the principle of respecting and safeguarding human rights.
> (Xi 2014, 156)

It can be seen from the above that the constitution of China, far from being an ideological artefact, codifies the gains of the revolution and acts as guide to state action.

1.5.2 Equality – Real and Ideational

Bourgeois constitutions speak in the name of *all* people. For example, the preamble to the United States and Indian constitutions begins with the words 'We the people…' (Constitution of India, Constitution of the United States). There is no recognition in the constitution of differences between classes or national/racial groups among citizens. Consequently, bourgeois constitutions treat unequals as equals. Treating unequals as equals reproduces injustices and inequalities, i.e. class relations in bourgeois societies. Socialist constitutions, in contrast, proclaim the class character of the state and society in unambiguous terms. They deliberately privilege working people over propertied sections of society. The constitution of the People's Republic of China, for example, states,

> Article 1: The People's Republic of China is a socialist state governed by a people's democratic dictatorship that is led by the working class and based on an alliance of workers and peasants.

The Soviet Constitution of 1936 stated,

> ARTICLE 1. The Union of Soviet Socialist Republics is a socialist state of workers and peasants.
> ARTICLE 2. The Soviets of Working People's Deputies, which grew and attained strength as a result of the overthrow of the landlords and capitalists and the achievement of the dictatorship of the proletariat, constitute the political foundation of the U.S.S.R.

By affirming the superior status of working people and privileging the underprivileged, socialist constitutions seek to bring about real equality as opposed to formal equality of bourgeois constitutions. The normative ideal is to transcend class oppression by correcting historical injustices of capitalism and imperialism.

1.5.3 Aspirational and Instrumental Constitutions

Bourgeois constitutions are aspirational. They articulate the normative ideals of the state in universalist language without clarifying how those ideals will be realised and the basis on which conflicting claims between people and property will be resolved. These aspects are left to the government of the day to adjudicate. Bereft of substantive provisions to actualise the aspirations,

> [T]he constitution is raised to the status of civil religion. The scale of this ambition is revealed once we realize that the instrumental and symbolic dimensions of the project directly conflict.
>
> (Loughlin 2022, 122)

The Basic Law in bourgeois constitutions imposes restrictions on the state, including the legislature, by limiting its constitutional powers to address conflicts between classes and nations and competing interests.

Socialist constitutions, in contrast, articulate concrete aims of the state that are feasible and achievable. According to Samantha Lomb (2018), when the drafting of the 1937 constitution was underway, Stalin insisted that the rights of citizens were carefully crafted to take into consideration feasibility and affordability appropriate for the stage of development because constitutional provisions obliged the state to establish programmes for implementation. For example, Stalin supported constitutional rights for women but (unlike formal gender equality in liberal constitutions) insisted that recognising women's rights in the constitution obliges the state to establish enabling conditions for women to exercise those rights by supporting maternity, childcare, children's education and family life. Lomb argues that in defining citizenship, popular sovereignty was not an abstract concept as in bourgeois constitutions but rather concretised in the soviets as primary institutions. The Chinese constitution guarantees freedom from national subjugation by foreign powers by recognising the 'patriotic united front', i.e. defence of national sovereignty as a constitutional duty of the state.

1.5.4 State and People's Sovereignty

The distinctions in (b) and (c) above present a radically different conception of sovereignty. In bourgeois constitutions, sovereignty vests in the state. As Loughin notes, 'Sovereignty is a correlative expression of the state. The state and sovereignty are codependent: state as intelligible scheme and sovereignty its authority (Loughlin 2022, 55). Being grounded in medieval European history, bourgeois constitutionalism excluded the sovereignty of all other nations and peoples (Loughlin 2022, 170–171). In contrast, sovereignty in socialist constitutions vests in working people, primarily workers and peasants (Chakste 1949). The Bolshevik constitution for the first time redefined sovereignty as sovereignty of working people (Marković 2017). The sovereignty of working people was achieved through struggles and therefore grounded in the materiality of working class and national liberation histories. Bourgeois constitutions fix state sovereignty within certain ground rules of constitutionalism in which private property is foundational. In contrast, working people as the source of sovereignty embedded in socialist constitutions provides a flexible framework for reorganising the state that is different from the Basic Law of neoliberal constitutions.

1.5.5 Writing Elite and People's Constitutions

Drafting of bourgeois constitutions was undertaken by a small group of people from privileged classes. For example, the United Kingdom's constitution is unwritten. It is a series of constitutional statutes enacted following negotiations between the monarchy and the merchants, aristocracy and anti-feudal intellectuals, and it remains so. Marx (1980 [1855]) described the British Constitution as follows:

> The British Constitution is indeed nothing but an antiquated, obsolete, out-of-date compromise between the bourgeoisie, which *rules not officially* but in fact in all decisive spheres of civil society, and the landed aristocracy, which *governs officially*. Originally, after the "glorious" revolution of 1688, only a section of the bourgeoisie, the *aristocracy of finance*, was included in the compromise. The Reform Bill of 1831 admitted another section, the *millocracy*[c] as the English call it, i.e. the high dignitaries of the *industrial* bourgeoisie. The history of legislation since 1831 is the history of the concessions which have been made to the industrial bourgeoisie, from the new Poor Law to the repeal of the Corn Laws and from the repeal of the Corn Laws to the death duties on landed property.

More sections of the bourgeoisie have been added since Marx's critique, for example, the so-called 'globalists' or the political class representing transnational finance capitalists. The American constitution was drafted by a small team of 55 delegates from different states, of whom only 39 delegates signed the constitution (America's Founding Documents n.d.).

Socialist constitutions, in contrast, are the products of revolutionary movements in which wide cross-sections of working people participated. The Bolsheviks were the first to initiate a nationwide consultative process of constitution making at the Congress of Victors in 1934 convened after victory in the imperialist fuelled Civil War and the NEP initiatives to revive the economy. Stalin saw constitution making as a state building project and initiated consultations with all classes and groups in society on the draft which was widely discussed, debated and voted on across the country and the Union (Lomb 2018). In the context of threats of external aggression and internal divisions within the ranks of socialists, the attempt to write the first socialist constitution floundered on divisions over questions of class struggle and alliances, and 'purist' versus pragmatic approaches to socialist construction. The fate of the former USSR held important lessons for the CPC which noted that the USSR collapsed after 69 years because 'it did not adapt socialist constitutionalism' (Wang 2013, 11). After a decade of the Cultural Revolution, which prioritised political mobilisations over economic development, the CPC determined that 'Left deviation' was attributable to the lack of a constitutional framework which was necessary for consistency in the exercise of state power, stability of the state and socialist construction (Wang 2013). Wang argues China should not mimic Western constitutions and instead find '[...] better solutions to prove the superiority of socialist democracy, legal systems and human rights (Wang 2013, 21).

1.5.6 Public/Private Divide

The foundations of bourgeois constitutionalism rest on the public/private divide (Loughlin 2022, 164). Public and private domains are established by bourgeois states to insulate private property and its institutions from the rest of society (Clunie 2011). Although the domains are legal artefacts that exclude working people from the economy and insulate private property from democratic politics, the domains give the illusion of really-existing social spaces. The institutional architecture in modern societies follows from the public/private divide as the basic constitutional structure within which debates centre around the extent of permissible deviation from the dividing line (Sampford 1991). These constitutional arrangements limit the role of the state to varying extents.

Socialist constitutions are characterised by the absence of the public and private domains as distinct political and economic spheres in society. Socialist constitutions invest states with the responsibility of governing society and establishing and managing socialist economies for working people. The Communist Party, as a distinct political institution outside of the constitutional state, acts as the political vanguard on behalf of the people to steer the state through historic socialist transitions in the present and the future. In this system, both state and economy are subject to the political direction of the communist party. The public/private divide restricts the powers of the state in the economy; the communist party, in contrast, is tasked with political oversight over the economy *and* state. The absence of public/private divide as the basis for the constitutional state has follow-on implications for the institutions of the state and society.

1.5.7 Rule of Law and Separation of Powers

A set of constitutional theories follows from the public/private divide that guides exercise of state power. The most important of these is 'Rule of Law', the idea that the constitution is superior to the state and the citizens. Backer (2017) makes a useful distinction in Western legal traditions between law understood as a set of norms derived from immutable sources, e.g. god/divine sources or tradition and custom to which states and citizens alike must defer, and governance/administration which is about managing the affairs of the state. Rule of Law, the ideological foundations of constitutionalism, is non-negotiable, whereas the administration/governance may be modified, changed or adapted. Rule of Law gives bourgeois states the external appearance of unified state power.

However, power in bourgeois states is internally divided. Bourgeois constitutional theory is not bourgeois without the theory of Separation of Powers that shadows Rule of Law. Separation of Powers became a salient feature of modern states with the induction on the one hand of 'civil society', i.e. organised competing interest groups into the legislature, and on the other, the separation of the pre-existing state apparatuses (bureaucracy and military) from civil (bourgeois) society. These arrangements developed from the modernisation of the pre-modern state and the compromises with the landed aristocracy and new merchant classes that the compromises entailed. Separation of Powers inducts multiple conflicting interests into the very core of the institution of the state (Marx 1833–1844). Marx's analysis of competing internal struggles within the state in France in the *Eighteenth Brumaire of Louis Bonaparte* (Marx 1950 [1851]) exemplifies the conflicts that occur at the very centre of state power. These constitutional arrangements mirror the competition between fractions of capital and contradictions between the circuits of money, capital and production that is the motor of bourgeois societies.

The bureaucracy and armed forces (including police) give the institution of the state the centralised command-control capacity that allows the state to present itself as a unified legal entity. Equally, it checks the representative character of the legislature in two ways, first, by assuming executive control over the day-to-day governance of the state; and second, by the notional representation of civil society in the legislature. The institutional design of representative democracy is such that the representatives do not sit in the legislature representing the actual interests of real people/groups in society – in other words, they do not sit in the legislature as delegates of civil society groups. 'Civil Society' assumes a corporate character in the legislature through political parties who represent society as incorporated entities independent of the electorate. One of Marx's strident criticisms of Hegel was about the ways in which Hegel delinked the representatives from the people in the so-called representative democracy (Marx 1833–1844). The corporatisation of civil society in representative democracy is achieved through multiparty democracy where multiple political parties compete for representative status in the legislature. Referring to representative democracy in America, Engels (1891) wrote,

> Here there exists no dynasty, no nobility, no standing army, beyond the few men keeping watch on the Indians, no bureaucracy with permanent posts or the right to pensions; and nevertheless we find here two great gangs of political speculators, who alternately take possession of the state power and exploit it by the most corrupt means and for the most corrupt ends – and the nation is

powerless against these two great cartels of politicians, who are ostensibly its servants, but in reality exploit and plunder it.

Amongst the most ideological aspects of constitutionalism is the idea of 'independence of the judiciary' in which the judiciary acts as referee between the legislature and executive, as well as conflicts between bureaucrats. The judiciary ensures both limbs of the state remain within the remit of the Basic Law of the constitution, the public/private divide, corporatisation of economy and polity and prevent the legislature from becoming truly representative of the people on the one hand and state capture by segments of the bourgeoisie on the other.

Socialist constitutions, in contrast, are founded on unity of powers, not separation, on legislative supremacy, not constitutional supremacy, on democratic centralism, not representative democracy and the vanguard role of the communist party in socialist transition not multiparty democracy in forever-capitalism. The Bolshevik revolution introduced a new type of constitutionality. The Soviet constitution offered unity of state powers as the alternative to separation of powers (Marković 2017). The unity of state power principle reflected the need for the unity of working people (not competition of interests) as the basis of the state and democracy. Representation was through a system of delegates sent by lower tiers of administration to the apex body which acted as the legislature (Lomb 2018, Marković 2017). The communist party played a key role in the assemblies across all levels of governance in the former Soviet Union (Lomb 2018). In China at community level, village, urban housing associations, public and private enterprises, self-governance is through community level congresses (Fang and Zhao 2020). Under the Chinese constitution, 'the National People's Congress (NPC) is the highest organ of state power. The president, the prime minister and the head of judiciary are all elected by the NPC deputies. [...] Above all the Chinese Communist Party (CCP) exerts unified leadership over all state organs' (Ying 2023). The leading role of the communist party more than any other issue has confounded Western legal scholars, including some Marxist legal scholars. The parallel roles of the multi-tiered people's congresses and the communist party means the socialist legal system and socialist constitutions cannot be understood through liberal lenses of Rule of Law, Separation of Powers, and multiparty representative democracy using binaries such as 'democracy vs totalitarian' or 'popular vs authoritarian' as many 'critical', 'post Marxist' and 'post structuralist' theorists tend to do.

The CPC has a large social base in China with membership across the country estimated at ten million, amounting to nearly 10 percent of the population, for eight to ten citizens there is a CPC member, from housing associations and village committees to private and public corporations (Backer 2018). The CPC's role is to provide political guidance to the state and all its institutions at all levels of governance (Backer 2018, Ding 2017). Thus, all public and private institutions are subject to political policies and programmes determined by congresses of working people. Programmes and policies proposed by the party undergo scrutiny bottom-up within the party hierarchy and once adopted at the top, the implementation by the state calls for supervision by the people (Xi 2014, 157). Under democratic centralism, '[...] the party views law as the party's and the people's will and self-discipline' (Ding 2017, 331), where the will is formed through the consultative processes of hierarchy of congresses and the discipline exercised through oversight of all aspects of governance and state under party supervision.

The separation of powers is between political processes and administration/governance of political decisions where both are distinct but related processes (Backer 2018). As Wang Zhenmin notes (2013, 21), 'It is extremely wrong to contradict constitutional politics and the Party's leadership. The Constitution of China was developed under the leadership of the Party, and each revision of the Constitution was proposed by the central committee of CPC.' Judicial autonomy in this context is about autonomy in the administration of state that excludes law making (Backer 2017). In liberal constitutionalism, in contrast, the act of interpreting constitutions and the law, and 'judicial activism', far from being actions of an 'independent judiciary' are deeply political acts (Backer 2017, Loughlin 2022).[3]

1.5.8 Constitutional Breakdown

It must be noted in conclusion that constitutional crisis in bourgeois political economy occurs when Separation of Powers breaks down and the contradictions between the three limbs of the state can no longer be reconciled (Marković 2017). Until such breakdown point, separation of powers, as Lenin noted, stabilises bourgeois rule. In socialist political economy, a systemic breakdown occurs when the communist party is unable or unwilling to lead the politics and the economics of the state and society or when the practice-theory-practice dialogue breaks down. For example, the beginning of the end of socialism in the former USSR began when the Communist Party in the Soviet Union abandoned Marxism and socialism after the death of Stalin in 1953 (Losurdo 2023 [2008], Mao 1964) and ended with the formal and legal end to the leading role of the Communist Party in developing state policy and the introduction of the multiparty bourgeois democracy under the Boris Yeltsin presidency in 1993 (Brovkin 1990, Gilison 1972).

What is interesting about the debates on socialist legality since the Reform and Opening Up era is that the legal modernisation debates in China have engaged Western, mainly mainstream American constitutional scholarship. There is very little engagement with scholarship in the Law and Marxism subfield within Western Legal Studies and their theories, approaches and legal histories. The focus on American legal scholarship underplays comparative socialist legal scholarship in other socialist jurisdictions. On the other side, confusion among Western/Scholastic Marxists on how to characterise China: is it socialist or capitalist, an emerging imperial power or a rallying point for oppressed states, together with an objective evaluation of the former USSR, the first socialist system, act as barriers to a broader understanding of the connections between socialist democracy, state and constitutions in socialist transition. By drawing attention to the limitations of Scholastic Marxism and proposing the three epistemic breaks as benchmarks for distinguishing socialist from bourgeois constitutions in the foregoing sections, this chapter makes way for wider reflections on theoretical aspects of Marxist approaches to socialist transitions and the role of socialist constitutions in them.

1.6 Reflections on Marxism, Socialist Transitions and Constitutional Change

The foregoing sections have focused on the structural aspects of the differences between bourgeois and socialist ideas of democracy, state and constitutions. The chapter has bookended the analysis with the Bolshevik and Chinese revolutions, the two most important socialist revolutions so far. It has taken the claims of the socialist states as articulated by them as the point of departure. This chapter has not evaluated those claims to socialist transition and the divergences between theories and practices of those claims. A serious research agenda on Marxism, law and socialism must begin by drawing a clear line between liberalism, the ideology of capitalism and Marxism, the theoretical guide for socialism. This chapter is limited to drawing that line in relation to key concepts in law and institutions: democracy, state (the most foundational institution) and constitutional principles. To remain methodologically consistent, this chapter has set out the normative claims of bourgeois democracy against normative claims of socialist democracy, not the deviations from it, as is often the case. Likewise, the depoliticised role of the judiciary in the socialist system led by a parallel institution, the communist party, must be compared with the political role of the judiciary using judicial interpretation and activism under the shield of Separation of Powers. In a nutshell, like must be compared to like, norms with norms, deviations with deviations, the stated goals of the two systems, and the differences must be assessed in their own terms. Scholastic Marxism scrambles these levels of analysis.

This chapter has not addressed the specific problems of socialism in the present historical conjuncture: the epoch of imperialism. Since the Bolshevik revolution, the single biggest obstacle to socialist construction has been the hostility and aggression of imperialist powers led by transnational monopoly finance capitalism to any alternate system of political economy anywhere. This reality of the epoch presents a larger political question for Marxism. For example, is a transition to the next stage of socialism in any single country possible under conditions of imperialist encirclement? To what extent is a democratic world order a necessary condition for socialism? What is the relationship between class struggle and the struggle for national independence in the present historical context? These questions cannot be addressed within the narrow disciplinary field of legal studies; they cannot be addressed in isolation from socialist political and economic practices.

Lastly, what are the benchmarks for socialist transition? This question is complicated by the ever-present possibilities of restoration of capitalism or reversals on the socialist road. At the present level of development of Marxist theory and practice, the benchmarks for socialist transition must remain intuitive theoretical generalisations. Historical socialist transition is about overcoming the fundamental dualisms and adversarial social relationships on which capitalism as a social system is founded. The dualist and adversarial relations between nature and labour are the most foundational of capitalism's social relations. Several others follow from this foundation, e.g. the adversarial dualisms of economy/polity, private property/wage labour, city/countryside, manual/intellectual labour, class/nation. These adversarial dualist social relationships distinguish capitalism from other social systems. The extent to which these contradictions can be addressed will always depend on the concrete historical conditions inherited by each generation of working people/socialists, the limits of possibilities within each historical condition, and the capacities of working people to lead the transitions to the next level, including Marxist modes of thought and being. Doing so calls for constant education, learning from practices, a grasp of fundamentals of Marxist philosophy, the political ability to evaluate and reevaluate the possibilities when conditions change, and build the capacities to organise for the next stage in socialist transition. Socialism is not a destination or a point of arrival. Socialism is the path to a different way of being human.

Notes

1 I use the term 'Scholastic Marxism' to refer to Marxist theory produced within academia interchangeably with 'Western Marxism' in a wider sense to refer to theories and practices that together form a particular tendency within Marxism with its roots in the Second International. For different understandings of Western Marxism see (Anderson 1989 [1976], Losurdo 2024).

2 For many Western Marxists Mao's use of the term 'stages' could invoke spectres of historical determinism common in scholastic debates on the historical unfolding of socialism in Marxist theory. During the World Wars, for communist parties in the colonial world more generally speaking, the 'stages' question was an immediate practical question about the position they should take when confronted with imperialist aggression. How this question was addressed has shaped the trajectory of socialism in the colonised world to an extent that has not been adequately studied. In China, the question was an immediate and practical one about what the Communist Party of China should do in the face of Japanese invasion of their nation. Mao was not writing a general treatise on historical materialism. Rather he was applying Marxist philosophy to the problem at hand, which was the liberation of their homeland. Anti-colonial movements everywhere, socialist or otherwise, strived for broad based national unity for national liberation or, in Mao's words, to 'unite the many to defeat the few.' The

question for Chinese communists, and indeed communists in anti-colonial struggles, was not one of determinism or voluntarism as a general theory of the historical trajectory of socialism but a contextually specific question of how socialists should respond to the concrete problems that history presented to them, and in so doing, how they could advance Marxist theory.

3 For four decades now a robust debate on modernisation of law, Rule of Law, socialist legality, socialist constitutionalism with Chinese characteristics has prevailed in China (Backer 2017, Can 2013, Ding 2017, Gong 2023, Han 2018, Hsiung 1970, Huang 2010, Jiang and von Appen 2022, Leng 1967, Li and Zhou 2019, Lin and Wu 2022, Liu 2021, Shigong 2010, 2014, Wang 2007, 2013, Xie 2015, Xin 2020, Zhenmin 2009). The CPC has led these legal innovations and reforms. These debates occur alongside extensive law reforms which includes developing socialist constitutional theory. In 2023 the CPC released *Opinions on Strengthening Legal Education and Legal Theory Research in the New Era* calling for developing legal research, theory, scholarly legal community and emphasising the need for grounding the agenda for legal innovations in Marxist jurisprudence (Wang 2024).

References

Ahmed, Faiz. 2016. "In the Name of a Law: Islamic Legal Modernism and the Making of Afghanistan's 1923 Constitution." *International Journal of Middle East Studies* 48 (4):655–677.

America's Founding Documents. n.d. "Meet the Framers of the Constitution." National Archives, accessed 20-01-2025. https://www.archives.gov/founding-docs/founding-fathers.

Anderson, Perry. 1989 [1976]. *Considerations on Western Marxism*. London; New York: Verso.

Backer, Larry Cata. 2017. "Between the Judge and the Law: Judicial Independence and Authority with Chinese Characteristics." *Connecticut Journal of International Law* 33 (1):1–42.

Backer, Larry Cata. 2018. "Chinese Constitutionalism in the "New Era": The Constitution in Emerging Idea and Practice." *Connecticut Journal of International Law* 33 (2):163–214.

Bilchitz, David. 2014. "Egalitarian Liberalism, Distributive Justice and the New Constitutionalism." *Theoria: A Journal of Social and Political Theory* 61 (140):47–69.

Brovkin, Vladimir N. 1990. "The Politics of Constitutional Reform: The New Power Structure and the Role of the Party." *Cornell International Law Journal* 23 (2):323–340.

Bui, Dat T. 2021. "A Quest for Due Process Doctrine in Vietnamese Law: From Soviet Legacy to Global Constitutionalism." *The Chinese Journal of Comparative Law* 9 (2):178–209. doi: 10.1093/cjcl/cxab009.

Can, Zhao. 2013. "Marching towards Rule of Law: An Analysis of the Content on Legal and Judicial Construction in CCP National Congress Reports from 1982 to 2012." *Tsinghua China Law Review* 5 (2):169–185.

Chakste, Mintauts. 1949. "Soviet Concepts of the State, Interntional Law and Sovereignty." *The American Journal of International Law* 43 (21):21–36.

Clunie, Gregor. 2011. "The Public/Private Dichotomy and the Unity of Capitalist (Re-) production." In *The Public in Law: Representations of the Political in Legal Discourse*, edited by Gregor Clunie, Claudio Michelon and Haris Psarras, 177–193. Oxford: Taylor & Francis Group.

Cobos, Felipe Curcó. 2018. "The New Latin American Constitutionalism: A Critical Review in the Context of Neo-Constitutionalism." *Canadian Journal of Latin American and Caribbean Studies/Revue canadienne des études latino-américaines et caraïbes* 43 (2):212–230. doi: 10.1080/08263663.2018.1456141.

Constitution of India, accessed 04-09-2025. https://lddashboard.legislative.gov.in/sites/default/files/coi/COI_2024.pdf.

Constitution of the United States, accessed 04-09-2025. https://constitution.congress.gov/constitution/.

Ding, Xiaodong. 2017. "Law According to the Chinese Communist Party: Constitutionalism and Socialist Rule of Law." *Modern China* 43 (3):322–352.

D'Souza, Radha. 2010. "The Rights Conundrum: Poverty of Philosophy Amidst Poverty." In *Rights in Context: Law and Justice in Late Modern Society*, edited by Reza Banakar, 55–69. Farnham, Surrey; Burlington, VT: Ashgate.

D'Souza, Radha. 2013. "Review Essay: Justice and Governance in Dystopia." *Journal of Critical Realism* 12 (4):518–537.

D'Souza, Radha. "Imperialism and Self-Determination: Revisiting the Nexus in Lenin." *Economic and Political Weekly* XLVIII 15 (April 13, 2013): 60–69.

D'Souza, Radha. 2018a. "The October Revolution and the Anti-colonial Movements in South Asia." *Economic & Political Weekly (Special Articles)* 52 (43):46–58.

D'Souza, Radha. 2018b. *What's Wrong with Rights?: Social Movements, Law and Liberal Imaginations*. London: Pluto Press.

D'Souza, Radha. 2021. "Transcending Disciplinary Fetishisms: Marxism, Neocolonialism, and International Law." In *Elgar Handbook on Law and Marxism*, edited by Paul O'Connell and Umut Ozsu, 335–355. Cheltenham, UK: Edward Elgar.

Engels, Frederick. 1891. "1891 Introduction by Frederick Engels: On the 20th Anniversary of the Paris Commune." Karl Marx: Civil War in France (1871). https://www.marxists.org/archive/marx/works/1871/civil-war-france/index.htm.

Engels, Fredrick. 1972 [1891]. *The Origin of the Family, Private Property and the State*. Moscow: Progress Publishers.

Fang, Ning, and Junhua Zhao. 2020. "Introduction: The Political System of Contemporary China." In *China's Political System*, edited by Ning Fang, xi–xxiii. Singapore: Springer.

Fernández, Albert Noguera. 2012. "Chapter 5 What Do We Mean When We Talk about 'Critical Constitutionalism'? Some Reflections on the New Latin American Constitutions." In *New Constitutionalism in Latin America: Promises and Practices*, edited by Almut Schilling-Vacaflor and Detlef Nolte, 99–119. Oxford: Taylor & Francis Group.

Fuchs, Sandhya. 2024. "The Authoritarian Leader's Playbook: How Narendra Modi Captured India's Legal System and Is Rewriting the Country's History in His Image." accessed 11-04-2024. https://theconversation.com/the-authoritarian-leaders-playbook-how-narendra-modi-captured-indias-legal-system-and-is-rewriting-the-countrys-history-in-his-image-226889.

Gilison, Jerome M. 1972. "Khrushchev, Brezhnev, and Constitutional Reform." *Problems of Communism* 21 (5):69–78.

Gong, Pixiang. 2023. "The Path Evolution of Chinese Modernization of the Rule of Law." *Frontiers of Law in China* 18 (3):348–378.

Han, Dayuan. 2018. "40 Years of Chinese Reform and Opening up Alongside Chinese Constitutional Study." *Frontiers of Law in China* 13 (4):458–496.

Head, Michael. 2020. "Soviet Legal Theory." In *Encyclopedia of the Philosophy of Law and Social Philosophy*, edited by Mortimer Sellers and Stephan Kirste, 1–9. Dordrecht: Springer Netherlands.

Hsiung, James C. 1970. "Peking's Attitudes Toward International Law." *Chinese Law & Government* 3 (1):3–6. doi: 10.2753/CLG0009-460903013.

Huang, Philip C. C. 2010. "Introduction to "Constitutionalism, Reform, and the Nature of the Chinese State: Dialogues among Western and Chinese Scholars, III"." *Modern China* 36 (1):3–11.

Jiang, Hao, and Antonia von Appen. 2022. "The New Validity Rules in Chinese Civil Code and Chinese State-owned Enterprises' Freedom in Contracting: One Step Too Far." *The Chinese Journal of Comparative Law* 10 (3): 1–19. doi: 10.1093/cjcl/cxac024.

Kamali, Mohamed Hashim. 1985. *Law in Afghanistan: A Study of the Constitutions, Matrimonial Law and the Judiciary*. Leiden: Brill.

Khaitan, Tarunabh. 2020. "Killing a Constitution with a Thousand Cuts: Executive Aggrandizement and Party-state Fusion in India." *Law & Ethics of Human Rights* 14 (1):49–95. doi: 10.1515/lehr-2020-2009.

Leng, Shao-Chuan. 1967. "Pre-1949 Development of the Communist Chinese System of Justice." *The China Quarterly* 30:93–114. doi: 10.1017/S0305741000029210.

Lenin, Vladimir Ilych. 1908 [1973]. "Marxism and Revisionism." In *Collected Works*, edited by Vladimir Ilych Lenin, 29–39. Moscow: Progress Publishers.

Lenin, Vladimir Ilych 1970 [1905]. "Two Tactics of Social-Democracy In the Democratic Revolution." In *Selected Works in Three Volumes - Vol 1*, edited by Vladimir Ilych Lenin, 459–563. Moscow: Progress Publishers.

Lenin, Vladimir Ilych 1970 [1917]. "Imperialism the Highest Stage of Capitalism." In *Selected Works in Three Volumes Vol. 1*, edited by Vladimir Ilych Lenin, 667–768. Moscow: Progress Publishers.

Lenin, Vladimir Ilych 1971 [1920]. "Speech at the Second Congress of the Communist International." In *Selected Works in Three Volumes*, edited by Vladimir Ilych Lenin, 449–464. Moscow: Progress Publishers.

Lenin, Vladimir Ilych 1972 [1908]. "Lessons of the Commune." In *Collected Works*, edited by Vladimir Ilych Lenin, 475–478. Moscow: Progress Publishers.

Lenin, Vladimir Ilych 1974. "Notebooks on Imperialism." In *Collected Works Vol. 39*, edited by Vladimir Ilych Lenin. Moscow: Progress publishers.

Leskinen, Anna. 2015. "Methodological Issues in Studies of Cultural Legacies in Post-Socialist Russia's Civil Society." *Nonprofit Policy Forum* 6 (2):145–165. doi: 10.1515/npf-2014-0005.

Li, Ling, and Wenzhang Zhou. 2019. "Governing the "Constitutional Vacuum"–Federalism, Rule of Law, and Politburo Politics in China." *China Law and Society Review* 4 (1):1–40. doi: 10.1163/25427466-00401001.

Lin, Xifen, and Wanqiang Wu. 2022. "Something Lost, Something Gained: Changes in China's Procuratorate in Response to the Reform of the National Supervision System." *China Law and Society Review* 6 (1):79–110. doi: 10.1163/25427466-07010002.

Liu, Sida. 2021. "Cage for the Birds: On the Social Transformation of Chinese Law, 1999–2019." *China Law and Society Review* 5 (2):66–87. doi: 10.1163/25427466-00502002.

Lomb, Samantha. 2018. *Stalin's Constitution: Soviet Participatory Politics and the Discussion of the 1936 Draft Constitution*. Abingdon; Oxon; New York: Routledge.

Losurdo, Domenico. 2003. "History of the Communist Movement: Failure, Betrayal, or Learning Process?" *Nature, Society, and Thought* 16 (1):33.

Losurdo, Domenico. 2023 [2008]. *Stalin: History And Crtique of a Black Legend*. Translated by Salvatore Engel-Di Mauro and Henry Hakamäki. New York; Dublin; London: Iskra Books.

Losurdo, Domenico. 2024. *Western Marxism: How It Was Born, How It Died, How It Can Be Reborn*. New York: Monthly Review Press.

Losurdo, Domenico. Oct 31, 2000. "Flight from History? The Communist Movement: Between Self-Criticism and Self-Contempt." *Nature, Society, and Thought* 13 (4):457–484.

Loughlin, Martin. 2022. *Against Constitutionalism*. Cambridge, MA; London: Harvard University Press.

LPE Project. 2020. "Symposia: Socialist Constitutionalism." *Law and Political Economy*, accessed 17-10-2024. https://lpeproject.org/symposia/socialist-constitutionalism/.

Mahmood Mamdani, Mamdani. 2020. *Neither Settler nor Native: The Making and Unmaking of Permanent Minorities*. Cambridge, Massachusetts; London, England: Harvard University Press.

Mao, Tse-tung. 1964. "On Khrushchov's Phoney Communism and Its Historical Lessons for the World: Comment on the Open Letter of the Central Committee of the CPSU (IX)." In *Pamphlet Published by Foriegn Languages Press*, edited by Renmin Ribao (People's Daily) and Hongqui (Red Flag) 14 July. Peking. https://www.marxists.org/reference/archive/mao/works/1964/phnycom.htm.

Mao, Tse-tung. 1965. "On Practice." In *Selected Works of Mao Tse-tung*, 295–309. Peking: Foriegn Languages Press.

Mao, Tse-tung. 1969 [1949]. "On the People's Democratic Dictatorship." In *Selected Works of Mao Tse-tung Vol.IV*, edited by Committee for the Publication of the Selected Works of Mao Tse-tung Central Committee of the Communist Party of China, 411–424. Peking: Foriegn Languages Press.

Mao, Tse-tung. 1975 [1940]. "On New Democracy." In *Selected Works of Mao Tse-Tung*, edited by Committee for the Publication of the Selected Works of Mao Tse-tung Central Committee of the Communist Party of China, Vol II, 339–384. Peking: Foreign Languages Press.

Mao, Tse-tung. 1977 [1928]. "Why Is It That Red Political Power Can Exist in China?" In *Selected Works of Mao Tse-tung Vol.I*, edited by Committee for the Publication of the Selected Works of Mao Tse-tung Central Committee of the Communist Party of China, 63–72. Peking: Foriegn Languages Press.

Marković, Goran. 2017. "Novelties of the Soviet Constitutionalism: The Principle of Unity of Powers." *International Critical Thought* 7 (3):345–363. doi: 10.1080/21598282.2017.1356234.

Marx, Karl. 1833–1844. "Introduction to A Contribution to the Critique of Hegel's Philosophy of Right (Translator: Josephy O'Malley)." *Marxist Internet Archive*. https://www.marxists.org/archive/marx/works/1843/critique-hpr/index.htm.

Marx, Karl. 1950 [1851]. "The Eighteenth Brumaire of Louis Bonaparte." In *Selected Works in Two Volumes - Vol 1*, edited by Karl Marx and Fredrick Engels, 221–311. Moscow: Foriegn Languages Publishing House.

Marx, Karl. 1980 [1855]. "The British Constitution." In *Collected Works*, edited by Karl Marx and Fredrick Engels, 53–56. Moscow: Progress Publishers.

Marx, Karl, and Frederick Engels. 1969 [1848]. "Manifesto of the Communist Party." In *Selected Works, Vol. I,* edited by Karl Marx and Fredrick Engels, 98–137. Moscow: Progress Publishers.

Marx, Karl, and Fredrick Engels. 1981 [1846]. *The German Ideology*, edited by C. J. Arthur. New York: International Publishers.

Marx-Engels-Lenin Institute. 1943. *Lenin: A Biography*. London: Hutchinson & Co (Publishers) Lts.

Menon, Annapurna. 2022. "Debunking Hindutva Appropriation of Decolonial Thought." *Interfere: Journal for Critical Thought and Radical Politics* 3 (3):36–57.

Nkrumah, Kwame. 1968. *Neo-colonialism: The Last Stage of Imperialism*. London: Heinemann Educational.

O'Connell, Paul, and Umut Özsu. 2021. *Research Handbook on Law and Marxism*. Cheltenham, UK: Edward Elgar Publishing.

Penington, Robert. 1931. "Origin of Corporations." *Corporate Practice Review* 3 (5):33–37.

Piers Beirne, and Alan Hunt. 1988. "Law and the Constitution of Soviet Society: The Case of Comrade Lenin." *Law and Society Review* 22 (3):575–614.

Riddell, John, ed. 2015. *To the Masses. Proceedings of the Third Congress of the Communist International, 1921, Historical Materialism Book Series. 91*. Leiden; Boston, MA: Brill.

Sampford, Charles. 1991. "Law, Institutions and the Public/Private Divide." *Federal Law Review* 20 (2):185–222.

Shigong, Jiang. 2010. "Written and Unwritten Constitutions: A New Approach to the Study of Constitutional Government in China." *Modern China* 36 (1):12–46.

Shigong, Jiang. 2014. "How to Explore the Chinese Path to Constitutionalism? A Response to Larry Catá Backer." *Modern China* 40 (2):196–213.

Stalin, Joseph Vissarionovich. 1974 [1927]. "Interview with the First American Labour Delegation, September 9, 1927." In *Selected Writings: J.V. Stalin*, edited by Sunil Basu, pp. 15–45. Calcutta: National Book Agency Private Ltd.

Teitel, Ruti. 1994. "Post-Communist Constitutionalism: A Transitional Perspective." *Columbia Human Rights Law Review* 26 (1):167–190.

The Central Committee of the C.P.S.U (B). 1945. *History of the Communist Party of the Soviet Union (Bolsheviks): A Short Course*. Moscow: Foriegn Lanugages Publishing House.

Tkatova, Rima. 2010. "Central Asian States and International Law: Between Post-Soviet Culture and Eurasian Civilization." *Chinese Journal of International Law* 9 (1):205–220. doi: 10.1093/chinesejil/jmp036.

Tomba, Massimiliano. 2017. "Politics beyond the State: The 1918 Soviet Constitution." *Constellations* 24:503–515.

Wang, Xigen. 2024. "Strengthening Research on the Basic Legal Theory and Adapting Marxist Jurisprudence to the Chinese Context and the Needs of the Times *." *Frontiers of Law in China* 19 (3):261–270. doi: 10.3868/s050-013-024-0017-3.

Wang, Zhenmin. 2013. "Constitutional Politics: The Road to Permanent Peace and Stability on How the Communist Party of China Can Escape from the Historical Cycle." *Tsinghua China Law Review* 6 (1):1–22.

Wang, Zhuojun. 2007. "Democsracy, Rule of Law and Human Rights Protection under Gradually Developed Constitutionalism - By the Clue of Administrative Law." *Frontiers of Law in China* 2:335–352.

Xi, Jinping. 2014. *The Governance of China.* Beijing: Foreign Languages Press.

Xie, Hongren. 2015. "Restore the Truth: Traditional Chinese Law and Its Distortion by the Western Knowledge System." *International Critical Thought* 5 (3):296–312. doi: 10.1080/21598282.2015.1065378.

Xin, Xiangyang. 2020. "Prominent Features of the System of Socialism with Chinese Characteristics and China's Governance System." *International Critical Thought* 10 (2):161–181. doi: 10.1080/21598282.2020.1778258.

Ying, Sun. 2023. The National People's Congress in China. In *Routledge Handbook of Asian Parliaments*, edited by Po Jen Yap and Rehan Abeyratne, pp. 125–136. London: Routledge.

Zhenmin, Wang. 2009. "The Tsinghua China Law Review." *Tsinghua China Law Review* 1 (1):v–vii.

2 Socialism, Working Class Self-Emancipation, and Democratic Forms

Paul O'Connell

2.1 Introduction

In July 2024, five members of the environmental protest group Just Stop Oil (JSO) were given sentences of between four and five years in prison for planning a peaceful protest to disrupt the M25 motorway around London. These sentences are thought to be the longest ever given for non-violent protest in Britain (Gayle, 2024). The sentences were widely condemned as draconian, with the UN Special Rapporteur on Environmental Defenders, Michel Forst, describing them as 'punitive and repressive' and warning that the case represented a dangerous ruling that would likely deter people across Britain from protesting on any number of issues (Gayle, Horton, and Quinn, 2024). While the sentences were reduced on appeal (Friends of the Earth, 2025), the JSO case nonetheless crystallises a number of crucially important issues concerning rights, democracy and social change. Climate activism, in its various forms, is one of the central sites of activity for social change today. Given the pressing nature of the unfolding climate catastrophe, many people have turned to forms of non-violent protest and direct action, in a desperate effort to provoke action. Invariably, they have been met, in Britain and elsewhere, with aggressive policing, opprobrium from mainstream media and politicians and a raft of new anti-protest laws.

It was under one such law, the Police, Crime, Sentencing and Courts Act 2022 (PCSCA), that the JSO activists were convicted and given their lengthy sentences. The PCSCA created several new protest related offences, as well as expanding the scope of existing police powers under the Public Order Act 1986 (Martin, 2021; European Centre for Not-for-Profit Law, 2021). It was followed by the Public Order Act 2023, which added even further police powers and protest related offences to the statute book. Taken together, these legislative changes, and the wider rhetorical assault on climate, anti-war and anti-capitalist protesters, constitute a fundamental assault on the right to protest in Britain (Türk, 2023). But, the British experience is not exceptional, instead it reflects part of a global trend, in the context of persistent capitalist crises, of states the world over opting to repress and police opposition to the crises of the system,

DOI: 10.4324/9781032621623-3

rather than an attempt to meaningfully address the root causes of these crises (Roberts, 2013; Wood, 2014; Selmini and Di Ronco, 2023). The conviction and sentencing of the JSO protesters, then, raises a set of questions about the nature of the contemporary global order, building resistance and alternatives to the crisis ridden system of neoliberal imperialist capitalism, and the role of democratic forms such as rights.

While there is, with much justification, scepticism, sometimes bordering on nihilism, to rights and democratic forms from different sections of the broad left, this chapter will argue that defending, expanding and moving beyond these democratic forms is essential to any movement which seeks fundamental change today. The chapter begins with a discussion of the attitude of Marx, Engels and leading figures of classical Marxism to the question of democratic forms. What becomes apparent is that while classical Marxists had no illusions in bourgeois rights and other democratic forms, they nonetheless saw them as essential weapons in the struggles of the working class. The next section of the chapter moves the focus to the principle of working class self-emancipation to make two related arguments: (i) this principle was central to Marx's entire theoretical and political project and should be central to contemporary efforts to mobilise Marxism, and (ii) the principle of working class self-emancipation has important implications for how we think through democratic forms today. In Section 2.3, a sketch is offered of the contemporary global order, to ground and contextualise the discussion of how we should approach democratic forms today. This section emphasises two tendencies, growing inequality and rising authoritarianism, as central to understanding the coordinates of struggle in the world today.

The final substantial section draws from all the foregoing to argue that in the context of neoliberal decline and authoritarianism, democratic forms must play a central role in building movements for fundamental social change. This is not based on some naive commitment to abstract right, or the presumed priority of legal or formal institutional mechanisms for struggle. Instead, the assertion, expansion and transgressive re-crafting of these inherited democratic forms is crucial both to facilitate working class self-emancipation in the twenty-first century and to frame a political project that critiques and points beyond neoliberal hegemony.

2.2 Marxism and Democratic Forms

For opponents and critics of Marxism and revolutionary socialism, it is a given that these traditions are hostile and inimical to the democratic forms (rights, liberties, institutions and so on) associated with the bourgeois revolutions of the eighteenth and nineteenth centuries (Lukes, 1981; Macfarlane, 1982; Kołakowski, 1983). While it is true that the relationship of movements for radical social change and the extant democratic forms of capitalist societies has long been the subject of some debate. It is also the case that for many socialists it has been axiomatic that their project, both the goal of socialism and the struggle to attain it, must be fundamentally democratic (Geras, 1994, p. 92). This section explores that aspect of the Marxist and socialist tradition. Not to produce some writ from the dead for or against democratic forms, but instead to understand how these forms were understood by revolutionaries and the role of working class movements in advancing and expanding these forms.

It has long been assumed without much ado that Marx was opposed to human rights and bourgeois democracy. This conclusion is usually reached with partial, decontextualised quotes from *On the Jewish Question*, or the *Critique of the Gotha Program*, and some vague gesturing towards the crimes of authoritarian regimes which purported to be Marxist, socialist or communist. The reality is very different. As Igor Shoikhedbrod has recently shown, a close reading of Marx's work demonstrates that while he was a radical critic of liberalism and certain liberal rights, his main objective was to show the inherent 'contradictions and limitations of rights in capitalist society', but he nonetheless saw 'these rights as preconditions for communist society' (Shoikhedbrod, 2019, p. 55).

Indeed, Marx's argument in *On the Jewish Question* is, in the first instance, a defence of the equal rights of Jews within Europe, and the core theoretical insight of his argument is that while the rights associated with the bourgeois revolutions are a huge step forward for human freedom, they simply do not, and cannot, go far enough. This is because these rights are hitched to the system of capitalist property relations, a system which necessarily and invariably produces hierarchy, exploitation, oppression and inequality, thus negating the promise of freedom contained in these rights (Marx, [1843] 1987). Marx draws the important distinction between formal freedom and substantive freedom and concludes that rights under capitalism can only ever deliver the former (Marx, [1843] 1987, pp. 149–155). This is progress, he argues, but for true freedom and liberation, we must go beyond the mere formality of bourgeois rights and the substantive inequality of capitalist property relations. Taken along with his consistent defence of free speech, fair elections and more, Marx, far from being against rights and democratic forms, was committed to the defence of the limited gains they represented, while also, always, pointing for the need to go beyond them. As Hal Draper puts it, for Marx, 'the fight for democratic forms… was a leading edge of the socialist effort; not its be-all and end-all but an integral part of it all' (Draper, 1977, p. 282).

Marx's long time intellectual and political collaborator Frederick Engels followed a similar line to Marx on these matters, but for present purposes, he also made some significant points about the value of democratic forms within capitalism for socialist and working class movements. In his 1865 article entitled *The Prussian Military Question and the German Workers' Party,* Engels addressed directly the importance of bourgeois rights for the working class, notwithstanding the limitations and contradictions of those rights. From the outset, Engels notes that 'despite [their] bourgeois character', the rights to freedom of the press, free association and assembly and universal suffrage were rights 'without which the workers can never win their emancipation' (Engels, [1865] 1985, p. 69). Engels notes the hypocrisy and cowardice of the newly ascendant bourgeois but notes also that in their struggles against the decaying feudal order, they cannot win their own rights without 'at the same time putting weapons into the hands of the proletariat' (Engels, [1865] 1985, p. 77). As distinct from the old feudal order, the bourgeois 'must proclaim human rights… freedom and self-government', and, following Marx, Engels notes that while these forms may often ring hollow, with their adoption,

> the proletariat will thereby… acquire all the weapons it needs for its ultimate victory. With freedom of the press and the right of assembly and association it will win universal suffrage, and with universal, direct suffrage, in conjunction with the above tools of agitation, it will win everything else.
>
> (Engels, [1865] 1985, p. 77)

While we may, with the benefit of experience, say that Engels optimism in the efficacy of universal suffrage and associated democratic forms to allow the working class and socialist movements to 'win everything else' was misplaced. His argument nonetheless shows the importance that he, and many in the classical Marxist tradition, placed on these democratic forms.

It should also be noted that while Engels was, arguably, overly optimistic in some respects, he was not at all starry-eyed. He noted that, as had already happened, the bourgeois would align with the forces of feudal reaction to defend property against the demands of the working class. But even allowing for this, Engels argued that it was still incumbent on the working class to defend the democratic forms and freedoms associated with the bourgeoisie. As Engels put it,

> Even if the worst came to the worst and the bourgeoisie was to scurry under the skirts of reaction for fear of the workers… even then the workers' party would have no choice but, notwithstanding the bourgeoisie, to continue its campaign for bourgeois freedom, freedom of the press and rights of assembly and association which the bourgeoisie had betrayed. Without these freedoms it will be unable to move freely itself; in this struggle it is fighting to establish the environment necessary for its existence, for the air it needs to breathe.
>
> (Engels, [1865] 1985, p. 79, emphasis added)

This shows two clear points. One, the resolute commitment of Engels (and we can add Marx) to the defence of bourgeois freedoms, notwithstanding their innate limitations. Secondly, it shows that this is not a commitment grounded in moralism or some abstract concept of right, but in the recognition of the importance of these democratic forms within capitalist societies to allow the working class to build the movements necessary to break with capitalism and move to a higher stage of freedom.

The views expressed by Engels were, for the most part, the common sense of the working class and socialist movement through the nineteenth and early twentieth century. There were exceptions, to be sure, usually in the form of what Draper calls 'self-styled radicals' (Draper, 1977, p. 284), who rejected bourgeois democracy and rights. The dominant trend, however, was to see the importance of these inherited democratic forms, alongside the need to push beyond them. Rosa Luxemburg, for example, referred to freedom of the press and the right to assembly as 'sacred rights' (Luxemburg, [1915] 1970a, p. 298), which constituted the 'most important guarantees of a healthy public life and of the political activity of the labouring masses' (Luxemburg, [1915] 1970b, p. 389). Like Engels, Luxemburg's commitment to rights is not born of some moral commitment to abstract right but firmly rooted in the importance of these democratic forms for working class self-activity. Interestingly, Norman Geras notes that when Luxemburg spoke of rights and other democratic forms, she did not speak of them as merely part of the liberal heritage but took it 'for granted that they are indigenous to revolutionary socialism, she invokes them just like that. Such was the world she inhabited' (Geras, 1994, p. 98).

James Connolly, a contemporary of Luxemburg, provides another illustration of the commitment that revolutionaries had to the defence of rights and other democratic forms in the early twentieth century. Connolly was very much enmeshed in revolutionary struggle and was not at all naive about rights and the law. In 1899, Connolly noted that all the 'pretended political freedom and rights of citizenship' in the British Constitution were 'ever at the mercy of the governing class of England', who had no respect for these rights and would be quick to suppress them through the police and military force (Connolly, [1899] 2011a, p. 157). Notwithstanding this, Connolly recognised the significance of the rights to free speech, assembly and fair elections, and viewed them as important victories won by the working class (a point we return to below). In this light, Connolly argued that experience had taught 'the working class to guard what rights it has whilst reaching out to win greater rights for the future' (Connolly, [1914] 2011b, p. 488). Writing in 1914, in the teeth of World War One, Connolly noted that one major consequence of the war was that the working class had lost 'in a great measure, in Britain at least, all those hard-won rights of combination and freedom of action, the possession of which was the foundation upon which they hoped to build the greater freedom of the future' (Connolly, [1914] 2011c, p. 571). The emphasis here, echoing Marx, Engels, Luxemburg and others, is on the importance of rights, in particular, as necessary to the attainment of the wider goals of the socialist and working class movements.

The foregoing speaks to the understanding of rights and democratic forms within much of the classical Marxist and revolutionary socialist tradition. An understanding which highlighted the inherent limitation of bourgeois rights and democratic forms within the context of capitalist property relations, but nonetheless expressed a commitment to the defence of these forms, while also pointing to the need to go beyond them. Alongside this theoretical perspective, it is also important to note the concrete, material contribution of working class and revolutionary movements to the advance and shaping of key rights and democratic forms. As Geras notes, socialists were routinely 'involved in, sometimes at the forefront of, movements for the defence and extension' of liberal rights and liberties (Geras, 1994, p. 92). Going even further, E.P. Thompson argued that,

> Our society today – our democratic liberties and our social services – is in great part the product of [the struggle between labour and capital], and of the adjustments to it on the part of capitalist interests. If campaigners can meet in Trafalgar Square today, it is because of the great struggles for freedom of speech and assembly waged by radical and socialist working men in the 1880s and 1890s.
>
> (Thompson, 1959, p. 54)

Michael Löwy makes a similar point, arguing that 'democratic rights—freedom of expression and organization, universal suffrage, political pluralism—are not "bourgeois institutions" but hard-won conquests of the labour movement' (Löwy, 2013, p. ix).

This is an important point, because while it is common to set up socialism and Marxism as the antithesis of bourgeois rights and democratic forms, the history is much more complex. As Geras noted of Luxemburg, she and many others in the Marxist and revolutionary socialist tradition spoke of rights and democratic forms as indigenous to their tradition, because the working class and socialists had been central in struggles to advance these rights. This can be seen in Michael Foot's magisterial work on the origins of universal suffrage, where he shows that it was the working classes and broader masses who won and defined the right to vote over centuries of protracted struggle (Foot, 2005). The same can be said for, among others, the rights to free speech and protest (Stammers, 2009, pp. 70–101). On the latter, Engels wrote in 1872 about how the Gladstone government imposed restrictions on protests in public parks around London, and in doing so 'destroyed with one stroke of the pen one of the most precious rights of London's working people'. But, Engels happily relates, in response to this decree the working class of London organised massive protests 'in defiance of the government's decree'. The regulation was made unenforceable by the mass civil disobedience of the working class and was quietly allowed to lapse (Engels, [1872] 1985, pp. 294–295). This episode, and there are many more besides (Navickas, 2022), drives home Draper's point that 'it is the constant threat from below that ensures the recognition of democratic rights in practice' (Draper, 1977, p. 309).

The classic liberal or bourgeois rights and democratic forms which we have inherited are, therefore, not purely liberal or bourgeois. Instead, history shows that they were decisively shaped by the struggles of the working class and socialist movements. The importance of this point is drawn out by Ambalavaner Sivanandan, writing during the ascendancy of neoliberalism, in a passage that merits quotation at length. Sivanandan noted that,

> the freedoms won in [the] great period of industrial working-class struggle are being threatened. The emancipation of Capital from Labour has left a moral vacuum at the heart of post-industrial society, which is itself material. The 'universalist' bourgeois values which Bill Warren wrote about – 'equality, justice, generosity, independence of spirit and mind, the spirit of inquiry and adventure, opposition to cruelty' – and which sprang precisely from the creative tension between Capital and Labour are endangered by Capital's emancipation. The Factory Acts which took children out of work and women from the mines and gave them the light of day, the Education Acts that opened their minds out to other worlds and the world, the Public Health Acts which stopped the spread of disease and plagues – all came out of the tension, the hostility, between Capital and Labour… Freedom of speech, of assembly, the right to withhold one's labour, universal suffrage, sprang not from bourgeois benefice but from working-class struggle. All the gains of the period of industrial capitalism were the creative outcome of social contradictions – the heart of dialectical materialism.
>
> (Sivanandan, 1989, pp. 23–24)

The dynamic tension produced by the conflict between labour and capital played a crucial role in shaping rights and democratic forms in the nineteenth and twentieth centuries. It was in this context that Marxists and socialists adopted the position of defending and advancing these rights, while always seeking to go beyond them. It was in this context that such rights and democratic forms were, in certain contexts, revolutionary, radical and transgressive.

That context, of course, has passed. As Sivanandan intimated, the triumph of capital over labour, what is referred to now as the ascendancy of neoliberalism, reflected a qualitative shift in the relationship of capital to labour. In this context, the dynamic tension which made rights tangible, significant or important to movements for radical change has been replaced by an era in which the language of human rights has become ubiquitous while the systemic denial of rights has become entrenched (Evans, 2005, p. 6), where universal suffrage has been undermined by the entrenchment of modern forms of public opinion management and democratic decay. Without in anyway painting the past of rights and democratic forms in purely rosy colours, this shift in context has transformed the nature of rights and the relationship of movements for radical change to them. Rather than being transgressive weapons in the hands of the working class, rights and the broader democratic forms are entrenched in an industry of non-governmental organisations (NGOs) and think tanks.

The entire purpose of rights, now, seems to be to act as a metric for the calibration of their own violation. The attitude of earlier generations of revolutionaries, instructive as it may be, cannot simply be embraced or reproduced in this changed context. Instead, the question arises on new terrain, how, considering the lessons of the past, should movements for radical social change, and in particular revolutionary socialists, engage with our inherited democratic forms in an era of authoritarianism, crisis and moribund democracy. To begin to essay an answer to this question, the next section turns to the principle of working class self-emancipation, a principle that is integral to Marx's work, and to the best elements of the revolutionary socialist tradition. This principle, it will be argued, provides a crucial orientation to inform our approach to the question of rights and democratic forms today.

2.3 Working Class Self-Emancipation

The core of Marx's political and theoretical project was to understand capitalist society, in order to change it. More importantly, Marx anticipated and sought a revolutionary break with the capitalist mode of production, with its attendant barbarism and degradation, and the development of a higher form of society. From his early years as a radical philosopher and political journalist, through to his later years as the critic par excellence of capitalism, Marx stressed that the working class must, and would, be the motor force of this historical transformation. Marx, breaking with the elitism of earlier socialisms, centred the self-activity of the working class in his understanding of socialism and revolutionary change.

On the significance of this orientation, Draper notes that 'against all varieties of socialism and reform which looked on the masses in the accusative case ("we will emancipate them"), Marx developed the principle of the self-emancipation of the working class' (Draper, 1977, p. 216). This approach, this focus on the centrality of working class self-activity and self-emancipation, is, as Geras notes, 'central, not incidental' to Marx's entire political and theoretical project (Geras, 1973, p. 20). Expanding on this, Dan Swain argues that the principle of working class self-emancipation shapes Marx's,

> conception of what is wrong with capitalism, his notions of freedom and domination. It influences his conception of both the form and content of any alternative to capitalism, and how much it is possible to say about it. Moreover, it influences his sense of himself as an activist and politically engaged critical theorist, and of the role of other activists and theorists.
>
> (Swain, 2019, p. 1)

It follows that in trying to think through how those committed to fundamental social change today should engage with the extant democratic forms of capitalist societies, it is appropriate that the principle of working class self-emancipation should occupy a central place in our analysis. Indeed, the argument here is that the principle of working class self-emancipation provides an essential element for thinking through how we mobilise the Marxist and revolutionary socialist tradition today.

The classic formulation of the principle can be found in the *Rules of the First International* (which Marx wrote), which state that 'the emancipation of the working classes must be conquered by the working classes themselves' (Marx, [1864] 1985, p. 14). Ted Stolze argues that this formulation translates into the understanding that emancipation 'is not a gift bestowed from on high; it is instead the fruit of the concerted and intergenerational efforts of millions of ordinary human beings to achieve a society worthy of their collective struggle' (Stolze, 2019, p. 275). Stolze argues, further, that a commitment to this principle was the 'defining feature of Marx's mature politics' (Stolze, 2019, p. 270), but, as Swain indicates above, Marx's commitment to the principle goes back much further than that.

In his Preface to the 1888 English edition of the *Communist Manifesto,* Engels wrote that the principle of working class self-emancipation had long since been his and Marx's guiding principle, that it had been their 'notion, from the very beginning' that working class self-emancipation was a defining feature of their analysis (Marx and Engels, [1848] [1888] 2002, p. 202). Indeed, as early as 1844 Marx, in his critique of Arnold Ruge, identified the working class not as the passive, and pitiable, objects of history, waiting for a benevolent (middle or upper class) subject to lead them to freedom. Instead, Marx centred the self-activity and development of the working class as the only meaningful basis for bringing about the social movement and transformation necessary to begin to break with capitalism (Draper, 1977, pp. 219–221).

Marx's engagement with this idea continued through his critique of the Young Hegelians, in *The Holy Family* and his *Theses on Feuerbach* (which we return to below), and by 1847 'the idea of self-emancipation merged in Marx's thinking with the view of the class struggle as the crux' of socialist politics (Draper, 1978, p. 150). From Marx, and Engels, the importance of working class self-emancipation was carried over into the First and Second Internationals and can 'be found in virtually all the political writers of classical Marxism' (Geras, 1994, p. 95). It can be seen clearly, for example, in the work of Luxemburg, who stressed, time and again, that socialism 'will not be and cannot be inaugurated by decrees; it cannot be established by any government, however admirably socialistic. Socialism must be created by the masses, must be made by every proletarian' (Luxemburg, [1918] 1970c, p. 419). In a similar vein, Connolly, Luxemburg's contemporary, summed up the same core principle, although writing specifically about the issue of women's liberation, with the aphorism that 'there are none so fit to break the chains as those who bear them' (Connolly, [1915] 2021, p. 60).

Another important idea in Marx's work which complements the principle of self-emancipation is the idea of revolutionary praxis. Returning to the *Theses on Feuerbach*, Marx notes in the third thesis that while the basic materialist insight that people are products of their circumstances was sound, it neglected the central fact that it is people who change their circumstances, and in the process change themselves. This 'coincidence of the changing of circumstances and of human activity', Marx argued, 'can be conceived and rationally understood only as revolutionising practice' (Marx, [1845] 1985, p. 3). Central to this third thesis was the rejection of the benighted leader (i.e. Robert Owen) leading the working class to their emancipation, with this top-down model replaced by the transformative self-activity, praxis, of the working class.

The third thesis is particularly relevant and important to the principle of working class self-emancipation, because it 'breaks the circle which cuts men off from the possibility of self-transformation and, doing so, liberates them from the need for liberators' (Geras, 1973, p. 21). This is important because, as Marx stressed numerous times, the consolidation of capitalism 'develops a working class which by education, tradition and habit looks upon the requirements of that mode of production as self-evident natural laws... the capitalist process of production, once it is fully developed, breaks down all resistance' (Marx, [1867] 1990, p. 899). Because capitalism, in myriad ways, inculcates, in those who are exploited most and suffer most under its operation, this sense that 'there is no alternative', aprolonged period of struggle, education and self-transformation is needed to empower people to break with this system and imagine an alternative to it.

This latter point was acknowledged and spelled out by Marx and Engels in *The German Ideology*, where they noted that,

> Both for the production on a mass scale of... communist consciousness, and for the success of the cause itself, the alteration of men on a mass scale is necessary, an alteration which can only take place in a practical movement, a revolution; this revolution is necessary, therefore, not only because the ruling class cannot be overthrown in any other way, but also because the class overthrowing it can only in a revolution succeed in ridding itself of all the muck of ages and become fitted to found society anew.
>
> (Marx and Engels, [1845] 1985, pp. 52–53)

This protracted, dialectical, process of the working classes changing their own ideas and aspirations through struggles for immediate concrete demands is essential for the working class to emancipate itself. As Swain notes, if 'society is to be transformed, it must be on the basis of a process of self-transformation, in which people change themselves as they change the world' (Swain, 2019, p. 45). The emphasis that Marx, Engels and others place on the need for this sort of transformation reflects a clear eyed understanding about how the ideologies of individualism, fatalism and so forth infuse the broad masses of people who labour under capitalism.

Working class self-activity, or revolutionary practice, is central to building alternatives to the alienating, degrading order produced by capitalist relations of production. As Thompson put it,

> For working people above all, the road to human fulfilment in capitalist society has been bound up, in one way or another, with political organisation. It is through conscious action against exploitation and class oppression that they have ceased to be victims of their environment, and have achieved the dignity of actors in the making of their own history.
>
> (Thompson, 1959, p. 53)

This idea of the working class becoming actors in the making of their own history is also stressed by Michael Lebowitz. Drawing both on recent political experiences, in Venezuela and Bolivia in particular, and on a close reading of Marx's work, Lebowitz argues that 'Marx's concept of revolutionary practice: the simultaneous changing of circumstances and human activity or self-change… is the basis for the recognition… of the importance of protagonism in the development of human capacity' (Lebowitz, 2020, p. 163).

Lebowitz' argument usefully brings us to a point where we can weave together the various strands of the principle of working class self-emancipation. In brief, the argument runs as follows: the core of Marxism and revolutionary socialism is the principle of working class self-emancipation; working class self-emancipation requires revolutionary practice, the simultaneous transformation of circumstance and the self; this process of practice builds and enhances the capacities of people; so that they, in turn, can cease to be the victims of circumstance, and instead become actors meaningfully engaged in processes to break with capitalism, and build a higher form of society centred on the fulfilment of human needs and the realisation of human capacities.

With this as a starting point, a number of other important points necessarily follow. As Lebowitz argues, once we recognise 'the centrality of revolutionary practice, we understand that organizational forms matter… You need, in short, to create spaces that allow people to take steps through which they transform themselves' (Lebowitz, 2020, p. 165). In this regard, Marta Harnecker, who was also heavily involved in the recent revolutionary movements in Venezuela, Bolivia and elsewhere, stresses the need for a 'political instrument' to provide the space and support for this self-activity. As Harnecker put it,

> Finally, we have the most important task, because without it we will never be able to build socialism. What is needed is a political instrument that encourages popular protagonism in the most varied social and political milieus… one that puts itself at the service of that participation so that it is the people

> themselves who build the new society… Only thus will we be true to the thesis that revolutionary practice is essential for workers' emancipation and that of the popular movement in general. It is through practice that full human development is reached, this being the most important goal we are aiming for.
> (Harnecker, 2015, p. 179)

Echoing this, Lebowitz argues that 'encouraging the development of the capacities of the working class is the most important task of the political instrument' (Lebowitz, 2020, p. 171). The pursuit of working class self-emancipation, then, requires organisations and spaces where the working classes can develop their capacities, build their confidence and transform themselves in the process of striving to transform society.

The question of political organisation, and specifically the role of a revolutionary party, is central to understanding how working class self-emancipation can be realised. As Dimitrios Kivotidis argues,

> the leading role of the party is essential to counter the formidable force of habit and false consciousness, not because party membership provides immunity from false consciousness but because it presupposes an awareness of capitalist contradictions and the need to overcome them.
> (Kivotidis, 2024, p. 246)

The party, understood properly, is not an external force imposing itself on the working class but rather the organised expression of the class's most conscious elements. It functions as a 'political instrument' that encourages popular protagonism while providing strategic direction and coordination (Harnecker, 2015, p. 179). This understanding rejects the view that mass organisations can, by themselves, spontaneously achieve the consciousness necessary to overcome 'the partial and sectoral interests and the long held and deeply ingrained views of bourgeois ideology' (Kivotidis, 2024, p. 246). At the same time, 'no revolutionary workers' party can be successful in building a communist society by itself without directing its forces and attention towards building the institutional forms of mass participation' (Kivotidis, 2024, p. 246). The party is therefore a necessary institutional form for socialist democracy, working together with councils, trade unions and other organisations in a process of bidirectional learning (Kivotidis, 2024, p. 247).

Alongside the party as political instrument, the historical experience of workers' councils provides a crucial example of how the principle of working class self-emancipation can be institutionalised in practice. Workers' councils, or Soviets, first arose during the 1905 Russian Revolution out of the big strike movements, as workers organised to represent their interests and struggle for greater self-determination (Muldoon, 2021, p. 20). Following Marx on the Paris Commune, council systems were generally conceived of as 'working institutions', which combined legislative and executive functions in order to directly create and administer laws (Muldoon, 2021, pp. 140–141). For Luxemburg, councils represented 'the institutional embodiment of the self-liberation of the working class', forming the basis of a socialist republic in which workplaces would become 'centres of power' electing representatives to the highest political institutions (Muldoon, 2021, p. 142). The council form addresses a fundamental problem with bourgeois democracy: whereas parliamentary elections can be isolated, individualistic processes susceptible to ruling class ideological domination, councils root democratic practice in the workplace, exposing workers to 'the views of the most class-conscious elements of their class' through collective deliberation (Kivotidis, 2024, p. 232). By making productive units—where workers meet collectively every day—centres of political decision-making, the Soviet model opened the possibility for mass participation in governance (Kivotidis, 2024, pp. 230–231).

This view of the importance of protagonism is an important extension, or rather application, of Marx's principle of working class self-emancipation in the twenty-first century. The focus on building organisations to develop working class capacities chimes with Swain's observation that

> Marx did not just believe that the good society was one in which people were emancipated, and thus capable of realising their human powers freely. He also believed that this society itself must be the product of self-directed emancipatory activity.
>
> (Swain, 2019, p. 2)

In terms of how this relates to the broader issue of rights and democratic forms, Stolze argues that,

> Here is a key point, then: as a movement of the oppressed takes shape, to the greatest feasible extent the oppressed must be able to deliberate among themselves regarding their own interests and objectives in lessening or eliminating the oppression they experience.
>
> (Stolze, 2019, p. 280)

Elaborating on this, Geras notes that consistent commitment to the pursuit of working class self-emancipation would require 'what would today generally be called liberal norms of political life', although Geras notes that for Luxemburg and others, democratic decision-making and respect for basic liberties and rights was not just part of the liberal tradition, rather it was an intrinsic part of the revolutionary socialist tradition (Geras, 1994, p. 98).

The value of these forms—formal democratic equality, regular elections, due process and the rights and liberties associated with free political activity—lies, going back to Engels, in providing the working class and socialist movements with 'the environment necessary for its existence, for the air it needs to breathe', without which 'it will be unable to move freely itself' (Engels, [1865] 1985, p. 78). In the context of a commitment to social change rooted in the self-emancipation of the working class, democratic forms provide crucial space for the formation and development of political organisations that can develop the capacities of the working class. It also provides the scope for the mobilisation of movements for change, the connecting of the various strands of disparate protest and campaigning into collective communities of struggle. In the absence of this space, it is not feasible to begin to build a meaningful alternative to the extant social order.

Engels may have been overly optimistic about the ultimate consequence of entrenching these democratic forms, but he was right to stress their importance in the ongoing struggles and development of the working class. On this latter point, Ellen Meiksins Wood argued that,

> One must go beyond the function of juridical and political freedom and equality in sustaining capitalist relations of production and the position of the dominant class, and take account of the value liberal democratic political forms have had for subordinate classes, indeed, the degree to which these political and legal forms are the legacy of historic struggles by subordinate classes.
>
> (Meiksins Wood, 1978, p. 230)

Following on from this, Wood concluded that any 'socialist strategy ignores at its peril', the central role of these democratic forms (Meiksins Wood, 1978, p. 230). Far from ignoring the importance of these forms, the argument advanced here is that a transformative politics centred on the principle of working class self-emancipation can provide a vantage point from which we engage with these democratic forms. A perspective which does not surrender to liberal mythologising but still recognises the role and importance of democratic forms in struggles to build the new society in the shell of the old.

2.4 The Terrain of Struggle

Reflecting on the apparent contradiction between revolutionary socialism and democratic forms, Draper argued that the point is not to try to resolve the issue in the abstract, but rather 'to grasp the social dynamics of the situation under which the apparent contradiction between the two is resolved' (Draper, 1977, p. 283). Or, in other words, to consider how the question of democratic forms should be approached in concrete circumstances. In this regard, an understanding of the broad political economy of the contemporary global order is crucial to begin to elaborate an argument on the relationship between movements for fundamental social change and democratic forms. The term polycrisis has gained some traction recently to describe the increasingly apparent overlapping crises of spiralling inequality, climate breakdown, rising populism, economic stagnation, authoritarianism and war. But this term obscures more than it reveals, for in truth, what we are confronted with is the deepening structural crisis of capitalism (Jayasuriya, 2023).

In this regard, the various morbid symptoms enumerated in the polycrisis thesis are very much present, but they all have their shared root cause in the systemic crisis of capitalism which began to unfold in the 1970s. As Samir Amin, writing in 2019, aptly put it, the present conjuncture is one in which the 'system of generalized monopoly capitalism, "globalized" (imperialist) and financialized, is imploding right before our eyes' (Amin, 2019, p. 37). The system, Amin argued, is structurally incapable of resolving 'its growing internal contradictions' and as such is 'condemned to pursue its mad rush' into deepening crisis (Amin, 2019). Amin described this dispensation as the 'autumn of capitalism'. However, and of particular relevance for present purposes, Amin noted that this autumn of capitalism 'does not coincide with a "springtime of the peoples"' (Amin, 2019, p. 38). To put it slightly differently, the present global order is marked by a deep, structural crisis of capitalism, but at present there is no working class or revolutionary alternative to the spiralling crisis.

Two of the defining characteristics of the structural crisis of capitalism are accelerating and deepening inequality and a generalised shift towards authoritarianism. Climate breakdown and war, of course, are crucially important and are also rooted in the dynamics of capital accumulation and crisis, but for the purposes of the present discussion, the focus here is on the issues of inequality and authoritarianism. With the onset of the structural crisis of capitalism in the late 1960s and early 1970s, one of the central responses of capital was to undo the post-war compromise with labour. This inaugurated the era of neoliberal retrenchment, which began with the US backed overthrow of Allende in Chile, followed by the elections of Reagan and Thatcher, the defeat of the miners in Britain, and the steady slide into the present. A central aspect of the neoliberal assault on the post-war compromise was weakening organised labour, undermining workers' pay and conditions and decimating public services through privatisation and commodification. This is the extended period, which Sivanandan noted above, in which organised labour was systematically crushed and marginalised, allowing capital to intensify exploitation without the countervailing power that workers' organisations had previously exerted (Harvey, 2005; Davidson, 2017).

Over the last 50 years, as forms of neoliberalisation have been entrenched, modified and resisted, one of the most striking characteristics has been the immense growth in income inequality and the concentration of wealth in the hands of fewer and fewer people. In the most comprehensive study of global inequality to date, the 2022 World Inequality Report, Thomas Piketty and his colleagues tracked this trend, noting that '[income] and wealth inequalities have been on the rise nearly everywhere since the 1980s, following a series of deregulation and liberalization programs which took different forms in different countries' (Chancel et al., 2022, p. 11). They also note that global wealth inequalities are even starker than income inequalities, with half the global population possessing just 2 percent of total wealth, while the richest 10 percent own 76 percent of all wealth (Chancel et al., 2022, p. 10). They conclude their analysis of the data by noting that global 'inequalities seem to be as great today as they were at the peak of Western imperialism in the early 20th century' (Chancel et al., 2022, p. 12).

In a recent report, Oxfam International noted that not only is income and wealth inequality increasing, but that it is doing so at an accelerating pace. They found that in 2024 the total wealth of billionaires increased by $2 trillion, with billionaire wealth growing three times faster in 2024 than it had in 2023 (Oxfam International, 2025). The report also notes that this concentration of wealth is linked to growing levels of inequality both between and within countries. Thus, the falling living standards, collapsing public services and general push towards penury experienced by most people in the world are the flip side of the billionaire's rising tide. The Oxfam report also notes, worryingly, that while 'the numbers are grim, the reality is probably worse', because national data on inequality, particularly in the Global South, is outdated (Oxfam International, 2025, pp. 20–21). The era of neoliberal ascendancy and consolidation is marked, then, by 'unprecedented social polarisation worldwide', by 'savage inequalities… [that] impose untold hardships on billions of people who face daily struggles for survival and uncertain futures' (Robinson and Baker, 2019, p. 377). It should be stressed that the inequality which characterises the contemporary global order is not some aberration but rather marks the very success of the neoliberal counter-revolution launched in the 1970s. As David Harvey argues,

> Masked by a lot of rhetoric about individual freedom, liberty, personal responsibility and the virtues of privatisation, the free market and free trade, [neoliberalism] legitimised draconian policies designed to restore and consolidate capitalist class power. This project has been successful, judging by the incredible centralisation of wealth and power observable in all those countries that took the neoliberal road.
>
> (Harvey, 2011, p. 10)

The immiseration, inequality and uncertainty produced by the extant global order are central facets that fuel the rise of so called populisms, and right wing reaction (Davidson, 2017, pp. 625–631; Elliott, 2021). But they can only do this because of the second salient feature that defines the contemporary global order—the generalised shift towards authoritarianism.

From its inception, on the margins of political and theoretical respectability, neoliberalism has been antagonistic to democracy. In 1939 Friedrich Hayek, one of the founding fathers of neoliberalism, argued for economic policy to be removed from democratic decision-making. As Hayek put it, 'democracy will work only if we do not overload it and if the majorities do not abuse their power', Hayek argued further that if 'the restriction of the power and scope of government', was the price to be paid for a functioning (neo)liberal order, then it was a price worth paying (Hayek, 1939). When the theory of neoliberalism was mobilised in the 1970s to facilitate a ruling class assault on the working class and the post-war compromise, this anti-democratic element remained central. As Harvey notes,

> Neoliberal theorists are… profoundly suspicious of democracy. Governance by majority rule is seen as a potential threat to individual rights and constitutional liberties. Democracy is viewed as a luxury, only possible under conditions of relative affluence coupled with a strong middle-class presence to guarantee political stability. Neoliberals therefore tend to favour governance by experts and elites. A strong preference exists for government by executive order and by judicial decision rather than democratic and parliamentary decision-making. Neoliberals prefer to insulate key institutions, such as the central bank, from democratic pressures.
>
> (Harvey, 2005, p. 66)

Throughout the various episodes and phases of neoliberalisation, this anti-democratic strain has remained constant. From the transferring of interest rate setting powers to central banks, to the European Union's entire legal apparatus, the era of neoliberalism has seen the institutional locking in of what Roberto Unger calls 'the dictatorship of no alternatives' (Unger, 2005).

As neoliberalism has consolidated as a global hegemonic ideology and practice, the institutional locking-in of anti-democratic processes has induced a broader decline in the quality of the democratic life of states. As Peter Mair noted, the neoliberal era witnessed 'a wide-ranging attempt to define democracy in a way that does not require any substantial emphasis on popular sovereignty – at the extreme, the projection of a kind of democracy without the demos at its centre' (Mair, 2013, p. 9). In response to the hollowing out of democratic institutions and forms, Mair notes that we have seen a steady withdrawal of electorates from formal, democratic politics. In other words, as people increasingly come to see they have no real choice in the electoral field, they choose not to choose. In response to this, and the broader anti-democratic and depoliticising tendency of neoliberalism, a caste of professional politicians and political parties have also withdrawn from the people and become more firmly ensconced as state managers of the status quo (Mair, 2013, p. 18). This hollowing out of democracy, coupled with the defeat of the working class, has meant that decision-making has become far less concerned with issues of legitimacy, and more focused on maintaining a favourable business climate and credit rating. This, in part, is how the crisis of capitalism—which manifested in financial form beginning in 2008, but whose roots lie in deeper contradictions of accumulation and profitability—was turned, by parties of all political stripes, into a public finance crisis, requiring devastating austerity to address it.

As popular movements emerged to oppose this austerity, and the general crisis of the neoliberal system, states the world over invariably turned to repression to police opposition to the system and its crises. Unable to countenance policy alternatives that might, in any way, upset the gods of finance and ruling economic elites, the political managers of capitalist states turned to repression to counter the protests and opposition that inevitably flow from the crises induced by the system itself. Linking this directly to the issue of growing inequality, Robinson and Baker note that,

> escalating inequalities and the inability of global capitalism to assure the survival of billions of people throw states into crises of legitimacy and push the system towards more openly repressive means of social control and domination that exacerbate political and social conflict.
>
> (Robinson and Baker, 2019, p. 377)

This, as Harvey notes, is entirely in keeping with neoliberal orthodoxy, for, notwithstanding the utopian rhetoric about individual freedom and a small state, under regimes of neoliberalism the 'coercive arm of the state is augmented to protect corporate interests and, if necessary, to repress dissent' (Harvey, 2005, p. 77).

From the crisis of 2008, the global picture has consistently worsened. Growing inequality, exacerbated by austerity, the Covid-19 pandemic, followed by Russia's invasion of Ukraine, Israel's Western-backed genocide in Gaza and the increasing urgency of climate breakdown, have all seen growing protest movements around the world (OECD, 2021). These growing protests have, in turn, seen increasing state repression. Britain provides a specific example, with its raft of new anti-protest laws adding to the already extensive powers the police had to limit protest. This is coupled with a rhetoric, from the state and mainstream media, which paints climate protesters or anti-war protesters as dangerous subversives. The same sort of tactic is applied to workers who organise to defend their collective interests, with the previous Conservative government provoking a conflict with transport unions, to justify the introduction of draconian anti-trade union legislation. As the structural crisis of capitalism deepens and nascent forms of opposition to it emerge, the anti-democratic element inherent in neoliberalism moves a step further into open authoritarianism. On this point, Issa Shivji notes that when 'the chips are down and the system is in deep crisis or facing a formidable political opposition of the working people, all pretence of at democracy is set aside' (Shivji, 2020, p. 21).

The contemporary global order is fundamentally marked by the structural crisis of capitalism and the class domination of the capitalist ruling class, while the working class movement remains in retreat. Among the deleterious consequences of this era, and there are many, growing inequality, precariousness and immiseration and deepening authoritarianism are two of the most salient. They have given rise to what Neil Davidson calls regimes of permanent exception, 'involving both pre-emptive repression and diversionary scapegoating of groups ranging from people with disabilities to the entire Muslim population' (Davidson, 2017, p. 625). The context then, in which we must discuss the attitude of socialists, Marxists and others to democratic forms, is one of deepening social crisis and moribund democracy. A simmering context in which the living standards of the world's working class deteriorates steadily, while the wealth of a tiny few grows exponentially. And where attempts to address the pressing crises produced by the extant system are met either with the enervating inertia of hollowed out democratic institutions, or outright repression. In the next section, we bring together the various strands of the argument set out so far, to essay an answer as to how we should approach democratic forms today.

2.5 The Battle for Democracy

In the *Communist Manifesto,* Marx and Engels argued that the 'first step' in building a revolutionary movement that could challenge and transcend capitalism was for the working class to 'win the battle' for democracy (Marx and Engels, [1848] 2002, p. 243). As noted above, for Marx, Engels and most of the leading figures of classical Marxism, a central part of and weapon in this battle would be the democratic forms associated with capitalism. However, a lot of water has passed under the bridge since then and now. The contemporary era of neoliberal capitalist imperialism has shown that it can make peace with at least formal commitments to rights and democracy, and indeed has crafted a specific conception of rights which bolsters and legitimates the extant order. This, among other things, has fuelled scepticism and hostility towards the democratic forms that are associated with capitalism and the bourgeois revolutions of the eighteenth and nineteenth centuries. This scepticism is captured well in Radhika Desai's observation that we 'can only conclude that democracy and human rights are not so much substantive realities of capitalist societies as they are weapons in the ideological armoury of their class oppression and imperialism' (Desai, 2022, p. 177). While there is much merit in Desai's analysis, and while it is undoubtedly the case that the language of human rights and democracy have been used for ruling class, neoliberal and imperialist purposes for centuries—they have never just been that.

As shown above, there have always been subaltern or counter-hegemonic perspectives and struggles which have pushed back against dominant accounts of rights and democracy, and in doing so, have shaped and re-shaped these concepts over time. At least, they have done so when they had the capacity to do so. Going back to Sivanandan's point above, it was in an era of relative working class strength, when there was dynamic, open antagonism between labour and capital, that the working classes were able to exact and define some of these key rights. The advent of neoliberalism began, everywhere, with direct and extensive attacks on the rights of workers—principally because it was the organised working class that forced capital into the post-war compromise that neoliberals and economic elites wanted to break with. But also, because, whatever the variety of capitalism, the fundamental structural antagonism within the system is between labour and capital. With a series of victories over organised labour, national and international working classes were cowed. This, in turn, has facilitated and produced the major upward transfer of income and wealth from the global working class to a tiny number of super wealthy capitalists.

Over the course of the last 50 years, there have been sporadic, and in some cases significant, fight backs, but broadly speaking the old institutions of the working class, trade unions and mass, revolutionary parties, have been eroded. As too have many of the wider social and community organisations that sustained working class struggles in the past. We have reached a point, then, where the extant system is in a prolonged, structural crisis, the political managers can only respond to the symptoms of this crisis with more of the same in terms of broadly neoliberal policy and repression, and the capacity of the working class to provide a counterbalance or alternative to this is greatly diminished. In this context, the battle for democracy, to rebuild working class capabilities and institutional power, comes centre stage. As Harvey notes, 'it is the profoundly anti-democratic nature of neoliberalism backed… authoritarianism… that should surely be the main focus of political struggle' (Harvey, 2005, p. 205). To this we might add that while Harvey is right, the struggle against the unequal, undemocratic and authoritarian order wrought by neoliberalism must be centred on the self-activity of the working class. To resist the authoritarian decline of neoliberal capitalism, working class self-emancipation must come centre stage.

For the working class, in different places and in different ways, to begin to build the capacities and institutional frameworks to contest the dictatorship of no alternatives, it will require, in Engels' words, air to breathe. In the context of deepening crisis and authoritarianism, defending and expanding the rights of freedom of association and protest, free speech, privacy and due process will be crucial to facilitate the emergence of new movements and organisations. As Shoikhedbrod argues,

> A contemporary Marxist approach… should reclaim the protections associated with the rule of law and constitutionalism, not least because these protections secure a minimal level of freedom and provide a forum for contesting neoliberal policies at a time when wealth is concentrated in fewer and fewer hands and democratic sovereignty is being undermined by the unprecedented power of transnational capital.
>
> (Shoikhedbrod, 2019, p. 198)

Defending and crucially expanding the meaning and content of these rights and democratic forms is also, in present circumstances, a transgressive position. As Michael Yates has argued, in the context of neoliberal decline and authoritarianism, 'all crusades to make freedom, substantive equality, and real democracy a reality are, by definition, radically anti-capitalist' (Yates, 2018, p. 56).

On this latter point, Harvey makes a similar argument, arguing that while the neoliberal articulation of rights and democracy fosters a legitimate and understandable scepticism about these concepts and forms, it would be unfortunate 'to abandon the field of rights to neoliberal hegemony' (Harvey, 2005, p. 179). Instead, Harvey argues that if 'class restoration entails the imposition of a distinctive set of rights, then resistance to that imposition entails struggle for entirely different rights' (Harvey, 2005, p. 179). Elaborating on this, Harvey argues that,

> analysis shows that certain dominant social processes throw up and rest upon certain conceptions of justice and of rights. To challenge those particular rights is to challenge the social process in which they inhere. Conversely, it proves impossible to wean society away from some dominant social process (such as that of capital accumulation through market exchange) to another (such as political democracy and collective action) without simultaneously shifting allegiance from one dominant conception of rights and of justice to another. The difficulty with all idealist specifications of rights and of justice is that they hide this connection. Only when they come to earth in relation to some social process do they find social meaning.
>
> (Harvey, 2005, p. 180)

With respect to democracy, Marta Harnecker makes a similar argument, noting that one of the key tasks of the left is to 'foster authentic degrees of popular power and democracy that are tangibly superior to bourgeois democracy. We have to fight for a new type of democracy from below, for those below' (Harnecker, 2007, p. 34).

In the context of building and developing working class organisations and institutions to combat the extant social order, it will be crucial to assert and go beyond the democratic forms associated with capitalism. This is so for two reasons: (i) because, as Marxists, socialists and working class radicals in the past knew full well, such forms can be important weapons in the class struggle, and in providing space to develop working class capacities; and (ii) because asserting a radical, transgressive conception of both rights and democracy is one way of articulating and rallying support for movements that oppose the extant order. Asserting expansive and transgressive conceptions of the right to protest, and to wider democratic participation, challenges the depoliticising, anti-democratic drive of neoliberalism. It provides a context for the protagonism which will be central to build sustainable movements to transform the status quo. Likewise, asserting a richer conception of democracy, one which restores and expands the social content of it, fundamentally challenges, both ideologically and practically, the low-intensity democracy that prevails today.

Just as the neoliberal era was inaugurated with the attack on workers and workers' rights, it is only a revitalised, protagonistic working class that can mount a serious challenge to the crisis ridden capitalist order, whether of the neoliberal or emergent fascistic kind. Rebuilding working class confidence, capacities and power is crucial to building this challenge. As Lebowitz notes, 'in the absence of a working class that has developed its capacity, dignity, and strength through its protagonism and practice, the immediate response of workers to crises is to accept the necessity for the reproduction of capitalism' (Lebowitz, 2020, p. 171). Fifty years of neoliberalisation has invested Thatcher's war cry that 'There is No Alternative' with a ring of indisputable truth, and, as Yates notes, a hegemonic 'ideology predisposed to take the system as given and unchangeable creates a powerful barrier to radical change' (Yates, 2018, p. 61). As such the prospects of working class self-emancipation in the present context, of the working class winning the battle for democracy, will require a long process of organisation, education and struggle. This process will be inconceivable without the defence and extension of the democratic forms inherited from earlier generations.

2.6 Conclusion

Although their sentences were reduced on appeal, the case of the JSO protesters who were handed draconian prison sentences under new, repressive anti-protest laws is a signal lesson for all of us committed to fundamental social change, in whatever form. The scientific evidence is incontrovertible that we are rapidly hurtling towards irreparable climate breakdown, which will have devastating consequences for the biosphere and billions of people around the world. The veracity of the science on this issue has been acknowledged for some time and yet world leaders continuously fail to do anything of substance to address this most central of issues. The core reason for this is that climate breakdown is rooted in the incessant drive for short-term profit that drives the capitalist system. The political managers of the states of the world, particularly the core imperialist states of the West, cannot countenance any policy options that would pose a meaningful threat to this incessant accumulation, and to the interests of the economic elites that benefit from it, and so they do nothing—or, at least, nothing of substance. Unable to address the root cause of a pressing and crucial social problem, they instead have opted, across the board, to adopt a position of repressing opposition to the symptoms of the crisis. It is in this web of authoritarian neoliberal decline that the JSO and other climate protesters have been caught.

But it does not stop with climate protesters. The spiralling inequality that also marks the contemporary era, and the concomitant collapse in the living standards of working class people the world over, are also rooted in the system of incessant, short-term profit seeking. Indeed, as several authors have noted, the entire impetus of the neoliberal counter-revolution of the 1970s and 1980s was, precisely, to restore the power and wealth of economic elites, at the expense of the working class. In this regard, at least, neoliberalism has been a resounding success. So, when working class people now try to organise, in the workplace or the community, to resist the stagnation of real wages, and the gutting of the social wage produced by the privatisation and defunding of public services, the political managers of the system respond by scapegoating migrants, disabled people or benefit 'scroungers', and by repressively policing trade unions and anti-austerity movements. The same can be said of the increasing march to war and industrial murder that is part of the contemporary crisis of capitalism. The most striking example is that while Israel prosecuted its genocide in Gaza from October 2023 to January 2025, killing tens of thousands of Palestinians with the complete support of the West, these same Western states, again unable to address root causes, opted to aggressively police and repress protesters against genocide and for peace.

This latter example is the starkest. In some ways, climate breakdown can still appear to many as an abstraction, something not quite real. Likewise, because of the uneven impact of deindustrialisation, casualisation and austerity, coupled with the ethic of atomised individualism inculcated by neoliberalism, the collapsing living standards and rising inequality that mark the contemporary era can seem somewhat abstract or ephemeral too. But with the Israeli genocide in Gaza people were, thanks to modern social media, exposed daily to a brutal remorseless genocide of primarily women and children. When people, in their hundreds of thousands, took to the streets to call for an end to this slaughter, the increasingly authoritarian state managers of neoliberal capitalism responded by seeking to denigrate and mischaracterise the protesters, and by repressing anti-war and pro-Palestine protests. All these instances, and there are many more that could be added, show that in the present context, building any opposition to the brutality of the extant global order will require a defence of the rights to protest and free speech. More than this, the current moment will require the shield of these democratic forms to allow movements and institutions to develop, but will also require a re-conceptualised, radical conception of these forms to act as a sword for a working class offensive against the death march of authoritarian imperialist neoliberalism.

Bibliography

Amin, S. (2019). The new imperialist structure. *Monthly Review*, 71(3), 32–38.

Chancel, L., Piketty, T., Saez, E., and Zucman, G. (2022). *The world inequality report 2022*. World Inequality Lab.

Connolly, J. (2011a). Our mad rulers. In Nevin (Ed.), *James Connolly political writings 1893–1916* (pp. 156–157). SIPTU.

Connolly, J. (2011b). Labour mans the breach. In Nevin (Ed.), *James Connolly political writings 1893–1916* (p. 488). SIPTU.

Connolly, J. (2011c). A war for civilisation. In Nevin (Ed.), *James Connolly political writings 1893–1916* (p. 571). SIPTU.
Connolly, J. (2021). *The re-conquest of Ireland (Originally published 1915)*. Foreign Languages Press.
Davidson, N. (2017). Crisis neoliberalism and regimes of permanent exception. *Critical Sociology*, 43, 615–631.
Desai, R. (2022). The imperialism of democracy and human rights vs the democracy and human rights of imperialism. *International Critical Thought*, 12, 169–182.
Draper, H. (1977). *Karl Marx's theory of revolution: Vol. 1*. Monthly Review Press.
Draper, H. (1978). *Karl Marx's theory of revolution: Vol. 2*. Monthly Review Press.
Elliott, B. (2021). *The roots of populism: Neoliberalism and working-class lives*. Manchester University Press.
Engels, F. (1985a). The Prussian military question and the German workers' party. In K. Marx and F. Engels (Eds.), *Collected works*: Vol. 20 (pp. 37–77). Lawrence and Wishart.
Engels, F. (1985b). Meeting in Hyde Park. In K. Marx and F. Engels (Eds.), *Collected works*: Vol. 23 (pp. 294–295). Lawrence and Wishart.
European Centre for Not-for-Profit Law. (2021). *The United Kingdom's Police, Crime, Sentencing and Courts Bill: Analysis of compliance with international human rights standards*.
Evans, T. (2005). *The politics of human rights* (2nd ed.). Pluto.
Foot, P. (2005). *The vote*. Viking.
Friends of the Earth. (2025, March 14). *Court of appeal judgment on Just Stop Oil sentencing*. Friends of the Earth UK. https://friendsoftheearth.uk/system-change/court-appeal-judgment-just-stop-oil-sentencing.
Gayle, D. (2024, July 18). Five Just Stop Oil activists receive record sentences for planning to block M25. *The Guardian*.
Gayle, D., Horton, H., and Quinn, B. (2024, July 19). 'Not acceptable in a democracy': UN expert condemns lengthy Just Stop Oil sentences. *The Guardian*.
Geras, N. (1973). Marxism and proletarian self-emancipation. *Radical Philosophy*, 6, 20–27.
Geras, N. (1994). Democracy and the ends of Marxism. *New Left Review*, I(203), 92–98.
Harnecker, M. (2007). *Rebuilding the left*. Zed Books.
Harnecker, M. (2015). *A world to build*. Monthly Review Press.
Harvey, D. (2005). *A brief history of neoliberalism*. Oxford University Press.
Harvey, D. (2011). *The enigma of capital*. Oxford University Press.
Hayek, F. (1939). The economic conditions of interstate federalism. *New Commonwealth Quarterly*, 5, 131–149.
Jayasuriya, K. (2023). Polycrisis or crisis of capitalist social reproduction. *Global Social Challenges Journal*, 2, 203–220.
Kivotidis, D. (2024). *The dialectics of democracy*. Routledge.
Kołakowski, L. (1983). Marxism and human rights. *Daedalus*, 112, 81–95.
Lebowitz, M. (2020). *Between capitalism and community*. Monthly Review Press.
Löwy, M. (2013). *On changing the world*. Haymarket.
Lukes, S. (1981). Can a Marxist believe in human rights? *Praxis International*, 4, 334–345.

Luxemburg, R. (1970a). The Junius pamphlet: The crisis in the German social democracy. In M.-A. Waters (Ed.), *Rosa Luxemburg speaks* (pp. 257–298). Pathfinder Press.

Luxemburg, R. (1970b). The Russian revolution. In M.-A. Waters (Ed.), *Rosa Luxemburg speaks* (pp. 365–389). Pathfinder Press.

Luxemburg, R. (1970c). Speech to the founding convention of the German communist party. In M.- A. Waters (Ed.), *Rosa Luxemburg speaks* (pp. 400–419). Pathfinder Press.

Macfarlane, L. J. (1982). Marxist theory and human rights. *Government and Opposition*, 17, 414–432.

Mair, P. (2013). *Ruling the void*. Verso.

Martin, R. (2021). The protest provisions of the Police, Crime, Sentencing and Courts Bill: A 'modest reset of the scales'? *Criminal Law Review*, 1008, 1008–1025.

Marx, K. (1987). On the Jewish question. In K. Marx and F. Engels (Eds.), *Collected works*: Vol. 3 (pp. 146–155). Lawrence and Wishart.

Marx, K. (1985). Theses on Feuerbach. In K. Marx and F. Engels (Eds.), *Collected works*: Vol. 5 (p. 3). Lawrence and Wishart.

Marx, K. (1990). *Capital: Vol. 1*. Penguin.

Marx, K., and Engels, F. (1985). The German ideology. In K. Marx and F. Engels (Eds.), *Collected works*: Vol. 5 (pp. 19, 52–53). Lawrence and Wishart.

Marx, K., and Engels, F. (1985). Provisional rules of the association. In K. Marx and F. Engels (Eds.), *Collected works*: Vol. 20 (p. 14). Lawrence and Wishart.

Marx, K., and Engels, F. (2002). *The Communist manifesto*. Penguin.

Meiksins Wood, E. (1978). *C.B. Macpherson: Liberalism, and the task of socialist political theory*. Socialist Register, 215–230.

Muldoon, J. (2021). *Building power to change the world: The political thought of the German council movements*. Oxford University Press.

Navickas, K. (2022). The contested right of public meeting in England from the Bill of Rights to the Public Order Acts. *Transactions of the Royal Historical Society*, 32, 199–220.

OECD. (2021). *Perspectives on global development 2021: From protest to progress?* OECD Publishing.

Oxfam International. (2025). *Takers not makers: The unjust poverty and unearned wealth of colonialism*.

Roberts, A. (2013). *The end of protest: How free-market capitalism learned to control dissent*. Cornell University Press.

Robinson, W. I., and Baker, Y. K. (2019). Savage inequalities: Capitalist crises and surplus humanity. *International Critical Thought*, 9(3), 376–389.

Selmini, R., and Di Ronco, A. (2023). The criminalisation of dissent and protest. *Crime and Justice*, 52, 197–230.

Shivji, I. (2020). Samir Amin on democracy and fascism. *Agrarian South Journal of Political Economy*, 9(1), 12–28.

Shoikhedbrod, I. (2019). *Revisiting Marx's critique of liberalism*. Palgrave Macmillan.

Sivanandan, A. (1989). All that melts into air is solid: The hokum of new times. *Race and Class*, 31(3), 1–24.

Stammers, N. (2009). *Human rights and social movements*. Pluto Press.

Stolze, T. (2019). *Becoming Marxist: Studies in philosophy, struggle and endurance*. Brill.

Swain, D. (2019). *None so fit to break the chains: Marx's ethics of self-emancipation*. Brill.
Thompson, E. P. (1959). Commitment in politics. *Universities and Left Review*, 6, 50–54.
Türk, V. (2023, May 28). The Public Order Act will have a chilling effect on your civic freedoms – it must be repealed. *The Independent*.
Unger, R. M. (2005). *The left alternative*. Verso.
Wood, L. (2014). *Crisis and control: The militarization of protest policing*. Pluto Press.
Yates, M. D. (2018). *Can the working class change the world?* Monthly Review Press.

3 Postponing Paradise

British Socialism and Constitutional Instrumentalisation

Maria Tzanakopoulou

3.1 Introduction

For a place without a written constitution, Britain has seen a socialist tradition unusually invested in constitutionalism. From the radical wing of civil war republicans to the short-lived radical turn of the Labour Party in the twenty-first century, constitutional thinking has been a constant for British socialists. The term constitutional thinking is used here to describe something broader than just constitutional discourse or rhetoric: it points to the way in which constitutionalism has often framed conceivable political possibilities in British radical and socialist thought; to a history, as it were, of a familial coupling of British socialism and constitutional limits. The sections that follow try to navigate this history. Like all histories, the one under discussion has been non-linear and non-tidy and if, at times, the narration conveys an impression of orderliness, the reader should be aware that this is only for the sake of analytical clarity when drawing out recurring patterns of socialists' usage of the constitution. As such, what follows does not claim to offer a comprehensive account of the history of British socialism, but focuses instead on key moments of (strategic) weaponisation of the constitution by socialists. Interestingly, even this narrowing down of the focus has still allowed a look into almost every key moment of the British socialist tradition.

Before moving on to a summary of the argument, a couple of terminological and conceptual clarifications are in order. First, the terminological shift from 'English radicalism' to 'British socialism' found in the next Section 3.2 reflects historical periodisation: 'radicalism' refers to pre-socialist working-class movements, while 'England' is used (rather than Britain) in reference to the seventeenth-century groups such as the Levellers. Where these terms appear inconsistently, it is either to reflect their usage in primary sources or to maintain clarity in historical context. Second, neither early radicals nor modern socialists have ever constituted ideologically homogeneous blocs. The focus is therefore on dominant tendencies within the tradition: early mass movements like the Levellers and Chartists (primarily via their leadership), and later, the Labour Party's left wing and associated intellectual circles. More marginal currents, such as the

DOI: 10.4324/9781032621623-4

Communist Party of Great Britain, are included primarily for contrast. Third, despite references to 'British socialism', the analysis is heavily weighted towards developments in England, as space forbade engagement with the rich tradition of the other countries. Finally, there is little in the way of doctrinal constitutional analysis in the following sections. Rather than looking at the substance of constitutional argument, reforms, and proposals, the focus is on deciphering the underlying logic of British socialist preoccupations with the constitution. For example, while there have been interesting shifts from a preference to a strong executive in the first half of the twentieth century to a focus on decentralisation after the 1970s to a blend of the two in the twenty-first century, these matters are dealt with summarily. Nor should the reader expect a discussion of major constitutional moments such as the Human Rights Act or Brexit. The focus is instead on what Section 3.3 refers to as the instrumentalist logic that underlies British socialism's constitutional maximalism.

Constitutional maximalism is understood as the overinvestment by British socialism in the ability of the constitution to yield socialist results, if correctly tweaked. This, it is argued, reflects an instrumentalist logic according to which constitutional reform can be used as the tool to economic democracy if the user so wishes. This logic which has permeated British socialism historically can be seen in two dominant, partly overlapping, tendencies: first, a conviction—espoused, for example, by Chartist rhetoric, the Fabian tradition and post-war Labour governments—that the route to socialism is already latent in the (ancient) constitution, and all that is required is releasing its energy, if need be by removing barriers; second, the conviction that constitutional and procedural reform can substitute for material or class-based transformation. The argument proceeds as follows.

Section 3.2 briefly discusses tendencies in precious centuries. It argues that, for reasons related to the nature of the English state, early English/British radicalism remained anchored to a reverential view of the common law and the ancient constitution. For all the transformative ambition of early radicals, this anchoring gave rise to a constitutional framing of emancipatory politics that has survived to this day. According to it, liberty—and therefore, for example, universal suffrage—was already latent in the ancient constitution, and simply required correct application through the removal of obstructive barriers, to be realised. This view, which resulted in a general deference to old shibboleth's, including private property, planted the seeds of an instrumentalist understanding according to which democracy, not just political but also economic, resides in the constitution awaiting proper activation once the working class assumes control. This outlook foreshadowed later tendencies—most notably the intense parliamentarianism and constitutionalism of the Fabians and, subsequently, the Labour Party, which did not waver even under the influence of the Bolshevik revolution.

Section 3.3 examines socialism and the constitution in the twentieth century, focusing on the postwar period onwards. This era was marked by contradictions.

The 1960s ushered in a spirit of challenge to established constitutional orthodoxies, driven in part by the rise of a left intelligentsia. The Nairn-Anderson debate on the British working class and the archaic British state shook the constitutional acquiescence of previous decades, but was, in a historical irony, eventually used as the theoretical framework for one of the most deradicalised socialist campaigns for constitutional reform—that of Charter 88. Socialist critics argued that the campaign treated constitutional reform as a political end in itself rather than a means to a socialist end. In fact, this section suggests, both the Charter 88 campaign and the criticism against it have revealed a deeper instrumentalist logic that had up to that historical point manifested in the two forms mentioned above: either as removal of barriers to release the constitution's already latent socialist energy and/or—as in the case of Charter 88—replacement of class-based politics with constitutional reform. This framework is summarised under the term constitutional maximalism.

The last Section 3.4 examines how these dynamics played out in the twenty-first century. It argues that the instrumentalist logic persisted in both Jeremy Corbyn's approach to politics and in the constitutional responses it provoked. Although Corbyn himself was no constitutional maximalist, his political project retained a fundamentally instrumentalist understanding of the state—namely, the belief that the more power workers acquire, the more effectively they can wield the state apparatus to their advantage. This perspective ultimately obscured deeper understandings of class. Interestingly, responses to Corbyn from the point of view of the 'socialist constitution' mirrored this same instrumentalist logic. Here, a familiar historical cycle reasserted itself—one traceable back to tendencies visible even in the Chartist era: the idea that socialism is latent within the constitution and can be realised through the removal of institutional barriers. But this conception reproduces the central flaw of Corbynism: it treats superstructural institutions as neutral and manipulable at will, rather than as structurally embedded expressions of social relations and class antagonisms.

This framing misconstrues the nature of the working class, treating it as a group pitted against capital in a zero-sum contest for institutional control, rather as a social relation constitutive of capitalism itself. From this perspective, the constitution cannot be separated from the class structure it encodes.

This, it is finally argued, may be the enduring problem of socialist constitutional maximalism—its persistent instrumentalisation of the constitution, a tendency that, across its various historical forms, has consistently obscured the relational and structural realities of class.

3.2 Historical Foundations of Radical Constitutional Thinking

From the early modern period through the twentieth century, British radicalism has been shaped by an ostensible paradox: demands for social transformation have often been articulated through the conservative grammar of constitutional legitimacy. Time and again, revolutionary energies were channelled through appeals to tradition, legality, and institutional continuity, revealing a tension between constitutional faith on the one hand and socialist aspiration on the other. The paradox is ostensible because early radicals' faith in the constitution had, in fact, firm historical roots in the country's economic and political evolution. Historians have documented how, in seventeenth- and eighteenth-century England, the political was conceptualised through lived experiences of the legal. This was the result, on one hand, of 'the state's use of the courts as the chief means of exercising authority' (Brewer & Styles, 1980, p. 13). On the other, understandings of justice and equality were mediated by the (common) law, which had the power to occasionally vindicate a rural poor or send an aristocrat to the gallows thus seemingly creating a class equilibrium (Hay, 1975). As such, contrary to a common aphorism (Brewer & Styles, 1980), the rule of law was *not* a fiction—it produced material results and the conceptual framework through which to channel material demands. Indeed, it gradually came to constitute the main framework in which social and political conflicts arose and were settled (Brewer & Styles, 1980).

The entrapment of radical thought within the confines of constitutional 'givens' has drawn sharp criticism by radical historians, most notably E.P. Thompson who attacked early radicals' sanctification of certain conventions, including the monarchy, the hereditary principle, the rights of landowners, the Established Church, and property rights: '[once] enmeshed in constitutionalist arguments (…) reformers became caught up in the trivia of piecemeal constitutional renovation. For a plebeian movement to arise it was essential to escape from these categories altogether and set forward far wider democratic claims' (1968, p. 96). Thompson's view has obvious purchase—it highlights the manifest contradiction between, on the one hand, the socialist ambition of undoing a system predicated on exploitation and economic domination, and, on the other hand, the conservational tendencies of constitutional reform, however radical said reform may be. That said, not everyone has subscribed to Thompson's reading. It has been said to obscure a more complicated reality, in which the constitution rather than providing a hegemonic, unitary or totalising narrative was characterised by a fundamental indeterminacy, opening boundaries rather than closing them:

> constitutional rhetoric (…) was continually reproduced in different and contrasting ways. (…) [The] language of the constitution (…) always intersected with other discourses, its boundaries continually shifting as it was used for different strategic purposes. (…). As a story without an end, in which paradise was always postponed, [constitutionalist discourse] could never realise its totalising ambitions.
>
> (Vernon, 1996, p. 9, 15)

Indeed, by common consent, radical appeals to the constitution were often tactical, with constitutional meanings and idiom constructed and reconstructed in response to power struggles (Belchem, 1981; Epstein, 1989, 1990). This included, importantly, the radicals' reliance on the constitution as a framework for the transformation of political dissatisfaction into popular protest (Belchem, 1981). Yet, whether this was a *peculiarity* of early radical uses of the English constitution is open to question. The ambiguity in constitutional meanings strategically exploited by radicals is an almost existential condition of every constitution. Designed to preserve and reproduce the status quo, constitutional frameworks by necessity provide avenues for the expression of discontent, all while remaining restrictive terrains. It is for this reason that constitutions, to ward off the possibility of uncontainable unrest, also authorise violent repression. This was, for example, the bitter story of the 1819 Peterloo massacre, a historic public protest that may have been encouraged by appeals to constitutional legitimacy, but the response to which also triggered the Six Acts—an array of authoritarian-style provisions aimed at suppressing radical dissent. Seen in the light of this bipole, the perpetual postponement of paradise was perhaps not a historical accident but a structural eventuality—an outcome inscribed in the very logic of the constitutional project itself.

The political trajectory of the most prominent radical groups of earlier centuries exemplifies the tensions between constitutional hope and containment. The seventeenth century's Levellers, undeniably revolutionary in reimagining popular sovereignty in ways resembling modern theories of constituent power as permanent revolution, remained nevertheless constrained by constitutional limits (Kennedy, 2008; Morgan, 1988; Rees, 2016; Wood, 2002).[1] Despite their challenge against the common dominant assumption that the Parliament enjoyed a monopoly in representing the people, their constitutionalist focus prevented them from questioning established social hierarchies or the sacredness of private property (Aylmer, 1975; Gurney, 2007; Wood, 2002).[2] Echoing E.P. Thompson's critique above, Marxist historian Christopher Hill had described Leveller politics as an aspiration to 'extend democracy within the limits of capitalist society' (1972/1991, p. 121), a flaw which other historical accounts have explicitly attributed to the Levellers' 'constitutional focus' (Wood, 2002, p. 165). The Leveller leadership couched demands for social justice in terms of tradition, precedent, the ancient constitution, and birthright, thus transferring political and social conflict into a framework simultaneously constitutional and patriotic (Wood, 2002).[3] Here, the constitution set the terms of acceptable dissent rendering demands beyond its codes either irrational or illegible (Christodoulidis, 1998). Leveller radicalism was filtered out by a dual limitation of constitutional language and political possibility confining Leveller politics to a reformist register.

Similar interpretations have been suggested with regard to the nineteenth century's Chartist movement. Despite the transformative potential and revolutionary energy of the Chartists, the movement locked demands for social justice into the language of the ancient constitution—a language which may have legitimised their political standing in the eyes of the working class but simultaneously limited the movement's revolutionary potential (Epstein, 1990). The Chartists' central demand for universal suffrage was often tied to the language of natural rights found in the ancient constitution, and ideas about the naturalness of common law and divine right often drove political dispute (Gibson, 2017). Commitment to received constitutional doctrine and the rule of law further solidified a belief among the Chartists that common law and the Parliament were the appropriate, if not exclusive, channels for the settlement of political and social conflict (Finn, 2004; McKibbin, 1990). Parliament came to be regarded by the working class as the 'repository of liberty', rendering elections the dominant moment in the political life of the nation, particularly post-1840 when the Chartists became less militant (McKibbin, 1990; Thompson, 1971). In her detailed study of Chartist radicalism, Margot Finn argues that their resort to common law

> served to affirm received beliefs in the impartiality of the institutions of the state, in a legal system responsive to just claims of the disadvantaged against the ruling elite, and in a parliamentary system capable of registering the decrees of the people.
>
> (Finn, 2004, p. 186)

Within this context of constitutional acquiescence, property rights also remained excluded from the field of contestation. According to James Epstein,

> [as] a final qualification to the dominance of the constitutionalist idiom within popular radicalism, we should note that certain assertions of political or social rights were not well served by the force of such reasoning. This is true, for instance, (…) of claims for redistribution of property (…). The linkage within constitutionalist thought from the seventeenth century through the nineteenth century, of civil and political liberty with the rights of private property was strong. Thus it became difficult to invoke constitutionalist claims (…) without acquiescence to the notion of preservation of private property.
>
> (1990, p. 565)

The constitutional focus of Chartist politics did not help them withstand a further pressure: liberal forces who feared that emerging working-class consciousness would result in political conflict escaping the institutional binary of government and opposition and spreading into society in the form of contestation between unionised workers on the one hand and parliament on the other (Finn, 2004). By 1850, as historians document, the working class had been assimilated into a bourgeois state anxious to consolidate the interests of capital against those of workers (Saville, 1990). Helpful to this cause was the repeal of the Corn Laws in 1846, alongside other fiscal reforms, which fostered the idea of a non-partisan state rising above class divisions (Parry, 2009). This is not to suggest, however, that the Chartists were lacking in their radical ambition. Contrary to a common assumption, Perry Anderson has argued that Chartism was not immature, but premature (1964). The nineteenth-century proletariat emerged alongside the first wave of industrialisation and had to reinvent everything, from its ideas to its organisation and tactics. Indeed, the ideology of socialism had not consolidated yet—the Communist Manifesto, for instance, was published shortly *after* the Chartists' collapse (Anderson, 1964). Even so, the 'catatonic defeat' of Chartism led to decades of working-class inactivity (Anderson, 1964, p. 36), and possibly inscribed a defeatist reflex in the heart of future British socialism.

After a few decades of working-class inactivity, pockets of revolutionary thought started to re-emerge. Such was, for example, the Social Democratic Federation founded in 1884, which was unconcerned with the ancient constitution or with constitutional reform but whose imprint on the trajectory of British socialism remained limited (Howell, 1983; Morton, 1938). The decades that had intervened saw the workers' movement become 'thrifty, sober, religious, cautious and respectable'—what in the words of Gladstone was now even more 'fit to come within the pale of the constitution' (Leys, 1983/1989, p. 53). During the same period, labourism, understood as 'the defence and advancement of the interests of labour within capitalism', established itself as a dominant ideology within socialist ranks (Leys, 1983/1989, p. 53). It was within this ideological climate that the Labour Party was founded, offering a vehicle for parliamentary representation, not least in order to channel potentially uncontainable extra-parliamentary collective action through tidy institutional routes (Leys, 1983/1989).

This context, part of a continuum stretching back to the Chartists' over-investment in the power of parliamentary politics, helps explain why the reformist Fabians, founded in the same year as the more radical Social Democratic Federation, gained far broader appeal and influence. The Fabians' intensely constitutional logic gained a foothold strong enough to shape socialist orthodoxy for the next decades. Despite having socialisation of the industry and independence from 'private capitalism' as their horizon, they declared their faith in the English constitution, sought to persuade people to make 'sensible use of the power they already [had]' instead of trying to 'secure a more political power', and begged those looking for 'a sensational historical crisis to join some other society' (Fabian society, 1896, p. 3, 4, 5). Their distinctly bourgeois, utilitarian, and paternalistic tendencies left, in the words of Anderson, a 'poisoned legacy' to the working class (1964, p. 43). Notably, it also defined the ideology of the newly founded Labour Party.

While socialist contentment with the British constitution continued well into the subsequent decades, it has been argued that there emerged moments of acute constitutional discontent in the 1920s and 1930s, presumably under the influence of the Bolshevik Revolution (Wright, 1990). A representative example of such discontent is traditionally considered to be prominent Labour Party member Sir Stafford Cripps (Cliff, 1986). In his pamphlet *Can Socialism Come by Constitutional Methods*, Cripps advocated for an Emergency Powers Bill to be passed as the socialist government's first step, which '[would] be wide enough (…) to allow all that [would] be immediately necessary to be done by ministerial orders, [which] (…) must be incapable of challenge in the courts or in any way except in the House of Commons' (Cliff, 1896, p. 21). It is not entirely clear why this proposal, reaffirming at once the power of the executive and that of the Commons, has been considered anti-constitutional and not for example simply anti-democratic. In a way, what the Cripps episode ultimately revealed was not so much the radicalism of his proposal, but the deep constitutional reflexes of the Labour Party, and indeed the Trade Union Congress, which were quick to denounce any deviation, however procedural, from the orthodoxies of the ancient constitution. In a speech given a year later, French historian Elie Halévy offered the following comment:

> There is nothing extremely revolutionary in [Cripps'] point of view. It is slightly dictatorial, but he asked for nothing that, considered as a matter of procedure, was exactly new. However, it was enough to rouse the whole Labour world to anger. Sir Stafford Cripps was denounced as a traitor to English liberties, first by the Trade Union Congress, then by a Labour Party Congress, and lastly, the Labour Party thought it necessary to have a special conference in January to say the same things once more and to insist that when in power they should confine themselves to use of strictly constitutional methods.
>
> (1933, p. 498)

A recurrent theme since the eighteenth century, the idea of English liberty guaranteed by the (ancient) constitution revealed a deep continuity with earlier radical thought. So did, as Halévy later in the same speech remarked, the idea of the Parliament as the repository of English liberty:

> The ideal of English liberty in the eighteenth century was the idea of a Parliament strictly controlling the aristocracy and the monarchy, the paradoxical idea that the basis of society was not to obey those who governed but to disobey them, control them, and make things difficult for them.
>
> (Halévy, 1934, p. 499)

This, he continued, created a fundamental identity clash in modern British socialism: British socialists were historically predisposed to protect the individual against the state, all while having their socialist ideology push them to the opposite direction—that of a 'State strong against capitalists' (Halévy, 1934,

p. 498). In a sense, this is all but an alternative version of the familiar ostensible paradox with which this section opened, namely that the demand for social transformation has historically cohabited with a demand to preserve the foundational qualities of the ancient constitution.

In the meantime, political actors on the far radical end of the socialist spectrum, such as the Communist Party of Great Britain (CPGB), embracing (at least initially) an anti-institutional and anti-parliamentary strategy, remained in the margins of the socialist mainstream. Some have attributed this to the Party's Bolshevisation, which contributed to a lack of theoretical clarity (Hinton & Hyman, 1987). Others have argued that the appeal of the CPGB was lost after 1926 when the party broke up with elements of working-class self-emancipation hitherto integrated into its party lines and party culture by politically self-educated workers (Macintyre, 1987). However, the influence of the Communist Party of the interwar period did leave a strong imprint on British socialism. The Labour Party's famous Clause IV of the 1918 Constitution pledged that workers would enjoy the full fruits of their industry on the basis of common ownership of the means of production (Labour Party, 1918). This great promise, never mind its eventual abandonment, may well have been the result of radical, if tacit, pressures by the CPGB and other non-mainstream socialist groups. That said, the influence was not able to withstand, let alone overcome, the Labour Party's deep constitutional ethos: the first bitter defeat of Clause IV came during the class struggles of the 1920s and, most notably, the general strike of 1924 where the Party asserted its commitment to parliamentary politics and its aversion to any extra-constitutional means—the latter were kept at bay and regarded as communist and dangerous, with fears that they could possibly be used against the Labour Party itself (Coates, 1975). Nothing attests more to this spirit of constitutional comfort than the words of a chairman in 1919:

> We are either constitutionalists or we are not constitutionalists. If we are constitutionalists, if we believe in the efficiency of the political weapon (and we do, or why do we have a Labour Party?) then it is both unwise and undemocratic because we fail to get a majority at the polls to turn round and demand that we should [employ the strike weapon for political purposes].
>
> (Miliband, 1964, p. 69)

Overall, the interwar period was characterised by a Fabian collectivism blended with some radical elements of guild socialism and syndicalism, while more revolutionary communist politics remained fringe. Thus, alongside traditional models of strong executive government—the socialist mantra of the period—key figures like G.D.H. Cole and Harold Laski advocated self-government, worker-organised production, and the direct expression of popular will (Cole, 1920; McIlroy & Campbell, 2020). This notwithstanding, there was still solid faith in constitutional arrangements; rather than bending the constitution to

Labour's will, even the party's more radical members proposed that Labour should adapt itself to fit within already existing constitutional parameters (Wright, 1990). Dominant within this context was Labour's 'dogmatic commitment to reformist parliamentary methods' (Toye, 2012, p. 2). Largely confirming the historical development of radicalism in previous centuries, that commitment has been described as *an existential condition* for the party, as opposed to a mere political proclivity to parliamentarianism (Pimlott, 1977). The past of English radicalism foreshadowed this turn of events, while the present historical conjuncture of the 1930s helped to further consolidate the mentality of constitutionalism and parliamentarianism. Social transformation through parliamentary power had *not* yet been tried by British socialists, and Stalinism was starting to paint extra-constitutional politics in a negative light (Coates, 1975). It is against this background that, in 1935, Clement Attlee rose to lead the party. A symbol of 'moderation, reformism, and gradualism', Attlee displayed deep belief in Labour's constitutionalism and adherence to the idea of personal liberty (Morgan, 1985, p. 15).

3.3 Postwar Constitutionalism, the Nairn-Anderson Debate, and the Road to Charter 88

In the immediate postwar period, there was a reshuffling in the Labour Party's internal arrangements. This was partly triggered by wartime radicalism, partly by Labour Left's discomfort with trade union leadership, and partly by the regained legitimacy of the Communist Party (Minkin, 1991). A major party reconstruction proposal, including affiliation with the Communist Party and restriction of trade union electoral influence, gained momentum but was to eventually subside in favour of the party's concerted focus on a public ownership programme (Minkin, 1991). Indeed, in the period after 1945, the Labour Party rediscovered socialism in the nationalisation of central industries (Rees, 2003). The 1945 electoral victory effectively silenced aspirations for left-wing and communist cooperation, targeting a programme grounded in a synthesis of Fabian gradualism and Keynesian economics (Morgan, 1985). Some reforms, like the creation of the National Health Service, were not immune from political confrontation and the question of nationalisation generally remained contentious lacking any cross-party consensus (Webster, 1998). However, while in its official rhetoric Labour ideologically sided with state socialism as opposed to free market capitalism, the leadership had already settled the matter in favour of realism and 'pragmatic reform in a mixed economy' (Addison, 1977, p. 14). Next to its hesitation over economic reform, Attlee's government also remained constitutionally conservative and cautious against institutional change. It showed 'almost a reverence for the constitution, from the monarchy and the House of Lords to the fabric of local government which remained much as Lord Salisbury had left it in 1888' (Morgan, 1985, p. 494).

How Attlee's Labour is to be assessed is a matter of political and ideological disposition. While postwar Labour undeniably left a legacy of welfarism, from the standpoint of socialism—or even socialist constitutionalism—there remains significant ambivalence about the broader legacy of his government. Ralph Miliband, for example, in his *Parliamentary Socialism* (1964), devoted one sentence to the NHS and an entire treatise to Labour's failure to bring socialism to the country through the parliamentary route. Indeed, by the mid-1950s, the party had sidelined Labour Left, which had long been in search of a third way between support for North Atlantic Treaty Organisation and uncritical Soviet support, and Hugh Gaitskell's revisionism had prevailed (Coates, 1975). Within this context, commitment to public ownership was almost abandoned, references to socialism in official party documents started to wane, and references to capitalism effectively eclipsed (Coates, 1975). As John Saville commented some time later,

> [in] the years immediately preceding his death in 1963, Labour Party policy was reduced to reformist objectives which now no longer even involved the rhetoric of the transformation of society into a socialist commonwealth. This was Gaitskell's main contribution to the history of the Labour Party.
>
> (1980, p. 164)

By the time Labour was to form its second majority government, in 1964, reformism had officially consolidated, although Harold Wilson often made Labour's agenda sound way more radical than it actually was (Saville, 1980). The historical conjuncture of the West in the 1960s is more or less known. Within the context of a more general radicalisation of the masses, the surge in social and political activism, the rise of a left-wing intelligentsia, and Khrushchev's denouncement of Stalin etc, there emerged the New Left, which in Britain took a distinctly anti-constitutionalist direction. This was possibly the first time since the civil war that a strand of British socialism critical of the constitution found itself not entirely consigned in the political margins. In retrospect, the period was marked by the prominent influence of socialist historians Tom Nairn and Perry Anderson who, through the pages of the then newly founded New Left Review, launched a rereading of the British class system, mounted a sustained attack against the ancient constitution, and emerged as intellectual precursors of the later Charter 88 movement.

There were two principal interconnected threads in the Nairn-Anderson 1960s discussion. First, there was the assertion that the British bourgeoisie, having emerged and evolved within a feudal framework dominated by the hegemony of the landed aristocracy, failed to develop its own unified class consciousness. Absence of bourgeois hegemony in turn blocked the development of independent consciousness of the working class: '[in] England, a supine bourgeoisie produced a subordinate proletariat. It handed on no impulse of liberation, no revolutionary values, no universal language' (Anderson, 1964, p. 43). Leaving aside the authors' exclusive coupling of hegemony and a unified class consciousness, their claim that a historically retarded bourgeoisie limited the radical potential of the working class—a view contested by many, most notably E.P. Thompson (1965)—led to the second, partly connected and partly self-standing, contention: parliamentary democracy and parliamentary sovereignty, though potential proletarian weapons, were in fact constitutionally designed to absorb emerging social forces—first the bourgeoisie, then the proletariat—into existing structures without disturbing the dominance of the ruling bloc (Anderson, 1964). The archaic English constitution therefore had to be dismantled. Therein lay the authors' profound anti-constitutionalism.

This was not atypical of the 1960s. As Anthony King (2007) argued, the postwar social reshuffling had radically transformed attitudes and defeated old tendencies to defer to social and political shibboleths. Nairn and Anderson expressed this from an epistemic standpoint that was also distinctly Marxist in its orientation. Hegemony was used in its Gramscian sense, while the anachronistic constitution and the 'corrupting fetish' of the 'ancient' 'supremacy' of parliament' were attacked as forces blocking the class struggle from finding its way into the political sphere (Nairn, 1964, p. 61). This was, for Nairn, the trap into which the Labour Party of the 1960s had fallen. The party's 'parliamentary servitude' would not let it see 'British constitutional custom' and the party system with 'its heavy brake on the class struggle' as the 'double defence against socialism' (Nairn, 1964, p. 61). In this way, the Nairn-Anderson thesis broke with the socialist past in at least two ways. First, there was a break with the historical understanding of an omnipotent Commons and a strong executive as key to socialism (Murphy, 2024a). Second, by equating bourgeois hegemony and therefore, according to their argument, working-class consciousness with modernity, all while blaming the ancient constitution for the social ills of Britain, they were making—perhaps inadvertently—a powerful conceptual and ideological case for constitutional modernisation. The latter was to be picked up and tailored to the historical context of the late 1980s by the socialists of that period. In between, British socialism and constitutional militancy had to a great extent parted ways.

The industrial defeats of the 1960s and 1970s and the collapse of the Soviet Union, combined with the Thatcherite experience of the 1980s, left socialists profoundly disorientated and demoralised. From the 1970s onwards, the ideological and theoretical influence of Marxism retreated, as did 'anti-capitalist working class concerns', in favour of a focus on state power and aspects of Britain's governance (Erdos, 2009, p. 540; Howe, 2009; Murphy, 2024b). The conditions were conducive to a renewed socialist engagement with questions of Britain's constitutional order. Dominant within this context became the idea of modernisation (Murphy, 2024b). The British constitution was antiquated and was, therefore, at least in part, responsible for the painful socialist defeat by Thatcher's administration, from the ban on unionisation for Government Communications

Headquarters to the ban on free speech for Sinn Fein (Erdos, 2009). The Nairn-Anderson debate, with its focus on the 'modern' versus the 'ancient', thus conveniently fell into the lap of socialist constitutional reformists—only this time recast in a deradicalised register, stripped off its original Marxist methodology, never mind flawed or otherwise, and redirected towards a technocratic project of constitutional modernisation.

As E.P. Thompson and others had objected, the Nairn-Anderson thesis suffered from a strong normative bias in its conception of the 'modern', with Thompson in particular accusing them of conflating the modern with the bourgeois (Finlayson, 2003; Howe, 2009). If the criticism is correct, then it transpires that, interestingly, the project of socialist constitutional modernisation that dominated the late 1980s was possibly an accident, partly caused by a misreading of historical events by the New Left Review editors. Misguided or not, their thesis marked British socialism in the 1980s, prompting a reconsideration of political economy in terms of constitutional law and constitutional reform. This historical juncture gave rise to Charter 88.

Charter 88, which was launched from the offices on New Statesman and Society during the same year, was a political project with hegemonic aspirations, seeking to elevate social-democratic constitutionalism as the dominant political opponent to Thatcherism (Murphy, 2024a, 2024b). This was a movement from 'within the left' and while there was no official affiliation to the Labour Party, the latter became at times quite receptive to the movement's proposals, at least at the level of rhetoric (Wright, 1990, p. 322). The movement's key target was constitutional reform with a focus on proportional representation, an elected second chamber, a Bill of Rights, and regional government. A key underlying idea, and a first for British socialists, was the decentralisation of governmental power.

For some, like Paul Hirst—Birkbeck professor of sociology and political theory and former Althusserian turned pluralist endorser of the ideas of Cole and Laski discussed above—decentralisation primarily meant corporatism, namely the incorporation of industrial interests into governance. The Winter of Discontent had proven the rigidity of the British constitutional settlement with its centralised majoritarian elements to be not merely ill-suited to accommodate a corporatist logic, but an active obstacle to it (Hirst, 1990; Murphy, 2024a). The barriers to industrial justice and democratic socialism had to be removed. For this strand of—more militant—socialists, constitutional reform opened the institutional way to economic democracy.[4] For others, decentralisation primarily embodied a constitutional promise for more effective control of the executive. This was mainly pursued through proportional representation but also the demand for a Bill of Rights and a fortified role for the judiciary. The latter, arguably unprecedented, claim for British socialism drew into its ranks not only the Labour Party leadership of that time but also former supporters of Tony Benn, with the latter however remaining against Charter 88 style constitutional reform

(Murphy, 2024a, 2024b). Even the Bennite left, however, endorsed the demand for constitutional reform towards decentralisation, which Benn himself argued was necessary to render the Prime Minister accountable and to transform Britain's system 'from an Absolute Premiership into a Constitutional Premiership' (Benn, 1985).

With the Charter 88 campaign resurfaced a familiar dilemma for socialists: whether to pursue demands for social justice through constitutional reform in order to secure broader political traction, or to maintain a more radical critique that risked marginalisation from mainstream political discourse. In truth, the reforms proposed fell short even of that dilemma. The constitutional ambition of Charter 88 hardly incorporated any strong demand for reversal of social injustices. In the words of Michael Rustin,

> It was not part of the purpose of Charter 88 in the minds of some of its key supporters to reverse the changes in the balance of power between social classes that Thatcherism had brought about. The Charter 88 coalition would have been placed under grave stress if its more socialist members had been able to insist, for example, on the restoration of trade union or welfare rights revoked under Thatcher, as constitutional entitlements. Many supporters of the Charter, (…), were antipathetic, for libertarian reasons, to (…) the 'democratic collectivist tradition' of Labour.
>
> (2009, p. 574)

Thus, with hindsight, while the campaign did achieve a broader appeal, it lost on all other fronts. It secured neither meaningful constitutional reform nor, by any measure, radical social change (Loughlin, 1992). In this sense, Charter 88 presented a paradox: although it was the first—and possibly sole—socialist initiative of mass appeal to directly confront the ancient constitution and openly challenge established institutions—contrary to the traditional socialist acquiescence to them—it ultimately proved to be one of the most deradicalised campaigns.

In the end, the broader appeal it had momentarily secured proved itself futile. On the one hand, New Labour's constitutional reform in the 1990s at best selectively adopted those reform proposals that suited its own interests. As Matthew Flinders has remarked, next to a 'bi-constitutionalism' where Labour adopted proportional representation for devolved parliaments only, while retaining centralisation for Westminster, Charter 88 also led to a 'constitutional anomie' 'reflected in the government's inability to (…) provide a set of underlying principles or a rationale for the reforms it [had] implemented since 1997' (Flinders, 2009, p. 646). On the other hand, no social or ideological change was effected, although it has been argued that the constitutional visibility brought about by the campaign has left a positive legacy to this day (Erdos, 2009).

Commenting on Charter 88, Michael Rustin had argued that its logic was underwritten by the defeatism Thatcher's government had left socialists with and that

> rather than trying to resolve differences of political ends by constitutional means, Charter 88 was (…) a movement which sought to formulate political ends in constitutional terms. Rather than standing above politics, this campaign for constitutional reform was essentially a form of politics.
>
> (2009, p. 570)

From a socialist perspective, Ruskin is right to object against constitutional reform as an end in itself, and to the extent that Charter 88 was such a campaign, that is indeed further attestation to its reformist character. There is, however, a tacit assumption in Ruskin's extract according to which the proper (socialist) route would be to instrumentalise the constitution—use it as a means to an end—which, the argument goes, would have elevated the constitutional campaign above politics. The assumption contains an ambiguity. It sees the instrumentalisation of the constitution as a practice standing above politics rather than as a tactic that incorporates itself a political premise. That premise is that the law, in a capitalist state, can be deployed, twisted, and turned according to the political aims and intentions of the actor who puts it into use. This mentality, to which I will return in the next and final section, has informed what may be termed the *constitutional maximalism* of British socialism. It captures the overinvestment in the ability of the constitution to yield socialist results, if correctly tweaked. The instrumentalist idea according to which constitutional reform is the tool to economic democracy has defined British socialism and has transpired through two partly overlapping tendencies: first, a conviction—espoused, for example, by Chartist rhetoric, the Fabian tradition, and postwar Labour governments—that the route to socialism is already latent in the (ancient) constitution, and all that is required is releasing its energy, if need be by removing barriers; second, the conviction that constitutional and procedural reform can substitute for material or class-based transformation. The last section discusses how these tendencies have made it to the twenty-first century while elaborating on the conceptual and strategic problems of constitutional maximalism and instrumentalisation.

3.4 The UK Socialist Constitution in the Twenty-First Century: Instrumentalisation and Class

3.4.1 Corbynism: The Instrumentalisation of the State

The embedment of the Thatcherite dogma that capitalism was the only available option, and the concomitant adoption by the Labour Party of a mentality of 'responsible capitalism' from the 1980s onwards ushered in a period of ideological hibernation for British socialism (Carr, 2018, p. 90). Corbyn's election to the leadership of the Labour Party in 2015 was the first major hit to the ideological straitjacket of pro-market neoliberal orthodoxies. The rise of Corbynism is usually associated with, if not attributed to, a younger generation of socialists unaffected by the defeatism of the 1980s and nurtured in the more militant framework of the anti-war and anti-globalisation, and later, anti-austerity and Occupy, movements of the twenty-first century (Young, 2018). Equally important has, however, been an older generation of socialists who insisted on socialist ideas through the years of Thatcherism and New Labour (Davis & McWilliam, 2018; Thomas, 2016). The latter part of the Corbynite cohort is often associated with the socialist politics of Tony Benn who, as remarked above, endorsed a shift to constitutional premiership—a participatory democracy with less power for the executive and more power for working people. Yet, in contrast to Benn and, indeed, against the grain of British socialist tradition, Corbyn's agenda was distinctly non-constitutional. This is not to say that his manifestos lacked proposals for constitutional reform. From proportional representation to an elected second chamber, the traditional socialist repertoire of institutional change—whether well thought through or not—was there. What was lacking was the constitutional maximalism of earlier periods. Corbyn's agenda was light on appeals to the constitution, heavier on class-based politics. Linguistically too, the slogan *For the Many not the Few,* implied a division so defining of society that in a sense replaced the logic of constitutional reform with that of social antagonism, and a demand for wealth redistribution and worker empowerment.

With that said, Corbyn's agenda has been criticised both in relation to its proposals for institutional reform and in relation to its understanding of class-based politics and classes in the capitalist state. Starting from the latter aspect, in an extensive commentary on the Corbynite approach to socialism, political theorists Matt Bolton and Frederick Harry Pitts (2018) have noted that Corbynism has misread the nature of capitalist production processes thus failing to provide a genuine alternative to capitalism. For Corbyn, as for Benn before him, so the authors contend, wealth in the form of value seemed to be understood as a fixed transhistorical category rather than an abstract social relation specific to the capitalist mode of production (Bolton & Pitts, 2018). In other words, the Corbynite agenda was concerned with redistributing resources once wealth was out in circulation, all while overlooking the structural elements of its production. This was an approach to the production process as a neutral field, into which capitalists intervene only externally and *post festum*, in order to appropriate the wealth supposedly created by workers (Bolton & Pitts, 2018). This reading of production, through which socialism becomes a matter of distributive justice rather than power structures, has been heavily influenced by Miliband's account of capitalist domination as a personalised circumstance instead of a structural component of the capitalist state. Poulantzas, writing in response to Miliband's view of the capitalist state—a view that has underlined British socialist thought resonating not only in the politics of Benn and Corbyn, but earlier partly also in the work of Nairn and Anderson—observed the following:

> [theirs] is a problematic of *social actors*, of individuals as the origin of *social action*: sociological research thus leads (…), not to the study of the objective coordinates that determine the distribution of agents into social classes and the contradictions between these classes, but to the search for *finalist* explanations founded on the *motivations of conduct* of the individual actors.
>
> (1969, p. 70)

The personification of capitalism, described by Poulantzas, has obvious repercussions for the socialist agenda. It implies that socialism will arrive as the inevitable outcome of gradual accumulation by workers of control over the production process and imposition of their own rationality, but overlooks the structural elements of the economic base. According to this view, the fate of structural elements of the capitalist state is contingent on the personal ideology of those in charge of them (Bolton & Pitts, 2018). As Bolton and Pitts further remark, 'socialism cannot mean (…) "the victory" of the working class in a struggle between "two camps", while leaving untouched the system of social labour and value which constitute "class struggle" as an objective, structural feature of capitalist society' (2018, p. 174).

Stretched to its logical limit, this framework leads to several constitutionally relevant conclusions. First, it refuses to see the economic and political spheres as relatively autonomous sets of social relations assuming instead that the political sphere—the state—is up for grabs, with its control determined by the degree of economic power a class is able to accumulate at a given historical moment. This leads, secondly, to an instrumentalisation of the state—a convenient schema whereby once control of the state has been assumed, workers will be able to use it in line with their own interests. Thirdly, this understanding of social totality, or in Marxist terms, of base and superstructure as a direct reflection of the former on the latter, informs an instrumentalist approach to the juridical element, including primarily the constitution. This way, despite its class-centred emphasis rather than an overt constitutional focus, Corbynite politics reproduced the same instrumentalist logic that has historically characterised British socialism.

The significance of this continuity lies not so much in the specific procedural reforms advocated—such as proportional representation or the recalibration of powers between the Commons and the Lords. While such institutional planning is certainly important, the more revealing constant is the underlying logic that drives investment in the idea that institutional change is sufficient to trigger wholesale transformation; the belief, in other words, that socialism can arrive through legal and constitutional adjustment. It is this instrumental understanding of law and the constitution—as tools for transforming capitalism—that I turn to in the final section. Notably, this logic persists even in some of the most sophisticated responses to Corbyn's proposals for constitutional and institutional amendment.

3.4.2 British Socialism and the Instrumentalisation of the Constitution

Corbyn's agenda for institutional reform elicited critical responses from sections of the left, some of which focused specifically on its constitutional dimensions. His constitutional framework has, for example, been criticised for failing to hold to the Bennite vision of a constitutional premiership, returning instead to the traditional British socialist line of centralisation and a strong executive (Daniels, 2021). Keith Ewing (2017, 2020) has maybe offered the most nuanced discussion of Corbyn's constitutional agenda. He has, for example, criticised Corbyn's manifesto's 'overindulgence' in the Human Rights Act 1998 pointing out the liberal, as opposed to socialist, underpinnings of such a choice (Ewing, 2017). He has also taken issue with Corbyn's proposal for an elected second chamber, pointing out quite compellingly the strategic disadvantages such reform would have for a socialist government (Ewing, 2017, 2020). Overall, he has offered a comprehensive review of Corbyn's institutional agenda set against the broader constitutional architecture and democratic deficit of the British state. Importantly, for present purposes, though, it has also been suggested that '[the] challenge for Corbyn is to reconnect with Labour's past and to rediscover the social democratic structures that will make social democratic politics possible, though it is surely likely that the former will follow inexorably from the latter' (Ewing, 2017, p. 346). Leaving aside whether Labour's past is where one should like to return to, the extract appears to reproduce—perhaps with a tweak—the Corbynite logic examined above: structural change will ensue, *inexorably*, from the implementation of socially sensitive politics.

That a scholar of the quality of Ewing should deploy this logic, which eventually leads to the instrumentalisation of the state and the law, is hardly accidental. He is explicit elsewhere that the constitution can—and should—be deployed instrumentally in the service of labour as part of the socialist strategy (Ewing, 2020). To this effect, he has put together an elaborate socialist constitutional framework, including from mandatory universal sectoral bargaining and a Ministry of Labour to the socialisation of economic departments and workers' involvement in legislation through an economic council (Ewing, 2020). At the same time, he is under no illusion that the liberal constitution is neutral. Instead, with Kautsky, he has argued that socialists should fully utilise the democratic rights the constitution confers, not as ends in themselves, but instead in a purely instrumental fashion as means to *empower* Labour (and labour forces) (Ewing, 2020). If the British constitution does not allow this goal to materialise, then 'by all means, remove the barriers' (Ewing, 2020, p. 33). Here, the existing constitutional framework can be used as an instrument because, for all its defects, it has an *enabling* potential; indeed, 'an unintended potential for opportunity (…) inherited from the seventeenth century revolution' (Ewing, 2020, p. 58).

Two interconnected elements in the above analytical framework reveal an enduring affinity with the instrumentalist assumptions of the constitutional maximalism of the British socialist tradition. One is the conviction that a socialist alternative already resides in the ancient constitution which, in turn, will unleash its emancipatory potential if optimally used. The second is a logic both presupposing and concluding that reforming the constitution will change the fate of the working class. This paradoxical coupling of institutional preservation and constitutional reform where both are simultaneously cast as vehicles for class emancipation seems inscribed in the British socialist imaginary. It produces certain further paradoxes, not least the continued insistence on longstanding shibboleths such as parliamentary sovereignty. Long upheld by socialists as an *enabling* institutional set-up, parliamentary sovereignty, as remarked in previous sections, has helped entrench an understanding of politics as the exclusive preserve of parliament, thereby delegitimising extra-parliamentary forms of mobilisation and struggle (Meiksins Wood, 1995). In this way, British socialism, while aspiring to popular democratic empowerment, has often stumbled upon the institutional limits that it itself has chosen to preserve.

In a similar way, the strategy of working-class emancipation through constitutional reform has stumbled upon the structural limits of the capitalist state. This is not to say that socialism should not take constitutional reform seriously. The constitution remains a terrain of contestation and struggle and, indeed, a crucial one. In addition, as E.P. Thompson observed, the law 'despite its class bound and mystifying functions' is not simply a superstructural reflection of the economic base operating unequivocally in the interests of the ruling class (as cited in Meiksins Wood, 1995, p. 73). Legal change can be emancipatory for the working class. Nonetheless, the constitutional maximalism of British socialism expressed through the instrumentalisation of the juridico-political level, has at times altogether obscured the nature of class—of the British working class—as a social relation. Because classes are not merely subjects pitted against each other, but the social relations constitutive of capitalism, constitutional reform cannot on its own undo class domination, however much it empowers one class against the other, through for example industrial democracy, universal sectoral bargaining and so forth. The same limitations apply to the removal of constitutional barriers—a logic which assumes that socialism is inherent in the capitalist state waiting to reveal itself once the capitalist obstacles embodied in the biases of the liberal constitution, are lifted.

3.5 Conclusion

Constitutional reform has a place in socialist politics. Questions concerning the structure of state institutions, the powers of the executive, the role of the judiciary, and, most crucially, the pursuit of industrial and economic democracy are indispensable to any serious political vision of a more just and emancipated society. In this respect, engagement with constitutional questions is a sine qua non for socialism, and the contributions of socialist constitutional scholars have, for all their possible limitations, been indispensable to the broader socialist project. However, to treat the constitution as the privileged terrain of socialist transformation is to mistake procedural reform at the outer layers of capitalism for a rupture with the material logic that underpins it. This article has argued that much of the British socialist tradition falls into this trap. It has revisited this tradition through a historical review of socialist engagements with the constitution—a history that has fluctuated from acquiescence with capitalist institutions to outright challenges to them, but which has always in the end returned to an instrumentalist logic: the belief that the constitution or state can be wielded as a neutral tool once power shifts to the working class. And yet, this critique should not eclipse what has been achieved. Paraphrasing Ralph Miliband—himself one of the sharpest critics of socialists' constitutional illusions— whatever radicals and socialists have said or done, 'these men and women have greatly helped to civilise Britain'—'without [them], government would have been even more closed than it is; society would have been even less democratic; civil and political rights would have been even less secure; and the political culture would have been even more impoverished' (Miliband, 1984, p. 28). This, undeniably, is a debt we owe.

Notes

1 References to the people as an uncontainable force are made, for example, in the Levellers' letter 'England's Misery and Remedy' (September 1645). Available here: https://quod.lib.umich.edu/e/eebo/A90235.0001.001/1:1?rgn=div1;view=fulltext.

2 Christopher Hill in his seminal work *The World Turned Upside Down* explains that only after their decay did the Levellers advocate abolition of base tenures.

3 Edward Sexby's speech cited in Wood is specifically illuminating on this. This also resonated with Thompson's argument that constitutionalism, liberty and patriotism formed a common nexus of ideas.

4 According to Leys (1989), however, the corporatist model of Britain was consensual and caused no anxiety to 'strict constitutionalists'.

References

Addison, P. (1977). *The road to 1945: British politics and the Second World War*. Quartet Books.

Anderson, P. (1964). Origins of the present crisis. *New Left Review,* 23, 26–53.

Aylmer, G. (1975). *Levellers in the English revolution.* Thames & Hudson Ltd.

Belchem, J. (1981). Republicanism, popular constitutionalism and the radical platform in early nineteenth-century England. *Social History*, 6(1), 1–32. https://www.jstor.org/stable/4285043

Benn, T. (1985). The case for a constitutional premiership. In: King, A. (Ed.), *The British prime minister.* (pp. 221–241). Palgrave. https://doi.org/10.1007/978-1-349-17887-2_10

Bolton, M., & Pitts, F. H. (2018). *Corbynism: A critical approach.* Emerald Publishing.

Brewer, J., & Styles, J. (1980). Introduction. In J. Brewer & J. Styles (Eds.), *An ungovernable people: The English and their law in the seventeenth and eighteenth centuries* (pp. 11–20). Hutchinson.

Carr, R. (2018). Responsible capitalism: Labour's industrial policy and the idea of a National Investment Bank during the long 1980s. In J. Davis & R. McWilliam (Eds.), *Labour and the left in the 1980s* (pp. 90–109). Manchester University Press.

Christodoulidis, E. (1998). *Law and reflexive politics.* Springer.

Cliff, T. (1986). Stafford Cripps: Another tale of betrayal. *Socialist Worker Review*, 88, 20–22.

Coates, D. (1975). *The Labour Party and the struggle for socialism.* Cambridge University Press.

Cole, G. D. H. (1920). *Guild socialism re-stated.* Leonard Parsons.

Cripps, S. (1933). *Can socialism come by constitutional methods?* Socialist League.

Daniels, S. (2021). Corbyn, the constitution and constitutional premiership: Breaking Bennism? In A. S. Roe-Crines (Ed.), *Corbynism in perspective: The Labour Party under Jeremy Corbyn. Building progressive alternatives* (pp. 185–204). Agenda Publishing.

Davis, J., & McWilliam, R. (2018). Introduction: New histories of labour and the left in the 1980s. In J. Davis & R. McWilliam (Eds.), *Labour and the left in the 1980s* (pp. 1–19). Manchester University Press.

Epstein, J. A. (1989). Understanding the cap of liberty - Symbolic practice and social conflict in early nineteenth-century England. *Past & Present*, 122(1), 75–118. https://doi.org/10.1093/past/122.1.75

Epstein, J. A. (1990). The constitutional idiom: Radical reasoning, rhetoric and action in early nineteenth-century England. *Journal of Social History*, 23(3), 553–574. https://www.jstor.org/stable/3788181

Erdos, D. (2009). Charter 88 and the constitutional reform agenda. *Parliamentary Affairs*, 62(4), 537–551.

Ewing, K. D. (2017). Jeremy Corbyn and the law of democracy. *King's Law Journal*, 28(2), 343–362. https://doi.org/10.1080/09615768.2017.1363541

Ewing, K. D. (2020). Socialism and the constitution. *Current Legal Problems*, 73(1), 27–58. https://doi.org/10.1093/clp/cuaa002

Fabian Society. (1896). *Report on Fabian policy and resolutions presented by the Fabian Society to the International Socialist Workers and Trade Union Congress, London, 1896* (Fabian Tract No. 70). The Fabian Society.

Finlayson, A. (2003). *Making sense of new labour.* Lawrence & Wishart.

Finn, M. C. (2004). *After Chartism: Class and nation in English radical politics 1848–1874.* Cambridge University Press.

Flinders, M. (2009). Charter 88, New Labour and constitutional anomie. *Parliamentary Affairs*, 62(4), 645–662. https://doi.org/10.1093/pa/gsp023

Gibson, J. (2017) The Chartists and the constitution: Revisiting British popular constitutionalism. *Journal of British Studies*, 56(1), 70–90. https://doi.org/10.1017/jbr.2016.121

Gurney, J. (2007). *Brave community: The Digger movement in the English revolution.* Manchester University Press.

Halévy, E. (1934). Socialism and the problem of democratic parliamentarianism. *International Affairs,* 13(4), 490–507. https://doi.org/10.2307/2603399.

Hay, D. (1975). Property, authority and the criminal law. In H. Douglas (Ed.), *Albion's fatal tree: Crime and society in eighteenth-century England* (pp. 17–63). Pantheon Books.

Hill, C. (1991). *The world turned upside down: Radical ideas during the English revolution.* Penguin. (Original work published 1972).

Hinton, J., & Hyman, R. (1987). *Trade unions and revolution: Industrial politics of the early British Communist Party.* Pluto Press.

Hirst, P. Q. (1990). From statism to pluralism. In B. Pimlott, T. Wright, & T. Flower (Eds.), *The alternative: Politics for a change* (pp. 19–31). W.H. Allen.

Howe, S. (2009). Some intellectual origins of Charter 88. *Parliamentary Affairs*, 62(4), 552–567. https://doi.org/10.1093/pa/gsp026

Howell, D. (1983). *British workers and the Independent Labour Party, 1888–1906.* Manchester University Press.

Kennedy, G. (2008). *Diggers, levellers and agrarian capitalism: Radical political thought in seventeenth century England.* Lexington Books.

King, A. (2007). *The British constitution.* Oxford University Press.

Labour Party. (1918). Constitution of the Labour Party: Clause IV. Retrieved from https://www.labourcounts.com/Clause_IV.htm [accessed 14 May 2025].

Leys, C. (1989). *Politics in Britain: From labourism to Thatcherism.* University of Toronto Press. (Original work published 1983).

Loughlin, M. (1992). *Public law and political theory*. Oxford University Press.

Macintyre, S. (1987). *A proletarian science: Marxism in Britain, 1917–1933.* Lawrence & Wishart Ltd.

McIlroy, J., & Campbell, A. (2020). The Socialist Labour Party and the leadership of early British communism. *Critique: Journal of Socialist Theory*, 48(4), 609–659. https://doi.org/10.1080/03017605.2020.1850817

McKibbin, R. (1990). *The ideologies of class: Social relations in Britain 1880–1950.* Clarendon Press.

Meiksins Wood, E. (1995). *Democracy against capitalism: Renewing historical materialism*. Cambridge University Press.

Miliband, R. (1964). *Parliamentary socialism: A study in the politics of Labour* (2nd ed.). Merlin Press.

Miliband, R. (1984). *Capitalist democracy in Britain.* Oxford University Press.

Minkin, L. (1991). *The contentious alliance: Trade unions and the Labour Party.* Edinburgh University Press.

Morgan, K. O. (1985). *Labour in power, 1945–1951.* Oxford University Press.

Morgan, S. (1988). *Inventing the people: The rise of popular sovereignty in England and America.* Norton & Company.

Morton, A. L. (1938). *A people's history of England.* Victor Gollancz.

Murphy, C. (2024a). 'Towards a modern democracy'? The constitutional politics of the 1990s British left. *Contemporary British History,* 38(4), 565–589. https://doi.org/10.1080/13619462.2024.2410554

Murphy, C. (2024b). *Futures of socialism: 'Modernisation', the Labour Party, and the British left, 1973–1997.* Cambridge University Press.

Nairn, T. (1964). The nature of the Labour Party (I). *New Left Review*, 27, 38–65.

Parry, J. (2006). *The politics of patriotism: English liberalism and national identity.* Cambridge University Press. https://doi.org/10.1017/CBO9780511495984

Pimlott, B. (1977). *Labour and the left in the 1930s*. Cambridge University Press.

Poulantzas, N. (1969). The problem of the capitalist state. *New Left Review,* 58, 67–78.

Rees, D. B. (2003). Socialism. In D. Loades (Ed.), *Reader's guide to British history* (Vol. 2). (p. 1210). Fitzroy Dearborn.

Rees, J. (2016). *The Leveller revolution.* Verso.

Rustin, M. (2009). Revisiting Charter 88. *Parliamentary Affairs,* 62(4), 568–579. https://doi.org/10.1093/pa/gsp025

Saville, J. (1980). Hugh Gaitskell: An assessment. *Socialist Register*, 17, 148–169.

Saville, J. (1990). *1848: The British state and the Chartist movement.* Cambridge University Press.

Thomas, M. L. (2016). A house divided: Jeremy Corbyn and the Labour Party. *International Socialism*, 149(2), 39–70.

Thompson, D. (1971). *The early Chartists.* Macmillan Publishers Ltd.

Thompson, E. P. (1965). The peculiarities of the English. *Socialist Register,* 2, 311–363.

Thompson, E.P. (1968). *The making of the working class in England.* Pelican Books.

Toye, R. (2012). 'Perfectly parliamentary'? The Labour Party and the House of Commons in the inter-war years. *Twentieth Century British History*, 25(1), 1–29. https://doi.org/10.1093/tcbh/hws049

Vernon, J. (1996). Notes towards an introduction. In J. Vernon (Ed.), *Re-reading the constitution: New narratives in the political history of England's long nineteenth century* (pp. 1–21). Cambridge University Press.

Webster, C. (1998). *The National Health Service: A political history*. Oxford University Press.

Wood, A. (2002). *Riot, rebellion and popular politics in early modern England.* Palgrave.

Wright, T. (1990). British socialists and the British constitution. *Parliamentary Affairs*, 43(3), 322–340. https://doi.org/10.1093/oxfordjournals.pa.a052255

Young, L. (2018). *Rise: How Jeremy Corbyn inspired the young to create a new socialism.* Simon & Schuster.

4 Gramsci's Politics and Socialist Constitutionalism

Alexandros Chrysis

4.1 Introduction

Long before his incarceration in the fascist prisons of Mussolini, Gramsci had already acknowledged the need for the revolutionary proletarian movement not only to smash the bourgeois state and its mechanisms, but also to create new social and political institutions corresponding to the demands of socialism as a transitional process towards a classless and stateless communist society. Just a few years after the Russian, Hungarian, and German revolutions, the young Italian Marxist, while denouncing the "cretinous tactics of parliamentarism", has made it clear that "the socialist state cannot be embodied in the institutions of the capitalist state" (Gramsci 1977b [1919], p. 76). In Gramsci's view, conquest of the state means neither more nor less than the starting point of a long-run working class's social and ethico-political revolution in pursuit of a mature communist society.

It is the aim of this chapter to raise the issue of socialist constitutionalism based on the corpus of Gramsci's *Prison Notebooks*. To this end, the introductory (first) section of the article brings to the fore the argument according to which the institutional formation of a socialist state is a topic *poorly* discussed throughout Marx's, Engels', and Lenin's political theory.

Gramsci's attempt to bridge the dramatically verified gap between the low productivity concerning the theory of socialist constitutionalism and the high practical significance of socialist institutions and political procedures during the transitional phase from capitalism to communism is the subject of the central (second) section of my contribution to this collective volume.

In the last (third) section of the chapter, I argue for a contemporary Gramscian-type constitutionalism as an alternative to the parliamentarism of the twenty-first-century capitalist societies and to the statism of the twentieth-century regimes of "actually existing socialism".

DOI: 10.4324/9781032621623-5

4.2 Socialist Constitutionalism: Posing a Challenge to Gramsci's Theory of State and Revolution

In his *Critique of the Gotha Programme,* Marx came face-to-face with the challenging question: "What transformation will the state undergo in communist society?" (Marx-Engels 1989, vol. 24, p. 95) Yet the revolutionary thinker proved reluctant to confront the problem at full length; he confined his critique to a brief, rather vague and sarcastic comment: "This question can only be answered scientifically, and one does not get a flea-hop nearer to the problem by a thousandfold combination of the word people with the word state" (Marx-Engels 1989, vol. 24, p. 95). But what is the meaning of a "scientific answer" to the question of the transformation of a capitalist to a workers' state?

As Marx himself mentioned in his *18th Brumaire of Louis Bonaparte* (Marx-Engels 1979, vol. 11, p. 186), and according to the historical proof provided by the Parisian proletariat during the glorious days of the Commune, a transformation of the bourgeois state to a state which meets the demands of a communist society *in the making* is not possible, unless the *break* of the capitalist state-mechanisms occurs (Marx-Engels 1988, vol. 23, p. 175). From Marx's point of view, in particular, such a break must take place during the revolutionary transformation of the capitalist to the communist society, that means during the *political* transition in which the *class* character of the state "can be nothing but the revolutionary dictatorship of the proletariat" (Marx-Engels 1989, vol. 24, p. 95). What about the constitution, the laws, the political institutions, and the legal forms of this revolutionary state, however?

In my view, the fact that Marx extols the "mandat impératif", the universal suffrage, the control from below and the revocability of the demos' delegates by the people, and other democratic regulations as endorsed by the Commune, is just a faint indication of how he might have conceived the constitution of a transitional polity in terms of a "possible communism".[1] Even when he exalted the Parisian Commune as "a working, not a parliamentary, body, executive and legislative at the same time" (Marx-Engels 1986, vol. 22, p. 331), that is as a "working-class government" that constitutes "the political form at last discovered under which to work out the economical emancipation of Labour" (Marx-Engels 1986, vol. 22, p. 334), the author of the International's Address on the *Civil War in France* stayed away from working on a coherent theory of the proletarian state's political and legal forms.[2]

Indeed, though the Paris Commune offered Marx some essential data on an "institutional format" for the dictatorship of the proletariat as an anti-bureaucratic/anti-statist and genuinely participatory democracy (Tabak 2000a), the intellectual defender of the Parisian proletariat did not advance a specific constitutional theory which would respond at full length and effectively to the institutional challenges of a future socialist republic[3] (contra Tabak 2000a, 2000b).

For his part, Engels seems to be moving in a quite similar direction. Defending without reservation the 1871 Paris Commune as a historical example of the dictatorship of the proletariat (Engels 1990a, vol. 27, p. 191), Engels places his emphasis on the class content of the proletarian state and pays marginal attention to its constitutional formation. Despite his admiration for the institutional outcome of the Parisian proletariat's attempt to break the bourgeois state-machine and to be self-constituted as a *demos*, Engels did not proceed to lay down a constitutional draft of an *anti-parliamentarian* socialist democracy. Furthermore, his laconic reference to the "demokratische Republik" as the "specific form for the dictatorship of the proletariat [that] the great French Revolution has already shown" (Engels 1990b, vol. 27, p. 227) proved nothing more than a hint about what a socialist constitution might be in the future.[4] The decisive issue raised but not systematically analysed by Marx himself – "What transformation will the state undergo in communist society?" – remained an open question without an elaborate answer in Engels's writings as well.

But what about Lenin? As regards the theoretical and political aspects of a socialist constitutionalism, his own attitude does not prove an exception to the Marx's and Engels' rule. Being fond of the 1871 Paris Commune, the Bolshevik leader aligned with Marx and Engels in admiring the proletariat's ability to *invent* political forms.

Meanwhile, Lenin was conscious of the fact that the dictatorship of the proletariat as the essence of the transition from capitalism to communism "is certainly bound to yield a tremendous abundance and variety of political forms" (Lenin 1964, vol. 25, p. 418). Nonetheless, he rejected the Utopians' out-of-the-blue way of "discovering" institutions and denounced the Anarchists' overall dismissal of the institutional problem. At the same time, the author of *The State and Revolution* condemned the deification of parliamentarism as expressed and supported by the opportunistic Social-Democracy (Lenin 1964, vol. 25, pp. 436–437). But even so, Lenin, following Marx's and Engels' example, did not move towards a direct confrontation with the enigma of socialist constitutionalism. Unfortunately, disregarding "the deceptive nature of the forms of the bourgeois parliamentary system" and praising the Soviets as *working-class* institutions "capable of overcoming the resistance of the propertied classes and of laying the foundations of socialist society" (Lenin 1964, vol. 26, pp. 434–435), proves just a starting point for a theory of socialist constitutionalism, that remained, however, a goal to be reached in the indefinite future.

At this point, I feel the time has come for me to sum up my hitherto introductory analysis:

Though holding fast to the class substance of the workers' revolutionary state, neither Marx and Engels, nor Lenin worked out a theory of political institutions, legal relations, social and political rights within the constitutional frame of a socialist/communist polity.[5] While focusing on the *class essence* of the dictatorship of the proletariat, all of them avoided dealing *in extenso* with the *institutional forms* such a state may take.

Be that as it may, I would like to propose the following hypothesis:

> There is an urgent need for Marxism to elaborate on the still underdeveloped theory of a socialist republic as a political synthesis of constitutional forms and citizens' ethos corresponding to the class content of a workers' state, i.e. a dictatorship of the proletariat in its way to become a mature communist polity.

In what sense and to what extent Gramsci's politics contribute to minimising the Marxist deficit of socialist constitutionalism is the question I am going to discuss in the central part of this chapter on which I turn now the lens of my inquiry.

4.3 Gramscian Constitutionalism: Paving the Way to a Communist Polity

In a delicately written review of Gramsci's politics, Eric Hobsbawm argued many years ago that "talking about two different sets of political problems: strategy and the nature of socialist societies, Gramsci tried to get to grips with both" (Hobsbawm 1977, p. 208). From a Gramscian point of view, Hobsbawm suggests, Marxist politics should pay attention not only to the strategy of winning socialism, but to socialism itself. According to the British historian, the construction of socialism as an institutional process leading to a communist polity attracted Gramsci's interest in socialisation not in the economic, but in the sociological and political sense of the term. In this context, Hobsbawm reaches the conclusion that Gramsci must be considered as an influential Marxist thinker who – against every sort of economism – conceives production in socialism not as a separate technical and economic problem, but especially as a problem of education and politics (Hobsbawm 1977, p. 209).

A decade later, Joseph Femia seems to diverge from Hobsbawm's evaluation of Gramsci's politics, at least in relation to the formation of a socialist/communist polity. "Gramsci's discussion of the future society", mentions Femia, "was vague and generalized. Like Marx, he was more interested in the process by which revolution would come about than in what society would look like after the revolution" (Femia 1987, p. 177).[6] Even Femia, however, admits that "Gramsci does provide some indications" concerning a future "non-coercive" and at the same time "self-regulative" communist society, that can be attained through a "catharsis", which means by "a leap from the realm of necessity to the realm of freedom" (Femia 1987, p. 177).

To be fair, Gramsci gave us handy hints about socialist democracy and communist polity even before writing his stimulating *Prison Notebooks*. Just in the aftermath of the First World War, the young Marxist journalist Antonio Gramsci proves ready to raise the critical question:

> How are the immense social forces unleashed by the war to be harnessed? How are they to be disciplined and given a political form which has the potential

> to develop normally and continuously into the skeleton of the socialist State in which the dictatorship of the proletariat will be embodied? How can the present be welded to the future, so that while satisfying the urgent necessities of the one we may work effectively to create and "anticipate" the other?
>
> (Gramsci 1977a, p. 65)

Gramsci has no illusion; a workers' democracy must not be conceived as the *evolutionary* upgrade of bourgeois parliamentarism. Contrary to the socialists, who believe in and fight for the amelioration of the parliamentary institutions, the communist revolutionaries are fully persuaded that the socialist state should be formed as a qualitatively new system of political power. In Gramsci's own words, "the formula 'conquest of the state' should be understood in the following sense: replacement of the democratic parliamentary state by a new type of state, one that is generated by the associative experience of the proletarian class" (Gramsci 1977b, p. 76). Consequently, from a Gramscian standpoint, parliamentary institutions must be regarded as incompatible with a socialist republic. Above all, the workers' democracy must attempt the destruction of the bourgeois state, while advancing its own transformation to a classless and stateless, which means a communist polity.

On the other hand, an original socialist democracy does not come out all of a sudden. "The creation of a proletarian state", writes Gramsci, "is not a thaumaturgical act: it is itself a process of development" (Gramsci 1977b, p. 78). From this point of view, he is willing to acknowledge that a revolutionary transformation of a capitalist to a communist social formation requires a future-oriented systematic study concerning the institutions and the everyday operation of the socialist/communist society. "Every aspect of the problem deserves special study, detailed elucidation, coherent extension and integration" (Gramsci 1977a, p. 68), mentions Gramsci. At the same time, however, the young Marxist intellectual does not miss the opportunity to commend highly the significance of communist practice:

> Concrete and complete solution to the problems of socialist living can only arise from communist practice: collective discussion, which sympathetically alters men's consciousness, unifies them and inspires them to industrious enthusiasm. To tell the truth, to arrive together at the truth, is a communist and revolutionary act. [...] The dictatorship of the proletariat represents the establishment of a new, proletarian State, which channels the institutional experiences of the oppressed class and transforms the social activity of the working class and peasantry into a widespread and powerfully organized system. This State cannot be improvised: the Russian Bolshevik communists laboured for eight months to broadcast and concretize their slogan: "All power to the Soviets"- and the Russian workers had been familiar with Soviets since 1905.
>
> (Gramsci 1977a, p. 68)

Thus, according to Gramsci, it is the life experience of the proletariat and not the prefigurative theoretical improvisation that offers efficient solutions to the fundamental problems of a socialist state. In this regard, the distinguished revolutionary seems fond of communist practice and eager to express his own admiration for workers' democracy as "a magnificent school of political and administrative experience" (Gramsci 1977a, p. 67). For my part, however, I really wonder whether this passionate belief in the working masses' ability to learn *directly* from their communist experience drives Gramsci to underrate up to a point, even unconsciously, the real value of a research project on socialist constitutionalism.[7]

Be that as it may, Gramsci never succumbed to the attraction of a spontaneous political activism. As a Marxist intellectual, he recognised the vital role of a theory of the state in the revolutionary transition from capitalism to communism. In truth, Gramsci was fully aware of the fact that without such a state-theory, a "system of workers' democracy" could neither *legislate* its constitutional structure nor achieve the *unconditional* commitment of the demos to the communist cause (Gramsci 1977a, pp. 67–68).

At this critical juncture, the concept of "statolatry", concretely stated and vividly described in the *Prison Notebooks*, proves to be highly inspiring for my theoretical attempt to set forth the main features of Gramsci's socialist constitutionalism.

Having defined "statolatria" as the "attitude of each social group towards its own state", Gramsci hastens to connect the term with his own conceptual division of the state in *società politica* and *società civile* (Gramsci 1971, p. 268). He refers to statolatry as a term "applied to a particular attitude towards the 'government of functionaries' or political society", while pointing out that such an attitude towards the political state *stricto sensu* is organically linked with a social process generating an "active culture", which means "a movement to create a new civilisation, a new type of man and of citizen" (Gramsci 1971, p. 268).[8]

After all, the main goal that pervades Gramsci's approach to statolatry consists in demonstrating the need for the demos "to construct within the husk of political society a complex and well-articulated civil society". From this point of view, statolatry connotes the citizens' love for their newly founded republic and their *pathos* for self-legislation and self-government as combustible materials for superseding (aufheben) the socialist state, which finally withers away.

Indeed, in this frame of analysis, it looks perhaps strange to realise that the Marxist defender of "statolatria" regards socialist civil society as the "normal continuation" and "organic complement" of political society (Gramsci 1971, p. 268). Nonetheless, it would be a serious mistake to draw the conclusion that Gramsci considers civil society's institutions and practices of secondary importance as compared to the political society's mechanisms. On the contrary! His specific reference to statolatry underscores the value he places on the institutional formation and the cultural identity of a socialist/communist *società civile*, the dynamics of which should render *società politica* superfluous.

Hence, not by chance, the virtuoso of Marxist dialectics provides a quoteworthy answer to the reasonable question "which are the particular conditions that make statolatry fundamental to constituting a new polity?":

> For some social groups, which before their ascent to autonomous State life have not had a long independent period of cultural and moral development on their own [...] a period of statolatry is necessary and indeed opportune. This "statolatry" is nothing other than the normal form of "State life", or at least of initiation to autonomous State life and to the creation of a "civil society" which it was not historically possible to create before the ascent to independent State life.
>
> (Gramsci 1971, p. 268)[9]

No doubt this comment on "statolatry" breaks new ground for further elaboration and research on the proletariat's attitude towards the socialist state in general and the Soviet Union state in particular.[10] In this vein, attention should be drawn to Gramsci's warning: "this kind of 'statolatry' must not be abandoned to itself, must not, especially, become theoretical fanaticism or be conceived as 'perpetual'" (Gramsci 1971, p. 268).

To make it clear: being already convinced that time has come for the Russian proletariat to enjoy what actually had missed during the previous decades, i.e. an intensive political and cultural activity,[11] the author of the *Prison Notebooks* pinpointed the risk that statolatry, that is citizens' love for and devotion to their socialist/communist polity, degenerates to an uncritical support for a state empowered and reproduced *in perpetuum*.

At all events, dealing with the Soviet Union as a case study on socialist constitutionalism without taking into serious account "statolatria" is out of the question.[12] And even though such applied research is beyond the scope of this chapter,[13] it proves necessary to point out and never ignore or underestimate the fact that, in Gramsci's evaluation of the soviet experiment, *statolatry* is permanently distinguished from and opposed to *statism*, this pathological condition of suffocating citizens' motive for sovereign self-constitution and collective activity.[14]

In this sense, I will make use of the statolatry/statism opposition to shed light on the key problem of this chapter, namely on the overall assessment of Gramsci's intellectual endeavour to formulate and enrich a still wanting Marxist theory of socialist constitutionalism. Yet, given the complexity and the breadth of the *constitutional question* regarding the socialist state and its transformation to a communist polity, I will confine myself to raising just a few of the pivotal challenges which Gramscian constitutionalism turns out to be quite unprocessed to confront.

There is no doubt that identifying the fundamentals of Gramscian constitutionalism in the puzzling universe of the *Prison Notebooks* requires a functional thematic approach. Consequently, while keeping in mind the statolatry/statism distinction, I suggest following Gramsci's intellectual path to a communist polity in three distinctive "moments". In the "objective/institutional" moment of his analysis, Gramsci focuses on the *institutional configuration* of the workers' state as a political and legal system that aims at its own disappearance. In its "subjective/ethical" moment the Gramscian diagnosis refers to a *cultural revolution* as a long-term process directed by the socialist state in its own troublesome transformation to a communist polity. Finally, I discern the "withering away" moment of Gramsci's constitutional approach that culminates in the *communist society* as a non-state "regulated society".

Starting from the "objective/institutional" moment, it may prove helpful to recall that, while confronting the historical end to establish a "new state", Gramsci came face-to-face with Machiavelli. Nonetheless, at variance with Machiavelli's conception of the Prince as an exceptional individual, Gramsci reached the conclusion that the Modern Prince should be a collective subject, the political party *par excellence*, a vanguard party organised and directed in a way compatible with the new state it strives to create (Gramsci 1971, p. 253).[15]

The limitations of this chapter notwithstanding, let me bring to the fore the debatable relation between the *revolutionary party* as the modern Prince who aims to found a new type of state and the *working demos* as the constitutionally established Sovereign of the socialist republic. So, getting straight to the point, I would like to remind the reader that, in sharp contrast to Rousseau's Legislator, who leaves the stage as soon as he executes his founding role, Gramsci's Prince does not withdraw from public life till a mature communist society takes shape.[16] As a result, the communist party remains a key protagonist of the ongoing revolutionary process and a leading political figure throughout the workers' state constitutional life.

Furthermore, extending this line of inquiry, one more crucial topic of Gramsci's constitutionalism, that of *pluralism*, deserves special mention. Focusing on the "objective/institutional" aspect of a socialist democracy, particularly during its founding period, the Gramscian theoretical and political stance towards plurality looks rather elliptical, if not downright cryptic. In fact, it is worth noting, as Anna Showstack Sassoon does, that Gramsci's institutional approach to the party issue "leaves little space for the autonomous activities of other parties and non-party organisations"; but it is equally valid, as the same scholar confesses, that the logic of Gramscian hegemony is unthinkable without "a continuing plurality of political and social organisations" (Showstack Sassoon 1987, p. 230).[17] Anyway, it goes against the grain to argue with certainty that Gramsci opted for a socialist/communist polity without institutional and procedural plurality.[18]

Especially, the already mentioned Gramscian critique of parliamentarism denotes that the Marxist intellectual's concern about the institutional vivacity and the operational plurality of a socialist republic – multi-party system included – must remain open to further consideration and not be bypassed.[19] All in all, Gramsci's interest in distinguishing between parliamentarism and an alternative type of representative system should be borne in mind:

> It has to be considered whether parliamentarism and representative system are synonymous, and whether a different solution is not possible -both for parliamentarism and for the bureaucratic system- with a new type of a representative system.
>
> (Gramsci 1971, p. 254)

In fact, looking for "a different solution", i.e. pursuing a non-parliamentary and a non-bureaucratic version of political representation, Antonio Gramsci raises the constitutional question of a "system of government" within the frame of which "the people's consent does not end at the moment of voting, quite the contrary. That consent is presumed to be permanently active [...]" (Gramsci 1971, p. 193). Obviously, both the Paris Commune and the Soviet institutional paradigm exert decisive influence on Gramsci's constitutionalism and make the revolutionary intellectual argue that elections should not be held on the basis of "vague, generic programmes" which meet just the demands of formal democracy.

In opposition to a conventional parliamentary democracy corresponding to a mass of "amorphous citizens", a socialist-type democracy, as Gramsci suggests, entails the all-round commitment of active citizens to the communist hypothesis. As a matter of fact, a socialist republic, in sharp contrast to bourgeois parliamentarism and bureaucratic statism, requires the ethico-political "statolatry" of the working men and women, these "skilled productive elements", whose political participation in the life of the *demos* is not restricted to the voting process (Gramsci 1971, pp. 193–194).

Meanwhile, holding fast to the strategic goal of a classless and stateless society, Gramsci refuses to comply with a political programme of partial changes; he fights for a total, that means an integral transformation, institutional and cultural concurrently. In this sense, he insists that the state to be constituted should be conceived as an "integral state" and not as "a government technically understood" (Gramsci 1971, p. 267). But what does Gramsci exactly mean by the term "integral state"?

According to the author of the *Prison Notebooks*, a workers' "integral state" appears as the institutional and ethical outcome of a revolutionary process raised to and integrated in the form of a socialist/communist polity. Consequently, the "integral state" – "political society + civil society, in other words hegemony protected by the armour of coercion" (Gramsci 1971, p. 263) – becomes at the same time the citizens' *self-legislated* institutional frame of life (constitution) and their own *self-imposed* object of love (statolatry). It would be, therefore, a grave mistake to regard the "integral state" as a derivative of statism, let alone totalitarianism and bureaucratism.[20]

As Christine Buci-Glucksmann mentions in a noteworthy remark,

> the concept of the integral state, far indeed from being restricted simply to the field of expansion of the mechanisms of class domination that were specific to fascism, is originally two-dimensional and with many functions. The methodological duplication of superstructures, the taking into account of the historic basis of the state and the hegemonic apparatuses, pave the way to an understanding of the life of the state under socialism, to the establishment of certain elements of a theory of the transitional state.
>
> (Buci-Glucksmann 1980, p. 282)

Practically speaking, it proves a complicated matter to apply Gramsci's theory of politics to the constitutional making of a socialist-type integral state. Thus, considering necessary to adopt a constructive research orientation, I unreservedly align with those who believe that Gramsci converges with Lenin's political thought. From this angle, it is worth mentioning that the Italian revolutionary confronts the institutional and ethical aspect of a socialist republic in terms of a protracted historic and organic process, i.e. a *molecular transformation*,[21] normatively conducted by and directed towards the goal of a communist polity (Buci-Glucksmann 1980, p. 283).

Actually, despite a conceptual originality, Gramsci's theory of workers' state dynamics, concurring with Lenin's analysis, seems adequately transparent: the dictatorship of the proletariat, this socialist hybrid of coercion and hegemony, while combining *società politica* and *società civile*, *coercion* and *hegemony*, is being painstakingly transformed and finally withers away taking the form of a communist society without distinctive coercive mechanisms.

At this point, it is worth giving the floor to Alberto Burgio, who accurately reviews the position mentioned above:

> As in Lenin, for Gramsci, the task of the workers' State is twofold and ambivalent: it must on one hand protect the development of a "new society" and in this way is a *dictatorship*, the power of the people, "democracy" in its real sense, as Marx had provocatively written; and, on the other hand, at the same time has to disappear, to become extinct as the "new society", under its armed protection, consolidates its own structures. Protect and extinguish; defend and "gradually reduce" their own "authoritarian and coercive interventions": this is, both in the *Quaderni del carcere* ("Prison Notebooks") and in Государство и революция ("The State and Revolution"), the procedural function of the workers' state, the "dictatorship of the proletariat".
>
> (Burgio 2020, p. 85)

Thus, close in spirit with Burgio's reasoning, let me now condense the objective/institutional moment of Gramsci's constitutionalism in the form of a legislative directive, or rather, in the form of a categorical imperative:

> Legislate for the socialist institutions that way so as to make the workers' state attain "its own end, its own disappearance, in other words the re-absorption of political society into civil society."
>
> (Gramsci 1971, p. 253)

In this context, while portraying the citizen as a passionate participant and an influential member of a self-constituted demos, Gramsci reaches the "subjective/ethical" moment of his constitutionalism. Commenting on the "educative and formative role of the state", the author of the *Prison Notebooks* conceives the state in general, and the socialist state in particular as the educator who "tends to create and maintain a certain type of civilisation and of citizen (and hence of collective life and of individual relations), and to eliminate certain customs and attitudes and to disseminate others" (Gramsci 1971, p. 246).

Obviously, the state must apply the law as "its instrument for this purpose (together with the school system, and other institutions and activities)" (Gramsci 1971, p. 246). Yet, it would be wrong, not to say detrimental to this analysis, to ignore that, following Gramsci, the law is just "the repressive and negative aspect of the entire positive, civilizing activity undertaken by the state" (Gramsci 1971, p. 247). This means that the workers' state is due to perform its educational role through a *cultural revolution* which, according to Buci-Glucksmann's apt description, constitutes "an on-going process of adequation between culture and practice, [that] is neither a luxury nor a simple guarantee, but rather an actual dimension of the self-government of the masses and of democracy" (Buci-Glucksmann 1980, p. 286).

Undoubtedly, the Gramscian focus on the "subjective/ethical" moment of the working demos' self-constitution into a "semi-state" (Lenin 1964, p. 402), that aims at its own withering away, recalls the *ethical state* of Hegel and Croce (Gramsci 1971, p. 262).[22] "In my opinion", writes Gramsci,

> the most reasonable and concrete thing that can be said about the ethical state, the cultural state, is this: every state is ethical in as much as one of its most important functions is to raise the great mass of the population to a particular cultural and moral level.
>
> (Gramsci 1971, p. 258).[23]

From this point of view, Walter Adamson gives the impression that he moves on the right track, when arguing that "the proletarian state, as an embodiment of Hegelian *Sittlichkeit*, is an expanding counter-hegemony which has burst the boundaries of civil society to encompass political society as well" (Adamson

1980, p. 225). The same scholar misses the point, however, when he depicts Gramsci as a *gradualist* whose divergence from Leninist strategy is "marked, if not total" (Adamson 1980, p. 226).[24]

In my view, the Gramscian constitutionalism does not conflict with the fundamentals of a Marxist theory of the state. Gramsci does not call into question the ultimately determinative role of the *società politica-mechanisms of coercion* in relation to the *società-civile institutions of hegemony*. In this vein, I personally come into line with Loris Caruso's crystal-clear position:

> Gramsci's perspective is the building of a socialist state where the division between the dominated and the dominating is overthrown. This hegemonic aim is not achievable without also overthrowing class domination. For this reason, it is misleading to state that a post-Marxist Gramsci entirely places social transformation in the superstructure, as Bobbio and reformist and liberal interpretations of Gramsci maintain. [...] Gramsci completes the dialectical logic of class conflict with the logic of cultural hegemony, but he doesn't substitute the first with the second one
>
> (Caruso 2016, p. 150).

Certainly, to retrace Gramsci's theoretical journey towards the constitution of a socialist state is a quite demanding issue. Nevertheless, to keep in step with the Italian Marxist's constitutionalism as he tries to bridge the gap between the socialist state and the stateless communist polity proves to be an even more difficult affair. I am insinuating, actually, the "third moment" of Gramsci's constitutional dialectics, i.e. the "withering away" moment, when the "regulated society", as the author of the *Prison Notebooks* defined the communist society, is being brought to light.

Referring to the long-lasting use of the terms "ethical state" and "civil society" as a proof that "the 'image' of a state without a state was present to the greatest political and legal thinkers" (Gramsci 1971, p. 263), Antonio Gramsci turns against statism, castigating this time Lassalle, whose doctrines, concerning the state, are "in contrast with Marxism" (Gramsci 1971, p. 263).

In the meantime, the Marxist critic of statism does not omit to maintain that confusing a class-state with a regulated society is nothing but a middle classes' and petty intellectuals' misleading utopia. Regardless its constitutional formation, Gramsci argues, a capitalist society can never be a "regulated society". In reality, only a stateless society may exist as a *stricto sensu* regulated society. "As long as the class-state exists the regulated society cannot exist, other than metaphorically" (Gramsci 1971, p. 257). From this point of view, it is self-evident, indeed, to maintain, as the author of the Prison Notebooks explicitly does, that only the proletariat "that poses the end of the state and its own end as the target to be achieved can create an ethical state" (Gramsci 1971, p. 259).

At all events, however, Gramsci's juxtaposition of class-state and regulated society must not be interpreted in a simplistic/mechanistic way. Above all, the Italian revolutionary – who does not hesitate to borrow from Lassalle the initially liberal term "nightwatchman" (*state-veilleur de nuit*) and match it to his own conception of regular society(!) (Gramsci 1971, p. 263)[25] – remains a Marxist, who conceives the transition from a socialist state to a communist polity in the sense of a long-term, burdensome "molecular" dialectics leading from a class-state to a stateless society:

> In a doctrine of the State which conceives the latter as tendentially capable of withering away and of being subsumed into regulated society, the argument is a fundamental one. It is possible to imagine the coercive element of the State withering away by degrees, as ever-more conspicuous elements of regulated society (or ethical State or civil society) make their appearance
>
> (Gramsci 1971, p. 263).

Summing up: in the third moment of his socialist constitutionalism, Gramsci draws his attention to a communism-oriented minimal state (*state-veilleur de nuit*). Thus, he upgrades his interest in the combined – formative and *at the same time* withering away – dynamics of a "coercive organisation which will safeguard the development of the continually proliferating elements of regulated society, and which will therefore progressively reduce its own authoritarian and forcible interventions" (Gramsci 1971, p. 263).

At this point, a critical reference to Lenin's and Gramsci's converging views on the socialist state-communist polity relation appears suitable for pushing forward the scope of my analysis. Thus, let me turn at first to the following Buci-Glucksmann's stimulating assessment:

> In Lenin's thought, organizational and hegemonic aspects, transition phase and communist goal are not rigidly separated, but rather form a historic and organic process that moves by stages. The process is extremely protracted. It is in this same perspective that Gramsci envisaged an entire historical period in which the state would be initially synonymous with the government, but would gradually come to be identified with the civil society.
>
> (Buci-Glucksmann, p. 283)

Elaborating on the same hypothesis, Alberto Burgio determines two distinctive phases of the (post)revolutionary molecular transition to a stateless/communist society: the inaugural phase, *mainly* coercive and authoritarian, materialised by the state of the dictatorship of the proletariat, and the second phase, *mainly* cultural,advanced by the nightwatchman state that dies away to a mature communist society without classes and state.

In his noteworthy remark, Burgio argues as follows:

> The dictatorship of the proletariat remains the key moment of revolutionary shock, the fundamental tool of the working class used for the construction of the 'new society'. The initial situation is followed, in Gramsci's schema, by the phase of the "night-watchman state", in which the "element of coercive state" "gradually" reduces its own "authoritative and coercive interventions" (that is to say, "exhausts" itself) as soon as – *thanks to these interventions* (the process is dialectic) – on the contrary, energies and expressions of autonomy ("organic freedom") of "civil society" are developing: the "elements" of the new "regulated society"
>
> (Burgio 2020, p. 84).

Needless to repeat, this kind of distinction must not be conceived in the form of a rigid opposition between two types of a workers' state. Be that as it may, it is imperative for me to add, however, that Burgio's attempt to distinguish between the state of the dictatorship of the proletariat and the nightwatchman state requires a crucial clarification, even a revision. In terms of Gramsci's constitutionalism, the transitional state in its way to a full-blown communist society, as Marx himself stated in his *Critique of the Gotha Programme*, "can be nothing but the revolutionary dictatorship of the proletariat". In this sense, the Gramscian "nightwatchman" state is not a state that comes *after* the dictatorship of the proletariat as Burgio seems to claim; the nightwatchman state constitutes a "moment" in the dialectics of the dictatorship of the proletariat as a *semi-state* that is dying out in a communist polity.

Aside from these theoretical guidelines and political milestones, however, it seems futile searching for an exhaustive research project and concrete proposals in Gramsci's writings as far as the institutional establishment and the ethical life of a socialist republic are concerned. Though acknowledging the necessity for a transitional workers' state in between the capitalist and the stateless communist society, Gramsci refrained from working on the legal forms and power mechanisms of this unique version of state, let alone the content and the form of a "regulated society".

From this point of view, it is worth noting that, despite the indisputable fact that Gramsci's ideal of self-determination "does not vanish into the clouds of pure metaphysics", as Femia correctly mentions, it seems to me exaggerating to suggest that the author of the *Prison Notebooks* gives a specific "institutional embodiment" to this ideal (Femia 1987, p. 183). For my part, I fully endorse Adamson's conclusion: "the central problem area in Gramsci's political theory [is] his failure to go much beyond general phrases in depicting the nature of the future society" (Adamson 1980, p. 242).

In any case, the time is ripe to reconsider in what sense and to what extent Gramsci's politics contribute to a Marxist theory of socialist constitutionalism.

On the basis of the hitherto analysis, I am now ready for an overall evaluation of Gramsci's constitutionalism as a theoretical and political rejoinder to my research hypothesis, which I find worth recalling just before proceeding to the last part of this chapter:

> There is an urgent need for Marxism to elaborate on the still underdeveloped theory of a socialist republic as a political synthesis of constitutional forms and citizens' ethos corresponding to the class content of a workers' state, i.e. of a dictatorship of the proletariat in its way to become a mature communist polity.

4.4 Gramscian Politics: Defending Socialist Democracy as an Alternative to Bourgeois Parliamentarism and "Actually Existing Socialism". Critical Remarks and Concluding Hints

As noted above, Gramsci did not fail to recognise the necessity of defining a "new type of representative system" in strong and simultaneous opposition to parliamentarism and bureaucratism (Gramsci 1971, p. 254). It is worth insisting and reiterating, however, that the "different solution", which the author of the *Prison Notebooks* proclaimed and searched for, never took the form of a systematically formulated version of socialist constitutionalism.

Though taking into serious consideration the institutional legacy of the 1871 Paris Commune, the proletarian experience of the 1919–1920 Turin factory councils and the fundamental role of the soviets during the first years of the Russian Revolution, Antonio Gramsci, who never stopped to believe that the institutions of bourgeois democracy are incompatible with the ethico-political demands of a socialist republic, did not reach an *all-round* and *original* approach to the challenging issue of a socialist constitution.

Even so, to recapitulate and point up several aspects of Gramscian politics in contradistinction to the twentieth-century constitutional models of bourgeois parliamentarism and "actually existing socialism" may prove at least a valuable reminder that a Marxist theory of socialist constitutionalism is still required to lay out the *legal frame* and to express the *political ethos* of a socialist democracy, in other words the *Sittlichkeit* of a communist polity in the making.

To found and set up a socialist state on Gramscian principles is a process dictated and regulated by the need to accomplish the "catharsis", i.e. "the passage from 'objective to subjective' and from 'necessity to freedom'" (Gramsci 1971, pp. 366–367). To this end, the transformative task of the proletariat seems really indisputable:

> A class claiming to be capable of assimilating the whole of society and which was at the same time really able to express such a process, would perfect this

> conception of the State and of law, so as to conceive the end of the State and of law-rendered useless since they will have exhausted their function and will have been absorbed by civil society.
>
> (Gramsci 1971, p. 260)

In this context, to cultivate and disseminate *statolatry* among the citizens of a newly constituted socialist republic, while openly combatting *statism* and advancing the withering away of the state, turns out to be one of the main duties for the Modern Prince, i.e. the communist party.

Yet, Gramsci does not miss the chance to sound the alarm: this educative duty will not be performed successfully, unless the revolutionary party i.e. the collective leader of the cathartic process is *institutionally* and *politically* separated from the government. At bottom, in one way or another, the demos of the socialist republic, that is to say the sovereign political subject of the dictatorship of the proletariat, must legislate for and guarantee that the "dominating party will not be organically confused with the government, while being the instrument of the passage from the 'società civile-politica' to the 'società regolata'" (Gramsci 1977c, Q 6 [VIII] p. 734).

And, even though the Italian Marxist did not proceed to a concrete, let alone a detailed analysis of the party – state relation within the institutional frame of a socialist/communist polity, it would be wrong to undervalue the impact of this position on the theory and practice of socialism.[26] A constitutionally guaranteed and practically applied distinction between the state's and the party's political role looks, indeed, like a golden rule of Gramsci's constitutionalism. Above all, what actually matters is Gramsci's warning that the hegemonic communist party must not be integrated in and absorbed by the power system of the (socialist) state mechanisms, as far as it fights to push forward and secure the maturation of a communist polity. No doubt, this thesis fires *de facto* a trenchant intellectual and political stance against the 1930s Stalinist dogma of the authoritarianism of the state and the depoliticisation of the soviets.[27]

It seems perhaps needless to repeat: whether Gramsci is in fact a supporter of a multi-party socialist republic remains a debatable issue that deserves an expanded evaluation that exceeds the strict limits of this chapter. Even so, a critical observation as included in the *Prison Notebooks* should not be omitted.

Certainly, Gramsci does not ignore that there are countries where there is "a single, totalitarian, governing party"[28] (Gramsci 1971, p. 149), the Soviet Union being a case in point. Yet, the communist revolutionary stepped forward to argue: "Even if no other legal parties exist, other parties in fact always do exist and other tendencies cannot be legally coerced" (Gramsci 1971, p. 149). In other words, wittingly or unwittingly, directly or indirectly, Gramsci dispatches a crucial notification and a dramatic warning message to the socialist legislator: *Whether formally constituted or not, a multi-party system actually exists! In the legal context of a one-party system, however, "political questions are disguised as cultural ones, and as such become insoluble"* (Gramsci 1971, p. 149).

At all events, the politics–culture relation, especially in a country like Russia, where the civil society was and remained "primordial and gelatinous" (Gramsci 1971, p. 239), proved a thorny question. In terms of Gramscian constitutionalism, the concept of "statolatry" that is repeatedly quoted in this chapter, as well as that of progressive "Caesarism", which constitutes an interventional process that "helps the progressive force to triumph" and may exist "even without a Caesar" (Gramsci 1971, pp. 219–220), testify to the challenging and endless conversion of politics to culture and vice versa.

In this context, Giuseppe Vacca's assertion that "Gramsci was thinking of the Union of Soviet Socialist Republics (USSR) as the expression of progressive Caesarism" (Vacca 1982, p. 47) seems to me rather reasonable and worth taking into further consideration in connection with statements as the following, made by the author of the *Prison Notebooks* himself:

> In the more recent period, there is a type of party constituted this time not by an elite but by masses -who as such have no other political function than a generic loyalty, of a military kind, to a visible or invisible political center. [...] The mass following is simply for "manoeuvre", and is kept happy by means of moralising sermons, emotional stimuli and messianic myths of an awaited golden age, in which all present contradictions and miseries will be automatically resolved and made well.
>
> (Gramsci 1971, p. 150)

To be just, Gramsci's analysis of Caesarism hinted not only at the case of Soviet Union, but at Fascism and Nazism as well. Yet, I insist, together with Vacca: if Gramsci disconnected in reality USSR from the phenomenon of Caesarism, then his own distinction between "progressive and reactionary forms of Caesarism" (Gramsci 1971, p. 219) would have made no sense (Vacca 1982, p. 47).

After all, it is in this historical and theoretical frame of reference that the politics-culture hybrid of Gramscian constitutionalism unfolds its particular dynamic. In his effort to determine and defend a Marxist-type socialist democracy, the revolutionary intellectual carved out and brought into play concepts such as "statolatry" and "Caesarism" that looked suitable for a two-sided demarcation of the socialist polity from bourgeois parliamentarism and quasi-proletarian statism.

In this vein, to confront the developments of the Soviet state in a critical way proved one of the main concerns of Antonio Gramsci as a political thinker. Following his own critique of Bukharin's *Historical Materialism* [*Popular Manual*], the Italian imprisoned leader does not hesitate to describe the Soviet state as a new type of an "economic-corporative" state that aims, at least for the time being, at "the reorganisation of the structure and real relations between men and the economic world or world of production" (Gramsci 1971, p. 263).

As regards the superstructural level of the USSR, however, Gramsci discerns a still existing atrophy, whichmeans a crucial insufficiency in terms of an all-round ethico-political development of the *società civile* (Gramsci 1971, p. 263). From this point of view, what actually troubled him the most is how to avoid the working masses' *depoliticisation* or, to put it the other way round, how to achieve, both institutionally and ethically, the working masses' *active participation* in the constitution and operation of a socialist republic, i.e. a communist polity in the making.[29]

In any event, Gramsci did not forget to mention that *political apathy* makes up the common ground of *bourgeois parliamentarism* and *bureaucratic centralism*, this "ossified form of thinking [that makes] a certain disordered unruliness preferable to the philistine defense of pre-constituted cultural positions" (Gramsci 1977c, 15[II] p. 1806).[30] It is, in fact, against every sort of *political indifferentism* that the Marxist revolutionary provided a rough sketch of socialist constitutionalism striving for upgrading politics to a first-class priority as far as the citizens' everyday life is concerned.[31]

In the last analysis, Gramsci's politics constitute a theoretical and political attempt to a "new model of public life" (Boggs 1976, p. 100), to an "extended notion of democracy" (Showstack-Sassoon 1987, p. 227) that meets both the formal/legal and the substantial/ethico-political requirements of a communist polity in the making. And from this angle, I am in a position to claim that Gramsci, without leaning to bourgeois parliamentarism, distanced himself convincingly from USSR statism and an alleged *socialist* legality, in the context of which socio-political rights and norms are undervalued or, even worse, suspended.

As a matter of fact, reaching the end of this journey in Gramsci's politics, I am confident that the author of the *Prison Notebooks*, should have signed without reservation the statement, written in the 1960s, by his compatriot Galvano della Volpe:

> So long as there is a state, even a democratic state advanced to the full like the socialist state, and so long as there is a society organized on the relation of governing and governed, the basic principle of the state of law, that of the limit of the power of the state regarding the persons of the citizens, must remain. It can be infringed only at the price of incalculable iniquities and human sufferings.
>
> (Galvano della Volpe 1978, p. 113)

Summing up, let me return for one last time to the key question of this research essay:

> In what sense and to what extent Gramsci's politics contribute to minimising the Marxist deficit of socialist constitutionalism?

Indeed, I have no problem to admit that the Gramscian constitutionalism failed in substantiating a mature Marxist theory of socialist democracy. Though wanting in content and form, however, Gramsci's conception of the socialist state sheds bright light on the hard struggle of a *self-legislating socialist demos* to reach a communist polity. In contrast to the 1930s authoritarianism and the bureaucratic centralism of the Soviet state, which characterised in addition the societies later named "actual existing socialism", the Gramscian constitutionalism succeeds in depicting especially the *ethico-political* activity of the socialist demos as a sovereign *self-emancipating* collectivity, while demonstrating communism as a movement to annihilate politics in the specific sense of the "government of functionaries".[32]

Selecting, therefore, Gramsci's masterfully crafted appraisal of the demos' self-legislation seems to me the right choice to mark the end of this chapter:

> The maximum of legislative capacity can be inferred when a perfect formulation of directives is matched by a perfect arrangement of the organisms of execution and verification, and by a perfect preparation of the "spontaneous" consent of the masses who must "live" those directives, modifying their own habits, their own will, their own convictions to conform with those directives and with the objectives which they propose to achieve. If everyone is a legislator in the broadest sense of the concept, he continues to be a legislator even if he accepts directives from others -if, as he carries them out, he makes certain that others are carrying them out too; if, having understood their spirit, he propagates them as though making them into rules specifically applicable to limited and definite zones of living.
>
> (Gramsci 1971, p. 266)

Notes

1 While evaluating the 1871 Commune, Marx draws a rough institutional scheme of a **possible communism** as follows: "if united cooperative societies are to regulate national production upon a common plan, thus taking it under their own control, and putting an end to the constant anarchy and periodical convulsions which are the fatality of Capitalist production — what else, gentlemen, would it be but Communism, "possible" Communism?" (Marx-Engels 1986, vol. 22, p. 335).

In this context, it is not of secondary importance to mention that, while advising the proletarians against *political indifferentism*, Marx insists on reminding them to cope with the "revolutionary and transitional form" of their future state (Marx-Engels 1988, p. 393).

2 As Hal Draper (1987, p. 35) rightly notes, for Marx the argument that the proletariat's state will be the dictatorship of the proletariat was "a statement about the societal content of the state, the class character of the political power. It was not a statement about the forms of the government machine or other structural aspects of government or policies".

Though considering Draper's argument "well documented", Ralph Miliband (1965, pp. 289–290) seems to follow a different direction, arguing that "for Marx, the dictatorship of the proletariat is *both* a statement of the class character of the political power *and* a description of the political power itself; it is in fact the nature of the political power which it describes which guarantees its class character".

Following his own path of analysis, Monty Johnstone (1971, p. 458) suggests that Marx took advantage of the Commune and "added a new dimension to his concept of the dictatorship of the proletariat. This entailed a thorough going participatory democracy, combining direct democracy at the base with the election at regional and national levels of delegates operating under continuous control and briefing from below".

3 Despite my objections to Mehmet Tabak's rather contradictory assessment of Marx's "scattered remarks" on the proletarian dictatorship as containing a "coherent logic" and his quite optimistic conclusion that, if pieced together, those remarks would lead to a "distinctive model of democracy" (Tabak 2000a, p. 87), I have to confess that Tabak's articles constitute a valuable contribution to the issue of a socialist/communist constitutionalism (Tabak 2000a, 2000b).

4 It is worth noting Miliband's rather extreme and emphatic comment on the issue: "Engels was clearly mistaken when he wrote in 1891 that the democratic republic was 'even the specific form of the dictatorship of the proletariat" (Miliband 1965, p. 292).

5 A useful historical survey and a valuable critical analysis of socialist constitutionalism as a political challenge and a research-programme are included in Dimitrios Kivotidis' *The Dialectics of Democracy. Towards a Socialist Constitutionalism* (Kivotidis 2024, especially pp. 217–289).

6 From her own point of view, Anne Showstack Sassoon (1987, p. 227) reaches a similar conclusion, insisting that Gramsci "gives us little indication of the precise form of the new State, which he would have considered a utopian exercise".

7 While commenting on the revolutionary party-new (socialist) state relation Anne Showstack Sassoon (1987, p. 227) makes a penetrating remark: "Gramsci is very explicit that the party does *not* provide the *form* of the new State which can only develop from the experience of the mass movement and which has no previous model".

8 I think Gramsci has in mind Hegel's distinction between the "strictly political state" and the "entire state", that means the distinction between the state as a set of institutions and the state referring to the citizens' life and patriotic sentiment as a whole (see paragraphs 267, 273, 276 of *Hegel's Philosophy of Right*).

9 It is worth mentioning that Francesca Antonini (2020, p. 182), while interpreting the Gramscian concept of statolatry, commented on this concrete excerpt from *Prison Notebooks* as follows: "Gramsci is here clearly hinting at the situation in the USSR".

10 In a well-balanced remark, Alberto Burgio (2020, p. 89) concludes: "What Gramsci writes, reasoning on the theory of historical transitions and in particular on the transition to Communism, does not depend on his reflection on the Soviet experience even though undoubtedly these reflections and the judgement that he formed on the "new type" of State born of the Bolshevik revolution contribute to giving shape to the theoretical elaboration".

For her part, Francesca Antonini (2020, p. 180) mentions that "Gramsci's interpretation of Soviet Russia in the *Prison Notebooks* still requires in-depth investigation by scholars in all its facets. In fact, despite the number of articles dedicated to Gramsci's relations with the Italian Communist Party and the Comintern, a thorough analysis of his interpretation in the prison writings is still absent".

11 Following Joseph Femia (1987, p. 176), "when firmly located in their textual context, Gramsci's observations on state worship seem rather harmless. Intended, perhaps, as a retrospective comment on the October revolution, they can be understood as encompassing only those underdeveloped countries, such as Russia, where revolution is possible *before* the development of a proletarian hegemony".

12 On this issue, I fall into line with Roger Simon's general remark: "The note on statolatry is valuable for analysing the Soviet Union" (Simon 1999, p. 87). According to the same scholar, "the period of statolatry in that country was exceptionally prolonged and not used to develop a 'complex and well-articulated civil society'" (Simon 1999, p. 87).

13 Especially the last part of Silvio Pons' essay "Gramsci e la Rivoluzione Russa: una riconsiderazione (1917–1935)" offers a well-documented overview of Gramsci's critical way of dealing with the so-called "construction of socialism" in the USSR (Pons 2017, p. 912 ff.).

14 Moving in the opposite direction, Roger Simon paradoxically suggests that, using the term *statolatry*, Gramsci "meant very much the same as the term *statism* which has come into use in recent years" (Simon 1999, p. 87).

15 As Showstack Sassoon accurately mentions "a new concept of politics begins within the party itself. It is in this sense that the party prefigures a new type of state" (Showstack Sassoon 1987, p. 172).

16 In regard to Rousseau's Legislator, see *Of the Social Contract*, Book II, Chapter VII.

17 Dealing with the party as a founding institution of the new polity, special attention should be drawn to the fact that Gramsci avoids endorsing, at least explicitly, the position of Rousseau, who unreservedly expels political parties from the new state (Rousseau 1997, p. 60).

18 On this issue, Loris Caruso's comment deserves to be quoted at length: "In Gramsci's view, communism does not end either pluralism or the conflict for hegemony. Gramsci's communism *is* conflict for hegemony; namely, it is a translation of social antagonism from the economic to the ethical-political arena. In communism civil society becomes hegemonic over the state, consent subordinates coercion, and the ethical-political catharsis of hegemony subordinates the economic and corporate dimension: political society is gradually absorbed by civil society. The precondition of these processes, however, lies in the end of class domination, and the complete democracy consists of the subalterns' hegemony" (Caruso 2016, p. 151).

19 Anne Showstack Sassoon's comment is to the point: "Since the building of a socialist State entails the creation of positive support on the widest possible basis, the logic of Gramsci's argument, while not providing us with any specific suggestions with regard to the modes of building that hegemony, points towards full discussion and debate. Unlike the bourgeois State which might achieve a balance between hegemony and coercion but never eliminates the element of force, the socialist State exists for a unique purpose -to develop civil society, to increase the area of hegemony until the coercive apparatuses are no longer necessary" (Showstack 1987, pp. 225–226).

20 Referring to Gramsci's ideal of self-government, Joseph Femia (1987, p. 183) argues: "Freedom is the converse of powerlessness; democracy of elite rule. There is a Rousseauian element here. Man attains freedom, or self-autonomy, by cooperating with his fellows in a participatory community. Thus, all the constraints, obligations and inhibitions of society are the very means by which freedom is attained".

21 To signify a long-term dynamic process, the author of the *Prison Notebooks* uses quite often the term "molecular". See, for example, Gramsci 1971, pp. 46, 109, 194, 195, 221, 267, 280, 370.

22 As Hegel himself argues in § 270 (Remark) of his *Philosophy of Right*, "since the state is not a mechanism but the rational life of self-conscious freedom, the system of the ethical world, it follows that an essential moment in the actual state is the *disposition* of the citizens and so also the consciousness of this disposition that is expressed in *principles*".

In an addition to the same paragraph, the German philosopher mentions: "Of course the state is essentially worldly and finite; it has particular ends and particular powers; but its worldly character is only one of its aspects, and it is only to a spiritless perception that it is finite and nothing more. For the state has a lifegiving soul, and the soul which animates it is subjectivity, which creates differences and yet at the same time holds them together in unity".

23 According to the instructive note of the editors of Antonio Gramsci, *Selections from the Prison Notebooks*, "the idea of the "ethical" State is associated with Croce. For the latter, the two moments of the State were the "ethical" and the "political" (or the "moral" and the "useful"); he saw these as being in perpetual dialectical contradiction a conflict which he represented symbolically as that between Church and State. The term was also adopted by fascism, see e.g. Mussolini, in "The Doctrine of Fascism", 1 932: "The fascist State has its own consciousness, its own will, and for that reason is called an 'ethical' State. In 1929…I said 'For fascism the State is not the night-watchman… it is a spiritual and moral fact…it educates the citizens to civil virtue …'" etc." (note 60, in Gramsci 1971, p. 258).

24 Actually, Adamson endorses Paul Piccone's remark on the alleged Lenin-Gramsci opposition: "Gramsci's problematic rotates around the notion of self-constitution into a new State. Clearly, in this context Gramsci returns to a Hegelian notion of the State seen as the highest expression of civil society rather than, as in the orthodox Marxist tradition, a mere tool of class domination. In this conception of the state, Gramsci again radically differs from Lenin. Whereas Lenin constantly stresses its class character and repressive nature, Gramsci concentrates on its cultural – hegemonic function" (Piccone 1976, p. 502).

25 As Alberto Burgio accurately notes, "Lassalle criticized the liberal theory of the "minimal" State, delegated only to the protection of bourgeois economic liberties. Now Gramsci takes up this idea again, certainly not to reevaluate the liberal schema […] but with the aim of highlighting, according to Lenin's model, the process of reducing the repressive component of the workers' new power in charge of supervising ("protecting") the results gradually achieved in the consolidation process" (Burgio 2020, pp. 84–85).

26 In my view, Showstack Sassoon's claim may prove way off the mark, when arguing that "Gramsci gives us very little idea of the precise nature of the relationship between the State and the party after the revolution" (Showstack Sassoon 1987, p. 223).

27 As Showstack Sassoon accurately mentions, "notes written in the first instance about fascism provide the basis for a criticism of Stalin's theory of the 'reinforcement' of the State and the elimination of pluralism in the Soviet Union. Indeed, it is the opposite of this attempt to absorb civil society into political society, that is, it is the expansion of civil society and the absorption by civil society of the political realm, in which State and society become reunited, which is precisely the measure by which a new socialist State had to be judged" (Showstack Sassoon 1987, p. 224; see also Showstack Sassoon's comment as she connects one-party Soviet state with bureaucratic centralism- p. 231).

28 Gramsci uses the word **totalitarian** not in the contemporary negative sense of the term but in the sense of an "all-round"/global political organism (See the editors' comment of the *Selections from Prison Notebooks* -Gramsci 1971, p. $147_{n.33}$).

29 Through a brief, though crystal-clear remark, Joseph Femia keeps the mind of his reader alert: "Gramsci never ceased his search for new forms of popular participation, qualitatively different from those of liberal democracy" (Femia 1987, p. 183).

30 While considering the efficacy of Gramsci's constitutional thinking, it proves worth keeping in mind, as V. G. Kiernan suggests, that Gramscian political *anthropology* "finds in the average man, long divorced from any real part in control of public affairs, a 'fetishistic' attitude towards all institutions, whether of State or party, a taking for granted that they will somehow go on functioning whether he [she] does anything or not" (Kiernan 1972, p. 20).

31 Commenting on Gramsci's politics, Eric Hobsbawm raises the crucial question: "How can we expect to transform human life, to create a socialist *society* (as distinct from a socially owned and managed economy) when the mass of the people is excluded from the political process, and may even be allowed to drift into depoliticisation and apathy about public matters?" (Hobsbawm 1977, pp. 212–213).

32 As Carlos Nelson Coutinho rightly mentions, Gramsci's notion of intellectual and moral reform, which "is a necessary condition for achieving hegemony in the complex 'Western' capitalist societies, it is also a decisive element in the battle for the end of 'statolatry' or 'the government of functionaries' within socialism, that is, it is decisive for the struggle to dissolve the coercive state and to establish the resulting 'self-government of the associated producers" (Coutinho 2012, p. 115).

References

Adamson, Walter L. 1980. *Hegemony and Revolution. A Study of Antonio Gramsci's Political and Cultural Theory*. Berkeley and Los Angeles: University of California Press.

Antonini, Francesca. 2020. *Caesarism and Bonapartism in Gramsci: Hegemony and the Crisis of Modernity*. Leiden: Brill.

Boggs, Carl. 1976. *Gramsci's Marxism*. London: Pluto Press.

Buci-Glucksmann, Christine. 1980. *Gramsci and the State*. London: Lawrence and Wishart.

Burgio, Alberto. 2020. "On the Transition to Communism" in Davide Cadeddu (ed.), *A Companion to Antonio Gramsci. Essays on History and Theories of History, Politics and Historiography*. Leiden and Boston: Brill, pp. 79–89.

Caruso. Loris. 2016. "Gramsci's Political Thought and the Contemporary Crisis of Politics". *Thesis Eleven* 136(1): 140–160.

Chrysis, Alexandros. 2022. *The Marx of Communism. Setting Limits in the Realm of Communism*. London: Palgrave Macmillan.

Coutinho, Carlos Nelson. 2012. *Gramsci's Political Thought*. Leiden and Boston: Brill.

Della Volpe, Galvano. 1978 [1964]. "More on Socialist Legality" in Galvano della Volpe (ed.), *Rousseau and Marx*. Translated and introduced by John Fraser. London: Lawrence and Wishart, pp. 107–125.

Draper, Hal.1987. *The Dictatorship of the Proletariat from Marx to Lenin*. New York: Monthly Review Press.

Engels, Friedrich. 1990a [1891]. "Introduction to Karl Marx's *The Civil War in France*" in Karl Marx and Frederick Engels (eds.), *Collected Works*. Moscow: Progress Publishers, vol. 27, pp. 179–191.

Engels, Friedrich. 1990b [1891]. "A Critique of the Draft Social-Democratic Programme of 1891" in Karl Marx and Frederick Engels (eds.), *Collected Works*. Moscow: Progress Publishers, vol. 27, pp. 217–232.

Femia, Joseph V. 1987. *Gramsci's Political Thought. Hegemony, Consciousness, and the Revolutionary Process*. Oxford: Clarendon Press.

Gramsci, Antonio. 1971. *Selections from the Prison Notebooks*. Edited and translated by Quintin Hoare and Geoffrey Nowell Smith New York: International Publishers.

Gramsci, Antonio. 1977a [1919], "Workers' Democracy". in Antonio Gramsci (ed.), *Selections from Political Writings (1910–1920)*. Selected and translated by Quintin Hoare. London: Lawrence & Wishart, pp. 65–68.

Gramsci, Antonio. 1977b [1919]. "The Conquest of the State" in Antonio Gramsci (ed.), *Selections from Political Writings (1910–1920)*. Selected and translated by Quintin Hoare. London: Lawrence & Wishart, pp. 73–78.

Gramsci, Antonio. 1977c [1930–1932]. *Quaderni del Carcere*. Roma: Giulio Einaudi editore, Edizione critica dell' Istituto Gramsci. A cura di Valentino Gerratana.

Hegel Georg Wilhelm Friedrich. 1959 [1821]. *Philosophy of Right*. Translated with Notes by Thomas Malcolm Knox, Oxford: Oxford University Press.

Hobsbawm, Eric John. 1977. "Gramsci and Political Theory". *Marxism Today* 21, 7 (July 1977): 205–213.

Johnstone, Monty.1971. "The Paris Commune and Marx's Conception of the Dictatorship of the Proletariat". *The Massachusetts Review* 12: 3 (Summer 1971): 447–462.

Kiernan, Victor Gordon. 1972. "Gramsci and Marxism". *The Socialist Register* 9: 1–33.

Kivotidis, Dimitrios. 2024. *The Dialectics of Democracy. Towards a Socialist Constitutionalism*. Oxon: Routledge.

Lenin, Vladimir Ilych. 1964 [1917]. "The State and Revolution. The Marxist Theory of the State and the Tasks of the Proletariat in the Revolution" in Vladimir Ilych Lenin (ed.), *Collected Works*. Moscow: Progress Publishers, vol. 25, pp. 385–497.

Marx, Karl. 1979 [1852]. "The Eighteenth Brumaire of Louis Bonaparte" in Karl Marx and Frederick Engels (eds.), *Collected Works.* Moscow: Progress Publishers, vol. 11, pp. 99–197.

Marx, Karl. 1986 [1871]. "The Civil War in France. Address of the General Council of the International Working Men's Association" in Karl Marx and Frederick Engels (eds.), *Collected Works.* Moscow: Progress Publishers, vol. 22, pp. 307–359.

Marx, Karl. 1988 [1873]. "Political Indifferentism" in Karl Marx and Frederick Engels (eds.), *Collected Works*. Moscow: Progress Publishers, vol. 23, pp. 392–397.

Marx, Karl. 1989 [1875]. "Critique of the Gotha Programme" in Karl Marx and Frederick Engels (eds.), *Collected Works.* Moscow: Progress Publishers, vol. 24, pp. 75–99.

Marx, Karl and Engels Friedrich. 1988 [1872]. "Preface to the 1872 German Edition of the *Manifesto of the Communist Party*" in Karl Marx and Frederick Engels (eds.), *Collected Works.* Moscow: Progress Publishers, vol. 23, pp. 174–175.

Miliband, Ralph. 1965. "Marx and the State". *The Socialist Register* 2: 278–296.

Piccone, Paul. 1976. "Gramsci's Marxism: Beyond Lenin and Togliatti". *Theory and Society* 3: 485–512.

Pons, Silvio.2017. "Gramsci e la rivoluzione russa: una riconderazione". *Studi Storici, Anno* 58(4): 883–928.

Rousseau, Jean-Jacques. 1997. "Of the Social Contract". in Jean-Jacques Rousseau (ed.), *The Social Contract and Other Later Political Writings*, Translated and edited by Victor Gourevitch. Cambridge: Cambridge University Press, pp. 39–152.

Showstack Sassoon, Anne. 1987. *Gramsci's Politics*. London: Hutchinson.

Simon, Roger. 1999. *Gramsci's Political Thought. An Introduction*. London: ElecBook.

Tabak, Mehmet. 2000a. "A Marxian Theory of Democracy". *Socialism and Democracy* 14: 2, 87–113.

Tabak, Mehmet. 2000b. "Marx's Theory of Proletarian Dictatorship Revisited". *Science & Society* 64: 3 (Fall 2000): 333–356.

Vacca, Giuseppe. 1982. "Intellectuals and the Marxist Theory of the State" in Showstack Sassoon and Anne (eds.), *Approaches to Gramsci*. London: Writers and Readers, pp. 37–69.

5 A Socialist Constitutionalism for the Twenty-First Century

Dimitrios Kivotidis

5.1 Introduction

To argue for a socialist constitutionalism at a time when free market rationality, in its various forms, dominates all legal and political discourse may sound counterintuitive, if not utopian and naïve, especially to a legal audience. How can it be otherwise, when less than a handful of constitutions globally refer to the values of socialism or mention the attempt to build socialist economic relations and institutional forms;[1] when social and economic rights, like the right to strike, to collective bargaining, to social security, public health and education, sanctioned in liberal regimes after decades of hard fought and bloody struggles of the working class and the popular strata are consistently scrapped, restricted and erased from legal memory (Katsaroumpas 2018; Kivotidis 2018)?

Nevertheless, in spite of the current discouraging state of the struggle for socialism, or maybe precisely because of this, arguing for socialism and a socialist constitutionalism is all the more urgent, especially when one considers that the dominance of free market constitutionalism is historically contingent. It should not be forgotten that the fathers of neoliberalism and market rationality, like Ludwig von Mises and Friedrich Hayek, began to wage their ideological struggle at a time when even Britain's Conservative party accepted the value of socialist planning (Cockshott, Cottrell, and Dapprich 2022). The victory of free market logic, despite the fact that this logic reflects the foundational values and principles of capitalist economy, was not certain in the post-war period in the context of intense ideological struggle conducted under the influence of 'actually existing' socialist countries and strong workers' and communist parties around the world. According to Milton Friedman, the duty of neoliberal thinkers was 'to develop alternatives to existing policies, to keep them alive and available until the politically impossible becomes politically inevitable' (Friedman 2002). When the multifaceted crisis in socialist regimes led to their overthrow and in the context of an altered and globalised process of capital accumulation, free market logic could reign uncontested.

DOI: 10.4324/9781032621623-6

Now, in an age of sepsis and decay of capitalism, alternative visions are urgently needed to inspire the movement necessary to challenge the hegemony of market rationality, as well as the extant social condition. In this context, socialist constitutionalism, which denotes a field of study interested in the exploration of institutional forms and principles that challenge and aim at the transformation of the existing social order from a jurisprudential and constitutionalist perspective, is a very fruitful field for intervention (O'Connell 2021, 473–475). There have been various attempts at relaunching this notion recently.[2] I have dealt with these and their theoretical shortcomings elsewhere (Kivotidis 2024, 193–216). In this chapter, I will elaborate on the role that Marxist theory can play in the struggle of ideas around the notion of socialist constitutionalism.

Marxist theory provides us with an analytical key to understanding the historical development of socio-economic relations, namely the contradiction between productive forces and relations of production (Marx 1990, 873–929). The exponential growth of the digital infrastructure and its multiple effects on social life can be understood in terms of this contradiction. Phenomena like the intensification of exploitation, the widespread alienation, and the manipulation of the electorate, which are characteristic of contemporary digital societies, should not obscure the unprecedented potential for social emancipation that the digital infrastructure offers, which can be actualised if the root cause of these phenomena, namely, capitalist relations of production, is eliminated. This potential is recognised in arguments that most of the problems with planned economies that Friedrich Hayek and neoliberal political economists identified, are now considered solved or solvable by algorithmic mediation (Grunberg 2023; Morozov 2019). The infrastructure for transcending market economy and replacing it with a rationally planned economy based on socialist relations of production now exists.

The growth of the social forces of production has reignited the contestation of capitalist relations of production. The calculation debate is, even modestly, re-opened and the debate of 'planning versus market' is back on the agenda. Yet, socialist planning was rejected not only for economic but also for constitutional reasons. The bureaucratically planned economy was accused of being both inefficient and authoritarian, a threat to freedom. The main aim of this chapter is to counter the authoritarian/bureaucratic critique of socialism by exploring what socialist democracy could look like in the twenty-first century. To do this, I will revisit the relationship between institutions of socialist democracy and socialist planning to arrive at a reconceptualisation of democracy, from a socialist standpoint, drawing from the historical experience of the Soviet Union. Challenging the liberal notion of the absolute antithesis between democracy and bureaucracy, the main research question is: how does socialist constitutionalism resolve the tension between workplace democracy and central planning?

To answer this, the chapter is structured as follows. The first section explores the contradiction between social forces of production and capitalist relations of production with a focus on digital society. It explores from a Marxist perspective the phenomenon of digital authoritarianism and the increase in exploitation and alienation resulting from the introduction of new technologies in almost every social sphere. It is argued that it is not the digital infrastructure but the capitalist relations of production that pose a threat to human dignity. The second section compares the principles of free market constitutionalism, on the one hand, and socialist constitutionalism, on the other, with a focus on democracy to show that only a radical restructuring of capitalist relations and institutional forms can eradicate the adverse effects of digital society on human dignity, and instead realise its emancipatory potential. Finally, Section 5.3 focuses on the relationship between workplace democracy and centralised institutions, from a socialist constitutionalist perspective, aiming to counter the liberal critique that posits democracy and socialist planning in terms of absolute opposition and enhance the normative appeal of a socialist constitutionalism. It also aims to show that the digital infrastructure now presents agents of revolutionary socialism with an infrastructural potential for resolving the contradiction between socialist democracy and socialist planning.

5.2 Digital Authoritarianism

The first two decades of the twenty-first century have been defined by the intensification of contradictions of capitalist society, which manifested in multiple ways, such as the Global Financial Crisis and its ripple effects, like the Eurozone crisis; the global pandemic of COVID-19 whose root causes arguably lie in the ways that capitalism is eroding the natural environment (Wallace, Liebman, Chaves, and Wallace 2020); a cost-of-living crisis triggered by the multiplication of wars, as well as the economic responses to the pandemic (Tonak and Savran 2020); the resurgence of imperialist wars and military conflicts; and last but not least, the sharpening of the contradiction between productive forces and relations of production, with the breakthroughs in artificial intelligence (AI) and information and communication technologies, colloquially known as the 'Fourth Industrial Revolution' and the fear that this causes over the future of jobs and socio-economic relations (Hughes and Southern 2019). This last point is what this chapter focuses on to illustrate how socialist constitutionalism can be a useful tool in the struggle to overcome the bounds of the capitalist relations of production and release the emancipatory potential of social forces of production.

Over the same period, digital technology has colonised almost every aspect of social existence. Digital platforms have come to play a major part in mediating the processes of mass communication, concentration and dissemination of information, as well as the formation of consciousness (political, social, class, etc.) (Kivotidis 2024, 164–189). The importance of algorithms for contemporary networks of information and processes of social consciousness formation cannot be overemphasised, as the vast majority of the population uses social media platforms as their primary source of information. Despite its neutral appearance, the newsfeed algorithm of a social platform can have a severe impact on political decision-making: algorithms determine the allocation of information and enable targeted advertising and suggestions for vote. In this way, digital platforms assume a constitutional role of vital importance for the functioning of democracy and the exercise of political rights (De Gregorio 2022).

The unregulated activity of digital platforms has already had quite adverse effects on democracy, even from a liberal perspective. Phenomena such as the spread of fake news or targeted political advertising, showcased in the case of Cambridge Analytica, arguably result in the distortion of the fundamental nucleus of liberal democracy—i.e. the expression of free will in democratic decision-making processes. What is more, from a Marxist standpoint, it can be argued that the digital infrastructure plays a crucial role in the reproduction of false consciousness and the translation of economic power into political power (Taplin 2018; Bartlett 2018). Algorithms create what in political science is called 'elective affinity' or 'selective exposure', i.e. 'a leaning towards spending our time and attention with the people or organisations we already know and like, thereby strengthening our ties with them' (Howard 2016). New social media facilitate the creation of 'echo chambers', where groups of individuals enclose themselves and reproduce their solidified opinions, due to a lack of randomly accessed (high quality) information that would challenge their worldviews (Solik 2017). This prevents members of the subordinate social strata from engaging with ideas that challenge the root causes of this system of alienation and exploitation, namely the capitalist relations of production, and instead channels their indignation towards reactionary political solutions. The phenomena could be further exacerbated through the use of AI, which can be a powerful tool for political micro-targeting as well as disinformation and misinformation.[3]

The dire effects of the digital infrastructure on social and political consciousness are combined with widespread intensification of exploitation and increase of alienation in the workplace. The democratic deficit in the workplace, as a result of decades of labour market deregulation and dismantling of employee protection against the managerial prerogative, has enabled the introduction of new technologies without any consultation of those primarily affected by this process, namely the employees (Katsaroumpas 2023). The term 'technological authoritarianism' has been used to denote the technological governance model, where the employer enjoys an unrestrained power to control the design, use and organisational integration of technology in the workplace (Katsaroumpas 2023, 245). More and more companies use wearable work instruments that enable registering their employees' movements and location minute by minute, and analyse the data collected by means of AI to assess productivity (Moore, Akhtar, and Upchurch 2018). For instance, the Amazon warehouse monitoring system has been emblematic of authoritarian practices, featuring the constant monitoring of workers with vibrators indicating their location and movement, creating conditions of enhanced exploitation (Katsaroumpas 2023, 256). It is now generally accepted that too much monitoring increases stress, fear[4] and incentives to 'beat the system' by breaking safety rules and not taking mandated breaks (Ajunwa, Crawford, and Schultz 2017).

It follows that the democratic deficit in the workplace enables the increase of exploitation and alienation through the introduction of new technology, as workers are subjected to constant surveillance (even outside the workplace) and are treated as mere 'cogs' rather than valued human beings (De Stefano 2018). Yet, it is not just the workplace where exploitation is taking place. Digital platforms prey on an individual's leisure time too. For Shoshanna Zuboff, 'surveillance capitalism unilaterally claims human experience as free raw material for translation into behavioural data' (Zuboff 2019, v). According to Christian Fuchs, usage of these platforms is productive labour and platform users create value, because their labour is objectified in the commodities produced by social media corporations (i.e. the portion of a user's screen filled with ad clients' commodity ideologies). Users are productive workers whose activities are necessary for 'transporting' use-value promises from companies to potential customers: in the twenty-first century, transportation labour is communication labour (Fuchs and Mosco 2016).

Liberal constitutional theory is not totally blind to the adverse effects of the digital infrastructure on socio-political relations. The term 'digital constitutionalism' has been coined to denote the set of values and principles that should inform and guide the generation of normative responses to the challenges of digital technology (Suzor 2018; Golia 2022). This approach recognises that the primary threats for constitutional democracies do not come any longer exclusively from public authorities, but primarily from 'private actors governing spaces which are formally private spaces, but exerting in practice, and without any safeguard, functions traditionally vested in public authorities without any safeguard' (De Gregorio 2022, 14). Yet, this liberal approach falls short of explaining the limitations of constitutional responses to digital authoritarianism because it lacks the methodological tools to explore the structural functions of platforms in contemporary capitalist processes of accumulation.

In particular, the issues of exploitation, alienation and false consciousness fall outside the scope of liberal constitutionalism. Additionally, the issue of democracy tends to be overlooked, and when it is discussed, it is done from an individualistic viewpoint, focusing on privacy and narrow calls for government regulation (De Gregorio 2022). But, as we saw above, the current threats to human dignity that constitutional texts are meant to eliminate among other things, cannot be countered unless we understand the exact ways in which human beings are treated as means instead of ends in contemporary societies. Once this happens, one realises that the adverse effects of digitalisation and AI cannot be adequately addressed by the current juridico-political framework determined by market constitutionalism. Rather, to safeguard human dignity, a more radical institutional response is necessary, embedded in different social relations where technology aims at social needs satisfaction and the digital infrastructure is repurposed to serve social goals.

The dystopian trajectory accelerated by digital technology and AI should not give rise to neo-Luddite solutions. As mentioned above, the grim reality of digital authoritarianism can be explained by focusing on the platforms' role in the process of capital accumulation. The capitalist relations of production pose insurmountable obstacles to achieving the emancipatory potential of the digital infrastructure. Indeed, Marxist analysis shows that digital capitalism is the direct result of contradictions inherent in the capitalist mode of production (Andrejevic 2012; Fuchs and Mosco 2016, 45). Phenomena like data mining and targeted advertising have revolutionised the processes of circulation and realisation of surplus value, and by radically increasing the velocity of capital's circulation, they operate as factors countering the tendency of the rate of profit to fall, i.e. the ultimate barrier of the capitalist mode of production.[5]

If the adverse and alienating effects of the digital infrastructure on working and living conditions are determined by the capitalist relations of production, then their emancipatory potential can only be realised in the context of a radical restructuring of socio-economic relations in a post-capitalist society that has transcended the contradictions of the capitalist market. The literature exploring socialist alternatives to the capitalist market is currently growing (Hahnel 2021). Theorists are revisiting the original 'calculation debate', which concerned the feasibility and viability of a socialist mode of production based on central planning (Lange 1936; Dobb 1970; Ellman 2014), in light of the development of the digital infrastructure, which can arguably replace the market in collecting and distributing information essential to economic transactions and coordination (Pistor 2020; Pałka 2020; Phillips and Rozworski 2019). Critical studies of the so-called 'platform capitalism' have also led to proposals for different forms and models of socialist planning that can potentially replace the market as the main regulator of economic activity (Morozov 2019; Muldoon 2022).

Yet, the re-opening of the calculation debate and the investigation of alternatives to the capitalist market stumbles upon a great obstacle, namely the idea that central planning is also a threat to freedom and necessarily leads to the rise of an authoritarian system whereby needs, discovery and social production are determined by a bureaucratic elite or a dystopian rule by algorithms (Feher, Heller, and Markus 1983). In other words, even if one accepts that the problems faced by planned economies in the twentieth century are now solved, or at least solvable, through algorithmic mediation, the threat of authoritarianism still exists and is a good reason to delegitimise any attempt to replace the 'free market' with a system of planned economy.

Even critics who recognise the failings of the capitalist market end up arguing against replacing it with a planned economy because of the authoritarian threat that this would pose. For instance, Przemysław Pałka accepts that 'advances in data processing technologies might render an economic order based on central planning possible to realize and potentially more efficient than a market economy relying on private property and contract exchange' (Pałka 2020). At the same time, he warns that this efficiency comes at the expense of freedom (Pałka 2020). Pałka cites Ronald Coase's distinction between markets and hierarchies and reproduces the liberal assumption according to which a planned economy consists of rigid hierarchical relations between the planners, the enterprises and the workers (Pałka 2020, 130–131). From the liberal standpoint, planners are alien entities and once they step in 'individuals are stripped not only of property, but also of choices regarding their preferences about small and large issues in their lives' (Pałka 2020, 132).

It follows that a system 'that endows an individual with normative freedom to choose her life path without providing the means necessary to exercise that freedom' is preferable to a 'system questioning the very idea that individuals decide their own life paths' (Pałka 2020, 131). From a liberal standpoint, planning is seen as a form of authoritarianism where an external entity tells us what to do and what to consume. Socialist planning is, under this lens, necessarily embedded in the institutional context of political dictatorship, where a ruling group imposes its will on society and deal with opposition by repression (Ellman 2014, 26).

The problem with this line of reasoning is that authoritarian phenomena and coercion, as well as the distortion of the process of social production and needs satisfaction, are essential characteristics of contemporary capitalist societies, where profit rules supreme. The current 'liberal' world is full of command and control, unfreedom and coercion, as was very briefly shown in the previous section. This realisation renders the dilemma between freedom and efficiency false. Yet, the main flaw of this kind of 'liberal' argumentation is that it overlooks the democratic emancipatory potential of an algorithmically mediated planned economy. The benefits of a planned economy in terms of efficiency and social welfare need not result from authoritarian practices; they can be the products of a democratically planned and collectively organised economy.

Releasing the normative force and increasing the normative appeal of arguments for socialist planning necessitates engagement with the institutional forms of the socialist state. The following sections challenge the liberal antithesis between democracy and bureaucracy so as to arrive at a socialist notion of democracy that can accommodate the struggle to transcend capitalism in the twenty-first century.

5.3 Market Constitutionalism versus Socialist Constitutionalism

Before we identify how socialist constitutionalism approaches the principle of democracy, we need to define socialist constitutionalism as opposed to free market constitutionalism. The dominant paradigm of free market constitutionalism views the market as the superior form of producing and distributing goods in a society, especially when compared to planned economies (Dellis 2021, 28). From a market constitutionalist perspective, law's purpose is not to subvert, change or even manipulate the economy to achieve social goals or ideals, but to ensure economic efficiency and reduce transaction costs (Coase 1960).[6] In this light, the ideal constitution is understood as reducing transaction costs by placing basic governmental arrangements beyond the scope of democratic processes, and therefore freeing the people's energies for productive private activities (Holmes 1988).

Furthermore, the notions of economic efficiency and economic growth that market constitutionalism draws upon rely on specific political conceptions of how an economy should be organised. From a market standpoint, labour is seen as a cost and reducing the cost of labour necessarily involves deregulating the labour market and removing the protection afforded by socio-economic rights.[7] This explains why since the 1980s and once labour protections were perceived as barriers to profit they have been replaced by economic regulation intended to attract investment (Dukes 2008). This also explains the increasing 'hollowing out' of democratic forms of decision-making through *de facto* and/or *de jure* restriction of constitutionally and legally guaranteed democratic freedoms (Kaltsonis 2021), as well as the tendency—which has now become an essential characteristic of liberal democratic states—to delegate important economic functions and competences (such as monetary policy or fiscal oversight and forecasting) to non-majoritarian institutions or independent regulatory agencies, whose members are not subject to re-election constraints (Majone 1996; Gilardi 2002).

Under this lens, democracy is evaluated as a 'necessary evil' which ensures social peace but reaches its limits when the transaction costs of redistribution hinder economic growth. On the one hand, democratically enabled redistribution can increase social stability by making it less attractive to engage in social protest, riots or revolutions; on the other hand, democratic pressures to redistribute wealth could compromise property rights and thus reduce the incentive to invest (Barro 2000). It has been argued, for instance, that referendums, the modern-day institutional manifestations of direct democracy, undermine the long-lasting, co-operative mission of the constitution because, 'behind their seemingly consensual character, they unbind the "People-Ulysses" from the mast, to make decisions under the influence of all kinds of Sirens' (Dellis 2021, 133). Therefore, the arguments against popular participation in the decision-making process, especially with regard to the running of the economy, stem from the fear of redistributive policies and the perception of these as transaction costs from a market constitutionalist perspective (Meltzer and Richard 1981).

Following from this, it can be argued that the principles of market constitutionalism are determined by the process of valorisation (i.e. the addition of value to the initial value of money-capital advanced in the market), which constitutes the 'need'[8] that puts in motion the process of material production, in capitalism.

According to Marx, valorisation takes place in a constantly renewed movement (Marx 1990, 253). The bearer of this movement is the capitalist and its purpose is not the profit of a single transaction, but the unceasing movement of profit-making (Marx 1990, 254). Profit-making is the 'need' that determines the totality of the capitalist process of production, i.e. production, circulation, distribution and consumption. Profitability is arguably the governing principle of market rationality, i.e. the 'need' lying at the root of capitalist rationality and determining the form and content of any other need, e.g. need for food, shelter, health, education, etc.

On the contrary, socialist constitutionalism signifies a different model of constitutionalism governed by a qualitatively different principle, namely the 'free and full development of every individual'. This principle appears in the 'Communist Manifesto' where Marx and Engels call for a society where 'the free development of each is the condition for the free development of all' (Marx and Engels 2010, 506), as well as in 'Capital', where Marx refers to a highest form of society where 'the full and free development of every individual forms the ruling principle (Marx 1990, 738)'. This constitutes the foundational principle for a socialist constitution, but also the fundamental principle lying at the roots of a social formation, permeating all sorts of institutional frameworks and systems of social practice, including decision-making and dispute-resolving processes.

According to Tony Smith, the notion of the 'free development of the individual' does not merely refer to the 'formal freedom to act without external interference so strongly emphasised in the republican constitutions of modern capitalism' (Smith 2025). It rather conveys that 'socialism does not aim at a state of well-being paternalistically bestowed on passive recipients' (Smith 2025). Instead, 'every individual must have a freedom to develop on the basis of their own actions' (Smith 2025). This freedom presupposes the existence of institutional forms for collective evaluation, planning and decision-making, which are 'created, continually renewed, and periodically modified through the collective actions of the members of the socialist society' (Smith 2025). In that sense, replacing market distortions and insufficiencies with a socialist economy focused on social needs satisfaction is seen from a Marxist perspective as conditioned upon the flourishing of democratic institutions.

In this chapter, I argue that, from a socialist constitutionalist perspective, it is important to understand socialist democracy as (i) a process, and (ii) a relation of production that impacts on social consciousness. Let us begin with the first characteristic. In its Marxist conception, socialism refers to a transitional society, a society in transition to communism. It is identified with immature communism, i.e. the historical period of building the conditions for a society where social contradictions have been abolished. The historical result of this process is a communist society based on the communist mode of production. It follows that, from a socialist constitutionalist perspective, the process of building socialist democracy coincides with the process of building a communist, classless and stateless society.

The destruction of the 'old state machine' is only the first step in this process (Colletti 1969, 19). It constitutes the passage from a 'narrow, restricted democracy to full democracy' (Colletti 1969, 21). The project of destroying the 'diaphragm that separates the working classes from power' is at the same time a creative process of transmitting power directly into the hands of the people (Colletti 1969, 21). In the work of the classics of Marxism, we find that the workers' state form is characterised by advanced democratic principles. These include the direct or indirect election of all representatives and offices, including the judiciary; the replacement of territorial constituencies by workplace democracy based on production units (Lenin 1976c, 466); the right to recall; the abolition of privileges and the establishment of workman's wages for all state officials (Lenin 1976e); the exercise of workers' and popular control, including mechanisms of accountability; a change in the mode of operation of representative institutions so that they constitute decisive instruments of concentrated power, legislating as well as executing the workers' and popular will (Kaltsonis 2009). All the above constitute a qualitatively different form of democracy compared to the bourgeois parliamentary model.

Yet, the process of 'smashing' the old state and creating new institutional forms of working-class power is a long and arduous historical process which also involves the creation of the material conditions for the proper functioning of such forms; material conditions which will enable the all-round development of both the physical and mental abilities of the social individual and the necessary social consciousness (Ilyenkov 1967). Moreover, their creation can only result from a socio-political process of struggle and social restructuring that affects every aspect of living and working conditions and social relations. As a result, from a socialist constitutionalist standpoint, democracy is the result of a long historical process of building the material conditions for its actualisation. This process coincides with the development of institutions of substantive democracy and culminates in the withering away of the state as an instrument of coercion.

With the above factors considered, it can be argued that the development of socialist democracy is not a spontaneous process. It rather necessitates the existence of institutional forms that mediate the transition from the false consciousness sustained by bourgeois institutional forms to socialist consciousness. The building—and deepening—of socialist democracy requires vigilant and conscious application of its principles and nourishment of its institutional forms. This can be facilitated by the ideological intervention of a vanguard institutional form, such as the workers' party. The party is a crucial institution in the process of building socialism and socialist democracy, in its role to guide, convince, present arguments, organise and motivate, without, however, substituting itself for the workers and people. We will return to this point in the following section.

Concerning the second characteristic of socialist democracy mentioned above, it is argued that democracy can be conceived as a socialist relation of production (like central planning) to be developed in the process of socialist construction. The democratic form can be approached as a form of collective decision-making, which must be cultivated as a relation of production in the transition to communism. If the expropriation of the means of production is the beginning of the process of revolutionary transformation of the relations of production, the end of this process cannot but involve the actual participation of workers in collective decision-making, enforcement and scrutiny of such decisions (Kaltsonis 2016). Socialist democracy is an essential element of socialist construction as well as a condition for the withering away of the state.

This point gives a very different meaning to the idea of economic democracy. Arguably, the most important condition for the actualisation of socialist democracy is the principle of workplace democracy, according to which productive units should be the centres of decision-making processes. This is economic democracy not just in name (as it is in bourgeois constitutions, in the few historical instances it has existed) but also in practice. Lenin recognised this when he pointed out that 'making the economic, industrial unit (factory) and not a territorial division the primary electoral unit and the nucleus of the state structure under Soviet power' ensures the 'closer contact between the state apparatus and the masses of advanced proletarians that capitalism has united' (Lenin 1976b, 106–108). This results in 'the more direct influence of the working masses on state structure and administration' and 'makes it possible to effect profound socialist reforms' (Lenin 1976b, 106–108). Furthermore, it can be argued that the aforementioned principles of substantive democracy, namely constant debate and right to recall, can most properly materialise in this state form. The constant level of debate and scrutiny that makes democratic election a reality is ensured by making productive units—and not a fictional unit such as a constituency—the organisational basis of socialist democracy (Gluckstein 1995, 230–231).

Workplace democracy complements the party in the process of building the necessary social consciousness for a communist society; one of the main material conditions for the transition to communism. The council becomes the best organ for the collective education of workers and the development of communist consciousness even for the 'most ignorant and backward of workers' and 'the most vain and 'civil' of engineers' through their experience of factory organisation (Gluckstein 1995, 230–231). In discussing political issues in the workplace, an individual necessarily becomes exposed to the views of co-workers, i.e. of members of the same class—indeed, to the views of the most class conscious elements of their class. It is, therefore, possible that they might more easily manage to overcome limitations in their own thought, as well as contribute to the overcoming of limitations in the thought of their fellow workers, including those in the vanguard, through a collective process of deliberation.

Following from the above, democracy can be conceived as a benchmark for the development of socialism. As Lucio Colletti put it, the level of development of socialism can be measured by the level of development of democracy; 'the further the withering away of the State has advanced and the self-government of the masses has been extended, the more progress has been made in the transition from socialism to communism' (Colletti 1969, 25). Ralph Miliband reaches a similar conclusion when he claims that, whatever the circumstances in which a revolution occurs, the kind of all-but unmediated popular rule which Lenin describes belongs in fact to a fairly distant future (Miliband 1970, 317). This unmediated popular rule will be the result of a long historical process which will have led to the fullness, ripeness and decomposition of democratic power, as well as to qualitatively different forms of collective decision-making. Until then, the state will endure in an abundance of political forms, including democratic and bureaucratic, combining elements of both.

5.4 Democracy, Bureaucracy and Socialism

According to Lenin, the process of socialist construction is a long historical process which may give rise to an abundance and variety of political forms (Lenin 1976e, 418)—a point confirmed by historical attempts at building socialism thus far. Full democracy, which is ripe to the point that it decomposes and withers away, is the end result of a process which is not spontaneous but needs the guidance and leadership of the independent political organisation of the working class. Therefore, strengthening the constitutional role of the party, or the elements of the state commonly perceived as bureaucratic or technocratic, may constitute crucial aspects of this process.

This point challenges the absolute antithesis between democracy and bureaucracy. The Soviet experience of building socialism is quite commonly dismissed as giving rise to a bureaucratic apparatus that had nothing to do with socialism, democracy, etc. This argument emerges from a formal understanding of democracy and reflects the liberal view point which pitches individual freedom against state power, neglecting socio-economic processes. Yet, this absolute antithesis has formed the basis for various social-democratic, democratic socialist, Eurocommunist or anarchosyndicalist critiques. From a Marxist perspective, it can be argued that far from being an offspring of socialist society, or a necessary component of it, bureaucratism has existed and continues to exist in bourgeois governments. One needs to go no further than to look at the complex bureaucratic structures of domestic civil service or at the supranational institutional architecture of the European Union.

In the process of socialist construction, the bureaucratic birthmarks of capitalism are meant to be overcome. Yet, bureaucratism persists for a certain period. Among the factors that have historically been put forward to explain its persistence, we find the following: the need to create the material basis for communism through a socialist primitive accumulation (Lukacs 1992); the bitter class struggle carried out by the bourgeoisie, involving civil wars, military interventions, economic blockades, etc., which results in the suspension of democratic functions and freedoms; the enormous economic difficulties due to the above; the low educational and cultural level of the peoples in countries where socialist revolutions took place, which complicated the task of their participation in the creation of a new state and economic system; the lack of previous experience in building a new society and administering a new kind of state by members of the working class; the lack of revolutionary consciousness of the popular strata, which resulted in the lack of inner motivation and interest in rendering a service to the state and community; the lack of institutional forms to promote organisation and centralisation; the 'lack of sufficiently developed technical knowledge to be able to make correct decisions on short notice' which led to discussions becoming endless and no-one having sufficient authority to settle things (Guevara 2001, 183–185).

It would be naïve to think that these causes could have been eliminated through spontaneous and uncoordinated attempts at self-management of the economy. Additionally, demonising centralised institutions, like the Vesenkha (the Supreme Soviet of the National Economy), responsible for the establishment of socialist relations of production based on a planned economy, misses the role that these institutions are meant to play in the process of socialist construction. In the context of the October Revolution, the Bolshevik party was aware of the differences between a communist and an anarchosyndicalist approach to workers' control, as well as the challenges that the latter would pose for the process of socialist construction. They recognised that the building of a socialist society 'requires and presupposes the greatest possible centralisation of large-scale production throughout the country' (Lenin 1976a, 96). They experienced first-hand in the process of revolutionary transformation that 'democratic' self-government of enterprises understood in the abstract and demanded as an end in itself might place obstacles and pose dangers in the process of socialist construction. This was the case with the form of syndicalism and 'local self-management', which had dominated the revolutionary organisation of the economy until the summer of 1918, hid behind slogans of 'democratic self-management', and had been causing friction and competition as well as hoarding and profiteering, and was ultimately crippling the economy (Lenin 1976a, 96).

In this context of intense class struggle, the principle of 'workers' self-management' often stood for the prioritisation by many labour leaders of the needs of their own enterprises (Lyon 2006). This particularism and parochialism could 'result in the same sort of atomisation as under the capitalist system' (Avrich 1971). In that context, the Bolsheviks sought ways to ensure that the economy would be controlled *democratically by the working-class as a whole*, and not just by the workers of individual factories (Lyon 2006). The establishment of the Vesenkha, on December 2, 1917, as the main institution of central economic planning, constituted a major step towards establishing and consolidating the main aspect of socialist relations of production, namely central planning. The Vesenkha was tasked with the far-reaching duties of developing general norms and a plan for regulating the economic life of the country, and coordinating and consolidating the activities of central and local regulatory agencies. To fulfil these tasks, it was given extensive powers of confiscation, requisition, sequestration, forced syndication of various industries in the field of production, distribution and public finances, as well as the power to reform all existing institutions.

It is easy to see why these centralising aspects of Soviet government came under attack by the forces of the counterrevolution, as well as by 'internal critics of the communist movement' (Waller 1981). Yet, abstract critiques neglect the class function of such institutional forms in the context of intensified class struggle. The same applies to the institution of the workers' (communist) party, the vanguard of the working class in the struggle for socialism. Rather than a bureaucratic institution or an element of the bureaucratic apparatus, the party can be conceived as a working-class organisation, an institutional form intended to battle bureaucracy and lead the process of socialist construction and building of democracy. For Lenin, the party principle is necessary because the revolutionary state is not yet a workers' state (Lenin 1976f, 24) since the working-class struggle continues in the process of socialist construction, not only against bourgeois counter-revolutionary forces but also against the small commodity producers, as well as against the forces of inertia and the traditions of old society.[9]

The leading role of the party is essential to counter the formidable force of habit and false consciousness. Not because party membership provides immunity to false consciousness but because it presupposes an awareness of capitalist contradictions and the need to overcome them. It signifies a level of consciousness already achieved and adequate to translate into constant concern, care and commitment to carry this process forward despite the lack of an infallible guide on how this should take place. No revolutionary workers' party can be successful in building a communist society by itself, without directing its forces and attention towards building the institutional forms of mass participation, and without submitting its advanced programme for 'fermentation' in the mass organisations of the working class and the popular strata. At the same time, these mass organisations are unlikely by themselves, spontaneously, to achieve the consciousness necessary to overcome the partial and sectoral interests, as well as the long held and deeply ingrained views of bourgeois ideology.

The party is therefore a necessary institutional form for the building and operation of socialist democracy, together with the councils, the trade unions and other institutional forms that may appear. Socialist constitutionalism, according to Lenin, consists of an *arrangement of cogwheels* (Lenin 1976f, 21). Since the dictatorship of the proletariat cannot be exercised by the proletariat as a whole, at least in the first stages of socialist construction as this process emerges out of the womb of capitalist society, a complex arrangement of cogwheels and multiple 'transmission belts'— 'running from the vanguard to the mass of the advanced class, and from the latter to the mass of the working people' and vice versa—is necessary (Lenin 1976f, 21).

This cogwheel mechanism involves several institutions which are necessary parts of socialist democracy and involved in a process of multidirectional learning. In the first place, there is the workers' party which leads, but does not rule, advances the struggle and organises proletarian hegemony over allied classes and proletarian rule over class enemies. The work of the party is carried on through the councils, which embrace the working masses, irrespective of occupation (Lenin 1976d, 49). The party leads the working class and popular strata through the system of councils which formulate and put into practice collective decisions on how to forward the process of social emancipation. The collective labourer becomes a collective decision-maker, engaged in a conscious struggle to transform society as a whole; not merely promoting a personal, sectoral or class interest but the general interest discovered through collective deliberation (in the Soviets, in the party, in the trade unions) and applied to practice.

Other institutions, such as trade unions and workers' conferences, could be examined as elements of this arrangement of cogwheels, but this is not the aim of this chapter. Our aim is rather to highlight that institutional forms of socialist constitutionalism should not be fetishised. Instead, their role must be assessed from the perspective of class struggle, the advancement of the goal of socialism and the building of socialist democracy. This is the meaning of conceiving of socialist constitutionalism as a cogwheel mechanism. Administrative institutional forms, such as centralised institutions responsible for central planning, are not bureaucratic 'top-down' elements, foreign to the process of building socialism, but instead essential to this process. Similarly, the party is a working-class organisation, an essential institutional form in the process of building socialist democracy, rather than a bureaucratic remnant of the past.

Such a dialectical understanding enables us to view the relationship between socialist democracy and central planning not in terms of absolute contradiction, but of co-determination and mutual reinforcement. Furthermore, the growth of the social forces of production has now given rise to a mediating force which may prove invaluable in securing the optimal operation of the transmission belts through which the different institutions communicate, and their coordination takes place. I am referring to the feedback infrastructure. The term 'feedback infrastructure' has been used to describe the data collected by big corporations through countless traces of online activity (Morozov 2019). It has been argued that this 'feedback infrastructure' may be recast in a collectively organised production process geared to the satisfaction of social needs. Instead of being a profit-generation mechanism, this infrastructure could be used to collectively identify social problems, either of local or of more general importance, so that 'public and civil society institutions, deploying the free and available to all digital infrastructure, could arrive at better solutions than the logic of the market and competition à la Hayek and neoliberalism' (Boucas 2020, 60).

This is where the socialism of the twenty-first century has an edge over attempts at building socialism in the twentieth century. The growth of productive forces not only makes more urgent the overcoming of the capitalist bounds. It also enables posing new questions and developing new visions of socialist institutional arrangements, taking into consideration the existing infrastructure. There have already been significant theoretical elaborations on the potential of information and communication technologies for the process of building a communist society, i.e. a society of self-governance by the associated producers. For instance, there have been proposals for planned economies where needs discovery would rely on 'needs profiles', where individuals would register their needs. Taking inspiration from the function of 'baskets' and 'wish lists' in existing digital platforms, these models foresee that individuals would register their needs online through accessing a 'General Catalog' of all existing use-values/products and assigning specific preferences, so as to kickstart the production process (Saros 2014, 171–226).

The problem with such approaches is that needs discovery and social production are not technical or individual issues, despite being predominantly perceived as such from a market perspective, but political issues *par excellence*. These socio-political processes cannot be determined from the standpoint of an individual consumer but only from the standpoint of the conscious individual as a member of society as a whole. In that sense, they necessitate the existence of democratic institutions which guarantee the collective discovery determination of needs (Hahnel 2021; Saros 2014; Phillips and Rozworski 2019). As Alexandros Chrysis puts it, the rational operation of the realm of necessity presupposes weighting processes, plans and decisions of conscious and autonomous personalities (Chrysis 2020, 221). Socialist relations of production cannot rely on depoliticised and technical mechanisms of arriving at the quintessentially political decisions but necessitate the existence of forms of association and collective decision-making and planning.

The digital infrastructure is not an adequate condition for socialism and socialist democracy, but it is a necessary one, and it is a crucial factor which can facilitate the overcoming of what in earlier attempts to build socialism appeared as insurmountable obstacles, such as the contradiction between central planning and workers' democracy. The problem of institutional forms for the management of the economy was crucial in earlier historical attempts of socialist construction in the twentieth century and the problematic solutions applied to this problem—to an extent—determined the process of restoration of capitalism.[10] The contemporary level of technological development, however, has the potential of solving the contradiction between workplace democracy and central planning by establishing a two-way transmission of information between local and centralised decision-making institutions, which might enable the basic units of social organisation to not merely manage production but, at the same time and primarily, be organs for popular self-management in all its aspects (Holman 2018, 136).

5.5 Conclusion

Elaborating on the principles of a socialist constitutionalism is a vast project of extreme significance for the enhancement of the normative appeal of socialism and the transcendence of capitalist relations of production. Such a project would need to engage with several interrelated issues that centre on the fate of principles of liberal constitutionalism in the institutional forms of socialism and the development of new principles for a socialist constitution. Issues like: a socialist conception of right which places emphasis on the notion of social needs and the foundational need of communist society, namely the 'full and free development of the individual'; a dialectical approach to the principle of separation of powers which might involve its supersession at different stages of the revolutionary process; a renewed approach to the system of courts and justice administration which may involve the establishment of peoples' courts or the electivity of judges. Indeed, other contributions to this edited volume touch upon some of these issues.

This chapter contributes to the debate on socialist constitutionalism in two ways. First, by approaching socialist constitutionalism as a 'cogwheel mechanism', where different institutional forms (democratic and technocratic, local and central) are engaged in the process of building the conditions for the full development and ultimate ripening of workers' democracy to the point that it withers away in a communist society. Understanding democracy as a process is crucial for moving beyond the false depiction of institutional forms essential to the building of socialist democracy and communist relations of production (such as the workers' party or institutions of central planning) as bureaucratic and authoritarian.

Behind the grim reality and the dystopian projections of digital society, we find the emancipatory potential of the digital infrastructure. From a socialist standpoint, the realisation of this emancipatory potential presupposes a radical change in the relations of production, as well as in the institutional forms of decision-making, with the capitalist market being replaced by socialist planning for the satisfaction of social needs. Yet, any attempt to argue for a planned economy stumbles upon the well-ingrained critique of socialist planning as bureaucratic and authoritarian. In addition to the aforementioned reconceptualisation of socialist democracy from a socialist constitutionalist standpoint, this chapter highlighted the emancipatory potential of the digital infrastructure for resolving the tension between central planning and socialist democracy. In particular, I showed how the growth of social forces of production provides any new attempt to build a socialist planned economy with unforeseen possibilities for the fast transmission of quality information between local and centralised decision-making institutions, thereby overcoming one of the main obstacles faced in earlier historical attempts at socialist construction.

The ultimate success of new historical attempts to building a communist polity ultimately depends on the main driver of history, namely class struggle. Yet, the ideological struggle conducted in the adverse conditions of the counterrevolutionary epoch we are living in is essential for providing the working classes once again with the necessary vision to contest the extant social condition.

Notes

1 An example is found in the Preamble of the 2019 Constitution of Cuba, which declares Cuba's commitment to never return to capitalism as a regime sustained by the exploitation of man by man.

2 There have been several recent calls for re-focusing attention on 'socialist constitutionalism'. One of the most influential is that put forward by the Law and Political Economy group. Indicatively see Forbath 2020. Governed by the same logic, a social democratic conception of constitutionalism, geared towards tweaking existing institutions while disregarding their historical role and class function, is put forward by Keith Ewing (Ewing 2020).

3 See European Parliament Briefing, *Artificial intelligence, democracy and elections*, (2023).

4 According to Marx, insecurity and fear of unemployment are structural characteristics of the workers' condition in capitalism because of the state of dependence of workers on their wages to sustain themselves and their families. See Marx 1976, 781–794.

5 For a more detailed analysis of the role of new media platforms in countering the tendency of the rate of profit to fall, see Kivotidis 2020.

6 For a full view on the theorem, see Ménard and Bertrand 2016.

7 See the European Commission, *White paper on growth, competitiveness, and employment* (White Paper, COM (93)700, 1993) 123. For a critical analysis of this, see Kivotidis 2018.

8 It is not entirely accurate to call this general law of capitalist production a 'need'. It is certainly not a need in the sense of the German word *Bedürfnis*, which refers to human needs. It may more accurately correspond to the German word *Not*, which refers to necessity and may thus describe the force of necessity of this economic law. We could also make the tentative suggestion of calling this a 'radical need' of the capitalist mode of production, i.e. a need that lies at its root and designates its purpose and without which it ceases to exist.

9 'Classes still remain, and will remain everywhere for years after the proletariat's conquest of power. […] The abolition of classes means, not merely ousting the landowners and the capitalists—that is something we accomplished with comparative ease; it also means abolishing the small commodity producers, and they cannot be ousted, or crushed; we must learn to live with them. They can (and must) be transformed and re-educated only by means of very prolonged, slow, and cautious organisational work. They surround the proletariat on every side with a petty-bourgeois atmosphere, which permeates and corrupts the proletariat, and constantly causes among the proletariat relapses into petty-bourgeois spinelessness, disunity, individualism, and alternating moods of exaltation and dejection' (Lenin 1976d, 44).

10 In the 1960s, the development of productive forces, and cybernetics in particular, provided the means to radically change the managerial system of the Soviet economy and eradicate market methods of calculating labour and consumption. Automated management systems, as well as the automation of design and construction work, were recognised during that period as creating the prospect for a complete revolution in the management of the economy. However, at the historical point when the productive forces reached a level of development that would allow for more efficient

and effective central planning mechanisms and, consequently, for the deepening of socialist relations of production, the Soviet state adopted reforms which reinstated market mechanisms, material incentives and profit as the primary motors of economic production. See Pichorowitz 2005 and Bland 1980.

References

Ajunwa, I., Crawford, K. and Schultz, J. (2017) 'Limitless Worker Surveillance', 105 *California Law Review*, 735–776.

Andrejevic, M. (2012) 'Exploitation in the Data Mine', in C. Fuchs, K. Boersma, A. Albrechtslund and M. Sandoval (eds.), *Internet and Surveillance: The Challenges of Web 2.0 and Social Media*, (Routledge), 71–88.

Avrich, P. (1971) *The Russian Anarchists*, (Princeton University Press).

Barro, R.J. (2000) 'Rule of Law, Democracy, and Economic Performance', in G. O'Driscoll, Jr., K. Holmes and M. Kirkpatrick (eds.), *2000 Index of Economic Freedom*, (The Heritage Foundation), 31–49.

Bartlett, J. (2018) *The People Vs Tech: How the Internet Is Killing Democracy (and How We Save It)*, (Ebury Press).

Bland, B. (1980) *The Restoration of Capitalism in the Soviet Union*, available at https://revolutionarydemocracy.org/archive/BlandRestoration.pdf.

Boucas, D. (2020) 'Theory, Reality, and Possibilities for a Digital/Communicative Socialist Society', in C. Fuchs (ed.), *Communicative Socialism/Digital Socialism*, 18 *tripleC: Communication, Capitalism & Critique*, 48–66.

Chrysis, A. (2020) *Marx of Communism* (in Greek), (Kapsimi).

Coase, R. (1960) 'The Problem of Social Cost', 3 *Journal of Law and Economics*, 1–44.

Cockshott, W.P., Cottrell, A. and Dapprich, J.P. (2022) *Economic Planning in an Age of Climate Crisis*, (Self–published).

Colletti, L. (1969) 'Power and Democracy in Socialist Society', 56 *New Left Review*, 19–26.

De Gregorio, G. (2022) *Digital Constitutionalism in Europe: Reframing Rights and Powers in the Algorithmic Society*, (Cambridge University Press).

De Stefano, V. (2018) 'Negotiating the algorithm': Automation, artificial intelligence and labour protection, ILO Working Paper 246.

Dellis, G. (2021) *An Economic Analysis of Public Law: Demos and Agora*, (Edward Elgar).

Dobb, M. (1970) *Socialist Planning: Some Problems*, (Lawrence and Wishart).

Dukes, R. (2008) 'Constitutionalizing Employment Relations: Sinzheimer, Kahn-Freund, and the Role of Labour Law', 35(3) *Journal of Law and Society*, 341–363.

Ellman, M. (2014) *Socialist Planning*, (Cambridge University Press).

Ewing, K. (2020) 'Socialism and the Constitution', 73(1) *Current Legal Problems*, 27–58.

Feher, F., Heller, A. and Markus, G. (1983) *Dictatorship over Needs*, (Basil Blackwell).

Forbath, W.E. (2020) *Socialism Past and Future: Part I*, available at https://lpeproject.org/blog/socialism-past-and-future-part-i-of-ii/.

Friedman, M. (2002) *Capitalism and Freedom*, (University of Chicago Press).

Fuchs, C. and Mosco, V. (eds.), (2016) *Marx in the Age of Digital Capitalism*, (Brill).

Gilardi, F. (2002) 'Policy Credibility and Delegation to Independent Regulatory Agencies: A Comparative Empirical Analysis', 9(6) *Journal of European Public Policy*, 873–893.

Gluckstein, D. (1995) *The Western Soviets: Workers' Councils versus Parliament 1915–1920*, (Bookmarks).

Golia, A. (2022) 'The Critique of Digital Constitutionalism', *Global Constitutionalism* (published online).

Grunberg, M. (2023) 'The Planning Daemon: Future Desire and Communal Production', 31(4) *Historical Materialism*, 115–159.

Guevara, E. (2001) *Che Guevara Reader: Writings on Politics & Revolution*, (Ocean Press).

Hahnel, R. (2021) 'Democratic Socialist Planning: Back to the Future', 57 *Socialist Register*, 291–309.

Holman, C. (2018) 'The Councils as Ontological Form: Cornelius Castoriadis and the Autonomous Potential of Council Democracy', in J. Muldoon (ed.), *Council Democracy: Towards a Democratic Socialist Politics*, (Routledge), 131–149.

Holmes, S. (1988) 'Precommitment and the Paradox of Democracy', in J. Elster and R. Slagstad (eds.), *Constitutionalism and Democracy*, (Cambridge University Press).

Howard, P. (2016) 'Is Social Media Killing Democracy?', *Oxford Internet Institute*, (15 November 2016), available at https://www.oii.ox.ac.uk/blog/is-social-media-killing-democracy/.

Hughes, C. and Southern, A. (2019) 'The World of Work and the Crisis of Capitalism: Marx and the Fourth Industrial Revolution', 19(1) *Journal of Classical Sociology*, 59–71.

Ilyenkov, E. (1967) 'From the Marxist-Leninist Point of View', in N. Lobkowicz (ed.), *Marx and the Western World*, (University of Notre Dame Press), 391–407.

Kaltsonis, D. (2009) *The Dilemma of Bolivarian Democracy* (in Greek), (Ksifaras).

Kaltsonis, D. (2016) *What Kind of Democracy Do We Need?* (in Greek), (Topos).

Kaltsonis, D. (2021) *The End of Democracy?*, (5 April 2021), available at https://legalform.blog/2021/04/05/the-end-of-democracy-dimitris-kaltsonis/.

Katsaroumpas, I. (2018) 'De-Constitutionalising Collective Labour Rights: The Case of Greece', 47(4) *Industrial Law Journal*, 465–503.

Katsaroumpas, I. (2023) 'United Kingdom: Labour Law and Technological Authoritarianism at Work: Past, Present, and Future', in M. De Vos, G. Anderson and E. Verhulp (eds.), *The Cambridge Handbook of Technological Disruption in Labour and Employment Law*, (Cambridge University Press), 245–267.

Kivotidis, D. (2018) 'The Form and Content of the Greek Crisis Legislation', 29(1) *Law and Critique*, 57–81.

Kivotidis, D. (2024) *The Dialectics of Democracy: Toward a Socialist Constitutionalism*, (Routledge).

Lange, O. (1936) 'On the Economic Theory of Socialism: Part One', 4(1) *The Review of Economic Studies*, 53–71.

Lenin, V.I. (1976a) 'Comments on the Draft "Regulations for the Management of the Nationalised Enterprises"', in *Collected Works: Volume 42*, (Progress Publishers), 96.

Lenin, V.I. (1976b) 'Draft Programme of the R.C.P.(B.)', in *Collected Works: Volume 29*, (Progress Publishers), 97–140.

Lenin, V.I. (1976c) 'First Congress of the Communist International: Theses and Report on Bourgeois Democracy and the Dictatorship of the Proletariat', in *Collected Works: Volume 28*, (Progress Publishers), 453–478.

Lenin, V.I. (1976d) 'Left-Wing Communism: An Infantile Disorder', in *Collected Works: Volume 31*, (Progress Publishers), 17–118.

Lenin, V.I. (1976e) 'The State and Revolution', in *Collected Works: Volume 25*, (Progress Publishers), 385–498.

Lenin, V.I. (1976f) 'The Trade Unions, the Present Situation and Trotsky's Mistakes', in *Collected Works: Volume 32*, (Progress Publishers), 19–42.

Lukacs, G. (1992) *The Process of Democratisation*, (SUNY Press).

Lyon, R. (2006) *Workers' Control and Nationalization*, (6 January 2006), available at https://www.marxist.com/workers-control-nationalization-part1.htm.

Majone, G. (1996) *Temporal Consistency and Policy Credibility: Why Democracies Need Non-Majoritarian Institutions*, Robert Schuman Centre Working Paper RSC No. 95/57.

Marx, K. (1990) *Capital: Volume 1*, (Penguin).

Marx, K. and Engels, F. (2010) 'Manifesto of the Communist Party', in *Marx and Engels Collected Works: Volume 6*, (Lawrence and Wishart), 477–519.

Meltzer, A.H. and Richard, S.F. (1981) 'A Rational Theory of the Size of Government', 89(5) *Journal of Political Economy*, 914–927.

Ménard, C. and Bertrand, E. (2016) *The Elgar Companion to Ronald H. Coase*, (Edward Elgar).

Miliband, R. (1970) 'Lenin's The State and Revolution', 7 *Socialist Register*, 309–319.

Moore, P.V., Akhtar, P. and Upchurch, M. (2018) 'Digitalisation of Work and Resistance', in P.V. Moore, M. Upchurch and X. Whittaker (eds.), *Humans and Machines at Work: Monitoring, Surveillance and Automation in Contemporary Capitalism*, (Palgrave Macmillan), 17–44.

Morozov, E. (2019) 'Digital Socialism? The Calculation Debate in the Age of Big Data', 116/117 *New Left Review*, 33–67.

Muldoon, J. (2022) 'Data-Owning Democracy or Digital Socialism?', 28 (4) *Critical Review of International Social and Political Philosophy*, 570–591.

O'Connell, P. (2021) 'The Poetry of the Future: Law, Marxism, and Social Change', in P. O'Connell and U. Özsu (eds.), *Research Handbook on Law and Marxism*, (Edward Elgar), 458–476.

Pałka, P. (2020) 'Algorithmic Central Planning: Between Efficiency and Freedom', 83 *Law and Contemporary Problems*, 125–149.

Phillips, L. and Rozworski, M. (2019) *People's Republic of Walmart*, (Verso).

Pichorowitz, V.D. (2005) 'E. V. Ilyenkov's Views on the Economic Nature of Socialism in the 1960s' (in Greek), *Communist Review* 5. Available at https://www.komep.gr/m-article/8d3717e2-ff2d-11e9-95d7-3ed1504937da/

Pistor, K. (2020) 'Rule By Data: The End of Markets?', 83 *Law and Contemporary Problems*, 101–124.

Saros, D. (2014) *Information Technology and Socialist Construction: The End of Capital and the Transition to Socialism*, (Routledge), 171–226.

Smith, T. (2025) *A Socialism for the Twenty-First Century: Towards the "Full and Free Development of Every Individual"*, (Brill).

Solik, M. (2017) *A Managed Democracy: Social Media and the Algorithmic Accountability*, available at https://www.academia.edu/37816159/A_managed_democracy_Social_media_and_the_algorithmic_accountability.

Suzor, N. (2018) 'Digital Constitutionalism: Using the Rule of Law to Evaluate the Legitimacy of Governance by Platforms', 4(3) *Social Media + Society*.

Taplin, J. (2018) *Move Fast and Break Things: How Facebook, Google and Amazon Have Cornered Culture and Undermined Democracy*, (Pan).

Tonak, E.A. and Savran, S. (2020) 'The World in Economic Depression: A Marxist Analysis of Crisis', *Tricontinental*, (10 October 2020), available at https://thetricontinental.org/dossier-notebook-4-economic-crisis/.

Wallace, R., Liebman, A., Chaves, L.F. and Wallace, R. (2020) 'COVID-19 and Circuits of Capital', 72(1) *Monthly Review*, available at https://monthlyreview.org/2020/05/01/covid-19-and-circuits-of-capital/.

Waller, M. (1981) *Democratic Centralism: An Historical Commentary*, (Manchester University Press).

Zuboff, S. (2019) *The Age of Surveillance Capitalism: The Fight for a Human Future and the New Frontier of Power*, (Profile Books).

6 Emergencies of the Possible

Exception, Revolution, and the Legal Past

Cosmin Cercel

6.1 Introduction: The Field of Emergency

The starting point for this investigation is the perhaps-now-(in)famous Agambenian observation that the state of exception is 'the reef on which the revolutions of the twentieth century have been shipwrecked' (Agamben 1998 [1995], 14). Regardless of what one might think about the concept of state of exception advanced and defended by Giorgio Agamben (Agamben 1998 [1995], 2005), and indeed about the philosophical luggage that this concept bears – of which the Heideggerian undertones are not to be easily dismissed or cherished (Cercel 2021a, 46; Tacik 2021, 60) – the fact of the matter is that the constitutional and social history of twentieth century have been marked by the experience of exceptional regimes and emergency powers.

If one aims to sketch out the conceptual structure of a possible constitutional framework that goes beyond the horizon of bourgeois constitutionalism and seeks to construct an image – be it even tentative – of what *socialist* constitutionalism might look like, the historical material of the yet active ruins of the twentieth century cannot be eschewed. To it, an understanding of the material legal history of emergency is crucial. Now, if the statement raised by Agamben can easily be read as a blank dismissal of the experience of state socialism as just another footnote in the history of the state of exception (Cercel 2018, 205–207), which in itself is just another name for the foundational modern confusion between *zoe* and *bios* (Zartaloudis 2010, 160), there is little to be done about breaking the biopolitical deadlock, and for an emancipatory, insurgent form of constitutional thought, other than by radically rethinking the very foundational coordinates of our political ontology (Agamben 2005, 87–88; Primera 2018, 130).

This is, of course, not the path I am willing to take here, not only because I believe that is a deadlock,[1] but also because of disciplinarian, epistemological, and political commitments. Even against the grain of the prevailing injunctions of the legal historical field, I do believe that an utopian project of insurgent constitutionalism (Negri 1999, 314) can be rendered operative and that a form of *socialist* constitutionalism – that is a way in which the power of the state can be

DOI: 10.4324/9781032621623-7

tamed, thought through, constrained and used to the benefit of the many – can be brought to the fore. However, if an insurgent constitutionalism is to be possible at all, then it has to grapple with two foundational conceptual and historical burdens, enmeshed in the very legacy of bourgeois constitution: emergency and the constitutional form.

To this end, in what follows, I aim to engage in a critical and historical reading of the intersections between emergency and emancipatory political projects. My endeavour is twofold: first I aim to reflect on the relationship between the intellectual and conceptual construction of emergency as an obscure object of bourgeois constitutionalism, a necessary 'excess' (Tacik 2025, 50) nested within the constitutional form. Second, by examining three moments in the history of this praxis, I aim to provide for a contextual understanding of the legal and material intricacies of emergency in its entanglement with constitutional history as a matter of revolutionary theory and praxis.

A first step I take is by considering a concept of emergency fit for the purposes of this analysis. From the outset, it is important to note that a distinction between state of exception and emergency is useful insofar as it situates the whole horizon of the matter at hand: is an emergency a temporarily bound suspension of legality, or a somewhat limited shortcut from procedural and institutional constraints, subjected to rules of transparency and judicial oversight? Or is it something deeper, a more direct suspension of the constitutional process, or of the legal order that retains something of the original sovereign excess of laying down the law or the constitution? In other words, do we follow the liberal dogma or Agambenian–Schmittian obscurantism? To this, the answer should be a resolute neither.

The fact that 'emergency' has been described within liberal bourgeois doctrine as a limited, temporarily bound, subjected to the scrutiny of the courts, and ultimately marginal phenomenon (Rossiter 1948; Ferejohn and Pasquino 2004; Gross and Ni Aolain 2006) has to do more to myth rather than historical truth. Not only does liberal constitutionalism – understood here broadly as an uneasy articulation of separation of powers, *Rechtsstaat* or checks and balances and fundamental rights (Sajó and Uitz 2017, 25–29) – an ambiguous relationship to say the least with emergency powers and exceptional regimes, but also it historically developed through them and was moulded by them. It would be useful here to recall not only the revolutionary moments in European or US history, but also those of restauration and social turmoil. This historical dynamic has obscured much of the actual material operation of the law and has distorted our understanding of constitutionalism, presenting it as necessarily a practice able to contain the material power of the organised state (Sajó and Uitz 2017, 3) a question which could fall under the label of constitutional ideology and to whose effects on legal scholarship and practice still require further consideration.

Ultimately, an astute and honest legal history of liberal constitutionalism in the centre and periphery abounds moments of crisis, suspension of fundamental rights, overriding of separation of powers principle and legal certainty (Fraser 2012; Skinner 2022a, 2022b; Neocleous 2014). To most of these, the reaction of the constitutional canon was at most a shudder of shoulders, rather that an answer able to integrate the way in which emergency has actually shaped and re-written constitutional provisions or constitutional orders. In this sense, the most important insights into the operation of the legal machinery came from its critics. As Mark Neocleous aptly observed, emergency powers are not a marginalia to the constitution or an outside of liberalism, they are actually an organic part of its operation: 'far from being outside the rule of law, emergency powers emerge from within it' (Neocleous 2006, 207), almost inasmuch as the constituted polity is the result of pacification (Neocleous 2014, 34). These elements of liberal constitutional ideology appear, thus, to be fundamentally built upon a specific caesura, an operation that expunges from the ambit of constitutional knowledge, from the outset, the possibility that constitutional arrangements are altered through emergency (Ferejohn and Pasquino 2004, 211; Albert and Roznai 2021). As Alan Greene, aptly remarked with regards to contemporary emergencies, permanent states of emergency today, (…) are potentially transformative but this transformative dimension is never expressly acknowledged' (Greene 2018, 212).

The operation of this closure of the legal mind runs, of course, deep in the intellectual history of the constitutional and jurisprudential enterprise and one can find countless examples and arguments in the defence of a constitutional thought grafted on a science of norms that is built on the postulation of an identity thesis (Kelsen 1992 [1934], 100). In Hans Kelsen's words, 'the state … is a legal system' and 'in situations of "national emergency"', the state's action 'cannot (…) go against the statute' (Kelsen 1992, 100). Yet, nonetheless, this position is not only ideological in the sense that it hides the historical reality of a rather murkier experience of suspensions of constitutional protections, process or constitutional order. It is, itself, a political stand, operative at the level of the politics of jurisprudence that sustains the bourgeois state apparatus.

6.2 Beyond 'Emergency': Constitutional Form, Exception, and History

This brings us to the postulation of the existence of a specifically bourgeois understanding of emergency as being essentially split between a normative layer that is publicly ostensible, and a praxis that keeps on being pushed into the ambit of various official bodies. In legalese, that is the split between constitutional provisions and adjudication and judicial practice as well as that of the praxis of various administrative bodies of the executive branch. The relationship between the two is not an easy one, and certainly not reducible to the crude distinction between the law in books and law in action (Pound 1910), or that between ideology as superstructure and material basis (Marx 1987 [1859]). Rather, it is an ideological tension between ideological state apparatuses (Althusser 1976, 93) functioning under the ambit of the law. As Premyslaw Tacik rightly observed with regards to legal liberalism,

> The exception is neither stable nor eternal; it does not have a firmly ontological or metaphysical status. It is rather permanently produced and reproduced by allocating exceptionality in particular loci. In turn, exceptionality can be seen as a quantum of energy that each legal system contains, which can be differently spread between various incarnations of 'exceptional' or 'normal' institutions and acts.
>
> (Tacik 2025, 50)

Nonetheless, regardless of these inner tensions, something like a concept of emergency, split between theory and praxis is articulated and possible to be identified in the historical development of constitutionally bounded polities, regardless of doctrinal musings, judicial attempts to covering its operation or attempts of covering its material effects. Now, if this concept of emergency is marked by this particular split between constitutional officialdom and executive practice, the other concept of exception reducing the operation to constitutional law to an entirely fluid structure, is also the result of a distinct political stand. The scholarship discussing exception and owing to Agamben's rendition of Schmitt's *Ausnahmezustand* (Agamben 1998, 2005; Schmitt 1985 [1922]) has done a lot in pointing towards the essentially mythical position of the liberal bourgeois understanding of emergency, insofar as 'the locus of exceptionality (…) is the legal institutional apparatus itself' (Fusco 2025, 38).

I have discussed elsewhere the need to distinguish between exception and emergency and the necessity for grounding historically the process through which bourgeois constitutions are effectively displaced by practices of emergency (Cercel 2021a). The crux of the distinction hinges upon the bounded character of emergency, that the concept of exception thoroughly negates. As Schmitt wrote, 'the exception is to be understood to refer to a general concept in the theory of the state, and not merely to a construct applied to any emergency decree or state of siege' (Schmitt 1985 [1922], 5). However, by the same gesture, both Agambenian and Schmittian renditions, move too fast, albeit in politically different directions, both ending up in different types of deadlocks that should be resisted intellectually and politically. For Schmitt the exception, as a true reality of the law, is the way of reconstructing a true form of authority that can introduce into the realm of the social the reactionary imagined postulates of a natural order of things: it is a way of instituting normalcy, insofar as 'for a legal order to make sense, a normal situation must exist, and he is sovereign who definitely decides whether this normal situation actually exists' (Schmitt 1985 [1922], 13).

For Agamben, the project started by revealing the ubiquity of the exception is that of an undoing of the essentially repressive power of the law that limits life in its structures and subsequently keeps on producing the bare life that can be dispensed with. As an absolute legal utopia (Johansen 2020), it aims at the possibility of rendering the killing machinery of the exception inoperative (Agamben 2005, 123). But both accounts fail to take material history seriously. Granted, they do acknowledge its existence, but in negative. For the reactionary later to be Nazi jurist, the whole point of exception is to be able to do away with the threat of revolution and most importantly for our times, with the legacy of French revolution and revolutionary thought (Schmitt 2013 [1921], 142–143; 178–179). In his adoption of Cortès, 'in the face of radical evil the only solution is dictatorship' (Schmitt 2005 [1922], 66). The exception, as the core of legality, is thus the locus for grounding authority and bringing about normalcy, in effectively reversing history.

For Agamben, the exception whilst operative historically, it is the political ontological presupposition of modernity, and therefore an attempt to overcoming it should go through a rethinking of the very coordinates of politics (Whyte 2013) – perhaps very much in line with an eternal deferral of its messianic potential (Johansen 2021, 86). I will leave aside a criticism of the idealistic roots of this politics of addressing this version of the 'exception', but it is perhaps worth mentioning to which extent it is dependant on a conflation between theological and political as 'the modern State inherits both aspects of the theological machine of the government of the world' (Agamben 2011, 143), that seems to command therefore the strategies for its overcoming within the sphere of messianic politics and intellectual resistance (Fusco 2023; Björk and Johansen 2025; Fusco 2025, 167).

To wrap up, I haste to underline the division between emergency and exception, and to label at least provisionally the three conflicting concepts as liberal, reactionary, and anarchist. What I aim to is to propose a concept of emergency that does not yield to the ideological commitments of liberal constitutionalism and is apt to describe emergency as thoroughly transformative without falling within the idealism or indeed obscurantism of the 'exception'. Being able to understand emergency as a concept grounded in a material history of practices that gain legal relevance is perhaps the first step in sketching even tentatively the coordinates of a socialist constitutionalism.

6.3 Emergency between Reaction and Revolution

Coming to this point, it is perhaps serviceable to trace the theoretical attempts of understanding emergency within the Marxist field. There is, of course, a thorough, even if at times somewhat bird-eye view, Marxian reflection on dictatorial practices of the bourgeois state (Marx 1978 [1850], 1979 [1852], 1986 [1871]). There is also a rather clear understanding of what a transitional regime under the label of the dictatorship of the proletariat might entail, both within the thought of Lenin and his followers (Lenin 1974 [1917], 1974 [1918]; Trotsky 2007 [1920]).

There is, alas, also the theory and practice of Stalinism and, of course, the constitutional history of the other forms of degenerated worker's states (Cercel 2018; Mańko 2020), obscuring and complicating further the entanglement between state power, revolutionary praxis, and political commitments.

Each of these encounters between Marxism and emergency powers needs to be documented and understood in its own context and intellectual horizon. They do resist being read as a systematic theory of dictatorship – being it one of the bourgeoisie or of the proletariat. More serious attempts of developing a Marxist theory of dictatorship and authoritarian state – such as Poulantzas', enmesh the question of emergency in a theoretical attempt to grasp the dynamics of bourgeois state in its normal and pathological, that is authoritarian form (Poulantzas 2000 [1978]). This step is salutary and important, by providing us with the tools for understanding how bourgeois reactions to political crisis are determining shifts in the machinery of the state. However, what remains a blind spot is the nature of these mechanisms, that of the minute, practical, instrumental tools at the threshold between formalised law and executive orders or policies that articulate emergency. This is not a matter of hair splitting, but a rather important utopian question about what to do with emergency powers within a socialist constitutional framework. Should emergency powers be accommodated constitutionally? Should they be simply equivocally recognised? Should they be completely and explicitly banned?

Explaining that emergency regulations have a basis in the class structured society and that they can be and are tools of oppression is an important first step in that direction. However, too abstract and general categories lend themselves to obscuring the contingency of the historical forces at play in situations of crisis. Empirical historical research not guided by theoretical framework able to integrate individual declarations of emergency and uses of these powers will probably be able to do even less in terms of serving of a guide for a socialist understanding of emergency.

Now, such a theoretical framework cannot dispense with at least pointing towards, be it even in negative, a theory of law and a theory of rights. Indeed, such a position should be understood as being integrated in a specific constitutional theory and discussed alongside broader questions of theory, political strategy or political commitment in relation to a socialist vision of constitutional rights. On this last point, I hasten to acknowledge that on the long run, too much confidence in law and its powers can derail revolutionary projects under historical strains marked by nationalist discourse and ideological confusion (Cercel 2018, 200–201). I am, of course, not going to be able to provide anything akin to a socialist constitutional theory here. However, I would like to raise the importance of taking into account the material history of emergency in relation to law and socialist projects of emancipation: the fact that emergency has a tendency to stick (Bishai 2020), and also to thwart political processes (Cercel 2018, 206), in the same manner in which law as such, as an ideology, or as a form, is able to undermine revolutionary commitments from within (Cercel 2018, 205). I therefore consider that these predicaments should be read against the background of an existing material constitutional agreement of sorts that places at least an inclusive community endowed with social rights at its core.

In this sense, it is useful then to recall the ambivalence with which Marx credited to the authoritarian measures of the bourgeoisie in its uses of emergency powers. For instance, when criticising the drafters of the constitution of the 2nd French Republic in building their new normative order on the trail of blood left after the June Days, he astutely pointed towards how constitutional law followed the reality of a constitutional and constitutive practice: in order for the bourgeois constitution to be brought to life, the reprisal of the proletarian uprising was necessary. In Marx's words, '[t]he emancipation of the workers—even as a phrase—became an unbearable danger to the new republic, for it was a standing protest against the restoration of credit, which rests on undisturbed and untroubled recognition of the existing economic class relations' (Marx 1978 [1850], 62). It should be noted that at the very moment when general Cavaignac – former governor general of Algeria – was repressing the workers in Paris,[2] the Constitutional Assembly was debating the drafts of the Constitution, expressing a clear connection between exceptional powers and constitutional order:

> the Constituent Assembly resembled the Chilean official who wanted to regulate property relations in land more firmly by a cadastral survey just at the moment when subterranean rumblings announced the volcanic eruption that was to hurl away the land from under his very feet. While in theory it accurately marked off the forms in which the rule of the bourgeoisie found republican expression, in reality it held its own only by the abolition of all formulas, by force sans phrase [without any exceptions], by the *state of siege*.
> (Marx 1978 [1850], 77)

This very inconsistency of the constitutional framework – reflecting the very inconsistency of the bourgeois and aristocratic elements of the French ruling class of 1848 enabled its own cynical exploitation by the president Louis Bonaparte soon to become Napoleon III: 'each paragraph of the Constitution contains its own antithesis, its own Upper and Lower House, namely, freedom in the general phrase, abrogation of freedom in the marginal note'(Marx 1979 [1852], 115). The brutal repression instituted by Bonaparte in the wake of the Coup d'état of December 1852 was that of an exceptional regime (Decree No. 721 of 8–10 December 1851) originating in the consensus over general Cavaignac quelling the proletarian uprising (Fourtanier 1849). However, for Marx, the potential of exceptional authoritarian rule, is not only about unfettered authoritarianism, but also one of the possibilities of unifying and transforming the society, it changed 'the motley pattern of conflicting medieval plenary powers into the regulated plan of a state authority whose work is divided and centralised as in a factory' (Marx 1979

[1852], 185) and in this way, strengthened the central government. Emergency is both an enabler of authoritarianism but, at the same time, can transform society and break the old relations of production, and arguably in the right hands could bring about a revolutionary transformation (Lenin 1974 [1917], 399).

The dictatorship of the proletariat – in its amphiboly as an overstretching of the state aimed at bringing its own destruction, and as a temporary material process through which the relations of production are replaced – is, of course, the crux for understanding the emancipatory potential of emergency. Yet, its practice, and especially the Stalinist turn decreeing precisely the end of revolutionary transformation, as a matter of law and less of material changes has obscured and effectively derailed the core of this process. It is precisely at this threshold in both intellectual history of constitutional thought and practice, that an important, albeit confused distinction between progressive emergency and reactionary emergency was brought about by Evgeny Pashukanis (Pashukanis 2025 [1927]).

We owe the focus on this distinction to the English translation recently published in Law and Critique to a speech delivered by Pashukanis in 1927 (Shoikhedbrod and Khachaturian 2025). In a nutshell, the speech offers a rather traditional doctrinal analysis of emergency legislation in effect at that time across Europe, at a time when the first wave of fascist takeover was taking place, and when bourgeois and landowners' reaction was getting official staple under a flurry of emergency measures (Barbusse 1926; Cercel 2024). The context is important, not only with regards to marking the threshold in Soviet jurisprudence, practice and politics between Leninist revolutionary politics and towards the Stalinist turn (Shoikhedbrod and Khachaturian 2025), but also in relation to the end of the European Civil War (Traverso 2017) and the revolutionary attempts across Europe in the wake of WW1 in establishing revolutionary governments (Lompar 2024; Skinner 2019). In this sense, the speech takes stock of the bourgeois and landowner's dictatorial measures in organising repression against the proletariat.

One needs to keep in mind to which extent by that time, extraordinary measures have been a marker of reactionary politics, starting at least with the response of aristocratic governments to the 1848 revolutions. There was, by that time, a strong argument in considering emergency measures as being enmeshed with a history of repressive practices directed against the proletariat and, at times, against the progressive elements of the bourgeoisie. Read against this background, the distinction Pashukanis operates is important, not in the way in which it is resolved, and the criteria it proposes, but as a measure or of an attempt of reclaiming a progressive element in the suspension of the constitutional order for the purposes of emancipatory revolutionary politics. In this sense, the crux of the argument lies with the fact of recuperating to the legal and revolutionary practices of proletarian government, the tools that have been used historically against it. The short historical examples he provides – the English Civil Wars of seventeenth century, the French Revolution and the American Civil war – alongside the Soviet Union and the rising anticolonial movement of his time, offer a level of continuity between the struggles of a rising bourgeoisie against the aristocracy and that of the proletariat against the bourgeois rule. The criterion for distinguishing between reactionary emergencies and the progressive ones is unsurprisingly the class character (Pashukanis 2025 [1927]). As he writes:

> the rising bourgeoisie issued these exceptional [emergency] laws against a reactionary class, namely, the feudal aristocracy and slave holders. These exceptional [emergency] laws are aimed at breaking down the resistance of reactionary classes and clearing the path for new and progressive social forms [...] However, when such laws are applied by imperialist countries with a view to staving off the inevitable collapse of capitalism, they are retrograde and reactionary, for then these laws are directed against the most progressive of all classes in present day society, namely, the proletariat. In such a case these laws serve only to preserve the privileges of a small capitalist group.

Now, while entirely historically accurate, this criterion is just the beginning for thinking and assessing the insurgent potential of emergency. In a purely political meaning, it does not offer more than an instrumental character: if it is the proletariat that uses emergency in its own interests, or the bourgeoisie in order to curb the working of reactionary classes, then it is progressive. If it is the bourgeoisie or the aristocracy that aim at crushing the proletariat, then it is reactionary. It seems to me that Pashukanis was able to make better jurisprudential arguments than this when he was pointing towards law's efficacy as an objective social relation (Pashukanis 1951 [1924], 167). Rather, at this particular junction, one can glimpse an echo of what Stalinist jurisprudence of the Vyshinsky kind will look like (Vyshinsky 1961).

However, the distinction raised is indeed consequential: it enables us to think about the possibility of emergency not only as a tool in the hand of bourgeoisie or of the landowners, of the 'bayonets turned against the people' (Marx 1979 [1852]), but as an instrument in the service of revolutionary politics. As a matter of constitutional theory, this position is consistent with Lenin's pre-revolutionary intuitions on the progressive character of rights in their protection granted to the workers (Lenin 1972 [1895]), as well as with the progressive nature of the constitutional form as a useful tool for laying down the necessary material foundations for mass mobilisation and building a revolutionary movement under the conditions of reactionary hegemony. As Lenin wrote in the wake of the 1905 revolution,

> What do the police and officials want? The absolute monarchy. What do the most liberal of the bourgeois (...) want? The constitutional monarchy. What do the class-conscious workers (...) want? The democratic republic.
>
> (Lenin 1962 [1905], 557)

In this sense, Pashukanis' distinction is able to refine further the notion of the dictatorship of the proletariat by addressing directly the nature of the legal tools of its implementation and of the nature of the legal framework at work. At the same time, it does come dangerously close to the idea of a 'socialist legality' that contradicts at least partially the core of Pashukanis' theory of the legal form as an essentially capitalist notion grafted on the reality of a commodity-based society (Pashukanis 1951 [1924], 127). As he wrote, 'a society which according to the condition of its production forces is constrained to preserve an equivalency between expenditures of labour and compensation … will be constrained to preserve also the form of law' (Pashukanis 1951 [1924], 124). Furthermore, it seems to pave the way in which to understand jurisprudentially the legal minutiae of the state apparatus, while at the same time – most likely do to the limitations of the genre – eschewing the more structural question of the relation between state power, legality, and constitutional law and constraints.

I do not want to append or engage in a further analysis of Pashukanis' legal theory, yet it is useful to recall the ways in which Pashukanis disregarded public law and dismissed constitutional thinking as simply ideology, as crude distortion of reality that does not have the grounding of the legal form in real social and economic processes, but effectively lives in the minds of the jurists: 'the idea of unconditional obedience to an external, norm-establishing authority has nothing in common with the legal form' (Pashukanis 1951 [1924], 154).

6.4 Insurgent Emergencies: A Historical Trajectory

If the speech is perhaps a step back from the theory of the legal form, it is a step taken in the right direction, precisely as a gesture of accommodating a reflection on state power under the guise of formal law. If this is the case, a reflection on how bourgeois public law operates at its different layers – constitution, statutory provisions, judicial and administrative practice – in its attempt of rationalising the material, ultimately military power, 'of the special bodies of armed men' (Lenin 1974 [1917], 393), could be the start of a historical reflection of the constitutional form. Such a concept of constitutional form would ground itself, unlike the 'formal' dimension of private law, not in a commodity theory of law, but would necessarily need to take into consideration the element of coercion and that of organised military power. While it would enable perhaps a better understanding of the operation of bourgeois constitutionalism, precisely by integrating into its ambit what it had traditionally and positively tried to hide as an other scene of its operation (Cercel 2021a, 53), such a concept would not be able to tell us much about the particular place of emergency into a socialist constitutional framework.

Rather, only a thorough historical analysis of forms of insurgent constitutionalism in modern context would enable us to think what would be the place of the emergency dispositive. Yet as for any other constitutional concept, their test would be that of concrete historical contexts, being to be decided and balanced only against political realities. There are however three fundamental moments that one could consider in relation to progressive uses of emergency that could act at least as a sketch guideline for what a revolutionary emergency would look like within a socialist constitutional framework. We can think of the French Revolution, the Paris Commune, and, of course, the October revolution. However, these moments can and should be complemented by a global constitutional history that waits to be written – one of the ephemeral political projects in the wake of WW1, of anticolonial struggles and the progressive political projects across the world: including both states, or zones of decolonisation. Within this tradition, a special place is occupied as mentioned earlier by the particular entrenchment of emergency within the structure of the Soviet Union, and the postwar socialist states, as perhaps experiences of a particular failure of revolutionary practice that fell prey to the traps of militarism and nationalism turning slowly but steadily in ethnonational projects.

If we consider the role of emergency within the context of the French revolution for the particular purposes of this investigation – necessarily implying a bird-eye view – the crux of the question is the moment of the so-called Terror. A specific temporality can be devised constitutionally between the abolition of feudal titles in August 1789, the declaration of the republic in September 1792 and from that moment on to the Thermidorian turn and the arrest of Robespierre in July 1794. While the first period is that of revolutionary turmoil within an ambiguous constitutional framework that was moving from royal absolutism to constitutional monarchy, the second one is what can be termed as a continual revolutionary emergency.

First, the emergency is gradually included within the ambit of the legal and constitutional mechanisms, but in Pashukanis parlance, it would be precisely an example of reactionary emergency, insofar as we are dealing with martial law directed against the peasant uprisings and with the first iteration of the state of siege. In the words of Mirabeau aptly describing the purpose of the martial law legislation of 1789, 'the people calls for bread and the government answers with gunshots' (Discussion, 475). It is perhaps no surprise that it found itself at the core of the Champ de Mars massacre, bringing the downfall of the project of constitutional monarchy, as the National Guard shot the representatives of the popular front of Cordeliers. For its part, the state of siege, safely hidden within the pages of a statute concerning military fortifications in wartime, was to become the paradigm of the repression through nineteenth century across the globe, being slowly extended from fortifications properly being under military siege, to any type of territory facing unrest and passing the test of time, while being efficient, with all modifications, in France until 1958 when brought to an arguably stricter constitutional oversight.

Once the republic being declared, already in the midst of the War of the First Coalition, there was clearly a time of turmoil, and the revolutionary government resorted to all possible instruments of emergency in its panoply from martial law, declaration of 'rebellion', or legal or illegal 'state of siege'. Within this context the *Comité de Salut Public*, emergency had barely any legal grounding – it was rather the work of the committee that sanctioned militarised repression through its own means in either Vendée, Ancenis and Noirmoutier, through orders that extended beyond the limits of the law the uses of the states of siege outside fortifications (Le Gal 2014). The model, simply put, was that of a civilian body that oversaw military operations directed against internal threats, mainly of civilian nature. In a sense, it was the very overturn of the logic of bourgeois emergency that was meant to be limited spatially and statutorily. The emergency is that of a fictitious state of siege that operates under and through the functioning of an emergency specific committee, that is in itself an embodiment of a 'permanent state of emergency'. Perhaps what is useful to note here is that the declaration of the republic and the 'terror' as a reaction to foreign intervention, internal strife (of either left or right), displaced the legal safeguards and, to some extent, changed the logic of the emergency and exception by placing it in a specifical institutional body exercising a plenitude of state power as an arm of the legislative.

Within the context of the Commune of Paris of 1871, the debate over the institution of a *Comité de salut public* is telling for the theoretical aims of such a debate over emergency powers within a revolutionary context. At that time, the short-lived Commune found itself within the midst of a civil war against the official government retreated in Versailles, while parts of France were under formal German military occupation following the jingoist adventure of Napoléon III. The point of the debate within the Council of the Commune, the representative body of the Commune functioning on an imperative mandate based on direct elections, was whether the Commune should institute such a committee overseeing all matters of public safety, that would be designed to exercise 'the most extensive powers over all the commissions' (*Les 31 Séances* 1871, 116), in order to respond to the 'gravity of the circumstances' (*Les 31 Séances* 1871, 116). Proposed by Jules Miot, a socialist and member of the First International, the draft decree aimed to address what was perceived as a lack of *efficacy* – and I would stress the Kelsenian undertones (Kelsen, 99–100) – of the decrees of the Commune. In the words of Jean-Jacques Pillot, close to Blanquism, 'all too often are the decrees of the commune a mere dead letter' (*Les 31 Séances* 1871, 137), while the dire situation called for swift action. As Miot spoke, 'there is a need for a committee who will provide a new impulse to the defence and has the courage, if necessary, to make the heads of the traitors fall' (*Les 31 Séances* 1871, 137).

On the side of the defenders of the project, Léo Melliet, another militant of the First International, demanded that such a committee be formed 'so as to centralise all powers' (*Les 31 Séances* 1871, 118). The position of those opposing is equally worth noting, insofar as the arguments advanced are about the political nature of the commune, and the danger that dictatorial powers put to such a democratic endeavour. While some arguments can be probably dismissed as idealist legalism – insofar as they call for clear delimitations between powers within the remit of the executive committee and the proposed committee for public safety (*Les 31 Séances* 1871, 120–121), and this while the National Guard of the Commune was fighting a siege from the Regulars of the Versailles government – others raise important questions about how such a committee can overturn the whole political gains in terms of direct democracy and constitutive power. For François-Charles Ostyn, Belgian anarchist member of the Commune, such a committee 'is disguised royal power' (*Les 31 Séances 1871*, 136), a formula echoed by citizen Babyck, a nurse member of the Council, who saw it as a 'return to the errors of monarchy' (*Les 31 Séances 1871*, 136). A straightforward and somewhat principled opposition to the creation of the committee was considering this a move beyond the imperative mandate and an usurpation of popular sovereignty (*Les 31 Séances 1871*, 140). This is indeed a recurring theme on the side of the opposition, considering that such a committee was against the social principles of the Commune and in dissonance with its democratic character, as it was essentially a dictatorial institution (*Les 31 Séances 1871*, 145).

A peculiar, yet interesting opposition was uttered by French realist painter Gustave Courbet, another member of the committee. In his position, he insisted that all the names designating concepts or institutional bodies that referred back to previous revolutionary experiences should be formally avoided: 'the titles: Public Safety, Montagnards, Girondins, Jacobins, etc., etc., cannot be used in this republican socialist movement' (*Les 31 Séances 1871*, 144). This opposition, based arguably on his realist position, but also on a radical understanding of the historical contingency of the situation was expressed in almost historical materialist terms: 'let's use those terms that our revolution suggests' (*Les 31 Séances 1871*, 144). I do not think it is in any way jurisprudentially meaningful to take sides in this debate. It is important to note that the proposal has passed and the Committee was formed, yet its activity was not able to bring the victory over the forces of the reaction. It might be true that as a matter of historical position the debate was just another one in a long series of discussions and utopian experiments. It is yet important as a historical document not that much in the debates between 'authoritarians' or 'democrats', but as a plurality of positions on what to do within the depth of a revolutionary catastrophe – it was less about emergency measures, as it was more about the political positioning on the path to be taken.

It would be a daunting task to compress the minute and rich historical experience of the October revolution between October 1917 and July 1918 under a label such as constitutional uncertainty or revolutionary government. The truth of the matter is that before the July Constitution of the RSRFR, official power rested with a fragmented plurality of bodies – local Soviets, the Sovnarkom, the All Russian Congress of Soviets, the Cheka, Military Soviets and at various degrees the Red Army, revolutionary tribunals. Thinking in terms of emergency in this particular context is perhaps of no serious constitutional meaning unless one would want to make a point about the essentially fragmented and plural sources of an insurgent revolutionary legality and officialdom. Yet, once the revolution articulated its own constitutional discourse – albeit in a resolutely messianic way that aimed to put an end to exploitation and autocracy – the question resurfaces. This is, of course, within a context of a civil war and foreign intervention in support of the Whites, while the territorial application of the constitution was under serious limitations. It is also, within a purely insurgent form of constitutionalism, which in many respects was a first step from within a specific historical experience marked by a reverence of a notion of legality grounded in either natural law or some form of higher morality: the constitution is grounded in the revolution itself and its political outcomes. The derailment of the revolutionary thrust by emergency powers might be an easy target, one that has been brandished and used by either anti-communist historiography or trotstkyism. But one should be careful about how this argument is deployed and in relation to which moment of the revolutionary transformation. While by the end of the Civil War, as Sheila Fitzpatrick observed, there were already signs of the Central Committee or the Politburo usurping state powers in the amphiboly between state and party (Fitzpatrick 2001, 88), the question needs to be understood within the unfolding of the revolutionary situation and the role that the Bolsheviks held within the radical rupture with Tsarist autocracy.

Three points raised by Lenin in relation to the excess and authority consubstantial to war communism should render clearer to which extent emergency was interwoven to the revolutionary situation marked by Civil War and imperialist encirclement, and what were the inner guidelines of this type of insurgent constitutional thinking. In response to the critique raised by Kautsky with regards to the dictatorship of the proletariat cutting away with parliamentary traditions of democracy the answer, written in the echo of the war, was blunt: 'The exploiter and the exploited cannot be equal' (Lenin 1974 [1918a], 252). By moving outside the formal scene sanctioned by history, into the unknown of building a proletarian state, the revolution has rendered bourgeois concepts and standards inoperative. Formal equality and constitutional rights, as well as matters of expediency are no longer to be understood through the normative lenses of liberal legality, but as concepts and normative statements contingent upon the class character of the new state brought about by the revolution (Lenin 1974 [1918b], 248). In other words, what matters as a guide or a standard is class position, 'presenting the question from the point of view of the oppressed classes' (Lenin 1974 [1918b], 248). Rebuilding constitutional discourse goes also hand in hand with shaping the administration of justice by the revolutionary tribunals.

From an internal perspective, their role is to be 'rapid and mercilessly severe in dealing with counter-revolutionaries, hooligans, idlers and disorganisers' (Lenin 1974 [1918b], 219). There is no question for getting caught within the cobweb of formal liberal legality under the conditions of class war. In a letter addressed to Kursky, the minister of Justice, Lenin emphasises the specific type of relation between the emerging legality and repression aimed at circumscribing the revolutionary action:

> The courts must not ban terror—to promise that would be deception or self-deception—but must formulate the motives underlying it, legalise it as a principle, plainly, without any make-believe or embellishment. It must be formulated in the broadest possible manner, for *only revolutionary law and revolutionary conscience can* more or less widely *determine the limits* within which it should be applied.
>
> (Lenin 1973 [1922b], 358; emphasis added)

6.5 Conclusion: Emergency and the Need for a Historical Materialist Legal History

If we are to take stock of these three formative moments of revolutionary emergency, there is certainly hard to find an overarching principle, yet if we read them diachronically we can grasp a certain trajectory of continuity. This moves from an improvisational construction, a sort of bricolage, building on older and reactionary forms towards integrating a sense of historical contingency that attains a full position within Lenin's time. The French revolution did not find an impediment in mixing martial law, royal ordinances harking back to 1670, or military doctrines in supporting the operation of the *Comité de Salut Public*. It also went beyond legality in its actions, as a matter of necessity. It was deposed by a return to some form of bourgeois legality that itself aimed to limit the civilian control over military matters. The Directorate, as another form of emergency, led by general Barras, who lead the troops of the Convention in arresting Robespierre, is the clear image of a return of emergency to its traditional forms: under a state of siege it is the military who take over civilian authority and not the other way around (Simonin 2008, 266).

The Commune was aware not only of the excesses of the *Comité*, but also of the danger emergency – or dictatorship, understood as a technical institution – posed to democratic rule and its possibility of altering the revolutionary project. On the other hand, it was also aware of the need for a centralisation of power in the face of the onslaught. Even if Marx had readers among the members of the Commune and saw in it a first proletarian state, the role of Marxism in its practice was rather limited. This is no longer the case for the October revolution which builds on the historical experience of previous revolutions, learns from previous failures of workers uprsings and engages in a specific attempt to link between Marxist theory and political practice. It is in this sense, that Lenin's position is important in moving away from a type of constitutional or jurisprudential horizon indebted to past forms. Not only as a trained lawyer was Lenin aware of the traps that such a move would put on revolutionary action, but his *State and Revolution* as well as his political work captures an important historical shift.

Under the conditions of a proletarian revolution that revendicates from Marx, the old categories can no longer function; sure, there is a dictatorship of the proletariat, but this is 'not strictly a state'. Emergency, then, needs to be understood within the horizon of the class war able to overcome imperial powers and that aims to transform the social material basis that renders it possible (Lukács 2009 [1924], 57). It should be understood in relation to its effective material force and less in relation to a guiding legal, constitutional or jurisprudential principle that would be able to limit its institution and operation.

This brings us to the provisional conclusion of this chapter which should be as succinct as possible. First, a theoretical framework for socialist constitutionalism cannot eschew the question of emergency. In formulating a position on emergency, a proper concept needs to be wrested from either liberal dogmas or reactionary and idealist positions. In doing so, Pashukanis distinction between progressive emergencies and reactionary ones is a useful contribution enabling us to think about emergency in the hands of an emancipatory project. The short historical excursus I have engaged in, should be able to at least point towards the fact that there is certainly not an easy or clear principle that could guide us in a satisfactory manner insofar as emergency read through historical materialist lenses is ultimately a matter of political commitment at wrest with material conditions. It is, in an eminent way, an illustration of how normative layers struggle to contain historically determined social forces. Lenin's position clearly alludes to this predicament – yet, there is a glimpse of a normative statement grasped in his use of 'revolutionary conscience'.

After the Stalinist purges, the failure of really (in)existing socialism, after the collapse of the Soviet Union, at a time when we are facing the resurgence of fascism, we are perhaps lacking that optimism and the political strength that Bolsheviks retained even at the times of full encirclement. The historical trajectory opened in October revolution was marked by a derailment of its emancipatory potential through emergency powers: the purges and Stalinism were a clear embodiment of how the constitutional form, in its ambivalence between written promises and hidden practices of repression survived. Martial law was turned against the workers in Poland, and the ethnonational Romania under Ceausescu ended in a state of emergency declared against the workers.

As Alain Badiou observed, 'if political subjectivity is not able to sustain itself by itself, in its thinking and in its act, by the singularity of its trajectory …, then it does not have any other referent than the state' (Badiou 1998, 24). A caveat might then be useful in relation to how emergency, once embedded within constitutional discourse is able to threaten political subjectivity, by tying emancipation to the power of the state, to territorialise its potential. The obscure disaster of socialism whose traces are now apparent in renewed

Russian imperialism are also part of this trajectory of emergency. Yet, this historical trajectory is not *fate*, and emergency need not be the necessary reef shipwrecking revolutions.

If we try to wrest from this materiality of practice a normative position, perhaps, Lenin's notion of the *position of the oppressed* would be of use, side by side with the concept of necessity – *Notrecht.* As Dimitrios Kivotidis aptly observed,

> Hegel's *Notrecht* is the 'right ofextreme need' of those who risk starving to death; not only do they have the right to steal the bread that will keep them alive, but the 'absolute right' to transgress the one-sided right of property, that legal norm which condemns theft. In the same manner, the exploited and the oppressed can invoke their 'right of need', the 'real state of necessity', to question not only the exceptional form which infringes upon their formal rights, but the validity of the capitalist property regime itself which thwarts the satisfaction of their vital social needs.
>
> (Kivotidis 2021)

If real emergency is that which cannot be accommodated as it is about material historical forces, what the constituted socialist polity can do in its necessary actions that are inherently extra-constitutional, is to integrate this particular "position of the oppressed" as an internal normative constraint, which is probably not a matter of law, but one of politics. The deployment of this emergency device should also be done in assessing the risks and the pitfalls in derailing socialist commitments and in considering past experiences. A future socialist constitutionalism will thus find a stable ground not in normative jurisprudential postulates, but rather in a global, comparative legal history written from the perspective of the oppressed.

Notes

1 Agamben's position during the COVID-19 pandemic made this argument even less tenable by exposing how it obscures the material conditions that shaped states' responses to the global health crisis (Cercel 2021b). But perhaps the easiest way to capture this deadlock is by referring to Walter Benjamin's understanding of the historical embeddedness of the exception: 'The current amazement that the things we are experiencing are "still" possible in twentieth century is *not* philosophical' (Benjamin 1968 [1940], 257).

2 It might be useful to note to which extent the practice of repressing revolts in the French colonies was connected to that of repression in Paris. In the last days of the Orléans monarchy, the King appointed Marshall Bugeaud, another Governor General of Algeria to repress the very republican revolution that was now turned against the workers (Bessonnet-Favre 1902, 14).

References

Assemblée Nationale/National Assembly. Discussion sur un projet de décret sur les attroupements, lors de la séance du 21 octobre 1789', in *Archives Parlementaires de 1787 à 1860 – Première série (1787–1799)* vol. IX. 474–475. Edited by Emile Laurent and Jérôme Mavidal. Paris: P. Dupont, 1877.

Assemblée Nationale/National Assembly. Les 31 *Séances officielles de la Commune de Paris 1871*. 1871. Paris: E Lachaud.

Agamben, Giorgio. 1998. *Homo Sacer: Sovereign Power and Bare Life*. Stanford: Stanford University Press.

Agamben, Giorgio. 2005. *State of Exception*. Chicago: University of Chicago Press.

Agamben, Giorgio. 2011. *The Kingdom and the Glory*. Stanford: Stanford University Press.

Albert, Richard, and Yaniv Roznai. 2021. "Emergency Unamendability: Limitations on Constitutional Amendment in Extreme Conditions." *Maryland Law Review* 81: 243–258.

Althusser, Louis. 1976. "Idéologie et appareils idéologiques d'État." In *Positions 1964–1975*, 67–125. Paris: Éditions Sociales.

Badiou, Alain. 1998. *D'un désastre obscur: Sur la fin de la vérité d'Etat*. Paris: Editions de l'Aube.

Barbusse, Henri. 1926. *Les bourreaux*. Flammarion: Paris.

Benjamin, Walter. 1968 [1940]. "Theses on the Concept of History." In *Illuminations*. 236–252. Edited by Hannah Arendt. New York: Shocken Books.

Bessonnet-Favre, C. 1902. *Février 1848 d'après des documents authentiques*. Paris: Librairie Geldage.

Bishai, Linda S. 2020. "The Inertia of the Exception." In *Law, Security and the State of Perpetual Emergency*, 11–36. Cham: Palgrave Macmillan.

Björk, Mårten, and Tormod Johansen. 2025. *The End of Law: Political Theology and the Crisis of Sovereignty*. Abingdon: Routledge.

Cercel, Cosmin. 2018. *Towards a Jurisprudence of State Communism: Law and the Failure of Revolution*. Abindgon: Routledge.

Cercel, Cosmin. 2021a. "Through a Glass, Darkly: Law, History and the Frontispiece of Exception." In *States of Exception: Law, History, Theory*. 35–40. Edited by Cosmin Cercel, Gian Giacomo Fusco and Simon Lavis. Abingdon: Routledge.

Cercel, Cosmin. 2021b. "Pandemic, Exception and the Law: Notes on the Shattered Nomos of Europe." *Acta Universitatis Lodziensis*: *Folia Iuridica* 96: 83–97.

Cercel, Cosmin. 2024. "Unearthing the Dark Side of the Law. Narratives of Law and Authority in the Tatarbunar Trials." *History of Communism in Europe* 14: 111–130.

Ferejohn, John, and Pasquale Pasquino. 2004. 'The Law of the Exception: A Typology of Emergency Powers', *International Journal of Constitutional Law* 2: 210–239.

Fitzpatrick, Sheila. 2001. *The Russian Revolution*, 2nd ed. Oxford: Oxford University Press.

Fourtanier, Alexandre. 1849. "Rapport fait par M. Alex. Fourtanier, au nom de la commission chargée d'examiner le projet de loi sur l'état de siège." In *Comptes Rendus des Séances de l'Assemblée Nationale Législative*, Vol. II, 127–131. Paris: Panckoucke.

Fraser, David. 2012. "Evil Law, Evil Lawyers: From the Justice Case to the Torture Memos." *Jurisprudence* 3(2): 391–428.

Fusco, Gian Giacomo. 2025. "What Is (State of) Exception the Name of?" In *Law and the Exception. Towards a New Paradigm.* 1–39. Edited by Gian-Giacomo Fusco and Przemysław Tacik. Abingdon: Routledge.

Fusco, Gian-Giacomo. 2023. *Form of Life: Agamben and the Destitution of Rules*. Edinburgh: Edinburgh University Press.

Greene, Alan. 2018. *Permanent States of Emergency and the Rule of Law: Constitutions in an Age of Crisis*. London: Hart.

Gross, Oren, and Fionnuala Ní Aolain. 2006. *Law in Times of Crisis: Emergency Powers in Theory and Practice*. Cambridge: Cambridge University Press.

Johansen, Tormod Otter. 2020. "Minor Law: Notes towards a Revolutionary Jurisprudence." In *States of Exception: Law, History, Theory*. 73–91. Edited by Cosmin Cercel, Gian Giacomo Fusco and Simon Lavis. Abingdon: Routledge.

Kelsen, Hans. 1992 [1934]. *Introduction to the Problems of Legal Theory*. Oxford: Oxford University Press.

Kivotidis, Dimitrios. 2021. "Norm and Exception: From the Weimar Republic to the Nazi StateForm." In *States of Exception: Law, History, Theory*. 119–139. Edited by Cosmin Cercel, GianGiacomo Fusco and Simon Lavis. Abingdon: Routledge.

Le Gal, Sébastien. 2014. "Réprimer les « villes en ébullition ». Le recours aux législations d'exception en France (XVIIIe-XXe siècle)." In *La ville en ébullition : Sociétés urbaines à l'épreuve*. 241–267. Edited by Pierre Bergel et Vincent Milliot. Presses Universitaires de Rennes.

Lenin, Vladimir Ilych. 1962 [1905]. In *Collected Works*, vol 8. 557–559. Edited by Vladimir Ilych Lenin. Moscow: Foreign Languages Publishing House.

Lenin, Vladimir Ilych. 1972 [1895]. "Explanation of the Law on Fines Imposed on Factory Workers." In *Collected Works*, vol. 1. 29–72. Edited by Vladimir Ilych Lenin. Moscow: International Publishers.

Lenin, Vladimir Ilych. 1973 [1922b]. "Letter to D I Kursky." In *Collected Works,* vol. 33. 358–359. Edited by Vladimir Ilych Lenin. Moscow: International Publishers.

Lenin, Vladimir Ilych. 1974 [1917]. "The State and Revolution." In *Collected Works*, vol. 25. 385–540. Edited by Vladimir Ilych Lenin. Moscow: International Publishers.

Lenin, Vladimir Ilych. 1974 [1918a]. "The Proletarian Revolution and the Renegade Kautsky." In *Collected Works*, vol. 28. 227–325. Edited by Vladimir Ilych Lenin. Moscow: International Publishers.

Lenin, Vladimir Ilych. 1974 [1918b]. "Concerning the Decree on Revolutionary Tribunals." In *Collected Works*, vol. 27. 219–220. Edited by Vladimir Ilych Lenin. Moscow: International Publishers.

Lompar, Rastko. 2024. "The Emergence and Evolution of Anti-Communist Legislation in Interwar Yugoslavia." *History of Communism in Europe* 14: 41–63.

Lukács, György. 2009 [1924]. *Lenin : A Study on the Unity of His Thought*. London : Verso.

Mańko, Rafał. 2020. "'Our Fatherland Has Found Itself on the Verge of an Abyss…': Poland's 1981 Martial Law, or the Unexpected Appearance of the State of Exception under Actually Existing Socialism." In *States of Exception: Law, History, Theory*. 140–166. Edited by Cosmin Cercel, Gian Giacomo Fusco, Simon Lavis. Abingdon: Routledge.

Marx, Karl. 1978. "The Class Struggles in France, 1848 to 1850" [1850]. In *Collected Works*. vol. 10. 45–146. Edited by Karl Marx and Frederick Engels. London: Lawrence & Wishart.

Marx, Karl. 1979. "The Eighteenth Brumaire of Louis Bonaparte" [1852]. In *Collected Works*. vol. 11. 99–197. Edited by Karl Marx and Frederick Engels. London: Lawrence & Wishart.

Marx, Karl. 1987 (1859). "Preface to a Contribution to the Critique of Political Economy." In Karl Marx and Friedrich Engels, *Collected Works*, Vol. 29, 252–420. Translated by Victor Schnittke and Yuri Sidobnikov. New York: International Publishers.

Marx, Karl. 1986. "The Civil War in France" [1871]. In *Collected Works*, vol. 22. Edited by Karl Marx and Frederick Engels. London: Lawrence & Wishart.

Negri, Antonio. 1999. *Insurgencies: Constituent Power and the Modern State*. Minneapolis: University of Minnesota Press.

Neocleous, Mark. 2006. "The Problem with Normality: Taking Exception to 'Permanent Emergency'." *Alternatives* 31: 191–213.

Neocleous, Mark. 2014. *War Power, Police Power*. Edinburgh University Press.

Pashukanis, Evgeny Bronislavovich. 1951 [1924]. "The General Theory of Law and Marxism." In *Soviet Legal Philosophy*. Edited by John N Hazard. Cambridge: Harvard University Press.

Pashukanis, Evgeny Bronislavovich. 2025 [1927]. "Exceptional [Emergency] Legislation against the Toilers and their Organisations (Speech Delivered in Moscow, 1927)." In Igor Shoikhedbrod and Rafael Khachaturian. 2025. "E. B. Pashukanis' 1927 Speech on 'Emergency Legislation Against the Toilers and Their Organisations': Explication and Critical Analysis." *Law and Critique*. https://doi.org/10.1007/s10978-025-09413-z.

Poulantzas, Nicos. 2000 [1978]. *State, Power, Socialism*. London: Verso.

Pound, Roscoe. 1910. "Law in Books and Law in Action." American Law Review 44: 12-36.

Primera, German Eduardo. 2018. *The Political Ontology of Giorgio Agamben: Signatures of Life and Power*. London: Bloomsbury.

Rossiter, Clinton. 1948. *Constitutional Dictatorship: Crisis Government in the Modern Democracies*. Princeton University Press.

Sajó, András and Renáta Uitz. 2017. *The Constitution of Freedom*. Oxford: Oxford University Press.

Schmitt, Carl. *Political Theology*. 1985 (1922). Translated by Georg Schwab. Cambridge: MIT Press.

Schmitt, Carl. 2013 (1921). *Dictatorship*. Cambridge: Polity.

Shoikhedbrod, Igor, and Rafael Khachaturian. 2025. "E. B. Pashukanis' 1927 Speech on 'Emergency Legislation Against the Toilers and Their Organisations': Explication and Critical Analysis." *Law and Critique*. https://doi.org/10.1007/s10978-025-09413-z.

Simonin, Anne. 2008. *Le déshonneur dans la République: Une histoire de l'indignité, 1791–1958*. Paris: Grasset.

Skinner, Stephen. 2019. "Criminal Law and the Use of Force: Ideology and State Power in Fascist Italy and England in the Interwar Period." In *Ideology and Criminal Law: Fascist, National Socialist and Authoritarian Regimes* 299–320. Edited by Stephen Skinnner. Oxford: Hart.

Skinner, Stephen. 2022a. "Inciting Military Disaffection in Interwar Britain and Fascist Italy: Security, Crime and Authoritarian Law." *Oxford Journal of Legal Studies* 42 (2): 578–605.

Skinner, Stephen. 2022b. "Identifying Dangers to Democracy: Fascism, the Rule of Law and the Relevance of History" In *Judicial Independence Under Threat*. 160–178. Edited by Dimitrios Giannoulopoulos and Yvonne McDermott. Oxford: Oxford University Press.

Tacik, Przemyslaw. 2021. "The Other Side of Exception. Sovereignty, Modernity and International Law" In *States of Exception: Law, History, Theory*. 54–72. Edited by Cosmin Cercel, Gian Giacomo Fusco and Simon Lavis. Abingdon: Routledge.

Tacik, Przemyslaw. 2025. "Exceptionality: Towards the General Theory of Exception." In *Law and the Exception. Towards a New Paradigm*. 40–71. Edited by Gian-Giacomo Fusco and Przemysław Tacik. Abingdon: Routledge.

Traverso, Enzo. 2017. *Fire and Blood The European Civil War, 1914–1945*. London: Verso.

Trotsky, Leon. 2007 [1920]. *Terrorism and Communism: A Reply to Karl Kautsky*. Edited by Slavoj Žižek. London: Verso.

Vyshinsky, Andrei. *The Law of the Soviet State*. Translated by Hugh W. Babb. New York: Macmillan, 1961.

Whyte, Jessica. 2013. *Catastrophe and Redemption: The Political Thought of Giorgio Agamben*. Albany: State University of New York Press.

Zartaloudis, Thanos. 2010. *Giorgio Agamben: Power, Law and the Uses of Criticism*. Abingdon: Routledge.

7 Right, Social Consciousness and the Dictatorship of the Proletariat

On the Philosophical Foundations of the Discussion on Socialist Constitutionalism

Dimitrios Kilakos

7.1 Introduction

Anyone acquainted with the basic corpus of the so-called classical Marxist-Leninist literature on scientific communism[1] would admit that there are very few mentions on what is nowadays called socialist constitutionalism and much more insights on the communist polity. It is, therefore, a legitimate question whether these insights on the latter could inform a reconstruction of an integrated approach on the former that is consistent with the views of the classics on scientific communism. The question becomes even more interesting once it is acknowledged that Lenin, who was personally involved in almost every aspect of the work of the newly established Soviet power after the victorious Great October Socialist Revolution, seems to have not been engaged in the preparation of the first Soviet Constitution, the theoretical questions that could be addressed on this occasion, and the discussions and disputes on relevant issues, as it can be inferred from the relatively few mentions on these issues that can be found in his *Collected Works*. In fact, Lenin seems to turn to the Soviet Constitution mostly to juxtapose it with constitutions of capitalist countries for propaganda reasons and not to draw theoretical inferences that promote the development of Marxist-Leninist theory.

This chapter is not meant to contribute to filling the aforementioned gap in Marxist-Leninist literature. It is rather meant to discuss the philosophical preconditions for undertaking this task, by delving into the importance of developing political and legal consciousness as parts of the development of social consciousness in the immature communist society. Specifically, instead of adding some more pages to the existing literature on the institutional manifestation of right in the legal superstructure of the immature communist society, as it is often the case with many contributions to the ongoing discussion on socialist constitutionalism, I focus on the rather overlooked aspect of how right[2] affects the development of social consciousness and its interaction with the legal superstructure.

DOI: 10.4324/9781032621623-8

Such a philosophical discussion may seem to be of narrow importance on the particular forms that the organisation of social regulation in the dictatorship of the proletariat[3] takes. However, questions about political mediations leading to particular social forms during the dictatorship of the proletariat should primarily be discussed as part of political strategies, which could be conceived as theoretico-political reflections on concrete circumstances (Garo 2023, p. 6). In this regard, a discussion on the legal form of social consciousness[4] may inform various aspects of the discussion on the formation of social relations during this period and the development of human subjectivity within their context. Moreover, it may contribute to the discussion on the withering away of the state and the law thesis.

This contextualisation of the discussion serves as a means to rebut the view, drawing on Thompson (1975), that socialist constitutionalism is an extension of liberalism aiming to transpose the rule of law and liberal rights onto a socialist order. Although in different context, the essential features of this view can also be traced in Sypnowich's claim that political and legal institutions are guarantors of democracy and preconditions of social emancipation (Sypnowich 1987). Similarly, Shoikhedbrod argues for legal rights in communist society as technical and cultural preconditions for the free development of individuals (Shoikhedbrod 2019). In one way or the other, these views seem to draw on Marx's view of the relationship between social relations and the legal and political superstructure, as outlined in the "Preface" to *A Contribution to the Critique of Political Economy* (Marx 1970). By focusing instead on the relationship between social Being and social consciousness, as outlined in the same passage, I intend to offer a new perspective in this discussion.

This new perspective may further inform a critique of a crucial feature of these views, which is the idea that while the content of law is historically contingent, the very nature of the legal form itself is transhistorical. Since an analogous idea is also applicable in the discussion on democracy, their conjunction in terms of the discussion on socialist constitutionalism informs a sort of constitutional fetishism, according to which socialist constitutions become an external constraint on the power of the dictatorship of the proletariat, via which the new political order is developed. In this regard, while I share with Sultany (2021) the inclination to argue that Marxism challenges the fetishism and mystifications of modern constitutionalism, I disagree with him on that socialist constitutionalism aims to deepen democracy – at least to the extent that this view seems to suggest that the democratic content of the dictatorship of the proletariat is merely a variation of the democratic content of liberal forms of the dictatorship of the bourgeoisie, as if it is the same content that is developed in these two forms.

In the following section, I attempt to pinpoint the significance of the discussion on social consciousness – and, particularly, its legal and political form – for the debate on socialist constitutionalism. I then proceed to discuss the issue of continuity and discontinuity in the development of legal and political forms of social consciousness in the transition from capitalism to full-blown communism. Specifically, I argue for the asymmetry between the content of the legal and the democratic forms in capitalism and socialism, conceived as the immature stage of development of the communist society. Before concluding, I discuss in more detail the specificity of the development of juridico-political forms during the transition to full-blown communism. Several loops throughout the text serve the goal to proffer a nuanced understanding of the legal and political content of the dictatorship of the proletariat, as described in several passages of Marx, Engels, and Lenin, in the light of what concerns each specific section of this chapter.

7.2 Social Consciousness, Dictatorship of the Proletariat and Socialist Constitutionalism

Arguably, the core philosophical issue in the discussion on socialist constitutionalism and the communist polity consists in the dialectical interaction of the base with the superstructure of the immature communist society and the role and function of the dictatorship of the proletariat – "the organisation of the vanguard of the oppressed as the ruling class for the purpose of suppressing the oppressors", as Lenin (1964b, p. 466) defined it – as the central pillar upon which the new social order is built.

In this respect, from a Marxist-Leninst standpoint the discussion on socialist constitutionalism and the communist polity is a discussion on how the institutionalisation of working-class power can be aligned with its objectives, to dismantle capitalist structures and remnants, and to build not only the foundations of communism, but the full-blown communist social relations and the new, communist type of human personality. Thus, it turns to be a discussion on how the dictatorship of the proletariat lays the groundwork for the development of communist social relations, on the grounds of the formation of the economic base of communism, which inevitably influences the evolution of the institutional framework and legal norms, including the constitutional framework. In other words, the discussion on socialist constitutionalism is a discussion on the transformation of social reality under the direction of the dictatorship of the proletariat, the collectively conscious agent of the communist social transformation.

The last phrase of the previous paragraph is deliberately formulated in a way that highlights the conscious transformation of social reality as the core content of the historical role of the dictatorship of the proletariat and its interlacement with the development and transformation of the constitutional framework of the immature communist society. This formulation brings forth the theme which is acknowledged by Marxism as the basic philosophical question in the field of social phenomena – that is the investigation of the relationship between the social Being, the totality of material relations that man develops with his physical and social environment, on the one hand, and social consciousness, the aggregate of ideas, theories, perceptions, social feelings, morals and customs in which the objective reality of nature and society is reflected, on the other. Specifically, it brings forth the significance for the discussion on socialist constitutionalism and the communist polity of the most fundamental discovery of Marxism, in which its revolutionary nature lies: the dependence of social consciousness on social Being and the dialectical interaction between them, the former being corollary of the latter, while also counteracting and in some instances enabling and advancing its further development.

For, since both the base and the superstructure of the immature communist society are parts of its social Being, it is the active role of social consciousness that explains how the creative force of the dictatorship of the proletariat manages to drive the society in its state of development in which it becomes able to develop itself on the grounds of the communist social relations without the interference of state power, as the state withers away and eventually becomes obsolete, together with its coercive enforcement of the law. It is exactly the creative force of the dictatorship of the proletariat that sets the ground for the development of the communist economic and other social relations, which cannot emerge and develop spontaneously, and their development presupposes the destruction of their capitalist predecessors and any remnants that may contain the seed for their re-emergence and restoration.

Admittedly though, it may seem that I have already jumped into the conclusion, without discussing the very issue of social consciousness and its legal form. Let's turn to this point, then.

In one of the most famous excerpts from his works, Marx notes:

> In the social production of their existence, men inevitably enter into definite relations, which are independent of their will, namely relations of production appropriate to a given stage in the development of their material forces of production. The totality of these relations of production constitutes the economic structure of society, the real foundation, on which arises a legal and political superstructure and to which correspond definite forms of social consciousness. The mode of production of material life conditions the general process of social, political and intellectual life. It is not the consciousness of men that determines their existence, but their social existence that determines their consciousness.
>
> (Marx 1970, pp. 20–21)

This excerpt, which is denseful in meanings, provides the core of the Marxist guidelines for the scientific study of socio-historical phenomena and their dialectical development.

As the eminent Soviet Marxist philosopher E.V. Ilyenkov notes, social consciousness "precedes individual consciousness as something pre-given, as something that exists before, outside and independently of individual consciousness".

This social consciousness "is being developed from one generation to the other" and "differs in principle from 'individual consciousness'". Ilyenkov notes that

> in its individualized form, in the form of the consciousness of those closest to us, and then in the form of that whole circle of people that appears in one's field of vision, shapes one's consciousness into a much larger degree than the 'material world'.

This is despite social consciousness being, according to Marx "the derivative of the social Being, that is, of the system of material and economic relations that exist among people" (Ilyenkov 1980, pp. 34–35). Our philosophical interest focuses on this "historically evolving whole" which is "the entire spiritual culture of mankind", which is "formed by a multitude of dialectically contradictory interactions" (Ilyenkov 1980, pp. 40–41). Among these interactions, Marxism pays special attention to the ones reflecting class struggle.

In order to discuss socialist constitutionalism and the communist polity in terms of social consciousness, one should delve deeper into the relationship between the legal and the political form of social consciousness, on the one hand, and the juridico-political forms of the superstructure, through which they are expressed and manifested, on the other. It is a complex philosophical issue, which is often – and, arguably, unduly – overlooked.

The legal form of social consciousness, as any other of its forms, reflects social reality and the material relations humans develop with their natural and social environment, and influences forms of social organisation. Among those relations, our main concern for our current purposes is legal relations, which are closely connected to various forms of social consciousness, primarily legal consciousness. As two distinguished Soviet Marxist philosophers write, legal consciousness, as a certain form of social consciousness,

> represents views, theories, teachings and concepts common in society about the legal and illegal, about the fair, proper and obligatory in relations between people, states, nations, and the assessment of the law in force in society that arose historically with the emergence of classes and changed with the change in the economic system.
>
> (Kelle and Kovalzon 1959, p. 69)

Reflecting the economic structure of society, "the legal system has a direct impact on the formation of the legal consciousness of society" (Kelle and Kovalzon 1959, p. 69). In its content, the legal form of social consciousness, as a reflection of social existence, encompasses ideas and perceptions of justice held by social forces representing the material interests prevailing in any given society. This content is expressed in legal forms and norms, as it is validated by political authority. As a form of social consciousness, right expresses and consolidates relationships of dominance and subjugation, the dictatorship of the ruling class within the socio-economic formation, and its leading role in society. Thus, the legal form of the reflection of social reality in social consciousness is expressed through a set of acts, rules, and regulations, which, under certain conditions, are enacted by political authority and govern the activities humans engage in within the context of their social relations. Through this legal superstructure, social life is regulated in its various aspects. This regulation bears the burden of the class character of the society, which is also reflected on how social classes with different positions and conflicting interests, populating a society, assess its legal system.

The legal form of social consciousness appears during the development of social Being at a stage where further social development is determined by the struggle between carriers of differentiated and opposing interests, which it reflects from the perspective of the dominant class and its needs. Thus, historically, the legal form of social consciousness appears along with class society and politics, expressing the need to maintain social unity according to the material interests of the dominant class, as if they expressed the needs of the entire society. What differentiates legal consciousness in the early, immature communist society from the previous ones in which class struggle also exists, though, is the fact that the dictatorship of the proletariat, on the ground of the developing communist social relations and active political engagement of the working masses, actually expresses the needs of the entire society, en route to its classless future. In previous class societies, it is the rule of a social minority, aiming to reproduce its mode of existence, that appears against society as if it embraced its needs.[5]

Parenthetically, this is the reason why I disagree with Shoikhedbrod on that the withering away of the legal form in communism "would mean reverting to pre-juridical relations in which human beings are not even formally recognised as persons" (Shoikhedbrod 2019, p. 120). The transition to the full-blown communist society is the forward movement towards a society of full-blown personalities. This movement consists in transcending the realm of the illusory recognition of supposedly equal legal and political rights in the essentially unequal capitalist society, in which a person is the one whose activity within the nexus of commodity-based relations should be regulated.

The political form of social consciousness reflects the relations between the various social groups within a society with the problem of power at its core. As such, its development begins with the division of society into classes (cf. Engels 1970a). The discrete elaboration on the political form of social consciousness allows us to see that the material and spiritual development of class societies takes place in a political context. Therefore, political consciousness highlights political relations as class relations in their essence. Any social problem acquires a political character if its solution, indirectly or directly, is linked to class interests and the problem of power. The political form of social consciousness is expressed in the activity of social subjects. Thus, politics is developed as a special form of social activity in class societies and will exist as long as classes exist. The political activity is developed within the political superstructure of society. Therefore, en route to the classless society, the political activity of people in the early, immature communist society aims to build the conditions for the dialectical negation of politics itself.

In classical Marxism-Leninism there is a profound link among right, state, and class, as well as among jurisprudence, politics and economy. Indeed, Lenin leaves zero margin of doubt on this, when he states that "[l]aws are political measures, politics. No political measure can prohibit economic phenomena" (Lenin 1964a, p. 48).

Therefore, in terms of our current discussion on social consciousness with regard to socialist constitutionalism and the communist polity, it is crucial to understand the interconnection of right and politics (in the sense of the legal and political form of social consciousness, respectively) as coexisting forms of social consciousness reflecting a given social Being, both in their historical development and their actuality and specificity in the case of the developing communist society. Taking into consideration that both the legal and the political form of social consciousness will become obsolete in the full-blown communist society, in a process driven by the activity of workers' power, the question of continuity and discontinuity in their development during the transition from capitalism to full-blown communism comes forth.

7.3 On the Discontinuity in the Development of Legal and Political Forms in the Transition from Capitalism to Full-Blown Communism

In the past of social history, the revolutionary leap from one stage of social development to the other, and thus from one form of class society to the next was characterised by the dominance of the social relations – and more significantly the economic relations in production – that characterise the new form. In every other case, these relations were already present and developed to a certain extent within the previous social formation. This made a certain institutional and political continuity inevitable. However, this is not the case for socialist revolution. During the socialist revolution, the working class assigns its dictatorship the duty to promote and establish the communist social relations from the very beginning of their formation, as they were not present in previous social order. Thus, there can be no institutional and political continuity in this case.

It is the newly founded proletarian state that has to actively promote the new social relations and organise its power (including its institutional forms) in the building of communism, thus providing the conditions for the realisation of true social emancipation. In this course, from its very beginning, the complete rupture with political and legal system of the bourgeois society is necessary. From the perspective of our concerns in this text, this suggests that legal norms, rules, and practices etc. of the bourgeois society cannot be given socialist content.

The idea that socialist content could be ascribed to the legal forms of the bourgeois society is an expression of legal fetishism, which, as Knox argues, is embedded with a type of rationality that encodes reality with an abstract and formal language that is functional for the reproduction of the capitalist system, precluding social struggles from targeting its roots (Knox 2009). In the context of the discussion on socialist constitutionalism, this kind of fetishism is usually expressed by the insistence on the transhistorical nature of legal forms (i.e. Shoikhedbrod 2019) and may be extended to the pertinence of bourgeois juridico-political forms in the communist society. On this, Kivotidis rightfully comments that legal form includes not only the institutional manifestations of legality but also the ideational elements of law (Kivotidis 2024a, p. 249). It is exactly on those ideational elements of the law that the discontinuity and the rupture between the bourgeois and the socialist context of development of the legal form become apparent. For, as the Soviet marxist philosopher E.V. Ilyenkov indicates, law is the "fetishised" or "reified" forms of collectively organised experience, while legal and political forms have crystallised in social consciousness and are reinforced by force of habit and tradition (Ilyenkov 1980). Therefore, one should turn to the previously discussed issue of the development of the legal and political forms of social consciousness to understand the differentiation of their actual content in the transition from capitalism to full-blown communism via the conscious activity of the dictatorship of the proletariat.

This suggests that the values and practices informing legal and political forms in the period of the dictatorship of the proletariat, emerge from its own initiative and serve its own needs and goals, being fundamentally assymetrical with legal and political forms of the capitalist society.

Legal and political forms are not predetermined and adjustable to any different content that may be given to them. On the contrary, given their historicity, it is the actual content of these forms that, in its development, determines them in their specificity. To put it simply, if capitalist society utilises its legal and political powers and forces to protect the right to individual property and the grounds of capitalist exploitation of labour, the early communist society utilises powers and forces to protect the collective property and the grounds of communist social emancipation. In the former case, the social majority, excluded from power, is suffering from the rule of the social minority, while in the latter, it is the social majority which, via its power, should prevent and deter the effect of anything that may lead to the restoration of the previous social order.

Let us delve deeper into this discussion on discontinuity. The legal form of social consciousness in capitalism, reflecting the social existence of bourgeois society, contributes to establishing the economic and political conditions of the system of bourgeois class domination and workers' exploitation, whose economic base is reflected in the legal superstructure of the bourgeois society. At this stage of social development, one could specify certain features of right that deserve special attention.

At first, it is only in capitalist society that right proclaims the formal equality of all citizens before the law. Bourgeois society presents itself as a society of formal equality among its citizens, who relate to each other as formally independent and equal commodity producers, and all relations among them – or, to be more exact, mostly those who bear economic interest, either directly or indirectly – are recorded in legal forms. Thus, while in pre-capitalist class socio-economic formations exploitation occurred under conditions of formal inequality among the members of the society (since exploitation of man by man was based not only on economic but also on extra-economic – physical – violence and coercion of various kinds), class exploitation in capitalism occurs under conditions of formal freedom and equality of rights for all members of bourgeois society. The legal consolidation of this formal equality is both a prerequisite for capitalist exploitation and a veil under which class contradictions and the substantial inequality that capitalism harbours are attempted to be concealed.

Besides formal equality, there are also other features of bourgeois rights which do not pertain to socialism/communism. Among them, one should also highlight abstract individualism. According to this conception, both individual justice and the legitimacy of political authority are justifiable with reference to the freestanding individual, without social characteristics or context. Such abstract individuals, becoming the basic unit of moral, political, and juridical analysis are deemed to represent the real-world human beings who are subject to that authority. In such a conception, the interests of such abstract individuals are prioritised over collective interests of social groups. Moreover, the latter are deemed to fundamentally contrast the former. This conception is obviously incompatible with the essential social nature essence that Marxism acknowledges to humans, who become personalities through their social interactions with their natural and social environments. Furthermore, this idea serves the class character of bourgeois society, since the protection on individual property as a right is the touchstone of its legal systems. However, it is rendered groundless by the distinct class character of the dictatorship of the proletariat, of the social majority who both owns and runs social production, since the dictatorship of the proletariat is meant to guide society to its classless future, where the potentiality of fully developed personalities will be realised.

A similar line of reasoning can be employed regarding other features of bourgeois right, such as the neutrality of the law, according to which courts supposedly decide impartially in disputes between abstract and formally equal individuals. In the case of the dictatorship of the proletariat, though, the essence of the class character of such a transitory form of state underdetermined such an ideal of impartiality. In turn, this fundamental difference undermines the applicability of the ideas of natural justice and natural judge, which are linked to the aforementioned impartiality in the case of the bourgeois state and law. It should also be noted that these two features of bourgeois right serve to reify law and the state in the dictatorship of the capital, while the rejection of their essence by the very nature of the dictatorship of the proletariat reify law and the state in the transition to full-blown communism. Finally, one could also discuss in a similar vein the element of coercion in bourgeois right and its transformation and dialectical negation, via the power of the dictatorship of the proletariat, in the transition to the classless society of full-blown communism. In such a society, coercion is abolished and replaced by conscious self-discipline for the advancement of social life of fully developed personalities as social beings, while formal freedom and equality are sublated by substantive freedom and equality.

Moreover, the role and significance of right increase significantly with the dominance of the bourgeoisie and the spread of capitalism, as bourgeois society is the most complex society humanity has known in its pre-communist history. This complexity, arising from the breadth and multitude of relations and mediations developed among social subjects, on the ground of the development of productive forces, is reflected both on social consciousness (hence in its legal form, too) and on the institutions and functions of the superstructure of bourgeois society (hence in the legal superstructure, too), compared to its predecessors. With regard to social consciousness, it is also reflected on the interplay among the legal and its other forms. With regard to the superstructure, it is reflected both on the diversification of the various bodies issuing rules, acts, laws, statutes that acquire legal status, and on the diversification of various branches of law, of judiciary institutions, and of law-enforcing mechanisms.

Since social consciousness is instilled in individuals through their practical experience and activity as contributors in the development of social life in all its manifestations and changes with the development of social formations, the same should be the case for the various forms of social consciousness, including the legal and the political. However, there is a profound difference in the case of socialism. In it, since the class struggle occurs with the social majority in power and tends to the development of the classless and stateless communist society which will constitute the new stage of development of the social Being, the legal consciousness also *tends* to be unified for the entire society. In this course, the content of socialist legality is subject to change, depending upon the circumstances and needs of the class struggle. It is only in this sense that it could be argued that socialist legal consciousness is embodied in socialist law, which safeguards the socialist legal order and serves as a means to cultivate citizens in the spirit of socialist legality. For it is in the dictatorship of the proletariat that the law becomes an actual – and not only formal – expression of the will of the social majority, being informed by its legal consciousness.

Thus, socialist legality is being developed in tandem with the development of communist economic and social relations, which set up the ground for the abolishment of the conditions that produce law and make legal regulations and processes necessary. In this regard, it could be argued that the actual essence of socialist legality is the preparation, in terms of social consciousness, of the non-legal social order of the communist society, of the non-legal social regulation in communism. If law is needed to give rights and impose duties on social subjects, then it withers away in the course of the preparation of the society that organises and runs its social life without the need for external forces of coercion and social regulation. This is also the case for the constitutional aspect of socialist legality. For, as Lenin argued, "[w]ritten and unwritten constitutions (…) are merely a record of the results of struggle obtained through a series of hard-won victories of the new over the old and a series of defeats inflicted on the new by the old" (Lenin 1963, p. 564). Since this struggle between the new and the old continues in the conditions of the dictatorship of the proletariat, this assessment remains in effect.

In the same vein, one can also discuss the discontinuity in the political forms, focusing especially in the democratic form which, in conjunction with the legal form, is mostly at stake in the discussion on socialist constitutionalism and the dictatorship of the proletariat.

Kivotidis (2024b) rightfully argues that in any class society, the institutional and the ideational features of democracy respond to the necessity of reproducing the relations that ensure the political rule of one social class over the others. On this ground, the discussion on the essence of democracy should not merely be a discussion on formal rules, procedures, and principles. By extrapolating this view, it could be argued that the quest for specific formal rules, procedures, and principles that distinguish bourgeois democracy from proletarian one is rendered untenable by the class character of any democracy. Obviously, this is not meant to suggest that a proletarian democracy is not distinguishable from a bourgeois democracy. However, their qualitative difference, stemming from the specific class character of each one of them, cannot be reduced to a specific set of formal elements, the mere existence of which would be sufficient to identify a democracy as a proletarian rather than a bourgeois one.

As both theory and history prove, the development of the immature communist society, the building of which begins once the working-class revolution overthrows the bourgeois class from power and destroys its governing mechanisms, is still guided by the development of class struggle, albeit with different forms and content, since "[c]lasses still remain, and will remain everywhere for years after the proletariat's conquest of power" (Lenin 1966, p. 44). The class struggle in the immature communist society develops on the grounds of conflicting tendencies in its social reality. The dictatorship of the proletariat, under the guidance of the communist party, strives to develop the communist relations by focusing on the development of central planning as a communist relation of production, in the course towards the full socialisation of the latter. This is the reason why Lenin stresses that the dictatorship of the proletariat is necessary "not only for the proletariat which has overthrown the bourgeoisie, but also for the entire historical period which separates capitalism from 'classless society', from communism" (Lenin 1964b, p. 418).

The new state machinery, the dictatorship of the proletariat, is the general political form which replaces the dictatorship of the bourgeoisie and may take various specific forms in different cases. As Lenin noted, "[t]he transition from capitalism to communism is certainly bound to yield a tremendous abundance and variety of political forms, but the essence will inevitably be the same: *the dictatorship of the proletariat*" (Lenin 1964b, p. 418 – italics in the original). Whichever the concrete specific forms may be, the dictatorship of the proletariat is essentially different from the dictatorship of the bourgeoisie, being the outcomes of two distinct – yet intertwined – trajectories of historical processes: the dictatorship of the bourgeoisie (in any democratic or non-democratic form) is the necessary outcome of the rise of bourgeoisie to power, the dictatorship of the proletariat is the necessary outcome of class struggle in bourgeois society and of the rise of the working class to power by the force of its revolution. In this regard, there is a profound asymmetry between the two, so that the particular norms and forms (including legal and political ones) of the former may only serve as part of the sociogenetic history of the latter, taking into consideration the dialectical leap performed with the socialist revolution.

At this point, one could discuss in more detail several aspects of the political form of social consciousness in bourgeois societies and proceed in discussing how these are abolished or sublated in the transition to full-blown communism, via the power of the dictatorship of the proletariat, in order to highlight several features its democratic content. In such a discussion, one could refer to formal democracy, to the formal principles of majority voting, the citizen as abstract individual/voter, etc.

Instead of such a detailed discussion, I restrain myself to a short discussion of bourgeois political consciousness as an ideological misrepresentation of the political reality of bourgeois society which serves the general political ends of the power of the capital. An exemplary case that may serve the needs of such a discussion is the confusion between voting and the exercise of political power that generates what may be called "voting fetishism". This is the mystical disguise of the profound difference between the registry of a preference to a candidate or a particular policy by the exercise of the democratic right to vote in elections, on the one hand, and the imposition of the ruling class' will and enforcement of its interests upon the society, so that it is forced to do something that otherwise would not be done, by means of coercion in a state-organised society, on the other hand. The latter is what political power actually consists in.

In this sense, "voting fetishism" becomes the necessary complement (or, if one prefers, symptom) of what Marx and Engels called "parliamentary cretinism", which is the "disorder", according to Engels, which penetrates its victims with "the solemn conviction that the whole world, its history and future, are governed and determined by a majority of votes" in a representative body in bourgeois societies (Engels 2021, p. 113). In this sense, it entails the confinement of civil society to an imaginary world (Carver 2002, p. 90). Such an illusion prevails in formal democracies, since the focal point of the political activity of the abstract individual as a citizen is the exercise of the right to cast a vote for the election of representative bodies as components of the political order of the society. In this sense, "voting fetishism" becomes necessary for the political institutions of the bourgeois society in order to succeed in their function for the reproduction of the capitalist regime of power, property, and productive relations.

However, as Marx has argued, the real world of politics taught that working-class access to the ballot does not amount to the actual exercise of political power as long as capitalist property and bourgeois relations prevailed, and should not be mistaken for it (Marx 1937). Following a similar line of reasoning, Lenin was argued against "the worship of 'consistent democracy'" and the belief that "extremely important political matters" could be solved "merely by voting", to attacking the illusion that the working people are capable, under capitalism, of acquiring the high degree of class consciousness needed to establish the rule of the working class in society. According to him, while universal suffrage is "an index of the level reached by the various classes in their understanding of their problems" and shows how they "are inclined to solve their problems", the actual solution of the problems "is not provided by voting, but by the class struggle in all its forms". Moreover, even when it has seized state power and formed its dictatorship, the proletariat should intensify class struggle, by other forms and means, in "order to destroy the pillars and foundations of actual inequality", and lead "all working people to the abolition of classes, i.e. to socialist equality, the only kind that is not a deception" (Lenin 1965a, pp. 266–275). Thus, the abolishment of "voting fetishism" turns to amount to the abolishment of formal equality and abstract individuality and the advancement of actual equality and fully developed personalities. On these grounds, it could be argued that the actualisation of the democratic content of the dictatorship of the proletariat is to be found in the transition from the former to the latter, the ideational reflection of which consists the essence of the political form of social consciousness in socialism.

Thus contextualised, the discussion on the democratic content of the dictatorship of the proletariat highlights this content in the active participation of the masses in organisation, performance, and running of state functions through institutionalised forms of governance of the society until, ultimately, social development attains its classless and stateless stage in full-blown communism, when actual and true self-governance of society will be effectuated. This is how I understand what Kivotidis calls "the dialectics of democracy", in the sense that "the struggle for democracy needs to turn into the struggle for communism", for "[r]eal democracy (…) will never exist until it will have become redundant together with all other state and political forms" (Kivotidis 2024b, p. 296).

The fortification and stability of the political regime that prepares the society for this forthcoming stage of social development is a prerequisite for its attainment. That is why the dictatorship of the proletariat, in its social essence, is not only a coercive, but also – and this is far more important for our current concerns – educative power, that is unrestrained by any laws in the quest for communism. To be exact, by any laws other than those pertaining to social development, i.e. the actual laws of history, of the dialectical development of social reality.

In this line of reasoning, Sultany's (2021) view that socialist constitutionalism aims to deepen democracy seems to counterpose the necessary emphasis that the dictatorship of the proletariat should place on the development of the productive forces of society in their interaction with the development of the communist relations of productions to the development of the democratic form of government.

Such an undialectical separation and juxtaposition of the former to the latter obscures and blurs the fact that the socialist order, including its constitutional aspect, is developed on the ground of the class content of democracy and not irrespectively of it. To put it differently, it is not the same democratic content, that, in different stages of its development, is organised in different forms. For, as Lenin highlights in his polemics against Kautsky, we can only speak of class democracy as long as different classes exist. While, in the course of history, proletarian democracy will take the place of bourgeois democracy, it is democracy itself that will *wither away* in communist society. Thus, the democratic character of the dictatorship of the proletariat is based on the class rule of the working class and derives from it and its historical perspective. With regard to the discussion on socialist constitutionalism and the communist polity, what is at stake in this debate is not merely whether the proletariat should utilise democracy in its struggle against the bourgeoisie, as it was the case in the dispute between Lenin and Kautsky. Rather, it is mostly whether an ideal of "pure democracy", that is to be reached by the deepening of democracy in socialism should inform the vision of the communist polity.

Moreover, the aformentioned separation and juxtaposition obscures the fact that the influence of the development of the communist relations of production concerns not only the development of the productive forces of the early communist society, but also gives impetus to the continuous and direct political action of the working class, of the people, as their definitive dominance is based precisely on this action. Both the development of production and the organs of power in socialism support and are supported by the power of the collective, social worker. Hence the dictatorship of the proletariat transforms the workers into protagonists of political action, which opens the way for social emancipation. This action, organised in terms of power, is what creates the material basis of a communist society. Moreover, it is exactly the functioning of the organs of this power that enhances the cultivation and development of communist consciousness. Therefore, the creation of the necessary material conditions for the development of a communist society, from the point of view of production and, more broadly, of the economy, is necessarily to be promoted through the development of the creative role of the organs of workers' power. This necessary relationship must also be reflected in the constitutional order. In this sense, the latter cannot function restrictively with regard to the development of this relationship.

It is these ideas materialised in social practice that attribute an increasingly determinant role in legal and political consciousness *en route* to full-blown communism. This role actually consists in laying the ground for rendering them obsolete: in full-blown communism there would be nothing left to be reflected on legal and political consciousness, since legal and political relations would not be anymore part of the social Being.

7.4 On the Specificity of the Juridico-Political Forms during the Transition to Full-Blown Communism

The line of reasoning that has been deployed thus far arguably suffices to highlight that there can be no constitutional answer to the question of how the political and legal consciousness of people is raised to the level that

> the society which organizes production anew on the basis of free and equal association of the producers will put the whole state machinery where it will then belong—into the museum of antiquities, next to the spinning wheel and the bronze axe.
>
> (Engels 1970a, p. 330)

Of course, if the dictatorship of the proletariat is the means through which the political awareness of people is raised to this level, then one should expect that socialist constitutional principles and structures should contribute to this. Other chapters in this volume discuss the types, qualities, and specificities of such principles and structures.

In terms of the main concerns of this text, it could be pointed out that the social character of property even in early communism also predetermines the framework for organising the social, class nature of state power. Those who produce material and intellectual goods can and must actively participate in decision-making in all aspects of social life. Here lies the supremacy of the dictatorship of the proletariat as the highest form of democratic organisation of a society that is still developing through class struggle. Ensuring the active participation of the collective worker, who constitutes the main productive force of society, in the administration of the workers' state consolidates and develops the new society. The active participation of the working class in making and controlling decisions is a prerequisite for the unhindered development of the productive forces and for the expansion and deepening of communist production relations. From this point of view, the importance of creating and ensuring appropriate material conditions for the effective involvement of workers in the problems of governing society stands out, as a necessary condition for upgrading the functioning of the institutions and organs of workers' power. This need goes hand in hand with the necessary priority afforded to the production of means of production in order to ensure expanded reproduction, socialist accumulation, and the social wealth necessary for the expansion of social well-being. In turn, the development of productive forces, the increase in productivity, and new technological capabilities entail the emergence and development of new needs, but also new problems. From this point of view, the class character of the workers' state policies emerges as decisive, and in particular the questioning of whether central planning is strengthened or weakened, in terms of matching existing possibilities with developing social needs. For, in the final analysis, the crucial issue is whether it is ensured that scientific central planning will be constantly upgraded to meet the new demands generated by the development of productive forces. In turn, this requires constant care so that the state of the dictatorship of the proletariat contributes to the formation of a responsible, communist attitude towards work, which plays a decisive role in socialist development.

In this sense, the democratic essence of the dictatorship of the proletariat, as a political form, lies in the socio-economic content of proletarian rule and it is manifested in the growingly conscious active participation of workers in the management of social and political affairs, in the course of development of the material conditions necessary for the eventual abolition of juridico-political forms. The final goal of this arduous process of transformation and reconfiguration of social order along communist social relations amounts, as Ilyenkov puts it, "to the converting of each individual from a one sided professional—from a slave of the division of labour system—into an all around personality, a real master (proprietor) of the material and spiritual culture created by all mankind" (Ilyenkov 1967).

The enduring and laborious struggle for the reorganisation of the society, for its re-foundation on a communist basis, until "people form the habit of performing their social duties without any special apparatus for coercion, and when unpaid work for the public good becomes a general phenomenon" (Lenin 1965b, pp. 284–285), affects all social relations and the social consciousness which, in its various forms and thus also in the legal one, reflects the developing new social reality.

In this regard, it makes absolutely no sense, from a Marxist-Leninist perspective, to think that state power begins to wither away immediately after the overthrow of the bourgeoisie and the seizure of power by the working class. While the bourgeois state is abolished by the proletariat in the course of the revolution, the remnants of the proletarian state after the socialist revolution wither away in due time, as Lenin explains to introduce his brilliant characterisation of the proletarian state, the dictatorship of the proletariat as a "semi-state" (Lenin 1964b, p. 402). It is this semi-state that should unleash its force in order to intensify the class struggle, until there is no need for it to exist, once this struggle is irretrievably won. In a certain sense, it is a unique type of state, its mission being to undermine its very existence. This may seem contradictory – indeed, it is an actual contradiction that the development of state power is the precondition for its withering away. However, a Marxist should not feel uncomfortable in such situations, since, according to materialistic dialectics, the heart of the development of reality (including social reality, of course) lies in the development of actual contradictions.

As Lenin suggested, "the dictatorship of the proletariat, the period of transition to communism, will for the first time create democracy for the people, for the majority, along with the necessary suppression of the exploiters, of the minority" (Lenin 1964b, p. 467) and it is the proletariat, via its dictatorship, that should judge who hinders the socialist revolution (Lenin 1965b, pp. 298–300). It is, therefore, the dictatorship of the proletariat that leads society – and, among other aspects of social life, the political and legal awareness of the people – to its level of development that "people will gradually become accustomed to observing the elementary rules of social intercourse (…) without force, without coercion, without subordination, without the special apparatus for coercion called the state" (Lenin 1964b, p. 467). Until then, as Lenin argued in discussions for the first Soviet Constitution, the dictatorship of the proletariat recognises "no freedom, no equality, no labour democracy if it conflicts with the cause of emancipating labour from the yoke of capital" (Lenin 1965b, p. 376).

It is rightfully argued by Kivotidis that the discussion on the withering away of the law might inspire the exploration of alternative constitutional arrangements and judicial structures in a society that has transcended the contradictions of capitalism, further suggesting that the legal form may be replaced by new forms of social consciousness based on the notion of "ethical community" and the principle of the "free and full development of the individual" in the communist society (Kivotidis 2024a, pp. 235–236).

The interest in the development of the reflection of the developing communist relations on legal forms and norms in the dictatorship of the proletariat should further be extended to the reflection of the transformations of social reality on social consciousness, in its various forms. For, it is the development of the socio-economic content of the proletarian rule that leads to the eventual abolition of the juridico-political forms. These forms will become obsolete along with the relevant forms of social consciousness, when there is nothing left on social Being to be reflected on them *per se,* since the new qualitative stage of its development requires a new structure of the social consciousness on which it is reflected.

As Lenin noted, the dictatorship of the proletariat is a "persistent struggle – bloody and bloodless, violent and peaceful, military and economic, educational and administrative – against the forces and traditions of the old society" (Lenin 1966, p. 44) that establishes the socialist social order, enacts the corresponding content of forms of social consciousness and paves the way for their definite and irreversible consolidation and prevalence by the force of habit. While the forces and traditions of the old society are still influencing the specificities of the juridico-political forms during the period of transition to full-blown communism, this influence is conditioned upon the political force of the proletariat, as the ruling class of the new society, organised in the form of its dictatorship.

Of course, this line of reasoning is not meant to suggest that in the future communist society there will be no administrative structures enabling deliberation, negotiation, and decision-making procedures, since the need for the implementation of means and regulations to organise social life and promote social order will not become obsolete. However, a thus conceived need for institutional organisation of the communist society does not amount to the perseverance of the political form of social consciousness in the future communist society.

In this regard, while Chrysis (2020) is right to argue that in the fully blown communist society the existence of forms of association and collective decision-making and planning will be necessary, his conclusion that a political character should be assigned to this kind of decions and plans made and implemented by the organised collective of fully developed personalities is not as straightforward as it may seem.

For, it is questionable which contradiction in the development of social Being that is reflected in the development of the political form of social consciousness during the transition from capitalism to full-blown communism is resolved in a way that prompts a new stage of development of the latter, now reflecting the new stage of development of the former. If there is nothing remniscent of the class character of the previous stage of social development and anything spurring it, what remains from its political order to be reflected in social consciousness? Since organisation and administration of the communist society need no coercion, then it is not only the law and the state that ultimately become obsolete as a result of their withering away, but it is also the legal and the political form of social consciousness (which, as it has been discussed thus far, should not be identified explicitly with legal constructs and state apparatus) that becomes diffused in other forms of social consciousness, which do not reflect in their essence the class character of the previous stage of social development. In fact, Chrysis himself actually points to this direction, since his view that the members of the future communist society will have "the ethical-political responsibility to evaluate, decide, and discern the criteria and limits, the measure of production and needs satisfaction" (Chrysis 2020, p. 220), may also be understood as if it points to a diffusion of the political in the ethical form, informing a process of free and creative life (Chrysis 2020, p. 234), as which he contents to be the characteristics of praxis that politics tend to assume in communism.

7.5 In Lieu of a Conclusion

In the superstructure of each society, institutions to which the ruling class has assigned the formulation and validation of the application of legal rules and practices, as well as the control and supervision of related processes, are articulated through the state. The properly organised structure and hierarchy of the institutions of the superstructure ensure the legitimation of power, aiming at the reproduction of the existing social order. The forms and methods of organising the social order, the processes of the state apparatus, as well as the framework and legal guarantees for the conditions of their exercise, are formally and institutionally secured through the functions of the legal and political superstructure. These features and functions of the legal superstructure and state apparatus enable the reproduction and further development of the social relations in production, in their interaction with the development of the productive forces of any given society, on which the power of the ruling class lies.

Here comes forth the role of the constitution, as an expression of the basic guidelines for these processes and their essence, in a given society. It is in this sense that the constitution becomes a "class category", expressing "the interests of the ruling class", the key to which, in the case of transition from capitalism to full-blown communism socialism, is its "socialist essence" (Grigoryan and Dolgopolov 1971, pp. 23–24).

In the period of building the communist society, which is the new stage of development of the class struggle that follows the revolutionary overthrow of capital from power, the dictatorship of the proletariat is assigned the duty to educate the masses of workers "to apply in practice the materialist analysis and the materialist estimate of all aspects of the life and activity of all classes, strata and groups of the population" (Lenin 1960, p. 412). Thus, it is via their active participation in and engagement with the political administration of society that the masses of working people become conscious of how the social, political, and economic system is operating in direct accordance with their interests and not in contradiction with them, as it was the case when Lenin wrote these lines.

The transitory nature of the immature communist society that is established by the socialist revolution and which the dictatorship of the proletariat leads to its maturity, to full-blown communism, thus becoming itself (i.e. the dictatorship of the proletariat, as the last historical type of state) obsolete, becomes evident in every instance and aspect of the dialectical development of the communist society. The outcome is a qualitatively new stage in the development of social Being, which is reflected on social consciousness. The latter, in its part, is an active factor in this dialectical process of development.

A society driven by the dictatorship of the proletariat, from the overthrow of bourgeois class from power to full-blown communism, is a society being developed amidst a social revolution and through it. This social revolution amounts to the development of the new, communist social relations. These relations and their relata form the new social Being, the material mode of existence of the new society, which is reflected in its developing social consciousness. Focusing on the development of social consciousness, we can shed new light on how the political action of the proletariat conditions the development of both the state and the right in the transition from the immature to the mature communist society.

Since the immature communist society remains one in which fierce class struggle takes place, the interconnection of right and politics on the grounds of the economy arguably bears significant impact on the constitutional issues pertaining the organisation of the dictatorship of the proletariat. In such a society, the constitution portrays the most general juridico-political framework via which the proletariat, as the ruling class of society and by the means of its dictatorship, under the guidance of the communist party, performs its organisational role, which, according to Lenin, is its principal role (Lenin 1966, p. 44). As long as the class struggle continues, the constitution of the socialist state should be in accordance with the conditions actually obtaining.

Notes

1 Scientific communism is considered to be one of the three component parts of Marxism-Leninism (next to materialistic dialectics in philosophy and political economy), dealing with the socio-political substantiation of the working class' historical mission and the means and ways of carrying it out. In the relevant literature, scientific communism is understood as arising out of the actual mass struggle of the proletariat against the bourgeoisie and the conscious leadership of the struggle on the part of the vanguard of the proletariat (the Communist Party), differing fundamentally from utopian and petty-bourgeois reformist socialism. It is based on the class struggle of the proletariat and the recognition of the necessity for the dictatorship of the proletariat. The theoretical statement of its principles is Marxism-Leninism, embracing general questions of philosophy and method as well as their concrete application, thus becoming essential to the proletariat in its struggles, since it imparts consciousness, self-assurance, and decision to the movement (Adoratsky 1934, p. 12). For further elaboration on the term see, for example, the relevant entry in the Dictionary of Scientific Communism (Rumyantsev 1984, p. 212); also (Seleznev and Fetisov 1985), among others.

2 I use the term "right" rather than "law", in the sense of the German term "Recht" rather than "Gesetz", or the Greek term "dikaion" rather than "nomos".

3 The term "dictatorship of the proletariat" is used throughout the text in the sense it is used in the classical Marxist-Leninist literature. That is, as a synonym for the conquest of political power by the working class and refers to the long historical process that begins with the revolutionary overthrow of the bourgeoisie from power and leads to full-blown communism, via the active engagement and participation of workers in the management of social and political affairs. In this sense, it signifies the state-form of the post-revolutionary class rule of the working class, as opposed to the pre-revolutionary domination and political rule of the bourgeoisie. For a detailed discussion on the history of the term and the relevant debates, see (Draper 1987) and (Kivotidis 2021).

4 Kivotidis (2024b) notes that the terms "legal form" and "political form" allow for the grasping of the unity of the ideational and institutional elements of plentiful social phenomena relevant to law and the state's social function. While focusing on this unity is necessary for a proper and comprehensive discussion on several issues that will also be dealt with in this text, I prefer to focus on the distinct constituents of this unity, in order to highlight some aspects of the interaction between these ideational and institutional elements. The reader should bear in mind this clarification to avoid a possible misunderstanding while reading the following pages, since the terms "legal form of social consciousness" (or, sometimes, "legal consciousness") and "political form of

social consciousness" (or, sometimes, "political consciousness") are used throughout the text referring to the aforementioned ideational elements, while the relevant institutional elements are included in the scope of the respective "superstructure".

5 While not intending to discuss in detail the relevant debates in Soviet legal scholarship and, particularly, it is probably obvious to the readers who are acquainted with it that this view differs from Pashukanis' views on the legal form, which have drawn significant scholar attention in discussions on Marxist legal theories. Pashukanis, by considering that the legal form is founded on commodity exchange, actually limits its scope only to the framework of social relations founded on commodity exchange. In doing so, however, he downplays the importance of the Marxist view of the primary role of production in the dialectical unity of production, distribution, exchange, and consumption, which constitute social production as a whole. Consequently, he downplays the importance of property and production relations in the very foundation of society—not only the bourgeois one, which is characterised by the capitalist mode of production and founded on the capitalist relations in production, but also the communist one (including the socialist one, in its pathway to full-blown communism). Thus, Pashukanis becomes oblivious to the active role that law is called upon to play as a means of influencing the workers' state for the consolidation and expansion of social property, towards the complete elimination of commodity-money relations. In fact, he actually turns to deny such a role. As such, Pashukanis' conception of the legal form amounts to disavowal of the importance and necessity of law for the conduct of the class struggle in socialism.

References

Adoratsky, V.V. (1934). *Dialectical Materialism: The Theoretical Foundation of Marxism-Leninism*. New York: International Publishers.

Carver, T. (2002). *Marx: Later Political Writings*. Cambridge: Cambridge University Press.

Chrysis, A. (2020). *Marx of Communism (in Greek)*. Athens: Kapsimi.

Draper, H. (1987). *The 'Dictatorship of the Proletariat' from Marx to Lenin*. New York: Monthly Review Press.

Engels, Fr. (1970). The Origin of the Family, Private Property and the State. In: K. Marx and Fr. Engels (eds.), *Selected Works,* Vol. 3 (pp. 191–334), Moscow: Progress Publishers.

Engels, Fr. (2021). *Revolution and Counterrevolution in Germany*. Paris: Foreign Language Press.

Engels, Fr. (1970). The Origin of the Family, Private Property and the State. In: K. Marx and Fr. Engels, *Selected Works,* Vol. 3 (pp. 191–334), Moscow: Progress Publishers.

Garo, I. (2023). *Communism and Strategy. Rethinking Political Mediations*. London: Verso.

Grigoryan, L. and Dolgopolov, V. (1971). *Fundamentals of Soviet State Law*. Moscow: Progress Publishers.

Ilyenkov, E.V. (1967). From the Marxist-Leninist Point of View. In: N. Lobkowicz (ed.), *Marx and the Western World* (pp. 391–407), London: University of Notre Dame Press.

Ilyenkov, E.V. (1980). *Leninskaya dialektika i metafizika pozitivizma [Lenin's Dialectics and the Metaphysics of Positivism]*. Moscow: Politizdat [in Russian].

Ilyenkov, E.V. (1967). From the Marxist-Leninist Point of View. In: Nicholas Lobkowicz (ed.), Marx and the Western World, pp. 391–407. London: University of Notre Dame Press.

Kelle, V. Zh. and Kovalzon, M.Y. (1959). *Formy obshchestvennogo soznaniya. [Forms of Social Consciousness]*. Moscow: Gospolitizdat (in Russian).

Kivotidis, D. (2021). *Dictatorship: New Trajectories in Law*. London: Routledge.

Kivotidis, D. (2024a). The Withering Away of the Legal Form: Revisiting Past Debates for Future Movements. In: C. Cercel, G.- G. Fusco and P. Tacik (eds.), *Legal Form and the End of Law: Pashukanis's Legacy* (pp. 234–257), London: Routledge.

Kivotidis, D. (2024b). *The Dialectics of Democracy: Towards a Socialist Constitutionalism*. London: Routledge.

Knox, R. (2009). Marxism, International Law, and Political Strategy. *Leiden Journal of International Law*, 22, pp. 429–434.

Lenin, V.I. (1960). What is to be Done? In: V. I. Lenin (ed.), *Collected Works*, Vol. 5, (pp. 347–530), Moscow: Progress Publishers.

Lenin, V.I. (1963). An Increasing Discrepancy. In: V. I. Lenin (ed.), *Collected Works*, Vol. 18, (pp. 562–579), Moscow: Progress Publishers.

Lenin, V.I. (1964a). A Caricature of Marxism and Imperialist Economism. In: V.I. Lenin (ed.), *Collected Works*, Vol. 23 (pp. 28–76), Moscow: Progress Publishers.

Lenin, V.I. (1964b). State and Revolution: The Marxist Theory of the State and the Tasks of the Proletariat in the Revolution. In: V.I. Lenin (ed.), *Collected Works*, Vol. 25 (pp. 385–540), Moscow: Progress Publishers.

Lenin, V.I. (1965a). The Constituent Assembly Elections and the Dictatorship of the Proletariat. In: V.I. Lenin (ed.), *Collected Works*, Vol. 30 (pp. 253–275), Moscow: Progress Publishers.

Lenin, V.I. (1965b). Report on Subotniks Delivered to a Moscow City Conference of the R.C.P. (B.). In: V.I. Lenin (ed.), *Collected Works*, Vol. 30 (pp. 283–290), Moscow: Progress Publishers.

Lenin, V.I. (1966). Left-Wing Communism – An Infantile Disorder. In: V.I. Lenin (ed.), *Collected Works*, Vol. 31 (pp. 17–118), Moscow: Progress Publishers.

Marx, K. (1937). *The Eighteenth Brumaire of Louis Bonaparte*. Moscow: Progress Publishers.

Marx, K. (1970). *A Contribution to the Critique of Political Economy*. Moscow: Progress Publishers.

Marx, K. (1937). The Eighteenth Brumaire of Louis Bonaparte. Moscow: Progress Publishers.

Rumyantsev, A.M. (ed.) (1984). *A Dictionary of Scientific Communism*. Moscow: Progress Publishers.

Seleznev, L. and Fetisov, V. (1985). *What Is Scientific Communism*. Moscow: Progress Publishers.

Shoikhedbrod, I. (2019). *Revisiting Marx's Critique of Liberalism: Rethinking Justice, Legality and Rights*. London: Palgrave Macmillan.

Sultany, N. (2021). Marx and Critical Constitutional Theory. In: P. O'Connell and U. Özsu (eds.), *Research Handbook on Marxism and Law,* (pp. 235–239), Cheltenham: Edward Elgar Publishing.

Sypnowich, C. (1987). Withering Away of Law. *Studies in Soviet Thought,* 33(4), pp. 327–328.

Thompson, E.P. (1975). *Whigs and Hunters: The Origins of the Black Act*. New York: Pantheon Books.

8 Freedom

The Normative Ground of Marx's Revolutionary Communism

Mehmet Tabak

8.1 Introduction

The main argument of the present chapter[1] is that Karl Marx's revolutionary communism is essentially a *normative theory*. To have such a "theory it is sufficient that one expresses an (essentially) consistent body of ethical judgments," which are both interconnected and derived "from some common foundation" (Brenkert, 1983, p. 8).[2] The chapter illustrates several related senses in which freedom is "the common foundation" of Marx's revolutionary communism, which entails a consistent body of interconnected normative judgments. These judgments are both critical and prescriptive.[3] Marx derives both aspects of this normative theory from a conception of human essence. This gives a humanist character to his revolutionary communism.

In outline, Marx's revolutionary communism conceives capitalism as a system of alienation (unfreedom and dehumanization), especially of the worker, and condemns it for this reason. Relatedly, it justifies political revolution as a necessary means to abolish alienation (Section 8.2). Revolutionary communism also prescribes expansively democratic, self-governing political and economic institutions (political communes and producers' cooperatives) for the post-capitalist society. The chief goal of these institutions is to achieve a truly emancipated society, called "communism" or "socialism"[4] (Section 8.3). Thus, freedom is both the organizing principle of such institutions and their normative-political end. Moreover, revolutionary communism calls for communistic distributive principles, or rights, which are justified as preconditions for a dignified life, based on human flourishing,[5] the antithesis of alienation. Ultimately, Marx describes communism as "a higher form of society" in which the all-around and free development of every individual becomes "the ruling principle" (Marx, 1867/1996, p. 588) (Section 8.4).[6] Revolutionary communism lends itself to a basic constitutional theory, which the conclusion of this chapter calls "communist constitutionalism." The concluding section both defines communist constitutionalism and briefly contemplates on its necessity.

DOI: 10.4324/9781032621623-9

8.2 Alienation and Revolutionary Consciousness

This section argues that Marx's critique of capitalism is, at bottom, a normative condemnation of, especially, the worker's alienation this system engenders. The argument is derived from three related types of evidence. First, Marx's various depictions of alienation consistently smack of normative disapproval. Second, his theory of revolutionary consciousness, which defends the necessity to overthrow capitalism, issues directly from his condemnation of alienation and desire to achieve a thoroughly free society. Third, Marx was consistently hostile to those who remained indifferent to workers' alienation/suffering, and to those who opposed their political struggles to abolish capitalism.

Marx's theory of alienation is too complex to adequately discuss in this brief space. Suffice it to mention the most foundational aspect of it, which highlights the worker's alienation in relation to the activity of production. Briefly put, Marx identifies four interrelated ways in which the worker is alienated in through capitalistic process of production: (1) from the products of labor, which—as capital—become an alien power over the worker; (2) through the loss of control over productive activity, resulting from commodification of labor power and, consequently, of human beings; (3) from other human beings, especially in relation to their social labor and its products; and (4) from human essence or "species-being," which encompasses all aspects of alienation.[7]

The following passage from *Capital*, Vol. 1, provides a useful, practical account of the alienation (estrangement) complex and its inhuman consequences:

> Within the capitalist system … all means for the development of production transform themselves into means of domination over, and exploitation of, the producers; they mutilate the laborer into a fragment of a man, degrade him to the level of an appendage of a machine, destroy every remnant of charm in his work and turn it into a hated toil; they estrange from him the intellectual potentialities of the labor process in the same proportion as science is incorporated in it as an independent power; they distort the conditions under which he works, subject him during the labor process to a despotism the more hateful for its meanness; they transform his life-time into working-time …
>
> (Marx, 1867/1996, pp. 639–640)

Overall, then "'alienation' is the name for … capitalist unfreedom" (Lukes, 1985, pp. 80–81), and for its dehumanizing effects. This is why Marx consistently associated alienated labor with slavery and inhumanity. For instance, in an early work, he calls capitalistic wage "payment for the slave," which commodifies workers and undermines their "human status and dignity" (Marx, 1844/1975d, p. 280). Alienation/unfreedom denotes dehumanization because it entails estrangement from human essence (Marx, 1844/1975d, 284; also see 1847/1977, p. 221; 1865/1985c, p. 129; 1875/1989b, p. 92). To associate alienation with a form of slavery and dehumanization, as did Marx repeatedly, is to express a certain normative disapproval of it. Marx was not indifferent to the effects of alienation.

Marx's condemnation of alienation directly informs his theory of revolutionary consciousness, as well as his related belief in the imperative to overthrow capitalism. We observe a version of this in his "Theses on Feuerbach." The tenth thesis states that "The standpoint of the old materialism is civil society; the standpoint of the new [i.e., Marx's] is human society, or social humanity." To rephrase, the standpoint of the likes of Feuerbach is the existing bourgeois society; the standpoint of Marx is the unalienated *human* society. The eleventh thesis compliments the tenth: "The philosophers have only interpreted the world in various ways; the point is to *change* it" (Marx, 1845/1975g, p. 5). The point, then, is to change the existing bourgeois society into one that transcends alienation. Without this normative desideratum, it is not clear why changing the world would be "the point." This "point" is the standpoint of Marx's revolutionary consciousness, as we are about to further see.

Marx famously states in an early work that "The weapon of criticism cannot, of course, replace criticism by weapons, material force must be overthrown by material force; but theory also becomes a material force as soon as it has gripped the masses." He thus treats critical theory itself as a crucial "weapon" of revolution and adds that such a theory must demonstrate "*ad hominem*, and it demonstrates *ad hominem* as soon as it becomes radical. To be radical is to grasp the root of the matter. But for man the root is man himself." This critical theory, which is consistent with "the teaching that man is the highest being for man," leads to "the *categorical imperative to overthrow all relations* in which man is debased, enslaved, forsaken, despicable being." That is, it leads to the revolutionary *categorical imperative* to abolish all relations of dehumanization (Marx, 1844/1975a, p. 182; also see 1844/1975b, p. 205).[8]

Evidently, a humanist-normative concern, derived from a conception of human nature, which also values human well-being, grounds Marx's revolutionary consciousness. In capitalism, said "*categorical imperative*" arises, especially, from the dehumanized and unfree condition of the proletariat, which is "a class with radical chains," and so "has a universal character by its universal suffering." This class, therefore, represents "the *complete loss* of man and hence can win itself only through the *complete rewinning of man*" (Marx, 1844/1975a, p. 186). Given its all-around alienation, Marx—the critical philosopher—not only calls upon the proletariat to invoke "a human title" for itself but also regards it as the only class capable of practically invoking this title universally.

In *The Holy Family*, Marx and Engels attribute their own revolutionary-normative consciousness directly to the proletariat, which "feels annihilated in estrangement," its "inhuman existence." Consequently, it develops "an *indignation* to which it is necessarily driven by the contradiction between its human *nature* and its condition of life, which is the outright, resolute and comprehensive negation of that nature." The consciousness of this contradiction leads to revolutionary consciousness:

> since man has lost himself in the proletariat, yet at the same time has not only gained theoretical consciousness of that loss, but through urgent, no longer removable, no longer disguisable, absolutely imperative need—the practical expression of necessity—is driven directly to revolt against this inhumanity, it follows that the proletariat can and must emancipate itself.
>
> (Marx and Engels, 1845/1975b, p. 37)

Likewise, Marx and Engels argue in *The German Ideology* that from the all-around alienation of the proletariat "emanates the consciousness of the necessity of a fundamental revolution, the communist consciousness, which may, of course, arise among the other classes too through the contemplation of the situation of this class" (Marx and Engels, 1846/1975a, p. 52).

We find compatible thoughts in the "materialist" *Manifesto*, which adumbrates a host of reasons that collectively provoke the emancipatory consciousness of the proletariat. These include the lamentations that workers in capitalism "must sell themselves piecemeal, [and so] are a commodity," and that they are consequently

> enslaved by the machine, by the overlooker, and, above all, by the individual bourgeois manufacturer himself. The more openly this despotism proclaims gain to be its end and aim, the more petty, the more hateful and the more embittering it is.
>
> (Marx and Engels, 1848/1976, pp. 490–491)

After discussing similar conditions of alienation–dehumanization in the *Grundrisse*, Marx adds:

> The recognition [by workers] of the products as … [their] own, and the judgment that its separation from the conditions of … [their self-] realization is improper [*ungehörig*] and forcibly imposed by force, is an enormous [advance in] consciousness …, and just as much the [death] KNELL TO ITS DOOM as the consciousness of the slave that he cannot be the *property of another*.
>
> (Marx, 1857–1858/1986b, pp. 390–391)

The improperness Marx has in mind here, as well as the "injustice" he detects in a very similar passage found elsewhere (Marx, 1861–1863/1994, pp. 245–246), urges the motivation for abolishing the conditions that engender it. Although Marx often attributes this revolutionary consciousness/motivation to the working class in his various works, it is undeniable that he himself was driven by it.

The claim that Marx's revolutionary consciousness is normatively grounded is further supported by his castigation of those who (1) refused to either call for emancipatory class struggle; (2) justified capitalism as the highest form of society; (3) or else remained indifferent to workers' "dehumanized life." An elaborate version of (1) is found in the *Manifesto*, where Marx and Engels criticize various socialist traditions for opposing workers' political struggles to emancipate themselves (Marx and Engels, 1948/1976, pp. 513–517). As for (2), Marx disparaged those who regarded capitalism as the final and highest form of society. For instance, he castigates Karl Heinzen for this reason (Marx, 1852/1983, p. 62), and in *Capital,* Vol. 1, he deprecates the "mystified form" of Hegel's dialectic, which "became the fashion in Germany, because it seemed to transfigure and to glorify the existing state of things" (Marx, 1867/1996, p. 18). The third type of castigation pertains to Marx's criticism of those who remained indifferent to the suffering of the working class. For instance, his *The Poverty of Philosophy* contains a critique of various "*fatalist* economists," who are as "indifferent ... as the bourgeois themselves are in practice to the sufferings of the proletarians..." These "economists now pose as blasé fatalists, who, from their elevated position, cast a proudly disdainful glance at the human machines who manufacture wealth" (Marx, 1847/1976, pp. 176–178).

"If one wanted to be an ox," Marx writes tellingly in a letter to Sigfrid Meyer, "one could, of course, turn one's back on the sufferings of humanity and look after one's own hide" (Marx, 1867/1987a, 366). This statement captures well the normative register of Marx's anti-indifferentist, revolutionary motivation, which urged him to repeatedly warn that the working class cannot emancipate itself without a revolution (e.g., Marx, 1844/1975b, p. 206; 1872/1988, p. 255; Marx and Engels, 1846/1975a, pp. 52–53; 1848/1976, p. 514, p. 519;). Emancipation ought to be brought about by a political revolution and, subsequently, by the institutions of the post-capitalist society.

8.3 The Governing Institutions of Communism: Political and Economic Communes

This section illustrates how Marx's vision of communism entails thoroughly democratic, self-governing political and economic institutions—communes and workers' cooperatives respectively, freedom being both their *modus operandi* and the principled aim. These institutions are prescribed and justified on normative grounds, even if Marx himself often denied resorting to such reasoning. Indeed, the governing institutions of communism are meant to overcome "political alienation" (Tabak, 2020, pp. 27–44), which the bourgeois constitutionalism legalizes and perpetuates (Sultany, 2021).

In *The Class Struggles in France*, Marx refers to the revolutionary rule of workers as *the dictatorship of the proletariat* for the first time,[9] describing it as "the necessary transit point to the *abolition of class distinctions generally*, to the abolition of all the relations of production on which they rest, to the abolition of all the social relations that correspond to these relations of production, to the revolutionizing of all the ideas that result from these social relations" (Marx, 1850/1978a, 127). Otherwise stated, the chief aim of the dictatorship of the proletariat is the abolition of all relations of alienation.

Another passage from the same text argues that "the revolutionary dictatorship" of the proletariat should be led by the working class, not by a "sectarian" group of leaders (Marx, 1850/1978a, p. 98). Thus, by 1850, Marx had dropped his momentary Blanquist-authoritarian-statist predilections (e.g., in Marx and Engels, 1848/1976, 505; 1850/1978, pp. 285–286). More generally, Marx had readopted his earlier anti-statist position. Accordingly, he argues in *The Eighteenth Brumaire* that the modern state "possesses an immense bureaucratic and military organization, with its extensive and artificial state machinery …, which enmeshes the body … society like a net and chokes all its pores." Marx then predicts that the next revolution in France would be against the bureaucratic state itself (Marx, 1851/1979, pp. 185 ff).

The Paris Commune of 1871 reminded Marx of this prediction (Marx, 1871/1989d, p. 131), as well as his animosity towards the state machinery. Thus, in *The Civil War in France*, his eulogy for the Commune, Marx disparagingly defines the state as the "centralized and organized governmental power usurping to be the master instead of the servant of society" (Marx, 1871/1986a, pp. 486–487), and maintains that "The working class cannot simply lay hold of ready-made state machinery and wield it for its own purposes" (Marx, 1871/1986d, p. 328; also see Marx and Engels 1872/1988, p. 175). It must replace it with "really democratic institutions," to be modelled after the Commune, "the direct antithesis" of the "state machinery" (Marx, 1871/1986d, p. 328, p. 330).

Had it survived, Marx argues rather wishfully, the Commune would consist of "really democratic institutions," based on direct "self-government" in all localities and representation regionally and nationally through *delegates*. Each delegate would "be at any time revocable and bound by the *mandat impératif* of his constituents." Moreover, the police and the officials of the entire executive branch would be "at once stripped of [their] political attributes, and turned into the responsible and at all times revocable agent of the Commune." Much "like the rest of public servants, magistrates and judges" would be "elective, responsible, and revocable." Lastly, "The unity of the nation" would "be organized by the Communal constitution" (Marx, 1871/1986d, pp. 331–332).

To Marx, the Commune was not simply a short-lived historical fact. It was also "the political form at last discovered under which to work out the economical emancipation of labor …, a lever for uprooting the economical foundations upon which rests the existence of classes, and therefore of class rule" (Marx, 1871/1986d, p. 334). As Engels further reiterates, he and Marx regarded the Commune as the proper form of communistic government, to be emulated in the future by other revolutionary societies (Engels, 1891/1990, p. 191). Marx himself continued to defend, as a desideratum, communal government for the future society after 1871. His conspectus of Bakunin's *Statism and Anarchy* is a case in point (Marx, 1874/1989g, pp. 519–520). Likewise, in his *Critique of the Gotha Program*, Marx insists that "Freedom consists in converting the state from an organ superimposed upon society into one completely subordinate to it" (Marx, 1875/1989b, pp. 94–95; also see Marx, 1879/1989a, 572). Evidently, Marx wanted to see an explicit demand for something like the Commune in the Gotha Program. This is also evident in Engels' remarkably similar critique of the Program:

> All the palaver about the state ought to be dropped, especially after the Commune, which had ceased to be a state in the true sense of the term. … We [Marx and Engels] would therefore suggest that *Gemeinwesen* be universally substituted for *state;* it is a good old German word that can very well do service for the French 'Commune'.
>
> (Engels, 1875/1989, p. 64)

In short, in Marx's view, the top-down bureaucratic state "cannot serve as the political instrument of … emancipation," since it is itself an instrument of unfreedom. For this reason, the future dictatorship of the proletariat ought to be modelled after the Paris Commune, the "antithesis" of the state, based on "really democratic institutions" (Marx, 1871/1986c, p. 533). Marx thought this model of self-government ought to remain in effect in the future classless society as well, except that it would no longer manifest itself as a transitional class dictatorship in such a society (Tabak, 2020, pp. 139–140). In any event, the political institutions of emancipation ought to function as free associations of self-governing citizens; the means and ends must coincide.

Marx's normative defense of workers' cooperatives dovetails his normative defense of the self-governing political communes as instruments of dealienation. The following comment, taken from his 1864 inaugural address of the International, captures the normativity entailed in his defense of the organically-formed workers' cooperatives—the economic communes:

> We speak of the co-operative movement, especially the co-operative factories raised by the unassisted efforts of a few bold "hands". … By deed, instead of by argument, they have shown that production on a large scale … may be carried on without the existence of a class of masters employing a class of hands; that to bear fruit, the means of labor need not be monopolized as a means of dominion over, and of extortion against, the laboring man himself … At the same time, … however excellent in principle, and however useful in practice, co-operative labor … ought to be developed to national dimensions, and, consequently, to be fostered by national means [under the democratic sway of the working class] … To conquer [national] political power has therefore become the great duty of the working classes.
>
> (Marx, 1864/1985a, pp. 11–12)

The main task of the International, Marx wrote on another occasion as a political demand, is "to combine and generalize the *spontaneous movements* of the working classes, but not to dictate or impose any doctrinaire system whatever." The International ought to recognize "the co-operative movement as one of the transforming forces of the present society based upon class antagonism." Marx further reasoned that this movement's "great merit is to practically show that the present pauperizing, and despotic system of *the subordination of labor* to capital can be superseded by the republican and beneficent system of *the association of free and equal producers*" (Marx, 1866/1985b, p. 190). In *The Civil War in France*, he once again speaks favorably of these "instruments of free and associated labor." "If," he adds,

> united co-operative societies are to regulate national production upon a common plan, thus taking it under their own control, and putting an end to the constant anarchy and periodical convulsions which are the fatality of Capitalist production—what else, gentlemen, would it be but Communism, 'possible' Communism?
>
> (Marx, 1871/1986d, p. 335)

Marx zealously repeats his longstanding defense of spontaneously-formed workers' cooperatives in his *Critique of the Gotha Program* (1875), especially against the Program's demand to establish "producers' co-operative societies *with state aid under the democratic control of the toiling people*." In this regard, the *Critique* specifically condemns the Program's demand to achieve workers' cooperatives with "state aid." The value of the existing "co-operative societies," Marx reiterates, emerges directly from the fact that "they are the independent creations of the workers and not protégés either of the governments or of the bourgeois" (Marx, 1875/1989b, pp. 93–94). This view is consistent with the anti-statist Marx's dual conviction that in communism, the direct producers must self-emancipate and self-govern. In this regard, the "co-operative factories of the laborers" represent the "first sprouts" of communism, as Marx also notes in the third volume of *Capital* (Marx, 1894/1998, p. 438).

Marx's comments on the possibility of Russia's transition to communism also reveal his persistent support for economic communes.[10] In this context, Marx argued that the underdeveloped Russia could indeed "acquire all the fruits of this [commune] system without suffering … [all the] torments [of capitalist development]" (Marx, 1877/1989e, p. 199). He is "convinced" that "this commune is the fulcrum of [communistic] social regeneration in Russia," provided that its "normal conditions of spontaneous development" are not thwarted by the state, the bourgeoisie, and the emergent class of *kulaks* (Marx, 1881/1989f, pp. 370–371). It would also "be necessary," Marx adds, "to replace the *volost*, the [regional] government body, with an assembly of peasants elected by the communes themselves, serving as the economic and administrative organ for their interests" (Marx, 1881/1987b, 353–354).

In conclusion, Marx had on many occasions envisioned as desiderata, the fundamental governing institutions of communism as "truly democratic" network of communes, political and economic. To freely collaborate with others to achieve common goals is to overcome social alienation and domination, to live in a meaningful community, as human nature requires. The human being, writes Marx accordingly, is "a *zoon politikon*" (social being) in the "most literal sense of the word" (Marx, 1857–1858, 1986b, p. 18). The achievement of such a community also depends on the institution of certain distributive and free-activity principles.

8.4 Principles of Distribution and True Freedom in Communism

In the *Critique of the Gotha Program*, Marx offers his most elaborate discussion of the communistic principles of distribution, even though some aspects of his discussion oddly smack of hostility towards proposing such principles or "rights." Here, Marx first outlines a list of public expenditures, which are to be deducted from "the total social product." These include the cost of both replenishing the means of production and further expanding their capacity, a "reserve or insurance fund to provide against accidents, disturbances caused by natural factors, etc.," as well as the deductions needed to cover "the general costs of administration." He also anticipates additional deductions to pay for "that which is intended for the common satisfaction of needs, such as schools, health services, etc.," as well as "funds for those unable to work, etc." These deductions will benefit "the producer ... directly or indirectly in his capacity as a member of society." Marx expects these expenditures to increase progressively "in proportion as the new society develops," (Marx, 1875/1989b, pp. 84–86; also see 1867/1996, p. 89; 1893/1997, p. 356).

Evidently, the satisfaction of the needs of persons is prioritized in Marx's foregoing distributive scheme, which demands the enhancement of need satisfaction "in proportion as the new society develops" its productive capacities. This is a transitional demand, as is the distributive principle of equal pay for equal amount of work. In the latter regard, Marx states that after all the aforementioned "deductions have been made," each individual producer of "the collective" (or co-operatives) is to receive "back from society ... exactly what he gives to it," namely, "the individual labor time of the individual producer." He presents two similar versions of the latter principle in the *Critique*, both of which he deems "defective" on the ground that they merely consider "individuals ... *only as workers*," ignoring "everything else" about them as human beings with different needs and abilities (Marx, 1875/1989b, pp. 86–87).[11]

Here, a hierarchy of normative *preferences* emerges. Even the "defective" principle of equal pay for equal contribution is still an "advance" over the principle of wages prevalent in bourgeois society because it "recognizes no class distinctions" and avoids the surplus-value pocketed by the capitalist. Relatedly, its implementation would mean that the ownership of the means of production cannot "pass to the ownership of individuals," which could then be used as instrument of exploitation and social domination; only "the individual means of consumption" can pass to the ownership of individuals (Marx, 1875/1989b, p. 86; also see Marx and Engels, 1948/1976, p. 500). Nevertheless, the principle of equal pay for equal contribution has its aforementioned "defects," which "are inevitable in the … [initial] phase of communist society as it is when it has just emerged after prolonged birth-pangs from capitalist society." Marx goes on to anticipate famously, and desirously, that "In a higher phase of communist society … the narrow horizon of bourgeois right [will] be crossed in its entirety and society inscribe on its banner: From each according to his abilities, to each according to his needs!" (Marx, 1875/1989b, p. 87).

Interestingly, Marx borrowed the utopian abilities–needs principle from certain socialist utopians.[12] It is seldom noted that he and Engels reflected favorably on it also in *The German Ideology*, where its normative register is more obviously revealed (Marx and Engels, 1846/1975a, p. 505 ff). The latter work refers to the principle as "one of the most vital principles of communism," arguing that unlike what other socialists maintain, "a *different form* of activity, of labor, does not justify *inequality*, confers no *privileges* in respect of possession and enjoyment [i.e., need satisfaction]." Therefore, "the false tenet, based upon existing circumstances, 'to each according to his abilities,' must be changed, insofar as it relates to enjoyment in its narrower sense, into the tenet, '*to each according to his need*'" (Marx and Engels, 1846/1975a, p. 537).[13] This "most vital principle of communism," *to each according to his need*, entitles individuals to satisfy their needs by virtue of being *humans*, regardless of their productive abilities, which inevitably vary. It thus implies the contributive principle: *from all according to their abilities*.

To demand a system of distribution based on individuals' needs and a system of contribution based on their unique abilities is to demand the wholesale abolition of the capitalistic system of wages. This was one of Marx's favorite demands. For instance, in his 1865 speech to the International, Marx (1865/1985c, pp. 148–149) maintains that "Instead of the [socialistic] conservative motto, '*A fair day's wage for a fair day's work!*'" workers "ought to inscribe on their banner the revolutionary watchword, '*Abolition of the wages system*!'" By the same token, the realization of this demand would contribute to the abolition of the system of alienation.

Evidently, Marx valued "the most vital principle of communism" because he deemed it essential to the chief aim of communism—to make "the *wealth* of human needs" the *object* of production, and thus make possible the "enrichment of *human* nature" (Marx, 1844/1975d, p. 306). In this sense, communism represents "the good society," which, "for Marx, is one in which people are rich in needs and rich in need satisfaction" (Elster, 1985, p. 68). Put from another vantagepoint, Marx's eudaemonism regards such satisfaction as a precondition for human flourishing (see Leopold, 2007, pp. 227–245).

"The *rich* human being," Marx writes in an early work, "is simultaneously the human being *in need of* a totality of human manifestations of life—the man in whom his own realization exists as an inner necessity, as *need*" (Marx, 1844/1975d, p. 304). Thus, *inter alia*, self-realization requires all-around free activity, which depends on implementing the principle of *from all according to their abilities*. As we are about to see, such free activity is necessary for human flourishing, which Marx regards as the highest human need.[14]

To begin with, Marx generally defines free activity as spontaneous, conscious activity, which he often contrasts with animal activity:

> Man makes his life-activity itself the object of his will and of his consciousness. He has conscious life-activity. It is not a determination with which he directly merges. Conscious life-activity distinguishes man immediately from animal life-activity ... Only because of that is his activity free activity.
>
> (Marx, 1844/1975d, p. 276)

In *Capital*, Vol. 1, Marx once again associates human essence with free, self-posited activity:

> A [spider's] operations ... resemble those of a weaver, and a bee puts to shame many an architect in the construction of her cells. But what distinguishes the worst architect from the best of bees is this, that the architect raises his structure in imagination before he erects it in reality. At the end of every labor-process, we get a result that already existed in the imagination [consciousness] of the laborer at its commencement. He not only effects a change of form in the material on which he works, but also realizes a purpose of his own that gives the law to his *modus operandi*.
>
> (Marx, 1867/1996, pp. 187–188)

Here, clarifies Marx, "We presuppose labor in a form that stamps it as exclusively human," not alienated, dehumanizing labor activity prevalent in capitalism (Marx, 1867/1996, p. 188). Marx's derivation of free, self-posited activity from human essence, as the human *ergon*—comes with normative implications, in the sense that such activity is an essential *human* need, and its satisfaction a *human* good. For this reason, as Marx reminds Adam Smith, self-posited activity is *travail attractif*, *even* when it demands "the most intensive effort" (Marx, 1857–1858/1986b, pp. 529–530).[15] Smith "is right, of course," adds Marx, that "in its historic forms as slave-labor, serf-labor, and wage-labor, labor always appears as repulsive, always as *external forced labor;* and not-labor, by contrast, as 'freedom, and happiness'" (Marx, 1857–1858/1986b, p. 530).[16] In communism, free activity ought to "become not only a means of life but life's prime want [or *need—Lebensbedürfnis*]" (Marx, 1875/1989b, p. 87).

Marx offers a compatible ranking system elsewhere, arguing that "FREE ACTIVITY which—unlike [socially necessary] LABOR—is not determined by a compelling extraneous purpose which must be fulfilled, and the fulfilment of which is regarded as a natural necessity or a social duty, according to one's inclination." Instead, free activity is undertaken for its own sake and is more satisfying than socially necessary labor, which would remain in effect even in communism to some extent. But, in communism, reasons Marx, even necessary labor is freer in comparison to its historical counterparts, precisely because it "is no longer performed for someone else," that is, for an alien/hostile force, and so does not entail "the social contradictions between MASTER AND MEN." Thus, in communism, necessary labor "acquires a quite different, free character" since "it becomes truly social [labor i.e., without any masters]" (Marx, 1861–1863/1989c, p. 391).

Marx makes a similar distinction between the two types of *free* activity in the third volume of *Capital*,[17] arguing that "labor which is determined by necessity and mundane considerations" cannot be fully eradicated even in developed communism.[18] "Freedom" in this "realm of necessity," Marx clarifies, "can only consist in socialized man, the associated producers, rationally [and collectively] regulating their interchange with Nature," and in "achieving this with the least expenditure of energy and under conditions most favorable to, and worthy of, their human nature." He regards the "shortening of the [necessary] working day" as an important condition of this kind. The "realm of [true] freedom," adds Marx, "actually begins only where labor which is determined by necessity and mundane considerations ceases," that is "beyond" the realm of necessity, in which is found "that development of human energy, which is an end in itself." In this sense, communism is "the true realm of freedom" (Marx, 1894/1998, p. 807). Elsewhere, Marx maintains that "The reduction of the necessary labor of society" would also contribute to "the artistic, scientific, etc., development of individuals," to "free development of individualities" in communism (Marx, 1861–1863/1989c, p. 91).

However, human flourishing depends not simply on spontaneous, conscious activity, undertaken for its own sake, but all-around free activity. In *The German Ideology*, Marx and Engels borrow Fourier's imagery to wishfully depict communism as a society in which

> nobody has one exclusive sphere of activity, but each can become accomplished in any branch he wishes, society regulates the general production and thus makes it possible for me to do one thing today and another tomorrow, … just as I have a mind…[19]

They favorably contrast all-around free activity with the *inferior* division of labor in capitalism, where "each man has a particular, exclusive sphere of activity, which is forced upon him ..." (Marx and Engels, 1846/1975a, p. 47). Inspired by another utopian, Saint-Simon,[20] Marx and Engels also associate all-around activity with the freedom of "every person ... to achieve all-round development of all his abilities" (Marx and Engels, 1846/1975a, p. 292). Such development is tantamount to a person's flourishing.

Elsewhere, Engels identifies flourishing as the chief *principle* of "the Communists," such as Marx and himself, who demand the organization of "society in such a way that every member of it can develop and use all his capabilities and powers in complete freedom and without thereby infringing the basic conditions of this society" (Engels, 1847/1976a, p. 96; also see Engels, 1847/1976b, p. 353). In the *Manifesto,* we likewise read: "In place of the old bourgeois society ..., we shall have an association, in which the free development of each is the precondition for the development of all" (Marx and Engels, 1848/1976, p. 506).[21] Moreover, Marx maintains in the *Grundrisse* that in communism, "the absolute unfolding of man's creative abilities [or potentialities]" would not be "measured by any *previously given [or predetermined] yardstick.*" Rather, "the development of all human powers as such" is to be posited as "the end-in-itself," making possible a life in which the individual "does not reproduce himself in any specific character but produces his totality ...; does not seek to remain something he has already become but is in the absolute movement of becoming" (Marx, 1857–1858/1986b, pp. 411–412).

The following famous lines from the *Critique of the Gotha Program* dovetail these thoughts, but add that the full realization of the communistic demand of human flourishing also depends on the further development of productive forces:

> In a higher phase of communist society, after the enslaving subordination of the individual to the division of labor, and thereby also the antithesis between mental and physical labor, has vanished; after labor has become not only a means of life but life's prime want [or need]; after the productive forces have also increased with the all-round development of the individual, and all the springs of common wealth flow more abundantly—only then can the narrow horizon of bourgeois right be crossed in its entirety and society inscribe on its banner: From each according to his abilities, to each according to his needs! (Marx, 1875/1989b, p. 87).

As such, developed communism represents the complete transcendence of alienation. Marx himself maintains that capitalism would "disappear with ... [the disappearance of] alienation" (Marx, 1861–1863/1989c, p. 446), and that "*Communism* is the *positive* transcendence of ... *human self-estrangement.*" Otherwise put, communism is "the real *appropriation* of the *human* essence by and for man" (Marx, 1844/1975d, p. 296). In this sense, the theory of communism is the culmination of Marx's eudaemonistic normative theory.

8.5 Conclusion: Revolutionary Communism as Constitutionalism

As we have seen, a humanist–eudaemonistic normativity grounds Marx's revolutionary communism, which has three systematically related features: it condemns capitalism for being the realm of alienation (unfreedom); justifies revolution as a "categorical imperative" to abolish alienation;[22] prescribes communism, defined as the realm of true freedom. The concept of communism is based on several fundamental *principles*, which are normative statements that collectively serve as the telos of this polity. As such, they are communism's constitutional principles, which are to be "inscribed on its banner."

In Marx's wording, communism is "a higher form of society, a society in which the full and free development of every individual forms the ruling principle" (Marx, 1867/1996, p. 588). This "ruling principle" posits a fundamental human right, which comes with several supporting principles that also imply rights. One of them is the well-known distributive principle: "From each according to his abilities, to each according to his needs!" (Marx, 1875/1989b, p. 87), which is to supersede the transitional principle of equal pay for equal contribution. Another principle calls for the gradual reduction of socially necessary labor. There are also foundational prohibitions, which are antithetical to the spirit of "bourgeois" constitutions. Important among them is the related prohibitions of exploitation and private ownership in the means of production (Marx, 1875/1989b, p. 86). Instead, in accordance with the principle of freedom, the communist polity ought to be based on collective ownership and democratic control of the means of production, which would render them "instruments of free and associated labor" (Marx, 1871/1986d, p. 335). Truly democratic institutions—communes—ought to replace the bureaucratic state also.

To recapitulate, revolutionary communism not only outlines the normative rationale for the transition from capitalism to communism (socialism) but also establishes, as desiderata, both the constitutive principles and institutional forms of the latter. In this sense, revolutionary communism may be called "communist constitutionalism," which is both critical and transformative.[23] It is critical because it highlights the economic, social, and political (including legal/juridical) shortcomings of capitalism (i.e., the "bourgeois society") as a whole. In this respect, the communistic emancipatory principles and institutions serve as humanist evaluative yardsticks, against which those of "the bourgeois society" are critically measured. It is transformative because it calls forth the replacement of this society with a polity that does not yet exist. In other words, it sanctions revolutionary-democratic transition from capitalism to communism, and defines the constitutive principles of the latter.

The futility of the major alternative anticipations of communism highlights the necessity of communist constitutionalism.[24] A popular anticipation of this kind, which can also be found in some of Marx's own works, expects the delivery of communism from capitalism's "laws of motion"—from such related "laws" as the declining rate of profit and overproduction, which presumably ensure both the ever so deepening of capitalism's endemic crisis and the arrival of communism. For this and related reasons, many Marxists have historically focused on the analysis of capitalist crisis, often as a way of heralding its impending abolition through its own "dialectic." Accordingly, "The criticism of capitalism … lacks a necessary connection to an elaborate communist alternative." Such a negation of capitalism

> does not take long to finally evaporate, since what once appeared as a socialist/communist alternative, i.e., the concrete negation of capitalism, as 'actually existing socialism', has proved to be a social system not only exploitative, but also dysfunctional, even by its own internal logic.
>
> (Chrysis, 2020, p. 13)

Another popular anticipation of communism was proposed by those who refused to wait for capitalism's dialectic to do its work. Based on the idea of "combined and uneven development," they justified a "dialectical leap" in economically underdeveloped countries by means of a political revolution. The (in)famous line from *The German Ideology* was conveniently cherrypicked as one of their slogans: "Communism is for us not a ... an *ideal* to which reality [will] have to adjust itself. We call communism the *real* movement which abolishes the present state of things" (Marx and Engels, 1846/1975a, p. 49). Such "things" were led by abolitionist "vanguard" forces, which hastened to establish communism chiefly by four means: (a) by capturing, strengthening, and utilizing the state machinery; (b) by eliminating capitalists; (c) by placing the means of production under bureaucratic command; and (d) subordinating the lives of their citizens both to the development of productive forces and the glorification of the state. Thusly was born the theory and practice of "actually existing socialism," defined merely as the abolition of capitalism. In this way, its antithesis became the very definition of communism.

A third anticipation is post-WWII social-democratic constitutionalism (associated with the welfare state), which resembles communist constitutionalism to a limited extent, due to their historical links.

> It is based on an instrumentalist view of the state and a formalist conception of democracy. … [I]t responds to capitalist contradictions by accommodating and reproducing them. Accordingly, social-democratic 'socialist' constitutionalism is more of a defence of liberal bourgeois constitutionalism than socialism.
>
> (Kivotidis, 2024, p. 193)

Inter alia, this form of constitutionalism lacks the (Marxian) communistic transitionality, which demands transcending class-based ownership and control of the means of production. Arguably, its retreat towards economic neoliberalism, the "neoliberal shift," during the 1980s was facilitated not only by the absence of a communistic transitional demand but also by the state-sanctioned ownership and control of the market-oriented means of production. By its very constitution, "the welfare state" was ultimately committed to the success of capitalism (Offe, 1984). Together with the collapse of the so-called "actually existing socialisms" in Eastern Europe and elsewhere, the retreat of the welfare state has enjoined the return to "a dictatorship of no alternatives" (Unger, 2005, p. 1).

The point of the foregoing is not that embracing communist constitutionalism would have prevented the pitfalls of other anticipations of communism. Rather, following the logic of Meno's Paradox, it is that the original idea of communism cannot be realized without explicating, *a priori*, its principles and institutional forms. However, the issue at hand goes beyond the need to envision the basic principles and institutions of communism. It also requires explaining why communism is necessary in the first place, especially since achieving communism requires the voluntary acceptance of its basic principles by a large segment of society. Marx's pertinent writings give as some of the most compelling answers in both regards, though they need to be further refined and updated.

Notes

1 The present chapter is largely derived from Tabak (2020).
2 Many scholars use the terms "ethical" and "moral" synonymously. To others, argue they mean different things. Except when unavoidable (e.g., in direct quotations), I will use the term "normative," which designates certain actions, social arrangement, or outcomes either as desiderata or as permissible, and others as undesirable, or impermissible.
3 My argument is not that Marx himself thought his works offered a normative theory—he did not; rather, it claims that such a theory can be attributed to him. Indeed, Marx's works contain several types of counterevidence that challenge the central claims of the present chapter. Due to space limitation, the counterevidence, which the present author deems irreconcilable with the evidence presented below, is ignored in what follows. Due to the same limitation, the chapter also largely ignores the rich secondary literature on the topics it covers. Tabak (2020, throughout) elaborates on such counterevidence and literature.
4 Marx generally uses the terms *socialism* and *communism* interchangeably, and not as appellations for different stages of post-capitalist society. For an informed discussion, see Chattopadhyay (2018, Ch. 1).
5 In "Marx's notion … to flourish is to realize both human capabilities and the conditions for freedom" (Lazarus, 2022, p. 417).
6 Nasser (1975, p. 485) aptly associates this "*ergon* argument" with Aristotelian ethics. According to Wood (2004, p. 128), Marx has a "recognizably Aristotelian conception of human self-actualization, the development and exercise of our 'human essential powers'." However, Wood denies that Marx's conception is in any way moral (or normative). For an excellent critique of Wood and others in this regard, see Groff (2015). For a rich discussion of the Aristotle-Marx connection, see ed. George E. McCarthy (ed.) (1992).
7 For a more detailed account of Marx's theory of alienation, including references to other such accounts, see Tabak (2020, pp. 12–26).
8 Comments such as this have inspired some authors to detect Kantian influence in Marx's writings (e.g., Karatani, 2005, p. 130).

9 Draper (1986, pp. 34–39, 111–171) offers an almost exhaustive treatment of the origin and uses of the concept of the proletarian dictatorship.
10 Wada (1983) provides an excellent account of Marx's approach to the question of Russia.
11 For an illuminating discussion, see Moore (1980, pp. 45 ff).
12 For an impressive survey of the origins of the principle, see Bovens and Lutz (2019). Also see Manuel and Manuel (1979, p. 710 ff).
13 The full version of the principle *from each according to one's ability, to each according to one's need,* was quoted by Engels in 1851, giving Louis Blanc as its source (Engels, 1852/1979, p. 555).
14 For excellent discussions of Marx theory of need, see Heller (1976), and Chitty (1993, 23–31).
15 Marx critically borrowed the idea of *travail attractif* and its opposite, *travail repugnant,* from the utopian Fourier. "Remember," one reads in The German Ideology, "that Fourier wished to see the present travail répugnant replaced by *travail attrayant*" (Marx and Engels, 1846/1975a, p. 481).
16 Smith also had a notion of workers' alienation that resembles that of Marx. For an interesting discussion, see Lamb (1973, pp. 275–285).
17 For good discussions, see Klagge (1986), and Kandiyali (2014).
18 In the *Manuscripts of* 1844, Marx seems to have a more optimistic view in this regard.
19 This portrayal of communism, penned down by Engels has puzzled many scholars. Some of them suppose that it was mocked by Marx (e.g., Carver 1988, and Rockmore 2018, p. 64). Wallimann (1981, Ch. 7), and Ware (1982, esp. pp. 57 ff) offer sound rebuttals of this supposition.
20 In this context, Marx and Engels approvingly speak of Saint-Simon's comment: "The reader will recall Saint-Simon's statement concerning *libre développement de toutes les facultés"* (Marx and Engels, 1846, 1975a, p. 481).
21 Unlike what a popular view maintains, Marx does not imagine a society in which the individual would exist for the sake of the community. For a lengthy list of authors who defend this view, and their judicious refutation, see Nordahl (1987).
22 As Bertell Ollman (1976, p. 132) aptly puts it, for Marx, "unalienation is the life man leads in communism."
23 Sultany (2001) offers an interesting and informed treatment of Marx's ideas as components of "critical constitutionalism." I prefer "communist constitutionalism" to stress the specificity of the constitutionalism *we attribute* to Marx. "Socialist constitutionalism" will also do, except that nowadays it calls to mind the former welfare states.
24 The following few paragraphs are not meant as adequate explanations of different anticipates and their consequences.

Bibliography

(Note *MECW* refers to *Marx and Engels Collected Works*)

Bovens, Luc & Adrien Lutz (2019) . "From Each according to Ability; To Each according to Needs": Origin, Meaning, and Development of Socialist Slogans. *History of Political Economy,* 51(2), 237–257.

Brenkert, George G. (1983). *Marx's Ethics of Freedom*. Routledge & Kegan Paul.

Carver, Terrell (1988). Communism for Critical Critics? "The German Ideology" and the Problem of Technology. *History of Political Thought,* 9(1), 129–136.

Chattopadhyay, Paresh (2018). *Socialism and Commodity Production: Essay in Marx Revival*. Brill.

Chitty, Andrew (1993). The Early Marx on Needs. *Radical Philosophy,* 64(2), 23–31.
Chrysis, Alexandros (2020). *The Marx of Communism: Setting Limits in the Realm of Communism.* Palgrave Macmillan.
Draper, Hal 1986. *Karl Marx's Theory of Revolution, Volume III: The "Dictatorship of the Proletariat."* Monthly Review Press.
Elster, Jon (1985). *Making Sense of Marx.* Cambridge University Press.
Engels, Frederick (1976a). Draft of a Communist Confession of Faith. In *MECW*, Vol. 6. Progress Publishers. (First appeared in 1847.)
Engels, Frederick (1976b). Principles of Communism. In *MECW*, Vol. 6. Progress Publishers. (First appeared in 1847.)
Engels, Frederick (1979). Critical Review of Proudhon's Book, *Idée générale de la révolution au XIXe siècle.* In *MECW*, Vol. 11. Progress Publishers. (First appeared in 1851.)
Engels, Frederick (1989). Engels to August Bebel, March 18–28, 1875. In *MECW*, Vol. 24. Progress Publishers. (First appeared in 1875.)
Engels, Frederick (1990). Introduction (to Marx's *The Civil War in France*). In *MECW*, Vol. 27. Progress Publishers. (First appeared in 1891.)
Groff, Ruth (2015). On the Ethical Contours of Thin Aristotelian Marxism. In Michael J. Thompson (Ed.), *Constructing Marxist Ethics: Critique, Normativity, Praxis* (pp. 313–335). Brill.
Heller, Agnes (1976). *The Theory of Need in Marx.* Allison & Busby.
Kandiyali, Jan (2014). Freedom and Necessity in Marx's Account of Communism. *British Journal for the History of Philosophy,* 22(1), 104–123.
Karatani, Kojin (2005). *Transcritique: On Kant and Marx.* The MIT Press.
Kivotidis, Dimitrios (2024). *The Dialectics of Democracy: Towards a Socialist Constitutionalism.* Routledge.
Klagge, James C. (1986). Marx's Realms of "Freedom" and "Necessity". *Canadian Journal of Philosophy,* 16(4), 769–777.
Lamb, Robert (1973). Adam Smith's Concept of Alienation. *Oxford Economic Papers,* 25(2), 275–285.
Lazarus, Michael (2022). Alienation and Action in the Young Marx, Aristotle, and Arendt. *Constellations,* 29, 417–433.
Leopold, David (2007). *The Young Karl Marx: German Philosophy, Modern Politics, and Human Flourishing.* Cambridge University Press.
Lukes, Steven (1985). *Marxism and Morality.* Oxford University Press.
Manuel, Frank E. and Manuel, Fritzie P. (1979). *Utopian Thought in the Western World.* Harvard University Press.
Marx, Karl (1975a). Contribution to the Critique of Hegel's Philosophy of Law: Introduction. In *MECW*, Vol. 3. Progress Publishers. (First appeared in 1844.)
Marx, Karl (1975b). Critical Marginal Notes on the Article "The King of Prussia and Social Reform" by a Prussian. In *MECW*, Vol. 3. Progress Publishers. (First appeared in 1844.)
Marx, Karl (1975c). Debates on Freedom of the Press and Publication of the Proceedings of the Assembly of the Estates. In *MECW*, Vol. 1. Progress Publishers. (First appeared in 1842.)
Marx, Karl (1975d). Economic and Philosophic Manuscripts of 1844. In *MECW*, Vol. 3. Progress Publishers. (First appeared in 1844.)
Marx, Karl (1975f). Proceedings of the Sixth Rhine Province Assembly. First Article. In *MECW*, Vol. 1. Progress Publishers. (First appeared in 1842.)

Marx, Karl (1975g). Theses on Feuerbach. In *MECW*, Vol. 5. Progress Publishers. (First appeared in 1845.)
Marx, Karl (1976). The Poverty of Philosophy. In *MECW*, Vol. 6. Progress Publishers. (First appeared in 1847.)
Marx, Karl (1977). Wage Labor and Capital. In *MECW*, Vol. 9. Progress Publishers. (First appeared in 1847.)
Marx, Karl (1978a). The Class Struggles in France, 1848 to 1850. In *MECW*, Vol. 10. Progress Publishers. (First appeared in 1850.)
Marx, Karl (1979). The Eighteenth Brumaire of Louis Bonaparte. In *MECW*, Vol. 11. Progress Publishers. (First appeared in 1852.)
Marx, Karl (1983). Marx to Joseph Weydemeyer, March 5, 1852. In *MECW*, Vol. 39. Progress Publishers. (First appeared in 1852.)
Marx, Karl (1985a). Inaugural Address of the Working Men's International Association. In *MECW*, Vol. 20. Progress Publishers. (First appeared in 1864.)
Marx, Karl (1985b). Instructions for the Delegates of the Provisional General Council: The Different Questions. In *MECW*, Vol. 20. Progress Publishers. (First appeared in 1866.)
Marx, Karl (1985c). Value, Price, and Profit. In *MECW*, Vol. 20. Progress Publishers. (First appeared in 1865.)
Marx, Karl (1986a). First Draft of *The Civil War in France*. In *MECW*, Vol. 22. Progress Publishers. (First appeared in 1871.)
Marx, Karl (1986b). *Outlines of the Critique of Political Economy*. In *MECW*, Vol. 28. Progress Publishers. (First appeared in 1857–1858.)
Marx, Karl (1986c). Second Draft of *The Civil War in France*. In *MECW*, Vol. 22. Progress Publishers. (First appeared in 1871.)
Marx, Karl (1986d). The Civil War in France. In *MECW*, Vol. 22. Progress Publishers. (First appeared in 1871.)
Marx, Karl (1987a). Marx to Sigfrid Meyer, April 30, 1867. In *MECW*, Vol. 42. Progress Publishers. (First appeared in 1867.)
Marx, Karl (1987b). Marx to Vera Zasulich (First Draft), March 3, 1881. In *MECW*, Vol. 42. Progress Publishers. (First appeared in 1881.)
Marx, Karl (1988). On the Hague Congress: A Correspondent's Report of a Speech Made at a Meeting in Amsterdam on September 8, 1872. In *MECW*, Vol. 23. Progress Publishers. (First appeared in 1872.)
Marx, Karl (1989a). Account of Karl Marx's Interview with *The Chicago Tribune* Correspondent. In *MECW*, Vol. 24. Progress Publishers. (First appeared in 1879.)
Marx, Karl (1989b). Critique of the Gotha Program. In *MECW*, Vol. 24. Progress Publishers. (First appeared in 1875.)
Marx, Karl (1989c). Economic Manuscript of 1861–63. In *MECW*, Vol. 32. Progress Publishers. (First appeared in 1861–1863.)
Marx, Karl (1989d). Marx to Ludwig Kugelmann, April 12, 1871. In *MECW*, Vol. 44. Progress Publishers. (First appeared in 1871.)
Marx, Karl (1989e). Marx to *Otechestvenniye Zapiski*, November 1877. In *MECW*, Vol. 24. Progress Publishers. (First appeared in 1877.)
Marx, Karl (1989f). Marx to Vera Zasulich, March 8, 1881. In *MECW*, Vol. 24. Progress Publishers. (First appeared in 1881.)
Marx, Karl (1989g). Notes on Bakunin's Book *Statehood and Anarchy*. In *MECW*, Vol. 24. Progress Publishers. (First appeared in 1874.)

Marx, Karl (1994). Economic Manuscript of 1861–63. In *MECW*, Vol. 34. Progress Publishers. (First appeared in 1861–1863.)

Marx, Karl (1996). Capital, Vol. 1. In *MECW*, Vol. 35. Progress Publishers. (First appeared in 1867.)

Marx, Karl (1997) Capital, Vol. 2. In *MECW*, Vol. 36. Progress Publishers. (First appeared in 1893.)

Marx, Karl (1998). Capital, Vol. 3. In *MECW*, Vol. 37. Progress Publishers. (First appeared in 1894.)

Marx, Karl and Frederick Engels (1975a/1846). The German Ideology. In *MECW*, Vol. 5. Progress Publishers.

Marx, Karl and Frederick Engels (1975b). The Holy Family, or Critique of Critical Criticism. In *MECW*, Vol. 4. Progress Publishers. (First appeared in 1845.)

Marx, Karl and Frederick Engels (1976). Manifesto of the Communist Party. In *MECW*, Vol. 6. Progress Publishers. (First appeared in 1848.)

Marx, Karl and Frederick Engels (1978). Address of the Central Authority to the League, March 1850. In *MECW*, Vol. 10. Progress Publishers. (First appeared in 1850.)

Marx, Karl and Frederick Engels (1988). Preface to the 1872 German Edition of the *Manifesto of the Communist Party*. In *MECW*, Vol. 23. Progress Publishers. (First appeared in 1872.)

McCarthy, George E. (Ed.) (1992). *Marx and Aristotle: Nineteenth Century German Social Theory and Classical Antiquity*. Rowman & Littlefield Publishers.

Moore, Stanley (1980). *Marx on the Choice between Socialism and Communism*. Harvard University Press.

Nasser, Alan G. (1975). Marx's Ethical Anthropology. *Philosophy and Phenomenological Research,* 35(4), 484–500.

Nordahl, Richard (1987). Marx and Utopia: A Critique of the "Orthodox" View. *Canadian Journal of Political Science,* 20(4), 755–783.

Offe, Claus (1984). *Contradictions of the Welfare State*. MIT Press.

Ollman, Bertell (1976). *Alienation: Marx's Conception of Man in Capitalist Society*. Cambridge University Press.

Rockmore, Tom (2018). *Marx's Dream: From Capitalism to Communism*. University of Chicago Press.

Sultany, Nimer (2021). Marx and Critical Constitutional Theory. In Paul O'Connell and Umut Özsu (Eds.), *Research Handbook on Law and Marxism*. Edward Elgar Publishing.

Tabak, Mehmet (2020). *Marx's Philosophy of Revolution and Freedom: A Critical Reconstruction.* Independent.

Unger, Roberto Mangabeira (2005). *The Left Alternative*. Verso.

Wada, Haruki (1983). Marx and Revolutionary Russia. In Teodor Shanin (Ed.), *Late Marx and the Russian Road: Marx and "the Peripheries of Capitalism."* Monthly Review Press.

Wallimann, Isidor (1981). *Estrangement: Marx's Conception of Human Nature and the Division of Labor*. Greenwood Press.

Ware, Robert (1982). Marx, the Division of Labor, and Human Nature. *Social Theory and Practice,* 8(1), 43–71.

Wood, Allen W. (2004). *Karl Marx.* Routledge.

9 Alternative Socialist/Communist Constitutional Futures in Pashukanis, Kojève, and Bloch[1]

Igor Shoikhedbrod

9.1 Introduction

In this chapter, I examine the alternative futures of right sketched out in the pioneering works of Evgeny Pashukanis, Alexandre Kojève, and Ernst Bloch with the aim of demonstrating their continued relevance for critical approaches to law and the possibility of 'socialist' and 'communist' constitutionalism. Each of these thinkers engaged in a critical analysis of law and theorised the nature, function, and future of right under emancipatory social conditions. Pashukanis, who remains the best known Soviet legal theorist in the West, theorised that 'legal regulation' and the 'opposition of private interests' in the capitalist market would be replaced by 'technical regulation' and thoroughgoing planning under communism, although he allowed for residual elements of the legal form to persist during the period of revolutionary transition from capitalism to communism. Kojève, for his part, theorised that 'bourgeois right' and its market-based standard of 'equivalence' would give way to a synthesised account of 'equity' in the Socialist Empire of private international socialist right. Finally, Bloch sought to retrieve for Marxism the radical heritage of natural law from below by reinscribing upon the banners of communism such values as human dignity, solidarity, and the reconstitution of juridical personhood. While Pashukanis and Kojève strive towards a definite finality in their respective futures or end-states, Bloch resists any such finality as foreign to the constitution of socialism in his speculative account of natural law from below. Far from reinforcing the paucity of Marxist reflections on right, the interventions of Pashukanis, Kojève, and Bloch serve as powerful reminders about the diverse futures of right that exist within the vibrant Marxist tradition. It is high time that we revisit the contributions of these largely neglected but imaginative thinkers when considering alternative futures of right and of constitutionalism beyond capitalism.

DOI: 10.4324/9781032621623-10

9.2 'Unity of the Diverse': Neglected Affinities between Pashukanis, Kojève, and Bloch

What do these three thinkers—a Russian Bolshevik of part Lithuanian ancestry, a Russo–Franco philosopher turned French civil servant, and an atheist German–Jewish philosopher have in common other than their 'heterodox' Marxisms? First, all three thinkers were profoundly impacted by the October Revolution and its world-historical aftermath. Evgeny Pashukanis was closest to that revolution, becoming the leading Soviet theoretician of law in the mid-1920s and rising in 1936 to the rank of the Deputy People's Commissar of Justice in the USSR, that is, before he was denounced as an 'enemy of the people' and executed in 1937 on trumped up charges of counter-revolutionary treason. Alexandre Kojève, who began as an enthusiastic supporter of the October Revolution in his youth and remained broadly sympathetic to the Soviet regime and especially to Stalin's leadership (Kojève [1929], 2021) did not share Pashukanis' fate owing in large part to his exile in France, where he became best known for his influential lectures on Hegel's *Phenomenology of Spirit*. Ernst Bloch also welcomed the October Revolution and at one point even zealously defended the notorious Moscow Show Trials. However, in the aftermath of World War II, Bloch experienced the East German instantiation of state socialism, which led him to reconsider his earlier views and to revalue the notion of subjective public rights in the tradition of natural law from below (on which see Negt and Jack Zipes 1975). A second area of affinity concerns the relative autonomy and specificity that each of these thinkers assign to right/law in contrast to class instrumentalist views that came to be associated with Marxist treatments of law more generally. Third, all three thinkers emphasise the foundational role of disputes between persons and the heritage of Roman private law for grasping the nature and specificity of legal relations. Finally, rather than simply counterposing right to revolutionary lawlessness, understood as the absence of *any* authoritative rules, all three thinkers formulate an alternative future of right beyond capitalism, which is to be grasped as a corrective to the shortcomings of the prevailing bourgeois/liberal legal form.

9.3 Pashukanis on the Disappearance of the Juridical Factor from (Communist) Social Relations and the Advent of Technical Regulation

Some readers will be perplexed by Evgeny Pashukanis' inclusion in this heterodox triad of Marxists. After all, did Pashukanis not theorise the 'withering away' of right/law as such? If so, does this not mean that he failed to offer *any* alternative future of right, thereby justifying his reputation as a 'legal nihilist' (Powell 1967)? As enticing as this interpretation may seem, it remains widely off the mark. First, Pashukanis' underlying claim of a 'homology' between commodity form and legal form, which he developed by following Marx's analysis of the commodity in *Capital*, extends to the period of the revolutionary transition from capitalism to communism. In other words, so long as generalised commodity exchange relations remain operative, including in societies like the Soviet Union during the phase of the New Economic Policy, the bourgeois/liberal legal form would necessarily remain intact. Second, although Pashukanis unambiguously anticipated the withering away of law under fully developed communism, it is not the case that he proposed nothing in its place, thereby earning his reputation as a 'legal nihilist'. Instead, Pashukanis maintained that 'technical regulation' would take the place of 'legal regulation' under full communism. Whatever one thinks of Pashukanis' concept of technical regulation, his future-oriented vision was not a communist society that is devoid of all authoritative rules or regulations; rather, the nature of those rules and regulations would be guided by technical rather than juridical considerations, informed by a background 'unity of purpose' and expediency rather than the 'opposition of private interests' and recourse to rights that underpin the bourgeois/liberal legal form.

One cannot fully appreciate the significance of Pashukanis' distinction between legal and technical regulation without first grasping his original account of the legal form and the extent to which it departed from prevailing class instrumental treatments of law that came to dominate Marxist jurisprudence. Pashukanis' underlying challenge to class instrumentalist treatments of law, which see the content of law as indisputably bound up with the project of class domination, is that they neglect law's distinctive form, which differs in important ways from other manifestations of authoritative regulation, such as the military and the church (Pashukanis [1929] 2017, p. 101). For similar reasons, class instrumentalists lack conceptual resources for addressing Pashukanis' medley of pointed queries in the *General Theory*, such as:

> why does class rule not remain what it is, the factual subjugation of one section of the population by the other? Why does it assume the form of official state rule, or - which is the same thing - why does the machinery of state coercion not come into being as the private machinery of the ruling class; why does it detach itself from the ruling class and take on the form of an impersonal apparatus of public power, separate from society?
>
> (Pashukanis [1929] 2017, p. 139)

It must be acknowledged that Pashukanis was not oblivious to the realities of class domination that obtain in the otherwise hidden sphere of capitalist production; his intention was to shed critical light on the formal side of capitalist processes that had been left undertheorised in classical Marxism. Pashukanis' decisive claim is that law finds its *differentia specifica* in the opposition of private interests between rival commodity owners in the capitalist market, each of whom is regarded as an equal legal person and is endowed with private rights in abstraction from their concrete material circumstances. In Pashukanis' words:

'The legal system differs from every other form of social system precisely in that it deals with private, isolated subjects. The legal norm acquires its *differentia specifica*, marking it out from the general mass of ethical, aesthetic, utilitarian, and other such regulations, precisely because it presupposes a person endowed with rights on the basis of which he actively makes claims' (Pashukanis [1929] 2017, pp. 100–101). Such a rendition of the 'legal form' allowed Pashukanis to establish the sociological basis for law's relative autonomy from direct class rule, to specify its distinct and increasingly hegemonic *form* relative to other varieties of authoritative regulation, and to treat legal phenomena, including 'legal fetishism', as possessing an objective basis in historically specific social relations.

Pashukanis' original account of the legal form provides a further basis for distinguishing between 'legal regulation', which is characterised by the opposition of private interests among commodity owners in the capitalist market, and 'technical regulation', which is informed by a background 'unity of purpose' that would be facilitated through centralised planning and the absence of markets under full communism. With respect to the former, Pashukanis maintains that

> a basic prerequisite for legal regulation is therefore the conflict of private interests. This is both the logical premise of the legal form and the actual origin of the development of the legal superstructure. Human conduct can be regulated by the most complex regulations, but the juridical factor in this regulation arises at the point when differentiation and opposition of interests begin.
>
> (Pashukanis [1929] 2017, p. 81)

Pashukanis provides two examples to demonstrate the striking differences between 'legal' and 'technical' regulation. Both examples boil down to the presence or absence of disputes between individuals, which can either be viewed from the prism of litigants pressing their private rights against each other before a judge, or as purely technical matters that call for the most expedient solution.

Pashukanis' first example is focused on the running of freight trains, which can be viewed from either the prism of legal or technical regulation. His second example concerns the doctor–patient relationship, which is the more interesting of the two examples because it touches on the enduring relevance of coercion, which is not limited to the bourgeois/liberal legal form. Under the prism of 'legal regulation', the doctor and patient are viewed as bearers of private rights, which they are ready to press against each other in the event of a dispute. Under the prism of 'technical regulation', however, the doctor and patient are not regarded as rights bearers at all, but as individuals united by a common interest or goal, that of healing and being healed. Pashukanis acknowledges in the same doctor–patient example that

> the enforcement of these rules [for healing sick persons] can be associated with some degree of constraint on the sick person. So long as this constraint is viewed from the standpoint of a goal which is the same for the person exercising the coercion as it is for the person coerced, it is a technically expedient act and no more.
> (Pashukanis [1929] 2017, p. 81)

Pashukanis is also clear about the criteria that is to be used in determining the content of technical rules in such cases:

> The content of the regulations is specified within these limits by medical science and undergoes change as medical science progresses. The lawyer has no place here. His role begins at the point where we are forced to leave this realm of unity of purpose and to take up another standpoint, that of mutually opposed separate subjects, each of whom represents his own private interests.
> (Pashukanis [1929] 2017, pp. 81–82)

Consequently, Pashukanis' intention is to mark out the characteristic differences between these two kinds of regulation and their background social preconditions, which is different from envisioning an emancipated communist society without *any* regulation. Pashukanis is challenging readers to consider the possibility that regulation need not assume a 'legal' character, which he links specifically to the presence of opposing private interests that then give way to the legal form and its corollary rights regime.

The need for an alternative conception of regulation becomes evident through Pashukanis' own admission—via the doctor–patient example—that some coercion will persist, even under fully developed communism. What distinguished Pashukanis' opposition between technical and legal regulation from other Soviet jurists is his anchoring of the latter firmly in the domain of private law and in the opposition of private interests. Such an anchoring was warranted on theoretical grounds because Pashukanis' 'commodity exchange theory of law', as it came to be called, holds that the legal form emerges together with the commodity form. The commodity form finds its natural home in the domain of private law that is concerned with transactions between market actors. Pashukanis affirms that 'no matter how ingeniously devised and unreal any one of the juridical constructs may appear, it is on firm ground so long as it remains within the bounds of private law, and of property law in particular' (Pashukanis [1929] 2017, p. 82). It is only under mature conditions of generalised commodity exchange that the legal subject, as an abstract commodity owner and rights-bearer, is 'raised to the heavens' (Pashukanis [1929] 2017, p. 121).

Pashukanis' anchoring of the legal form in private law did not mean that he dismissed public law as fictive or illusory, even when inferring that

> the very concept of "public law" can only be developed through its workings, in which it is continually repulsed by private law; so much so that it attempts to define itself as the antithesis of private law, to which it returns, however, as to its centre of gravity.
>
> (Pashukanis [1929] 2017, p. 106)

Pashukanis' crucial point here is that the 'antithesis' between public and private law is an objective one, rooted in the perpetual opposition between the individual and social interest in capitalist society. For this reason, Pashukanis takes issue with the views of some of his Soviet contemporaries, according to whom the antithesis between public and private law was the product of an arbitrary division 'dreamt up' (Pashukanis' words) by bourgeois jurists, and that such a division was no longer tenable in Soviet society, where economic activity had come under public control and therefore assumed a different function (Pashukanis [1929] 2017, pp. 104–105). Against such views, Pashukanis maintains that the division between public and private law can only be overcome, together with the legal form and legal ideology, in 'a society in which the contradiction between individual and social interests has broken down' (Pashukanis [1929] 2017, p. 106). Consequently, for Pashukanis the solution to this objectively existing 'antithesis' between public and private law is to be sought in the revolutionary transformation of the material conditions of life, which would eventually give way to a communist society that is guided by technical regulation and 'unity of purpose'.

Pashukanis departed from fellow Soviet revolutionists of law in another decisive respect, by registering his fierce and otherwise consistent opposition to the categories of 'proletarian', 'Soviet', and 'socialist' law, which he regarded as implausible theoretically and dubious politically. Pashukanis went further still by rejecting the category of 'public administrative law' in Soviet legal curricula on the grounds that it too would eventually be replaced by a new branch of study known as 'economic policy'—a view that he advanced with his collaborator Leonid Gintsburg as late as 1935 (Pashukanis [1935] 1980a, pp. 304–305). The basis for Pashukanis' reasoning was, once again, rooted in his strict conceptual distinction between legal and technical regulation, between background conditions of market exchange and those of consolidated centralised planning. Pashukanis already expressed misgivings about the category of 'proletarian law' in his *General Theory*, where he observed the following:

> The withering away of certain categories of bourgeois law (the categories as such, not this or that precept) in no way implies their replacement by new categories of proletarian law, just as the withering away of the categories of

> value, capital, profit and so forth in the transition to fully-developed socialism will not mean the emergence of new proletarian categories of value, capital and so on. The withering away of the categories of bourgeois law will, under these conditions, mean the withering away of law altogether, that is to say the disappearance of the juridical factor from social relations.
>
> (Pashukanis [1929] 2017, p. 61)

Although Pashukanis ended up conceding the existence of 'feudal law' in 1927, his position on the implausibility of post-capitalist categories of law remained unchanged. If anything, Pashukanis became more resolute on this point in later writings, inferring in his article, 'Economics and Legal Regulation' (1929), that

> the problem of the withering away of law is the yardstick by which we measure the degree of proximity of a jurist to Marxism…One who does not admit that the planned organizational base eradicates the formal legal basis is, essentially speaking, convinced that the relationships of commodity-capitalist economy are eternal, and that their loss at the present moment is merely an abnormality which will be eliminated in the future.
>
> (Pashukanis [1929] 1980b, p. 268)

Once again, we see Pashukanis' counterposing of legal regulation and technical regulation, except now with the subtle admission that

> we must take full account of the fact that, so long as the element of state coercion remains in operation, even in the sphere of relationships having nothing in common with the market and exchange, we will be dealing with legal regulation.
>
> (Pashukanis [1929] 1980b, p. 269)

Up to this point, Pashukanis was relatively mum on the issue of state coercion, especially since the bourgeois *Rechtsstaat* only comes on the scene in a derivative manner, that is, after the quintessential dispute between two commodity owners occurs, and in any case, it too was bound to 'wither away' with the displacement of commodity exchange by planned production. Pashukanis now had to contend with an avowed 'proletarian state' whose coercion was intensifying rather than dwindling with the introduction of forced collectivisation in the Soviet countryside.

One would think that such a striking contradiction between classical Marxist theory and Soviet political reality would lead Pashukanis to finally embrace the category of 'Soviet law'—if not for theoretical reasons, then certainly for political-strategic ones. However, the opposite proved to be the case. In the process of delivering an address concerning 'The Situation on the Legal Theory Front' (1930), Pashukanis was prompted by his more senior colleague Pyotr Stuchka to clarify his position on the place of 'revolutionary proletarian legality' during the period of revolutionary transition, to which he gave the following determined response:

> Answering Stuchka, I must say that for us revolutionary legality is a problem which is 99 percent political. We shall not solve it otherwise than by being oriented in policy. This does not mean that we should wave aside the work of creating principles and codes—we should perform this work, because if we turn aside from it, it will be taken in hand by the old jurists and they will smuggle in their reactionary ideas; but we must not put in the place of a movement forward—in company with the working class and the party—any system that has been frozen into immobility, even though it be dubbed proletarian law.
>
> (Pashukanis [1930], 1951, p. 280)

In placing the overriding emphasis on unrestrained revolutionary policy over law, Pashukanis doubled down on his view that the legal form and its surviving remnants were already in the process of 'withering away' in the Soviet proletarian state. However, by insisting on the prioritisation of revolutionary policy and centralised planning, which remained consistent with his earlier account of technical regulation, Pashukanis embraced a novel type of 'politicism', which imbued the same juridically unconstrained proletarian state with unprecedented transformative capacities.

It was not until his final reflections and recantations on this issue in 'State and Law Under Socialism' (1936) that Pashukanis gave up entirely on his tenacious commitment to the withering away of law and state in the transition to fully developed communism. In a fateful attempt at survival, Pashukanis bowed down to the reigning Stalinist regime and censured the main premises of his *General Theory*, according to which 'law, state and morality were simply declared to be bourgeois forms which cannot be filled with a socialist content and which must wither away in proportion to the realization of such content' (Pashukanis [1936] 1980c, p. 355). Now Pashukanis admits that

> this [his] grossly mistaken position, foreign to Marxism-Leninism, distorts the meaning of the proletarian state, distorts the meaning of proletarian communist morality, and distorts the meaning of Soviet law as the law of the proletarian state which serves as an instrument in the construction of socialism.
>
> (Pashukanis [1936] 1980c, p. 355)

Accordingly, Pashukanis reluctantly joined the growing 'normativist' chorus led by Andrei Vyshinsky (his erstwhile adversary on the 'legal theory front'), which deferred the withering away of state and law indefinitely (Sharlet 1978, p. 188).

Pashukanis' tragic demise is usually read against the political–historical context of the time (Head 2007; Bayer 2021). However, it is also worth looking into Pashukanis' tragedy from a more substantive theoretical angle, which moves beyond the usual refrain that Pashukanis was a casualty of his unyielding commitment to the withering away of law and rights under communism. On the view being advanced here, Pashukanis' chief error consisted in his rigid distinction between legal and technical regulation, and more precisely, in his claim that technical regulation would be characterised by a background 'unity of purpose'. Such a position, as we saw from Pashukanis' doctor–patient example, did not rule out recourse to coercion, even under fully developed communism. However, it would rule out the possibility that individuals could have *any* opposing interests whatsoever, even if these individuals unanimously agreed *ex-ante* about the superiority of the communist dispensation. In other words, Pashukanis' treatment of technical regulation assumed that even if residual coercion continues to be deployed under fully developed communism, there would be no social need for the institutionalisation of rights and protections against possible abuses of *political* power, however rare, since the goals of individuals would always coincide. In practice, this meant that Pashukanis wrote out the possibility of any lingering conflicts of interests between the proletarian state that was destined to wither away, the lone Communist Party (Bolshevik) at its helm, and the toilers. In yearning for such a culminating 'unity of purpose', Pashukanis' theory disarmed the emancipated producers of the most elementary formal rights granted to them by the hypocritical *Rechtsstaat*, and it did so without providing any alternative safeguards for ensuring that the free development of each would remain the condition for the free development of all.

If one wishes to be charitable to Pashukanis, one could argue that he was concerned all along with democratising the legal form (on which see Buckel 2020, pp. 275–276) through simplifying legal procedures and popularising justice, in which case 'technical regulation' could only mean the collective self-determination of the associated producers. However, Pashukanis' cumulative writings and political interventions consistently militate against such a democratising future vision because he placed uncritical faith in 'intra-party democracy' at a time when it ceased to exist while interpreting the politics of planning from above as a purely technical matter that did not call for any juridical safeguards against those tasked with the responsibility of issuing plans and executing them. For all intents and purposes, Pashukanis prioritised Party loyalty above all else (Melkevik 2023). More generally, Pashukanis was convinced that the politics of centralised planning would thoroughly displace the legal form. One can, of course, conceive of political rather than juridical safeguards against potential abuses of power under full communism (on which see Mandel 1986), but this would presuppose a robust democratic ethos of empowered soviets/councils that had by then been politically eviscerated in the Soviet Union. While Pashukanis was one of the most prominent victims of the 'counter-revolution' of law in the Soviet Union, it is important to recognise that his errors were, at least, partly theoretical in origin, rooted in an alternative future vision that ruled out the very possibility of conflicting interests among the emancipated producers.

9.4 Kojève and the Universal Realisation of Right in the Socialist Empire/UHS

Whereas Pashukanis' future-oriented vision anticipates the withering away of the legal form along with the political form of the state under full communism, Alexandre Kojève's *Outline of a Phenomenology of Right* (1943) is oriented towards the global realisation of the legal form in the 'Socialist Empire'(hereafter SE)/'Universal Homogenous State' (hereafter UHS), which would be accompanied by the disappearance of the political form of the state that Kojève interprets through the prism of Carl Schmitt's concept of the 'political'. Despite important differences in their respective end-states, Kojève shares Pashukanis' view that the specificity of the legal form is best captured by the characteristic dispute between two legally recognised persons, which necessitates judgement by an impartial and disinterested third. More specifically, Kojève submits that right can be grasped as a strictly juridical phenomenon whenever A's action infringes on the rights of B and provokes a reaction by B, which requires intervention by an impartial and disinterested third, C (Kojève [1943] 2000, p. 94). However, Kojève's understanding of what drives this characteristic dispute sets him apart from both Pashukanis and Bloch. Kojève locates the driving force of this dispute in the primordial 'struggle for recognition', which he understands as originating in a specifically human, 'anthropogenic desire' (Kojève [1947] 1969, p. 7). Elsewhere, Kojève refers to human history as being characterised by 'bloody fights for pure prestige carried on with a view to universal recognition' (Kojève [1946] 1970, p. 33). Whereas the dialectic of 'Lordship and Bondage' represents only a rudimentary 'moment' in Hegel's rich phenomenological odyssey, it becomes the *sine qua non* for Kojève's understanding of being, historical transformation, and his future-oriented vision of the SE/UHS.

The struggle for recognition remains the cornerstone of Kojève's influential lectures on Hegel's *Phenomenology of Spirit*, but Kojève only makes passing references to his future-oriented UHS in that work. Kojève's *Outline of a Phenomenology of Right*, which continues to be neglected in Anglophone scholarship relative to his famous lectures on Hegel, offers the most elaborate account of the juridical framework of the SE/UHS. The *Outline* concerns the concept of *Droit* (Right) and its realisation, which requires nothing short of universal recognition. In his review of contemporary interpretations of Hegel, Kojève submits that 'the analysis of the notion of Recognition therefore reveals to us the origin and the nature of the legal, political and social constitutive elements of human or historical existence' (Kojève [1946] 1970, p. 32). Referring to legal reality more specifically, Kojève writes:

> the reality constituted by the struggle for recognition is also a *legal* reality. For if this fight is started over a thing or a woman, it is not for the pure and simple possession of the thing or the woman that it is carried on (otherwise it would be a purely animal fight). The one fights against the other in order

> to make this other "recognize" his "exclusive right" to the thing or to the woman: man therefore fights in the final analysis for right [*pour le droit*]. And that is why, at the end of the fight for recognition, the thing as *legal property* (legitimate wife) as well as man as owner (husband) or as "legal person" ["*sujet juridique*"] in general are created.
>
> (Kojève [1946] 1970, p. 32)

It is worth noting here that Kojève, like Pashukanis, locates 'legal reality' primarily in the sphere of private law, which deals with the ownership and exchange of private property. This also speaks to the enduring legacy of Roman law, which on Kojève's idiosyncratic reading, originated in the 'aristocratic right' and the equality between masters.

While Kojève's status as a Marxist continues to be disputed in the scholarly literature (Shoikhedbrod 2022), he shares another important affinity with Pashukanis and Bloch, namely a trenchant critique of educing Right/law to ruling class interests. Although Kojève grants the existence of the phenomenon of 'class justice', he thinks that Marxists are profoundly mistaken when they reduce Right to economic epiphenomena, which has the consequence of robbing it of its relative autonomy and specificity. Kojève writes:

> Generally speaking, to the extent that *Droit* [Right] is determined by the interactions to which the idea of Justice that is at its base is being applied, it will be broadly determined by the economic, notably commercial, state of the Society where it is in force. Therefore, it is not at all futile to speak of a "class justice" along with the Marxists. But one must not forget that *Droit* [Right] is also something different from the economic interactions governed by *Droit* [Right]. It is an application to these interactions of a certain idea of Justice. And this idea, while generally being in harmony with the economic conditions, is autonomous in relation to them.
>
> (Kojève [1943] 2000, pp. 180–181)

Legal reality is a form of objective reality for Kojève, even if it is conditioned by economic phenomena and is actively repulsed by ruling class interests, principally originating in the generalised commodity exchange of Economic (Civil) Society and its related standards of market reward and equivalence. For Kojève, the phenomenon of 'class justice' unavoidably begets recurring revolutions and bloody wars–violent processes that will persist until the time that universal recognition is finally achieved in the SE/UHS. Kojève provides a striking sketch of all previous society, which he grasps in terms of struggles for recognition that will culminate in the 'classless society comprising the whole of humanity':

> History is therefore a more or less uninterrupted sequence of foreign wars and bloody revolutions. But this sequence has an aim and, consequently, an end.

> For being born from the desire for recognition, history will necessarily stop at the moment at which this desire will be fully satisfied. Now this desire will be satisfied when each will be recognized in his reality and in his human dignity by *all* the others, these others being recognized by each in their reality and dignity [a reality and dignity which are recognized as being] equal to his own. In other words, history will stop when man will be perfectly satisfied by the fact of being a recognized citizen of *a universal and homogeneous State*, or, if you prefer, of a classless society comprising the whole of humanity.
>
> (Kojève [1946] 1970, pp. 33–34)

Although Kojève's *Outline* is not modelled on Hegel's *Rechtsphilosophie*, which is guided by the logical development of the concept of Right and its actualisation, his account of the historical transformation of right mirrors most closely Hegel's diachronic approach in the *Phenomenology of Spirit*, which is informed by epochal historical developments, including the world-historical French Revolution. After identifying the specificity and (relative) autonomy of Right, Kojève outlines the various 'sublations' that accompany the historical transformation of Right, beginning with the movement from aristocratic right of equality (the right of masters, who first prevailed in the dyadic struggle for recognition) to the bourgeois right of equivalence (the right of slaves, who inaugurated through their transformative labour Economic Society and its contractual ethos), before culminating in the right of socialist equity (the right of citizens of the SE/UHS), which synthesises in a context-sensitive manner elements of aristocratic equality and bourgeois equivalence under the juridical standard of private international socialist right (Kojève [1943] 2000, p. 470).

It is telling that Kojève's SE/UHS is ultimately guided by the juridical standard of private international socialist right, and not public international socialist right. The reason for this becomes clearer when we grasp that for Kojève only private law adequately captures the specificity and (relative) autonomy of Right, which is informed by the quintessential dispute between A and B, necessitating judgement by an impartial and disinterested third, C. By the time that we arrive at Kojève's future-oriented SE/UHS, however, *anyone* can assume the role of C (the impartial and disinterested judge) precisely because a single concept of justice will have been universalised globally, while the individual, rather than the family or society as a whole, will remain the quintessential juridical unit of socialist Economic Society (Kojève [1943] 2000, p. 91). Kojève's conclusions should not be taken to suggest the corresponding absence of any differences in administrative techniques or uniformity in the positive laws of different territorial jurisdictions within the transnational SE/UHS (Howse 2006, 96). Rather, Kojève's decisive point is that such differences in administrative techniques and in positive law will not disturb the universalised conception of Right in the SE/UHS.

Kojève provides a more elaborate treatment of the preconditions for the realisation of the SE/UHS in the *Outline*. He writes:

> If a Society is *homogenous*, one can eliminate the words, "of an exclusive group." If it is *universal*, one can eliminate the words, "of a given Society." If it is homogenous *and* universal, one can eliminate the whole parenthetical expression—that is, the whole restriction introduced in this section. The definition of the *essence* of *Droit* will also then be applied to the *existence* of *Droit*, precisely because existence and essence will be but one: the essence of *Droit* will be fully realized and the existence will be entirely penetrated by the fullness of the juridical essence. Justice will be fully realised in and by *Droit* because all human existence will be determined by Justice.
>
> (Kojève [1943] 2000, p. 94)

Kojève was equally convinced that the SE/UHS would have to eliminate the political form of the state as a basic precondition for the universal realisation of Right. Such a process would also eliminate the vertical relationship between 'Governors' and 'Governed,' which is usually considered a defining feature of public law. Kojève submits:

> Let us not forget, moreover, that the socialist Empire is a *universal* and *homogenous* State: this means, on the one hand, that it has no Enemy, does not make war; on the other hand, because of its homogeneity, there is not in it an exclusive political Group, i.e., relations between Governors and the Governed (although there is a distinction between Administrators and the Administered). In other words, the Empire will be deprived of the two essential characteristics of the State. It will not have, so to speak, any political "interest." It will be "disinterested" in respect to its Citizens. This is why it will be able to continue to play the role of the juridical Third in respect to them.
>
> (Kojève [1943] 2000, p. 474)

What follows from Kojève's sketch of the SE/UHS is the anticipated twilight of the political form of the state and its thoroughgoing replacement by the legal form, which is made possible through that form's realisation and universalisation. Universal recognition is made possible in the SE/UHS in virtue of the thoroughgoing application of Right and the fact that everyone can become an 'impartial and disinterested' judge/third. History can finally come to an end because everyone will be recognised and there will be no further reasons for struggle. For this to happen, it is crucial that the fullest realisation of the legal form is accompanied by the disappearance of the political form of the state. Kojève's end state would require nothing short of an empire in which there are no more warring parties or nations but solidaristic relations between 'citizens' of the SE/UHS. For Kojève,

> the Citizen of the Empire will not be a Warrior; and he will be neither Governor nor the Governed. He will only be a Citizen in and by his equality and equivalence with others, with *all* the others, all men in general. To be a Citizen, therefore, will be nothing other than being a human being in the full and strong sense of the term.
>
> (Kojève [1943] 2000, p. 474)

Once the SE/UHS is consolidated, there will no longer be reasons for 'action' and change, including the spectre of revolutionary upheavals against perceived forms of injustice. Kojève affirms that 'when, at the limit, the State and politics will be overcome in the universal Society (i.e., without "enemies"), there will no longer be conflict over Droit—that is, no longer political revolutions or evolutions for juridical causes' (Kojève [1943] 2000, p. 158).

Kojève's end-state is worth comparing with Pashukanis'. Whereas Pashukanis looks forward to the 'withering away' of both the legal form and the political form of the state under full communism, Kojève envisions the fullest realisation and universalisation of the legal form in the SE/UHS. Unlike Pashukanis' insistence on the abolition of commodity exchange under full communism, however, Kojève also makes it clear that commodity exchange will remain integral to the institutional structure of the SE/UHG, as would a transformed understanding of the family, property, value, price, and even criminal right (Kojève [1943] 2000, p. 449).

Even as Kojève allows for the possibility that the *perfected* SE/UHS and its synthesised juridical standard 'may never be realized, given the finitude of human existence' (Kojève [1943] 2000, p. 470) at no point does he exhibit any doubt about the plausibility of the SE/UHS. The SE/UHS is never depicted by Kojève as an unattainable utopia, nor is the *Outline* intended as a warning against misguided utopian thinking. Kojève remained adamant about the prospect of the SE/UHS in finite history. It is also true that Kojève left open the precise means by which the SE/UHS could be realised (i.e., through evolutionary or revolutionary routes), just as he allowed for different catalysts and harbingers (e.g., Soviet communism, American Fordism, Japanese culture) that would help usher the ultimate end-state, namely the SE/UHS.

Despite their undeniable differences, Kojève's alternative future of right shares with Pashukanis' vision a longing for the cessation of conflict in a 'post-political' dispensation, with the obvious difference that Kojève regards the perfection and global realisation of the legal form as a precondition to such an end-state, whereas Pashukanis sees it as a characteristic barrier to his preferred end-state—a communist society—that is characterised by 'unity of purpose'. In Kojève's case, the realisation of the SE/UHS rests on the cessation of struggles for recognition and of action more broadly. For Pashukanis, technological inroads and centralised planning were to usher the anticipated 'unity of purpose', whereas for Kojève global integration, facilitated through a combination of market-based trade, technological development, and legal harmonisation, would free individuals from the 'realm of necessity' and help bring history to a close.

The 'end of history' in the SE/UHS would be marked by the progressive animalisation of human life and the concern with satisfying creature comforts. While such a vision of the end-state mirrors Friedrich Nietzsche's dreaded 'last man' (a parallel that scarcely troubled Kojève in his correspondence with Leo Strauss, on which see Strauss 2013), its basic outlines run contrary to Marx's vision of the future communist social formation as bringing the 'pre-history of human society to a close' (Marx [1859], 1978, p. 5). Consequently, no cessation of 'action' is anticipated in Marx's work that is comparable to Kojève's rendition of the end of history in the SE/UHG. Nor does Marx assign nearly the same importance to the historical 'struggle for recognition', for which he is explicitly criticised by Kojève on ostensibly Hegelian grounds (Kojève [1943] 2000, p. 177). However, Kojève does not provide any reasons for inferring, as he does, that his dyadic-existentialist struggle for recognition is more compelling than Marx's concern with historically-specific class struggles over material interests.

Although Kojève's future oriented SE/UHG rules out the possibility of an end-state without a perfectly realised legal form, it also assumes away the possibility of any lingering conflicts over the meaning of Right once the SE/UHG is consolidated. Here one need not accept Leo Strauss' conclusion that the SE/UHS would inevitably result in a technological tyranny of unprecedented magnitude (on which see Strauss 2013) to appreciate the perils of assuming away the possibility of disputes over the meaning of Right. Such disputes have been the harbingers of the most profound evolutionary and revolutionary political transformations known to human beings, Contrary to Kojève, there is little reason to think that disputes over the meaning of Right and the upheavals to which they have historically given rise will disappear in the near or distant future, and doubly so given that differences between 'Administrators' and 'Administered' will continue to inform the horizon of the SE/UHS. Kojève was so perturbed by Carl Schmitt's concept of the 'political' that he sought to write out the very prospect of revolutions against perceived injustices from the normative horizon of the SE/UHS. For how could there be any longing for revolution in an emancipatory context where Right is perfected and applied universally? In the final analysis, Kojève's yearning for a culminating *stasis* proves flawed because it assumes away the problematic of continuity and change in the meaning of Right upon the consolidation of the SE/UHS.

9.5 Bloch: Retrieving the 'Upright Carriage' in the Tradition of Classical Natural Law from Below

Among the three thinkers considered in this essay, Ernst Bloch stands out for his refusal to cast the emancipated society of the future and its right in terms of having reached a definitive culmination or finality. Bloch's position is informed by his critical-utopian orientation in *The Principle of Hope*, where he insists that 'only with the farewell to the closed, static concept of being does the real dimension of hope open' (Bloch [1954] 1986a, p. 18; for a more recent exploration, see Thompson and Zizek 2014). Bloch's work is also distinguished by his attempt at critically revaluing the classical natural law tradition with the aim of vindicating human dignity. Naturally, such an approach to right is likely to be met with scepticism and even derision from orthodox Marxist quarters because natural law has traditionally been invoked to justify the *status quo ante* and to condemn revolutionary transformation. Bloch's sensitivity to this problem leads him to contrast justice and the tradition of 'natural law from above' with justice and 'natural law from below' (Bloch [1961] 1986b, p. 199). It is precisely this operative distinction that allows Bloch to affirm that

> in the cradle of Marxism we find not only economic partiality on behalf of the *exploited* and *oppressed*, but also, in the spirit of natural law, an economic partiality for the humiliated and the degraded—a partiality that understands itself in the fight for human dignity, the constitutive heritage of classical natural law.
>
> (Bloch [1961] 1986b, p. 187)[2]

In order to further distance himself from traditional natural law theory, Bloch reiterates that there is no such thing as 'innate rights' and insists that all rights are acquired, typically through battle (Bloch [1961] 1986b, p. 188).

Bloch's awareness of the traditional 'Marxist distance to right' leads him to reconstruct the young Marx's critique of the so-called 'rights of man' in 'On the Jewish Question' through the 'Critique of Hegel's Philosophy of Right' and *The Holy Family* (jointly authored with Engels), while also showing the continued relevance of the very young Marx's critique of the 'Historical School of Law' (Bloch [1961] 1986b, p. 186). Bloch does this by observing that 'Marx demonstrated the bourgeois class content in them [human rights], but he also pointed out their future content, which at that time still did not have a basis' (Bloch [1961] 1986b, p. 177). The determination of that future (socialist/communist) content, according to Bloch, would depend on protracted struggles over rights, especially in the face of fascism and dictatorship, and that these struggles would be directed at expanding freedom of assembly, association, freedom of the press, security, and the resistance of working people to exploitation and oppression, all of which are indispensable to the project of 'socialist construction' (Bloch [1961] 1986b, p. 178). Furthermore, drawing on the lived experiences of actually-existing socialist societies, Bloch insists that in the absence of such struggles over rights, 'authoritarian socialism will prevail' (Bloch [1961] 1986b, p. 178).

Notwithstanding Bloch's explicit anchoring in natural law theory, he shares with Pashukanis and Kojève the view that the specificity and relative autonomy of law is to be found in the domain of private law. Bloch's *Natural Law and Human Dignity* begins with the perennial question of what justice is, which is promptly followed by the need for an impartial and disinterested 'third' to adjudicate disputes between two private wills (Bloch [1961] 1986b, p. 2). Although Bloch allows that disputes of this sort could conceivably be resolved within the ambit of public law, he later affirms that 'because the oldest and best-formed part of jurisprudence is private right and not public right, the publicist method has most of its difficulties in purely juridical matters' (Bloch [1961] 1986b, p. 213). Elsewhere, in a manner reminiscent of Pashukanis, whom he cites approvingly in that context, Bloch writes that 'even during the apogee of bourgeois democracy these last rights [public rights of the citizen] were made of a significantly less solid material than were the claims of the law of liens' (Bloch [1961] 1986b, p. 218). Bloch repeatedly returns to Roman law, which distinguished between the *Norma Agendi* and the *Facultas Agendi*, between objective right and subjective right. The *Facultas Agendi*, which corresponds to subjective right, presupposes an active legal subject (a juridical person) who is 'armed' with rights (Bloch [1961] 1986b, p. 212). The distinction between the *Norma Agendi* and the *Facultas Agendi* leads Bloch to demarcate two competing traditions in legal philosophy, the civilist and the publicist. Bloch submits:

> The *civilist* conception (particularly in Romanist jurists) in general only admits to subjective right, and to objective right only insofar as it touches upon the process of validating the subjective rights of others ...Conversely, the *publicist* conception (especially among German jurists) does not admit any subjective rights, but only subjective duties; the sole source of right is the state, the sole content of right is the collective interest.
>
> (Bloch [1961] 1986b, p. 213)

Rather than embracing the *publicist* conception, which would seem to follow from the collectivism customarily associated with the communist horizon, Bloch reappraises the *civilist conception* and makes it clear that classical natural law, which includes the claims of the oppressed and the dominated, takes its inspiration primarily from the civilist conception. Accordingly, Bloch writes that 'it [socialism] intends public order of a *norma agendi* only as an *unreified order of a freedom that has become publicly possible* as a facultas agendi of *all*' (Bloch [1961] 1986b, p. 227).

At the same time, Bloch readily acknowledges that the category of the juridical person has been bound up historically with private property and the power of ownership as absolute dominion, such that the juridical person has become unrecognisable, indeed so much so that even corporations are recognised as persons (Bloch [1961] 1986b, p. 217). The recognition of this historical fact does not prevent Bloch from concluding that 'subjective-public rights, in their real consequence and plenitude, contain the abolition of all exploitation, that is, of private property of the means of production, which makes exploitation possible and first made subjective rights known according to their first origin' (Bloch [1961] 1986b, p. 221). Rather than seeking the disappearance of 'subjective-public rights' and the concept of the juridical person on which they rest, Bloch calls for their reconstitution and more consistent realisation in the classless society of the future:

> In a classless society without money markets there are no owners of merchandise [commodities], but there are producers of goods who are legal subjects (juridical persons), and not least among their rights is the right not to be compelled to be a producer of goods. Thus the ultimate *subjective right* would be the license to *produce according to one's capabilities*, *to consume according to one's needs*; this license is guaranteed by means of the ultimate norm of subjective right: solidarity. It is only this solidarity—insofar as it thrived socialistically—that could bring to a happy conclusion the requisite liberal predominance of subjective rights (and the individual moral conscience) over objective rights (and their public, their social morality).
>
> (Bloch [1961] 1986b, p. 222)

Consequently, unlike Pashukanis, Bloch is convinced that the juridical factor cannot be expunged from communist social relations.

Although Bloch agrees with Pashukanis that the category of the juridical person emerges alongside private property and commodity exchange, it should not 'wither' with them in full communism. Bloch also takes issue with Pashukanis' attempt at prognosing the disappearance of all morality under full communism, which can only produce heteronomy and tyranny (Bloch [1961] 1986b, pp. 240–241). Bloch extends his criticism of the politically absolutist implications of such amoralist thinking to Pashukanis' perilous disregard for subjective-private rights and its tragic consequences. For Bloch, there is a symbiotic relationship between morality and law, which teaches that a 'politics, which tries to create precisely these conditions of human purity, will not be able to take one step in this direction unless it sees human law as in accord with the intentions of human ethicality…morals, in order not to be hypocritical or ideology, require the construction of public law, and the start of the construction of this law is not only a ceremonial ribbon-cutting, but also serves as the necessary preparatory construction internal to morals itself' (Bloch [1961] 1986b, pp. 241–242). As regards the sphere of right, however, it is not Pashukanis but Andrey Vyshinsky for whom Bloch reserves his harshest criticism. On the face of it, Vyshinsky sought to provide the sturdiest theoretical foundation for Soviet law and its catalogue of subjective-public rights. Bloch undertakes his criticism of Vyshinsky against the background of his earlier treatment of the *Norma Agendi*, the objective right that transforms everything into a subjective duty and renders the state omnipotent. Bloch associates the contemporary predominance of the *Norma Agendi* with the tradition of normativist-inspired legal positivism. In Vyshinsky's hands, writes Bloch, 'as is the consequence of such predominance of the *norma agendi* from above, not only civil law, the right to a trial, but also the right to work is completely limited and dominated by the objective sphere of right' (Bloch [1961] 1986b, p. 224). The broader implication of Vyshinsky's grounding of rights in the sphere of objective right from above is the dissolution of the juridical person and the emancipatory protections afforded by it, foremost the right to resistance against an otherwise omnipotent state. Rather than working towards the 'withering away of the state', to which Pashukanis was committed no less than Marx, Engels, and Lenin before him, Vyshinsky and his master, Stalin, sought to strengthen the state and its repressive laws (Bloch [1961] 1986b, p. 223). However, the '*jus pacis* [law of peace]', which Bloch associates with socialism, does not kneel before the omnipotent state, even if it styles itself with reference to 'socialist right', which leads to Bloch's most powerful conclusion in *Natural Law and Human Dignity*, namely that

> it is alien to the very essence of socialism on account of a finality that perpetually impedes but cannot be eliminated, and that—constantly claimed—is called the upright carriage on a habitable earth, one without the tyranny of the factory, without the factory of tyranny.
>
> (Bloch [1961] 1986b, p. 225)

In the end, Vyshinsky sought to legitimise the factory of tyranny, which remains 'alien' to the constitution of socialism.

The upright carriage remains the cornerstone of Bloch's future-oriented account of communist right and its acquired system of subjective-public rights. Bloch affirms that 'the wish of natural law was and is *uprightness* as a right, so that it might be respected in *persons* and guaranteed in their *collective*' (Bloch [1961] 1986b, p. 208). Such a position, which takes its theoretical bearings from Bloch's critical-utopian arguments in *The Principle of Hope* places the right to resistance at the centre of all subjective-public rights. It is hardly surprising, then, that the socialist dissidents of the erstwhile Yugoslav Praxis School saw in Bloch's work an inspiration for their own critiques of state-socialism. As Lubomir Tadić put it at the time,

> as long as the possibility of domination still exists, as long as there is still the phantom of the state, and as long as people can be kept in silence, one must reserve a concern for the right to stay upright, a concern that derives from natural law.
>
> (Tadić 1981, p. 426)

In recent years, Costas Douzinas has similarly argued that 'Bloch retains the main elements of Marx's critique of rights but discovers in the tradition of natural law the historically variable but eternal human trait to resist domination and oppression, and to imagine, fight, and achieve a society in which 'man will walk upright' (Douzinas 2019, pp. 126–127; see also Douzinas and Zizek 2010, pp. 85–86). Bloch's refusal to embrace a culminating finality in the communist horizon distinguishes him in important respects from Pashukanis and Kojève for whom the right to resistance and revolution could only become antiquated relics in their respective end-states. The distinctive merit of Bloch's 'speculative materialist' (on which see Moir 2019) approach to communist right is its principled refusal to treat the right of resistance in the past tense when addressing the future communist dispensation and to demonstrate, contrary to conventional liberal and orthodox Marxist assumptions, that right and revolution are not inherently at loggerheads, for both get their inspiration from the 'upright carriage'. On the other hand, despite Bloch's insistence on the concreteness of the 'upright carriage' and of the utopian horizon more generally, his alternative future of right remains characteristically abstract (on which see Geoghegan 1996, p. 142).

9.6 Conclusion

Our survey of Pashukanis, Kojève, and Bloch has sought to bring into critical relief the diverse futures of right that exist within the vibrant and heterodox Marxist tradition. Among the surprising findings of this study is that for all their differences, each of these thinkers holds that the project of socialist or communist constitutionalism must take its initial bearings from the sphere of private right, and not public right, which most public law scholars regard as the *terra firma* of the constitution. This important insight about private right, which will have to be explored further in another work, is interpreted most clearly, if idiosyncratically, by Bloch, who refers to Marx's insistence, in 'On the Jewish Question', that human emancipation will only be realised when the private individual of civil society reabsorbs the abstract citizen of the state in their everyday social and economic interactions (Bloch [1961] 1986b, p. 176).[3] However, unlike most commentators in the tradition of liberal political philosophy, Bloch does not think that Marx is calling for the dissolution of the private individual in an abstract collectivity that is devoid of rights. To be sure, the respective end-states and futures of right vary considerably among the three thinkers considered in this essay—unity of social purpose on the basis of technical regulation and centralised planning (Pashukanis), universal recognition and the perfection of the legal form in the SE/UHS (Kojève), and the reconstitution of juridical personhood and subjective-public rights, foremost among them being the right to resistance as inspired by the ineliminable 'upright carriage' (Bloch). It should be clear by now that the Marxist tradition, for all its strengths and weaknesses, does not suffer from a creative paucity of alternative conceptions of right beyond capitalism. Consequently, it is high time that we reconsider the contributions of Pashukanis, Kojève, and Bloch in connection with the ongoing projects of socialist and communist constitutionalism.

Notes

1 The original version of this essay was published as an article: Igor Shoikhedbrod, "Alternative Futures of Right in Pashukanis, Kojève, and Bloch." Law and Critique (2026): 21–39 DOI: https://doi.org/10.1007/s10978-025-09434-8. I thank the journal Law and Critique and its publisher, Springer, for granting me permission to reuse my original article for publication in the present volume.

2 Such statements by Bloch push against the grain of Glinka's (2023, p. 155) puzzling assertion that 'Bloch has a relatively superficial understanding of Marxist social theory; indeed, he views Marxism largely as an economic theory.'

3 Incidentally, Bloch's view is powerfully echoed in Marx's 1849 speech to Cologne jurors, where he submits: 'To maintain the old laws in face of the new needs and demands of social development is essentially the same as hypocritically upholding out-of-date particular interests in face of the up-to-date general interests. *This maintenance of the legal basis* aims at asserting such particular interests as if they were the *predominant* interests when they are *no longer dominant*; it aims at imposing on society laws *which have been condemned by the conditions of life in this society, by the way the members of this society earn their living, by their commerce and their material production* [my emphasis]; it aims at retaining in function legislators who are concerned only with particular interests; it seeks to misuse political power in order forcibly to place the interests of a minority above the interests of the majority. The maintenance of the legal basis is therefore in constant conflict with the existing needs, it hampers commerce and industry, it prepares the way for social crises, which erupt in *political revolutions*' (Marx [1849], 1977, p. 328).

References

Bayer, D. 2021. *Tragödie des Rechts*, Duncker & Humblot.

Bloch, E. 1986a [1954]. *The Principle of Hope, volume I*, translated by N. Plaice, S. Plaice and P. Knight, MIT.

Bloch, E. 1986b [1961]. *Natural Law and Human Dignity*, translated by D. Schmidt. MIT.

Buckel, S. 2020. *Subjectivation and Cohesion: Towards the Reconstruction of a Materialist Theory of Law*, translated by M. Vykoukal. Brill.

Douzinas, C. 2019. *The Radical Philosophy of Rights*. Routledge.

Douzinas, C. 2010. Adikia: On Communism and Rights. In C. Douzinas and S. Zizek (Eds.), *The Idea of Communism*. Verso, pp. 81–100

Geoghegan, V. 1996. *Ernst Bloch*. Routledge.

Head, M. 2007. *Evgeny Pashukanis: A Critical Reappraisal*, Routledge.

Howse, R. 2006. Europe and the New World Order: Lessons from Alexandre Kojève's Engagement with Schmitt's 'Nomos der Erde'. *Leiden Journal of International Law, 19*(1), pp. 93–103.

Kojève, A. 2021 [1929]. Philosophy and the Communist Party. *Radical Philosophy*, translated by T. Wilson, *2*(11), pp. 31–33.

Kojève, A. 2000 [1943]. *Outline of a Phenomenology of Right*, translated by B.P. Frost and R. Howse. Rowman & Littlefield.

Kojève, A. 1970 [1946]. Hegel, Marx, and Christianity. translated by H. Gildin. *Interpretation, 1*(1), pp. 21–42.

Kojève, A. 1969 [1947]. *Introduction to the Reading of Hegel: Lectures on the Phenomenology of Spirit*, edited by A. Bloom and translated by J.H. Nichols Jr. Cornell University Press.

Melkevik, B. 2023. Pashukanis, Evgeny Bronislavovich. In M. Sellers & S. Kirste (Eds.), *Encyclopedia of the Philosophy of Law and Social Philosophy*, pp. 2643–2646. Springer.

Mandel, M. 1986. Marxism and the Rule of Law. *UNBLJ*, *35*, pp. 7–33.

Marx, K. 1978. Preface to a Contribution to the Critique of Political Economy. In R. Tucker (Ed.), *The Marx-Engels Reader*, *2*, pp. 3–6.

Marx, K. 1977 [1849]. The Trial of the Rhenish District Committee of Democrats. In *MECW*, *8*. International Publishers, pp. 323–339.

Moir, C. 2019. *Ernst Bloch's Speculative Materialism: Ontology, Epistemology, Politics*. Brill.

Negt, O. and Zipes, J. 1975. Ernst Bloch, the German Philosopher of the October Revolution. *New German Critique*, 4, pp. 3–16.

Pashukanis, E. 2017 [1929]. *The General Theory of Law and Marxism*, translated by B. Einhorn. Routledge.

Pashukanis, E.B. 1980a [1935]. A Course on Economic Law. In P. Beirne and R. Sharlet (Eds.), *Pashukanis: Selected Writings on Marxism and Law*, pp. 304–345. Academic Press.

Pashukanis, E.B. 1980b [1929]. Economics and Legal regulation. In P. Beirne and R. Sharlet (Eds.), *Pashukanis: Selected Writings on Marxism and Law*, pp. 132–164. Academic Press.

Pashukanis, E.B. 1980c [1936]. State and Law under Socialism. In P. Beirne and R. Sharlet (Eds.), *Pashukanis: Selected Writings on Marxism and Law*, pp. 346–361. Academic Press.

Pashukanis, E.B. 1951 [1930]. The Situation on the Legal Theory Front. In H. W. Babb (trans.) and J. N. Hazard (Ed.), *Soviet Legal Philosophy*, pp. 237–280. Harvard University Press.

Powell, S.J. 1967. The Legal Nihilism of Pashukanis. *University of Florida Law Review*, *20*, pp. 18–32.

Sharlet, R. 1978. Pashukanis and the Withering Away of Law in the USSR. In S. Fitzpatrick (Ed.), *Cultural Revolution in Russia, 1928–1931*, pp. 169–188. Indiana University Press.

Shoikhedbrod, I., 2022. Kojève and Marx: Elusive Affinities and Divergences. In L. Pedrazuela (Ed.), *Kojève: A Man of Influence*, pp. 103–119. Lexington Books.

Strauss, L. 2013. *On Tyranny: Corrected and Expanded Edition, Including the Strauss-Kojeve Correspondence*. V. Gourevitch (Ed.) University of Chicago Press.

Tadić, L. 1981. The Marxist Critique of Right in the Philosophy of Ernst Bloch. *Praxis international*, *1*(4), pp. 422–429.

Thompson, P. and Zizek, S, 2014. (Eds.) *The Privatization of Hope: Ernst Bloch and the Future of Utopia*. Verso.

10 Proposals for a Socialist Constitution

Tony Smith

10.1 Introduction

The socialist project is not limited to the critique of capitalism. The ultimate goal is a world historical advance beyond it. Reflecting on what constitutes a "true advance" is one moment in this process, and anticipating the content of a socialist constitution is one form this reflection can take.

There are good reasons for socialists to be wary of constitutional proposals. Past justifications for constitutions have been utterly unacceptable. Constitutions are not divine decrees. They are not based on what is "natural" or "self-evident." Nor do they rest on the (supposedly) immemorial traditions of a (fictional) homogenous political community. They most certainly are not transcendental deductions of pure reason. These sorts of claims obscure how rulers have employed constitutions to legitimate their claims to power and delegitimate previous regimes (Colley 2021).

The constitutions of capitalist republics add another dimension of obfuscation. A system of generalized commodity exchange is based on contractual exchanges. And so in a sense,

> The sphere of circulation and commodity exchange … is in fact a very Eden of the innate rights of man. It is the exclusive realm of Freedom [and] Equality … Freedom, because both buyer and seller of a commodity … are determined only by their own free will. They contract as free persons, who are equal before the law … Equality, because each enters into relation with the other, as with a simple owner of commodities, and they exchange equivalent for equivalent.
>
> (Marx 1976, p. 280)

In other words, the rights to "freedom" and "equality" promised in the constitutions of capitalist republics are extrapolations from the (formal) freedom and equality of contractual exchanges.[1] When these rights are then used to justify the

DOI: 10.4324/9781032621623-11

very system of generalized commodity exchange they have been extrapolated from, the "argument" is viciously circular.

It would be a mistake, however, to conclude that a constitution has no place in socialism. Historical struggles provide lessons for socialists to build upon when formulating core commitments of the socialist project. A socialist constitution can be seen as a document affirming these core commitments, based on a collective learning process tied to emancipatory historical struggles.

Marx formulated the main historical lesson to be learned succinctly: the merely political emancipation promised by capitalist republics is inadequate (Marx 1975). This lesson is confirmed practically in the lived experience of the vast majority of social agents. Separated from the objective material preconditions of human life – means of subsistence and the means of production to produce them, both taking the social form of commodities owned by others – they are forced to put their capacities for activity at the disposal of the relative few who own and control investment funds for most of their adult waking life. In countless other respects too the constitutional guarantees of formal (legal) equality and freedom prove to be compatible with substantive coercion and systematic inequalities of life chances.

The lesson is confirmed theoretically in Marx's critique of political economy. In generalized commodity production, units of production invest money to purchase commodity inputs for the given round of production. They are able to continue operating in the future only if net monetary returns from the sale of output today enable them to compete successfully tomorrow. In this social context units of production *must* make monetary returns (M′) exceeding their initial monetary investment (M) their first and foremost goal, or risk being at a severe competitive disadvantage. Similarly, in generalized commodity production and exchange social agents generally *must* obtain monetary resources to purchase the goods and services required to address their wants and needs. This generally means that they *must* be somehow associated with units of production and distribution that make monetary returns their primary end. As Marx concludes, societies incorporating generalized commodity production and exchange generalize these social compulsions. The society as a whole is subjected to the *valorization imperative (M must become M′!)*, with each M′ forming the basis of a new M in the next period. "Capital" is Marx's name for this impersonal power, a bizarre "subject" retaining its identity as it moves from M to M′ and then to M″, M‴, and so on indefinitely. Even if political emancipation is accomplished, human ends will continue to be systematically subordinated to capital accumulation as an end in itself.

The practical implication of this historical lesson is clear: emancipatory struggles must aim at universal human emancipation, and not mere political emancipation. But what does "universal emancipation" mean?

Once again Marx provides a succinct answer. In the *Communist Manifesto* he called for a society where "the free development of each is the condition for the free development of all" (Marx and Engels 1976, p. 506). Similarly, in the *Grundrisse* Marx anticipated "a society of free individuality, based on the universal development of individuals" (Marx 1973, pp. 158, 708). Marx later endorsed another version of this goal in the first volume of *Capital,* calling for a society where "(T)he full and free development of every individual forms the ruling principle" (Marx 1976, p. 739). This last formulation can serve as the "ruling principle" for a socialist constitution defensible from a historical materialist standpoint.

The (indented and italicized) proposals that follow draw out implications of this principle and preconditions for its concrete actualization. Needless to say, any brief anticipation of such a document today will be incomplete, contestable, and revisable. The constitutional principles introduced below are suggestions for on-going collective deliberation.[2] They will be grouped under two headings, "political forms" and "social production."

10.2 Democratic Political Forms and Practices

An explicit affirmation of the collective freedom of social individuals to transform their social world belongs at the beginning of a socialist constitution:

> *We affirm our collective social freedom to establish and maintain a solidarity society whose ruling principle is the full and free development of every individual.*

Who is this "we"? A constitution for a society whose ruling purpose is the full and free development of *every* individual in principle extends to *all*, those "outside" any given (ultimately arbitrary) territorial boundary no less than those within. The social freedom affirmed in the making of a socialist constitution is not the act of a people trapped within given political borders, anxious about the "other" outside them. It is a free expression of universal solidarity. Socialism is inherently *internationalist*. This suggests a second principle for a socialist constitution, affirming its universal scope:

> *We affirm the collective social freedom to establish international socialism based on universal solidarity.*

An adequate model of socialism must incorporate institutions and practices of self-governance on an international level. This internationalist dimension of the socialist project is no more incompatible with a special concern for more limited (national, regional, local) communities than belonging to one of those communities is incompatible with special concern for family and friends. There are universally acceptable reasons justifying universal concerns, and there are universally acceptable reasons justifying concern for particular relationships. The immense importance of special bonds of love and responsibility in social life provide an impartial reason to justify certain forms of partiality, while solidarity rules out other forms.

10.2.1 Democratic Organizational Forms

There are four main forms of democratic decision-making (Landemore 2020). When freed from the limits and distortions imposed by capitalism and other systems of personal or impersonal domination, they are to be endorsed:

Socialist self-governance is exercised within four democratic social forms:

- *voluntary activist groups representing socialist civil society;*
- *elected representative bodies;*
- *representative bodies selected by sortition; and*
- *direct decision making by the political community as a whole.*

Each form has strengths and weaknesses. Activist groups bring public attention to significant issues that might otherwise be neglected. But the members of self-selecting particular groups may not sufficiently take into account legitimate perspectives and concerns of non-members about other issues. With universal suffrage citizens are able to hold members of elected representative assemblies accountable. But ordinary citizens do not themselves exercise decision making power in these assemblies. When the members of representative bodies are randomly selected, ordinary citizens are able to engage directly in political decision making. But this opportunity is restricted to those who happen to be selected. Referenda allow for universal participation in decision making. But no participant can be extensively informed about all issues. Insisting that all become adequately informed about everything imposes unreasonable demands of time and effort.

The proper conclusion for socialists, I think, is that the strengths of each democratic form must be mobilized in a way compensating for the weaknesses of the others.

Decision making within the organizations of socialist self-governance must discourage decision makers from neglecting the foreseeable effects of their decisions on other individuals and groups, the larger society, and the planet. Democratic decisions in socialism should not merely aggregate the present preferences of individuals and groups. They must result from exchanges of ideas and perspectives that may prove too require initial preferences to be modified or even abandoned.[3]

Democratic decision making in socialist society occurs after a period of deliberation:

- *When decisions are made within representative bodies, they occur after deliberation within those bodies, open to public input, public scrutiny, and public assessment.*
- *When decisions are made by referendums, they occur after public deliberation open to all in formal and informal public forums.*

10.2.2 Civil and Political Rights

Setting aside ample time for deliberation is only one precondition for decisions furthering the good of both the political community as a whole and the particular groups and individuals within it. A number of rights are required, including:

> *Every person in the relevant political unit has the right to form or join a Citizen Activist Group, to be selected for membership in a representative body formed by sortition, and to run for an elected position in an elected representative body.*

> *Every person in the relevant political unit has the right to vote (by secret ballot) in elections of members of representative bodies and in public referendums.*

In addition,

> *The socialist constitution explicitly acknowledges universal rights to freedom of speech and freedom of assembly,*

Marx saw freedom of speech and freedom of assembly as necessary preconditions for critical analyses and informed collective political actions in capitalism (see Shoikhedbrod 2019). They remain necessary precondition for critical analyses and informed collective political action in socialism, where no one should presuppose either that everyone else shares their perspectives and interests, or that they already understand the perspectives and interests of others. Others must be able to speak for themselves and form voluntary associations with others who share their perspectives and concerns (so long as they do not contravene the full and free development of others).

For free speech and freedom of association to have material actuality those speaking and associating cannot be systematically excluded from the means of social communication. A socialist constitution must affirm "media for the people":

> *The circulation of ideas in the public sphere of a socialist society reflects a core commitment to socialist pluralism. All reasonable perspectives must have a reasonable opportunity to have their voices heard in the social world.*[4]

Collective self-governance is also impossible when social individuals are subjected to domination. The socialist constitution anticipated here also affirms:

> *Rights to bodily freedom, including freedom to emigrate, reproductive freedom, and freedom from bodily harm and psychological abuse (and from the threat of harm and abuse);*

> *Freedom to own and use personal property;*

Freedom from arbitrary search and seizure of personal property;

Freedom from arbitrary arrest;

Right to due process in a judicial system upholding the core commitments of the socialist project;

Freedom of occupation; and

Freedom of conscience.

Systematic discrimination is an especially pernicious form of domination. A socialism for the twenty-first century must eliminate any persisting legacy of racism, sexism, and other forms of systematic oppression, and prevent such oppressive practices from re-emerging. A clear expression of this core commitment belongs in a socialist constitution:

Socialism rejects all forms of systematic discrimination incompatible with universal solidarity.

A socialist society will also not impose social roles fixed by custom, authoritarian decree, or lack of feasible options. Social identities in socialism can be expected to be fluid and experimental, based on the right of particular individuals (and voluntary associations) to discover particular interests, develop particular capabilities, and undertake particular projects that matter to them as the social individuals they are (or are striving to become). This is not a right to do whatever you want, whenever you want. There is no "right to particularity" when it undermines collective self-governance or is incompatible with the freedom of others to choose to live the particular sorts of lives *they* chose to live.[5] The point here is not that the demands of solidarity conflict with individual rights. The point is instead that the content of individual rights in socialism incorporates solidarity from the start:

The socialist project includes the freedom to live the particular sort of life one choses to live, consistent with solidarity with others.

The socialist commitment to substantive democracy is actualized in the adoption and modification of the socialist constitution, and in political self-governance after socialism has been established. Proposals for constitutional principles regarding these two processes follow.

10.2.3 Adoption/Modification of a Socialist Constitution

The original act of socialist self-governance is the collective adoption of a constitution. There are undoubtedly a number of reasonable ways this could be accomplished. Whichever is selected should be affirmed in the resulting document. The process sketched here illustrates one possibility.[6]

> *The adaptation of the socialist constitution took place within political forms of substantive democracy.*
>
> *At the time of adoption social agents operating within those political forms were from the territories initially undertaking the construction of socialism. This did not affect either the inherently internationalist scope of the socialist project or the inherently universal scope of the constitution expressing the core commitments of that project.*
>
> *The coalition of social movements that undertook the transition to socialism organized a Provisional Democratic Assembly, each member representing an approximately equal number of people; as well as a Citizens' Constitutional Committee selected by lot, whose composition broadly reflected the composition of the populace as a whole in the territories undertaking the transition.*
>
> *Members of the Provisional Democratic Assembly and members of the Citizens' Constitutional Committee separately composed initial drafts of the socialist constitution, taking into account input from Community Activist Groups. They then met jointly to compose a final draft [or, perhaps, two alternatives]. The document(s) were then submitted for public deliberation, with revisions made when they had majority support in both the Democratic Assembly and the Citizens' Committee. A revised document was accepted upon meeting the required minimum of sixty percent approval in a referendum.*[7]

If no proposal receives the required votes, the Democratic Assembly and the Citizens' Committee could propose a new alternative (or alternatives) for discussion prior to a second referendum, repeating the process until 60 percent approval is reached. It is unlikely the process of adopting a socialist constitution would be prolonged, so long as struggles against capitalism include extensive discussions of the sort of socialism worth struggling for.

Who affirms the initial constitution and where they are from is a matter of historical contingencies. They could be from two or more nations, two or more regions within different nations, two or more combinations of regions and nations. The important point is that the scope of the socialist project is internationalist from the start.

Since different territories will join the socialist international community at different times, a principle like the following is needed:

> *When forces struggling to establish socialism in a territory are successful after the socialist constitution has already been adopted elsewhere, a series*

of public forums is held to discuss whether they should adopt the socialist constitution. When sixty percent of the adult population votes in favour, the constitution is adopted.

Like all forms of human learning, the collective learning process that is the basis of the socialist constitution is fallible. Mistakes need to be corrected, omissions need to be rectified. A socialist constitution, then, must include rules for modification:

Every fifteen years the international-level Democratic Assembly (to be introduced below) will consider whether changes should be made to the socialist constitution. A Citizens' Committee devoted to this question will be randomly selected to reflect the composition of the international socialist community. If two-thirds of the membership of either group support an amendment, a series of in-person and virtual public forums will be organized. The proposal will be adopted upon receiving sixty percent of votes of adult members of the international socialist community in a subsequent referendum.

Any activist group in the society can initiate public deliberation and a subsequent referendum about a proposal to amend the constitution at any time by obtaining the signatures of twenty percent of the adult population in the international socialist community.

10.2.4 Self-Governance of Political Communities after the Constitution Has Been Adopted

The same democratic forms actualized in processes of adopting and revising a socialist constitution must also be actualized in the institutional framework and social practices of established socialist society:

The ultimate sovereign power of a socialist society lies in the collective ensemble of social individuals in their social interactions, mobilised within activist groups, representative bodies of socialist self-governance, public forums, and referendums.

Representative Democratic Assemblies and representative Community Associations are delegated powers to make laws and determine public policies, subject to democratic oversight by the collective ensemble of social individuals in general, and Community Activist Groups in particular.

All members of Representative Assemblies are elected for fixed terms and subject to recall.

The members of Community Associations are selected for fixed terms by lot to be broadly representative of the political community.

All proceedings of Democratic Assemblies and Community Associations are open to the public; all documents introduced in the course of deliberations are publicly available.

Public comments on the deliberations of Democratic Assemblies and Community Associations are posted on the websites where electronic public forums (supplementing those in-person) are held. Summaries of the content of these comments conveying the full range of viewpoints and the relative weight of support for each are to be introduced and discussed during the deliberations of the representative bodies.

If a Community Activist Group (or Groups) obtains signatures of twenty percent of the population calling for a referendum overturning a decision by a Democratic Assembly, a series of public forums on that proposal must be held, followed by a referendum. If sixty percent of voters in the referendum vote to overturn a law or policy, it is overturned.[8]

The inherently internationalist socialist project includes instituting democratic political forms on the international level. They are required on other geographical scales as well:

Democratic Assemblies, Community Associations, and other institutions of collective self-governance are established and maintained on local, regional, national, and international levels.

If the effects of a law or policy decision can be reasonably foreseen to have the greatest impact on a specific nation, region, or locality, the members of that community and their representatives have special weight in the decision-making process.

This *subsidiarity principle* is a corollary of the general principle that we are free only when we live under laws we have given ourselves. It is also based on the historical lesson that excessive centralization in decision-making tends to result in decisions reflecting the interests, beliefs, and powers of decision makers more than the good of those affected by the decisions. And it is based as well on the lesson that too much decentralization tends to undermine solidarity.[9]

Throughout world history, states and empires have appeared as transcendental powers dominating societies. The appearance of transcendence was (and is) illusionary; the power to dominate all too real. The constitutional proposals made in this section express the core socialist commitment to abolish both.

10.3 Social Production for Social Needs

10.3.1 Socialized Production

In the constitutions of capitalist republics the principle that those exercising political authority are accountable to those over whom the authority is exercised is often asserted. Even the most democratic forms of capitalist states have not established anything close to that. They have been systematically limited and distorted by a system defined by vast concentrations of economic power and the impersonal domination of capital. The restricted scope of "political" in these societies is an essential feature of this system.

In capitalism, the only decisions categorized as "political" are made by those occupying state offices. The production and appropriation of surplus value (the difference between monetary return M′ and initial capital investment M) is treated as an essentially private matter, left to the contractual agreements of individual economic agents. But the class relationship between those who own and control a critical mass of investment capital and those who do not is an inherently political matter. The structural coercion in the labor market faced by those separated from the objective preconditions of human life is an inherently political matter. The social domination representatives of capital exert over subordinates in the labor process is an essentially political matter. The systematic physical and psychological harms inflicted on the workforce in the extraction of surplus value are inherently political matters. The power to appropriate the social surplus and allocate its use are inherently political matters. The gendered and racialized ways class relations are concretely lived are inherently political matters. These supposedly private matters determine the general path taken by the polity no less than the laws and public policies adopted by state officials. The limitations of "merely political emancipation" (rule by law, formally equal citizenship, and so on) with its illegitimately narrow sense of "political" is, as Marx rightly insisted, one of the most important lessons of history. The property and production relations of capitalism, then, must be transformed.[10]

"Property" refers to an external relationship between an owning subject and an owned thing. The relationships defining a political community do not have this externality. *A unit of production is a political community where social agents cooperate for shared goals.* Forcing political communities into the social form of private property is a category mistake in theory and a social contradiction in practice.

This reasoning rules out private ownership by the community's members as well. State ownership or ownership by local communities are also inappropriate social forms. Units of production and distribution, like all communities in socialism, are sites of self-governance, part of a shared "Commons":

> *All sites of collective self-governance – including Democratic Assemblies, Community Associations, Public Forums, and Worker Collectives are active – are part of the Commons, and as such cannot be privately owned.*

The members of workplace communities have use rights in workplaces, specifically the right to use a share of the society's productive resources. These means of production are intrinsically part of the Commons as well:

Means of production are part of the extended Commons, and as such cannot be privately owned.

These principles might at first seem compatible with a market socialism where Worker Cooperatives compete in markets regulated by the state to maintain fairness in opportunities and results. There is, however, a good reason to reject market socialism.

Many models of market socialism exclude a distinct capitalist class. But they depict market societies incorporating generalized commodity production and exchange. The investments production enterprises would undertake, and the income their members would receive, would both be functions of enterprises' retained earnings. It would be the case that enterprises *must* make accumulating retained earnings their foremost goal or fall behind competing enterprises and ultimately be unable to continue. Competition among units of production for retained earnings would invariably shape and distort social life. "Capital" would once again emerge behind the backs of social agents, and once again dominate the society it has emerged from. The valorization imperative would define the "ruling purpose" of the society. Market socialism, in short, would be a society of "capital without capitalists."

The socialism defended here is not a market society where particular enterprises' investments stem in part from retained earnings and in part from loans and equity. Instead:

All investments in units of production in socialism are socialised.

Different models of socialism have proposed different ways to socialize investment in production. There is not space here to compare and contrast them in detail. As I have attempted to show elsewhere, socialist production should not center on constructing and implementing a comprehensive central plan of inputs and outputs (see Smith 2025). A technocratic elite making use of state-of-the-art computing to construct such a matrix and impose it on units of production is incompatible with socialist self-governance. More democratic forms of comprehensive central planning are likely to make excessive demands of time and effort on the populace at large. And any comprehensive central plan necessarily tends to inadequately incorporate tacit and local knowledge regarding both production (embodied in social agents engaged in production) and social needs (embodied in the social individuals whose needs they are). Comprehensive plans either must forbid (or strongly discourage) flexible responses to changing circumstances by producers and final users, attempt to prevent circumstances from changing (by systematically discouraging innovations, for example), or be almost continually modified in response to changing circumstances (making the present plan as obsolete as its successor is doomed to soon become). Comprehensive matrixes of inputs and outputs may be useful in some respects for limited purposes. They are not the alpha and omega of socialized production and exchange.

The model of socialism underlying the constitutional proposals that follow aims instead at a dynamic system of cooperative indicative planning. The illusionary goal of a perfect equilibrium of inputs and outputs is replaced with a continuously evolving co-ordination of production for democratically determined social needs by self-governing Worker Collectives that creatively respond to changed circumstances.

10.3.2 Production for Social Needs

The ruling purpose of production in capitalist market societies is the valorization of capital investment. A socialist constitution expresses a commitment to institute a form of production with a quite different purpose:

> *The purpose of production in socialism is to address democratically determined needs as effectively as possible in the given historical context.*

More specifically,

> *The purpose of production in socialist societies is to provide the goods and services needed for human flourishing, defined as the development and exercise of essential human capabilities.*

Somewhere in a socialist constitution, there should be a statement of what those capabilities are, recognizing that what counts as "essential" is open to revision.

> *Present understanding enables us to affirm as essential to human well-being capabilities to:*
>
> - *Live healthy lives of normal length;*
> - *Exercise agency in creative ways;*
> - *Engage in sensation, imagination, theoretical, and practical thought;*
> - *Have appropriate emotional connections with other social beings;*
> - *Experience ourselves as part of the natural world in relationship with other parts;*
> - *Engage in play;*
> - *Cooperate with others in households, workplaces and other organizations and associations; and*
> - *Participate as an equal in social practices of self-governance.*[11]

Capabilities mean little in the absence of opportunities to exercise them, suggesting the following:

> *A socialist society is committed to providing each individual with opportunities to exercise their essential capabilities to the greatest feasible extent in the given historical conditions.*

The development and exercise of the essential capabilities of *social* individuals is inherently a social matter, requiring social interactions within formal organizations and in the informal settings of everyday life. Self-governing Worker Collectives are one essential part of this story. There are others.

The development and exercise of these capabilities also generally require resources addressing three main categories of social needs.[12]

> *A socialist society must effectively address the universal needs that all members of a political community have as members of that community, including the collective universal need for the essential institutions and organizations of collective self-governance, for a natural environment within which human beings can flourish, for an effective innovation system, and for a built social environment conducive to the full development of social individuals.*[13]

In addition,

> *A socialist society must effectively address the universal ("basic") needs that all social individuals have as embodied individuals for the necessary means for their "full and free development," including adequate levels of food, shelter, clothing, education, cultural enrichment, physical and mental health treatment when required, and other forms of care.*[14]

Finally, "full and free development" requires being able to choose to live a particular sort of life with the particular goods it involves, so long as no unreasonable demands are imposed on others:

> *The socialist project includes a strong commitment to provide individuals with the particular goods they require for their particular life plans to the greatest feasible extent compatible with universal solidarity.*

The organizational forms of democracy discussed above come into play here, beginning with the democratic determination of needs in a given political community.

> *Prior to the commencement of a five-year period, three Community Associations are formed on each level (local, regional, national, and international), their membership randomly selected to reflect the make-up of the particular*

community. Each Association is charged with evaluating how adequately a specific category of social needs has been addressed in the period coming to a conclusion, and to consider how needs falling under that category might be better addressed in the future.

Community Associations and the public at large have free access to (anonymized) information regarding goods and services used to address social needs in the past, extrapolations of future trends based on this past data, surveys of individuals and community organizations regarding their evaluations of the goods and services they have used in the past and their suggestions and hopes for improvements, the innovations likely to become available in the short-to-medium term, and any other relevant matters. The Community Associations and subcommittees of the Democratic Assemblies must also solicit input on relevant issues from the public at large and independent Community Activist Groups.

The Associations then meet with subcommittees established in the relevant (local, regional, national, or international) elected Democratic Assembly to address the same matters. The members of the two groups then formulate what they consider to be the main alternative priorities for social production in the coming period. In some cases, the need for specific goods will be asserted. In most cases reference will be made to general sorts of goods. All the Associations and subcommittees then meet together to establish the two main alternative proposals taking all three categories of social needs into account.

After the main alternative priorities for production have been articulated, they are deliberated by the public at large in a series of virtual and in-person public forums, followed by a referendum affirming priorities for production in the given community in the coming five years.[15]

As noted above, the socialist constitution proposed here does not endorse Worker Collectives being commanded to produce certain sorts of outputs as part of a comprehensive plan. It calls instead for freely mobilizing the collective creative intelligence of workers. A first step in this process occurs when the members of each Collective deliberate and decide for themselves how they might best contribute to addressing the democratically determined social needs in the coming period (including the decision whether to produce consumption goods, inputs for other Production Collectives, or both).

The members of each Production Collectives collectively make a commitment to produce certain goods (or provide certain services). This collective commitment is expressed in a general plan for Collective over the coming period, formulated with the understanding that the Collective's plan must be appropriately adjusted when innovations or feedback from users establishes that adjustment is warranted.

To fulfill its commitments over the course of the period, a Collective must be able to obtain the requisite means of production and its members must be able to obtain means of consumption. Since there are no retained earnings to fund production and provide income, and no banks or capital markets providing funds, some other social process is required.

A Collective's proposed general plan includes an estimate of the funds needed to acquire necessary inputs from other Collectives and the income members require for obtaining means of consumption.

Initial drafts of Collectives' plans are reviewed by co-workers in the same sector, randomly selected from a set of those nominated by their co-workers. The members of these Sector Agencies provide feedback regarding estimates of costs, how the various plans might fit together (is there a danger of too much investment in certain areas, not enough in others?), and other relevant matters. Worker Collectives engaged in production then have opportunity to voluntarily revise their proposal on the basis of this feedback.

Final plans are then incorporated in requests for social funding for the coming period submitted to (local, regional, national, or international) Social Investment Centres.

10.3.3 Social Investment

The reference to funding above points to the role of "money" in the socialism anticipated in this chapter. Quotation marks are fully appropriate here (although they will be omitted in what follows) since there are profound qualitative differences from any form of pre-capitalist or capitalist money. Money here is not created by merchants, temples, or autocratic rulers. It is not created by private banks, public banks, or central banks. It cannot be accumulated as a store of private or public wealth. It cannot take the forms of investment capital or realized capital. It does not grant its holders social power over the living labor of others.

Whatever the social form of money in a given place and time, it always plays a constitutive role in making the society the specific sort of society that it is (Desan 2017). Constitutions in world history have conspicuously failed to incorporate this constituting role. A socialist constitution must remedy this defect while expressing that socialist money must be as internationalist as the socialist project:

An international Social Transaction Centre whose members are appointed and overseen by the international Democratic Assembly creates the units of account used by Worker Collectives to acquire means of production and by

> *individuals and community organizations to acquire means of individual and social consumption.*

In a society whose ruling purpose is the full and free development of *every* individual,

> *No individual's development should be systematically hampered by the contingent fact of being born in one place rather than another.*

This implies that eliminating the systematic tendencies to severe global disparities inherent in the capitalist world market is a core component of the socialist project:[16]

> *Serious disparities in life chances must not result from geographical disparities in flows of investment.*

The proposals that follow describe institutions and practices capable of actualizing these abstract constitutional principles in concrete social life. A crucial requirement for this is that the members of the international Social Transaction Centre have no discretion whatsoever over how the money they create is allocated:

> *The proportion of funds supporting production for social needs on the international level is fixed by the international Democratic Assembly.*

> *Each local, regional, and national political community in socialism receives a share of the remaining social investment funds directly proportional to the size of its population.*

Similarly, in a solidarity society, no person, group, nation, or generation has an intrinsic right to impose an environmental footprint greater than any other person, group, nation, or generation. This suggests a further core commitment of the socialist project, warranting a place in a socialist constitution:

> *Every political territory is allowed a share of the aggregate allowable environmental footprint directly proportional to the size of its population.*[17]

Members of Social Investment Centres are charged with allocating their community's share of social funding for production in a manner addressing democratically determined social needs without exceeding the environmental constraint.[18] Given how crucial this task is, the selection of members with knowledge, experience, and appropriate dispositions could not be more important.

> *The members of Social Investment Centres are randomly selected from the set of those who have 1) held positions of authority in any organization of*

> *socialist self-governance and 2) have been endorsed for positions in a Centre by a supermajority of those over whom their authority was exercised.*

Each Centre, on a given level, is randomly assigned a share of requests for social investment.[19] If Centres on a given level are informed of allocation decisions of others in real time, and allocations on local, regional, national, and international levels are staggered in overlapping five-year periods, social needs can be addressed comprehensively, excessive duplication can be avoided, and a flexible and dynamic balance between suppliers and users of production goods can be maintained.

Worker Collectives whose requests for social funding are granted now must mobilize the creative collective intelligence of their members once again:

> *The members of Worker Collectives whose requests for social funding are granted have the freedom to decide for themselves the means of production they employ, from which other Collectives production goods will be acquired, how production will be organized, their specific product lines (when the accepted proposals for social funding leave that open), when to abandon product lines and introduce new ones, and similar matters.*

Reference to the use of allocated funds to acquire production inputs raises the question how the prices of these (and other) goods are determined. There are no retained earnings here for producers to accumulate internally, no profits for external lenders or investors to demand a share of. Nothing corresponding to surplus value (or to the "mark-up" some heterodox economists refer to). The social form of price proposed here is equal to the social cost of production and use.

> *All products, whether means of production or means of individual and social consumption, are priced at their costs of production and use.*[20]

The quantities of final output acquired at cost to address needs of production, individual consumption, or social consumption provide evidence of the degree Collectives have fulfilled the commitments made in requests for social funding. Additional evidence regarding the quality of their output can be obtained from surveys of users. Judgements regarding opportunity costs can be based on this evidence. If, for example, a production good or good for individual or social consumption is quickly acquired in appropriate quantities at its cost price with few concerns raised by its users, that is a sign the opportunity cost was relatively low and the Worker Collective producing it should consider expanding production. If few acquire it at cost price and those that do have complaints, that is a sign of a high opportunity cost, and the relevant unit of production is expected to make improvements.

In addition,

> *Annual reviews of Worker Collectives contributing to the production for social needs are undertaken by Sector Agencies, and Social Investment Centres, with extensive input from Community Activist Groups, Democratic Assemblies, and Community Associations.*
>
> *Collectives receiving unsatisfactory reviews are given a reasonable period of time to improve and encouraged to take advantage of support offered by Sector Agencies and Research Centres for adopting "best practices" and undertaking innovations.*

Socialists should take seriously Kornai's claim that a major reason for the failures of state socialism in the twentieth century was the lack of hard budget constraints (Kornai 1992, pp. 140–145). His conclusion that there is no acceptable alternative to capitalism, however, does not follow. A socialism for the twenty-first century can incorporate the lesson.

> *No Production Collective has a right to continued social funding if it fails to address social needs effectively over time.*

The possibility of a reduction or even complete withdrawal of social investment provides a strong incentive for efficient production, measured by effectiveness in addressing social needs (as opposed to capitalist efficiency, measured by the transformation of M into M′).[21]

10.3.4 Social Labor

We turn next to constitutional principles regarding social labor and the acquisition of means of individual and social consumption.

For the foreseeable future most members of a socialist society will spend a significant portion of their lives engaged in the social labor required to reproduce the institutional framework and systems of social practices of socialism. Solidarity demands that,

> *Every individual has a right to contribute socially necessary labour in some form or other, and to receive appropriate social acknowledgement for that contribution.*
>
> *Every individual able to do so has a responsibility to contribute socially necessary labour in some form or other.*

"In some form or other" implies there are a variety of forms of socially necessary labor. One is activity within formal organizations (Worker Collectives, institutions of socialist self-governance, such as Democratic Assemblies). There are others:

> *All labour contributing to addressing social needs warrants explicit recognition as social labour, whether or not it is undertaken within formal organizations. In specific, care labour undertaken informally in households or communities must be acknowledged as the socially necessary labour that it is.*
>
> *Average worker income is set by the international Democratic Assembly.*
>
> *Allocations to Production Collectives for the income of their members are determined by multiplying average worker income by the number of members.*[22]
>
> *Those contributing necessary social labour outside Production Collectives receive average worker income.*
>
> *Individuals have the freedom to decide for themselves how to use their income to acquire the means of individual consumption.*
>
> *Local, Regional, National, and International Communities receive funds for social consumption proportional to their population size. These funds are allocated by Community Agencies established and overseen by the Democratic Assembly of the relevant level. Half of the members of these Agencies are selected by lot from the relevant community, with the other half appointed by the Democratic Assembly. Community Agencies have the freedom to decide the Production Collectives from which means of social consumption addressing community needs are obtained.*

The final proposals for a socialist constitution offered here build on Marx's profound distinction between a realm of necessity and a realm of freedom. The former centers on social actions required for the social reproduction of a socialist society. It is, of course, crucially important activities are performed. But that is not sufficient for "the full and free development of every individual." A *realm of freedom* is required.[23]

In capitalism, the "freedom" of leisure time is systematically limited and distorted. So-called free time tends to become colonized within *capital's time*, dominated by the imperatives of commodification, monetarization, and valorization. This tendency is eliminated with the quite different politics of time in socialism. A second difference is that in socialism the realm of necessity tends to contract while the realm of freedom expands over time, while in capitalism, the dominant tendency is for ratio of the two to be relatively stable. Productivity advances in capitalism's realm of necessity tend to result in an expansion of surplus labor producing surplus value, rather than a lessening of workers' time in that realm. A third relevant point is that the emancipatory potential of freely undertaken and freely organized commons-based peer production, producing knowledge goods freely available to anyone who wishes to use them, will be fully unleashed in a republican socialist society. While the expansion of the realm of freedom is in itself an important advance in world history, the unimaginably immense potential for commons-based peer production to further human flourishing is central to the case for socialism as well.

> *An expanding realm of freedom is essential to the socialist project, providing time to forge deeper social relationships with family members and friends, participate in community life in ways besides those necessary for social reproduction, and to purse projects of our own choosing.*

> *The international Democratic Assembly is charged with reducing the length of work time spent in Worker Collectives when advances in the general level of productivity allow that to occur without jeopardizing provision of resources required for developing and exercising essential human capabilities.*

10.4 Conclusion

This very provisional and incomplete set of proposals for a socialist constitution will almost certainly require modification and correction. But the underlying thesis of this chapter can be defended with confidence: marginal improvements leaving the property and production relationships of capitalism in place are not sufficient responses to the challenges of our historical moment. We need a socialism ambitious enough to eliminate impersonal and personal domination, as well as the social pathologies and environmental destruction domination generates. Anticipating a socialist constitution is only a part of this immense collective project. But it is an essential part.

Notes

1. Promised, but all too often not delivered. See Gerstenberger (2022).
2. A more comprehensive discussion is in Smith (2025, Ch.4).
3. Marx's defence of the Paris Commune highlights the importance of such deliberations (Marx 1986).
4. The crucial term "reasonable" excludes those who themselves attempt to exclude the voices of others by force or threats. And it excludes the distortions of public discourse occurring when private owners and their agents have the power to determine which ideas are allowed to circulate in society and which are not (Kivotidis 2023).

"Media for the people" can and should be implemented in a number of ways, including allocating prime media space to defenders of different positions roughly proportional to the number of adherents, allocating it randomly, and having access to key public media curated by rotating activist groups.

5 Assuming, of course, that *their* actions do not undermine collective self-governance or conflict with the legitimate claims of others.

6 The constitutional proposals presented in this paper are for a socialist constitution that has already been adopted. The section describing its adaptation is accordingly written in the past tense.

7 I do not regard the 60 percent requirement here and below as an essential feature of the socialist project. Some number seems required, and this one seems reasonable. Within an indeterminate range others would be reasonable too.

8 These percentages could be increased or decreased within a certain range without affecting the substantive point.

9 See Suvin's account of socialist Yugoslavia, whose different republics had functional autonomy (2016).

10 Fishkin and Forbath (2022) provide a comprehensive overview of how the political emancipation promised by some aspects of the US constitution has been limited, distorted, and reversed due to the power of economic oligopolies and their political supporters. Their response is to call for more political emancipation, specifically a resurgence of progressive movements for constitutional reforms. This agenda leaves in place the power that limits, distorts, and makes precarious what progressive movements are able to achieve. They fail, in other words, to learn the main lesson of their own book.

11 This list is adapted from Nussbaum (2001, pp. 416–418).

12 A rigid distinction between "needs" and "wants" cannot be justified. A world class musician does not merely "want" an instrument; a painter *needs* to have a brush.

13 The built environment includes infrastructure goods (roads, bridges, harbors, airports, energy networks, communication networks, and so on), public schools, public housing, public hospitals, playgrounds, hiking trails and other to public recreational facilities, cultural venues such as museums, theatres, concert halls, outdoor amphitheatres, and research centers. (The provision of means of production can also be categorized as a universal need of the community as a whole, with particular units of production having particular needs for particular means of production. The democratic determination of these needs is treated separately below.)

14 Advances in productive capacity and our understanding of human flourishing justify expanding what counts as "basic" needs over time.

15 See the discussion of participatory city planning in Porte Allegre in Mahendra et al. (2021).

16 These disparities are examined in Smith (2018, Chs.6, 11).

17 "Allowable" here is defined in terms of the planetary boundaries compatible with human flourishing, as determined by the best available environmental science (Wackernagel and Beyers 2019). As Marx wrote, "From the standpoint of a higher socio-economic formation, the private property of particular individuals in the earth will appear just as absurd as the private property of one man in other men. Even an entire society, a nation or all simultaneously existing societies taken together are not owners of the earth, they are simply its possessors, its beneficiaries, and have to bequeath it in an improved state to succeeding generations" (Marx 1981, p. 911).

18 The cumulative impact of economic disparities, environmental racism, and other discriminatory social pathologies afflicting capitalism, justify a transition period when systematically disadvantaged communities receive more funds for investment

and a greater share of the aggregate environmental footprint than their population size would otherwise determine. The socialist constitution anticipated here concerns socialism after this transition has been completed.

19 Alternatively, requests from specific sectors could be assigned to specializing Centers.

20 The first point to stress is that measuring costs in terms of "market prices" is another example of an intrinsically political matter that is incoherently treated as essentially unpolitical in capitalism. In that system, labor costs (and therefore the distribution of effective demand) reflect the political disciplining of workers. The systematic neglect of environmental costs is a political matter. The price system, as a whole, is profoundly shaped by government subsides (for R&D, etc.), taxes, the assignment of intellectual property rights, and so on. The question isn't whether the measurement of social costs of production is politicized; the only question is how they are. Very briefly, in the model of socialism developed in Smith 2025 the main costs are the costs to human beings of indirect and indirect (concrete) labor time in the "realm of necessity" (see below), environmental costs of depleting resources and generating wastes, and the opportunity costs when selecting one path of production requires foregoing another. Members of Sector Agencies and Worker Collectives making use of various information technologies calculate indirect and indirect labor time and assign it to a reasonable position in a numerical ordering (whether 0 to 100, 0 to 1,000, or some other range does not matter). Research Centers specializing in environmental science use the same scale to measure the relative environmental footprint of the given product's production and use. The numbers are then just added together to determine the cost price. (Evidence regarding opportunity costs is provided in ways described in the main text below.) Here, as elsewhere in the model, the claim is not that socialism is the Garden of Eden come to life. The claim here is simply that costs in socialism reasonably reflect the full range of social and environmental costs of production and use better than when they are measured by capitalist market prices (with or without modification by contingent political factors). The absence of individuals and groups privately benefitting from misstatements of social costs is an immensely important consideration. (A fuller treatment of the complex issues regarding prices in socialism is found in Smith 2025, Ch.5).

21 In capitalist market societies, individual consumption needs are, for the most part, treated as private matters, with needs for social consumption addressed by the state. Individual needs that cannot be addressed by the consumption of commodities, or those of social agents lacking sufficient purchasing power, tend to be systematically neglected. State provision of means of social consumption necessarily tend to prioritize providing preconditions for private capital accumulation while systematically neglecting other needs. It is absurd to think this is the best humanity can do.

22 Collectives are not mandated to distribute this amount equally among members. Perhaps special incentives (within narrow bounds) will prove necessary for especially onerous or dangerous forms of necessary activities.

23 "(T)he associated producers govern the human metabolism with nature in a rational way … accomplishing it with the least expenditure of energy and in conditions most worthy and appropriate for their human nature. But this always remains a realm of necessity. The true realm of freedom, the development of human powers as an end in itself, begins beyond it, though it can only flourish with this realm of necessity as its basis. The reduction of the working day is the basic prerequisite" (Marx 1981, pp. 958–959).

Bibliography

Colley, Linda 2021, *The Gun, The Ship, and The Pen: Warfare, Constitutions, and the Making of the Modern World*, New York: Liveright Publishing.

Desan, Christine 2017, "The Constitutional Approach to Money," in Nina Bandelj, F. Wherry, and V. Zelizer (eds), *Money Talks: Explaining How Money Really Works*, Princeton, NJ: Princeton.

Fishkin, Josephy and William Forbath 2022, *The Anti-Oligarchy Constitution*, Cambridge, MA: Harvard University Press.

Gerstenberger, Heidi 2022, *Markets and Violence: The Functioning of Capitalism in History*, Leiden: Brill.

Kivotidis, Dimitrios 2023, "'Bursting Asunder the Integument': Democracy, Digitalization, and the State'," in Hunter, Khachaturian, and Nanopoulos (eds), *Marxism and the Capitalist State: Towards a New Debate*, Cham: Palgrave MacMillan.

Kornai, János 1992, *The Socialist System: The Political Economy of Communism*, Princeton, NJ: Princeton University Press.

Landemore, Helene 2020, *Open Democracy: Reinventing Popular Rule for the Twenty-First Century*, Princeton, NJ: Princeton University Press.

Mahendra, Anjali, Robin King, Jillian Du, Ani Dasgupta, Victoria A. Beard, Achilles Kallergis, and Kathleen Schalch 2021, "Seven Transformations for More Equitable and Sustainable Cities," in *Towards a More Equal City*. Washington, DC: World Resources Institute.

Marx, Karl 1973 [1939], *Grundrisse*, New York: Vintage Books.

Marx, Karl 1975 [1844], "On the Jewish Question," in *Marx and Engels Collected Works, Volume 3*, New York: International Publishers.

Marx, Karl 1976 [1867], *Capital, Volume I*, New York: Penguin.

Marx, Karl 1981 [1894], *Capital*, Volume *III*, New York: Penguin.

Marx, Karl 1986 [1871], "The Civil War in France," in *Marx and Engels Collected Works, Volume 22*, New York: International Publishers.

Marx, Karl and Frederick Engels 1976 [1848], 'The Communist Manifesto', in *Marx and Engels Collected Works, Volume 6*, New York: International Publishers.

Nussbaum, Martha 2001, *Women and Human Development*, New York: Cambridge University Press.

Shoikhedbrod, Igor 2019, *Revisiting Marx's Critique of Liberalism: Rethinking Justice, Legality and Right*, New York: Palgrave Macmillan.

Smith, Tony 2018, *Beyond Liberal Egalitarianism*, Chicago, IL: Haymarket.

Smith, Tony 2025, *A Socialism for The Twenty-First Century: Towards "The Full and Free Development of Every Individual,"* Leiden: Brill.

Suvin, Darko 2016, *Splendour, Misery, and Possibilities: An X-Ray of Socialist Yugoslavia*, Leiden: Brill.

Wackernagel, Mathis and Bert Beyers 2019, *Ecological Footprint: Managing our Biocapacity Budget*, Gabriola Island, Canada: New Society Publishers.

Index

For Product Safety Concerns and Information please contact our EU representative GPSR@taylorandfrancis.com
Taylor & Francis Verlag GmbH, Kaufingerstraße 24, 80331 München, Germany

www.ingramcontent.com/pod-product-compliance
Lightning Source LLC
LaVergne TN
LVHW010635300926
849161LV00005B/950

* 9 7 8 1 0 3 2 6 2 1 6 0 9 *